DO MEN MOTHER?
FATHERING, CARE, AND DOMESTIC RESPONSIBILITY

D0011887

For a variety of reasons, more and more fathers are deciding to stay at home and care for their children rather than work full-time outside of the home. In addition, an increasing number of Canadian families are led by single fathers. In *Do Men Mother?* Andrea Doucet looks at the experiences of stay-at-home dads and single fathers and explores these fathers' impact on family life in Canada in recent years.

Using evidence gathered in a four-year in-depth qualitative study, including interviews with over one hundred fathers – from truck drivers to insurance salesmen, physicians to artists – Doucet illustrates how men are breaking the mould of traditional parenting models. Her research examines key questions such as: What leads fathers to trade earning for caring? How do fathers navigate through the 'maternal worlds' of mothers and infants? Are men mothering or are they redefining fatherhood?

Do Men Mother? illuminates fathers' candid reflections on caring and the intricate social worlds that men and women inhabit as they 'love and let go' of their children. In asking and unravelling the question 'Do men mother?' this study tells a compelling story about Canadian parents radically re-envisioning child care and domestic responsibilities at the beginning of the twenty-first century.

ANDREA DOUCET is an associate professor in the Department of Sociology and Anthropology at Carleton University.

ANDREA DOUCET

Do Men Mother?

Fathering, Care, and Domestic Responsibility

UNIVERSITY OF TORONTO PRESS
Toronto Buffalo London

© University of Toronto Press Incorporated 2006
Toronto Buffalo London
Printed in Canada

Reprinted 2007

ISBN-13: 978-0-8020-8731-7 (cloth)
ISBN-10: 0-8020-8731-0 (cloth)

ISBN-13: 978-0-8020-8546-7 (paper)
ISBN-10: 0-8020-8546-6 (paper)

∞

Printed on acid-free paper

Library and Archives Canada Cataloguing in Publication

Doucet, Andrea
  Do men mother? : fathering, care, and domestic responsibility /
  Andrea Doucet.

  Includes bibliographical references and index.

  ISBN-13: 978-0-8020-8731-7 (bound)
  ISBN-10: 0-8020-8731-0 (bound)
  ISBN-13: 978-0-8020-8546-7 (pbk.)
  ISBN-10: 0-8020-8546-6 (pbk.)

  1. Father and child – Canada.   2. Parenting – Canada.   I. Title.

  HQ756.D578 2006   306.874'20971   C2006-904038-9

This book has been published with the help of a grant from the Canadian
Federation for the Humanities and Social Sciences, through the Aid to
Scholarly Publications Programme, using funds provided by the Social
Sciences and Humanities Research Council of Canada.

University of Toronto Press acknowledges the financial assistance to its
publishing program of the Canada Council for the Arts and the Ontario
Arts Council.

University of Toronto Press acknowledges the financial support for its
publishing activities of the Government of Canada through the Book
Publishing Industry Development Program (BPIDP).

For Derek, Dad, and in memory of Dave –
three really great dads

Contents

viii   Contents

Acknowledgments

I am very grateful to the 118 fathers, and fourteen mothers, who gave generously of their time and insights to the research project that informs this book.

There are many capable people who participated in this research and writing endeavor at varied stages and in different capacities. Many thanks to my initial collaborators who assisted with the conceptualization of the research project proposal (Martha MacDonald, Patricia M. Connelly, Martin Richards, and Oriel Sullivan); my excellent research assistants (Erin Mills, Phil Robinson, Kelly McDonald, Chris Blahout, Maureen Flynn-Burhoe, Pete Andrachyk, and Liz Hall); and colleagues who assisted with group data analysis (Janet Siltanen, Allete Willis, Willow Scobie, and Jen Budney). In getting the book from draft to completion, thanks to Anne Laughlin and Virgil Duff at University of Toronto Press for their interest and assistance throughout; Alison Reid for meticulous copy-editing; Jane Butler for editing; Noeline Bridge for the index; John Hoffman for assisting in my search to find the cover photograph (and for his many articles on fathering in *Today's Parent*); Nancy Falconi for the beautiful cover photo; Lin Moody at Carleton and Doré Dunne at SSHRC for media promotion of my work.

Methodological inspiration for the work in this book comes from my teacher in participatory methods from the United Nations Development Program, Lyra Srinivason, and from Carol Gilligan for her generous facilitation of my learning of the Listening Guide. It is also important to mention that my reflections on reflexivity, relational knowing, and the Listening Guide, as described in chapter 2, are very much part of my ongoing collaborative work on methodology and epistemology with Natasha Mauthner at the University of Aberdeen.

My research on fathering was funded by a Standard Research Grant from the Social Sciences and Humanities Research Council as well as several internal research grants from Carleton University. I am especially grateful to the Faculty of Arts at Carleton University (and the family of Marston LaFrance) for the Marston LaFrance Fellowship in 2003–2004, which gave me the time to finish the research for this book and to get much of it written.

While the book consumed five years of my life, it has been about fifteen years in the making, as my thinking on mothering and fathering began shortly after the birth of my eldest daughter, Vanessa. There are thus many people to thank. The theoretical and substantive work behind this book began with my doctoral work at the University of Cambridge, where I benefited enormously from the stimulating academic environment and the rich influences of many professors and colleagues; these include first and foremost Robert M. Blackburn, Martin Richards, Carol Gilligan, Natasha Mauthner, Karen Hughes, Gillian Dunne and Ginny Morrow. I am also very grateful to conversations and critiques of my work provided by Rosalind Edwards, Jane Ribbens, Julia Brannen, Jane Ireland, Anne Marie Goetz, Sara Radcliff, Cathy Nesmith, Sharon Dolovich, and Jenny Jarmen. Special thanks to the Groovy Gang that met for many years in the attic of the old SPS building on Free school Lane in Cambridge. I will always be indebted to the late Suzanne Mackenzie, who was persistent in her encouragement that I should apply for a Commonwealth scholarship and take up doctoral studies in England.

Since my return to Canada in 1995, many colleagues have assisted me with my thinking on issues of gender, masculinities, methodology, and epistemology through varied reading groups, conversations, and comments on my work. I want to acknowledge with appreciation Janet Siltanen, Bruce Curtis, Alan Hunt, Wallace Clement, Rianne Mahon, Pat O'Mally, Aaron Doyle, Doris Buss, Fran Klodwosky, Daiva Stasiulis, Willow Scobie, Alette Willis, Rick Taylor, Meg Luxton, Claudia Malacrida, Glenda Wall, Gillian Ranson, Patricia M. Connelly, Martha MacDonald, John McMullin, Kiran Mirchandani, and Wendy Chan. My ongoing work on a SSHRC-CURA grant on fatherhood with Ed Bader, Kerry Daly, and Tim Paquette has been invaluable in thinking through what it means to be a father. I am especially grateful to Ed for his openness with ideas, his knowledge gleaned from many years working with fathers, and his enthusiastic support of my work.

As this is a book on family, parenting, and caring, I would be remiss not to acknowledge the large influence and support of my own circle of family and friends, beginning with Derek for twenty years of support and companionship, and my children – Vanessa, Hannah, and Lilly – whose daily lives remind me of the importance of scholarship that values the work of caring. Thank you, girls, for constantly reminding me – as my deadline seemed longer and longer – that J.K. Rowling, also a mother, managed to write six books and that the last one was over six hundred pages. A debt of gratitude goes to my larger family – Mom and Dad (Norma and Clarence/Boo), Kevin and Cheryl, Paula and Paul, Mark and Kathy, Richard and Julie, and to my parents-in-law, Mary Claire and in memory of Dave – for being good models of strong families and for providing quiet testimony to the ebb and flow of gendered family relations. A special heartfelt thanks to my sister, Lyse, for many conversations, for cards of encouragement from around the world, and for connecting me with the importance of writing for a wider audience. Last, but certainly not least, two very close academic friendships are tied up with the writing of this book from start to finish and I want to thank – from the bottom of my heart – Natasha Mauthner and Karen Hughes for being such generous colleagues and caring friends.

Some of the material in this book appears in modified form in several published or forthcoming journal articles and I want to thank the following publishers for granting permission to include it here: *Signs: Journal of Women in Culture and Society* (forthcoming, 2007) (University Chicago Press); *The Sociological Review*, 54(4) (2006) (Blackwell Publishing); *Atlantis: A Women's Studies Journal*, 28(2) (Spring/Summer 2004); and *Fathering: A Journal of Theory and Research about Men as Parents*, 2(3) (2005).

I have written this book with two distinct audiences in mind: academics and students as well as a wider general audience of people who have a keen interest in changes in mothering and fathering. Chapter 1 is likely the chapter that will appeal the least to non-academic readers and I encourage such readers to skim over the intricacies of theoretical debates, and to move on to the other chapters where the narrative flow is more central. I am grateful to Don Coles, award-winning poet and author and one of my former teachers at York University, for his advice on writing: 'My point: that clarity matters, subtlety matters, it *is* possible to be both demanding (of one's reader) *and* accessible, it *is* possible to speak suggestively and elusively *and* at the same time in a recognizably human voice. Not just possible, *necessary*' (www.library.utoronto.ca/canpoetry/coles).

A final word of appreciation to three fathers whose impact here is profound: to Derek Roche for being a loving dad to our three girls and for being a sounding board for many of the ideas that are in this book; to my own father, Boo Doucet, for his kindnesses and gentle words of wisdom through the years; and to my late father-in-law, David J. Roche, for his intellect, his interest in my work, and his challenging questions. The book is dedicated to the three of you.

DO MEN MOTHER?
FATHERING, CARE, AND DOMESTIC RESPONSIBILITY

Introduction: Do Men Mother?

Introduction

It was a crisp Canadian day in late autumn when I met Sam[1] for our second interview in a Tim Hortons coffee shop near his home in the Ottawa suburbs. A soft-spoken stay-at-home father of two young children, he is one of over 100 Canadian fathers interviewed as part of this study of primary caregiving fathers. Now looking back to this interview a few years later, I can still vividly remember when he spoke a few simple sentences that seemed to pull the conversation to a complete halt. It seemed odd to hear these words from a male voice: 'The other thing I would say is that if we had another child, I would want to go back to work and have my wife stay at home. If you don't have that chance to raise them yourself, it's a great loss. I have to say that every day I learn something from my kids. If you can swing it, do it. That's the way I see it.'[2]

Another father, Tom, spoke with conviction about the social and personal importance of the work that he was doing as a stay-at-home father. Although admitting that there are times when the stress of attending to children makes him feel overwhelmed, he nevertheless appreciates, like Sam, that he has had 'the chance' to do this. As we sat together on a summer morning in 2002, at the backyard picnic table outside his home in a small Quebec town, I interviewed Tom while his three young children ran and played around us.

There are times when I go insane. There are times where I think the demands at home are too much, the responsibilities, and the constant nagging and the whining of the kids and the diapers and the crap and doing the domestic life and being the home dad. Being the guy who has to clean the fridge, or do whatever, and that sucks. It would be a lot more fun to be with other people my age and to have interesting, stimulating conversations. I wouldn't have to answer 'Where's my hammer?' which my son can sometimes say fifteen, seventeen million times in one day. And I have to find ways of breaking up fights constantly. Sometimes I think, By God, my life would be a lot less complicated if I just had a nine-to-five job, and we were trying to negotiate that 'quality time' with them on evenings and weekends. But there are other times – just being with them in the summer, being in the backyard, colouring or doing puzzles or hanging out with them, just playing squirt-gun games for an entire hour – that are just great. There is nothing that can replace that. In a couple of years they won't want to do that anymore. They will want to play with their friends. And this time with them will be gone.

Across Canada, in the western province of Alberta, Rory's voice boomed through the telephone line as I interviewed him about his experiences as a stay-at-home father. He had just dropped his son off at his French immersion school and was on the speakerphone with me in his kitchen as he prepared millet burgers and rice bread, part of the weekly supply of allergen-free foods that he cooks for his seven-year-old son, Tristan. Four years ago, Rory closed up his consulting business as a quality control expert on gas pipelines to stay at home with his son, who was suffering with debilitating food allergies and a persistent stuttering problem. Now, he dabbles in paid work but finds himself pulling back if there is too much going on in Tristan's life: 'I know what my job is here ... I will make sure that everything is going right in Tristan's life, because *that is my job*.'

Speaking about how it is a 'real chance to stay home and raise them,' the joys of 'just being with them,' and how caring for a child is a man's 'job' are perspectives *not* often voiced by men. As highlighted in the work of feminist philosophers, sociologists, political scientists, and developmental psychologists over the past few decades, the dominant social conditions of men's lives often give rise to particular ways of being and seeing. These have been named differently across academic disciplines and theoretical perspectives, and include, for example; 'an ethic of justice' (Gilligan, 1982; Noddings, 2003), a 'male work norm' (Sassoon, 1987), a 'malestream' perspective (Balbo, 1987), the privileges of a 'patriarchal dividend' (Connell, 1995, 2000; Messner, 1987), 'hegemonic masculinity' (Connell, 1987, 1995, 2000), and the 'boy code'

(Pollack, 1998). Central words that connect these perspectives include *autonomy, domination, independence, power, disconnection*, and *individual rights*. However the concepts are named or framed, and however much this simple flow of theory and words is confounded by the complexities and intersections of ethnicity, class, sexuality, age, and culture, many theorists and social commentators nevertheless remain puzzled by the persistence of gendered ways of being, of difference and privilege that exist in the world, both historically and cross-culturally.

Against this backdrop of historical and theoretical understandings of men's lives, what constantly took me by surprise in my interviews with fathers were these clear and loud male voices speaking in what scholars would call a 'language of care' or an 'ethic of care' that embraces qualities of relationality, connections, interdependence, responsiveness, and responsibility (Gilligan, 1982; Larrabee, 1993; Noddings, 2003; Tronto, 1989, 1993). I remember each and every instance where fathers spoke within this 'language of care.' Something within the interview would change. Metaphorically, it was akin to listening to a familiar song or symphony and suddenly hearing a note off key. Could it be that when men speak in a language of care, it creates a sense of social and political vertigo?

Mothering, Fathering, and Vertigo Moments

Vertigo: A condition in which somebody feels a sensation of whirling or tilting that causes a loss of balance

(Oxford English Dictionary)

The sense of vertigo brought on by male voices speaking in a language of care may well be related not only to what we know about the gender differences in men's and women's lives but also to the vastly different experiences of *parenting* for women and men. Indeed, many researchers have argued that more than any other single life event, the arrival of children most profoundly marks long-term systemic inequalities between women and men (Brannen & Moss, 1991; Dowd, 2000; Fox, 1998, 2001; Hochschild, 1989).

This is not to say that fathering and mothering have been static over time. Throughout the past millennium, they have been radically altered by changing state policies on balancing employment and child rearing, shifting labour market configurations in relation to gender (e.g., full-time and part-time work, flexible working), diverse ideologies, and by mothers' and fathers' varied choices in relation to all these factors. Mothering has been particularly affected by rising employment rates for women, and especially for mothers of young children, throughout all Western industrialized countries (K. Daly, 2002; O'Connor, Orloff, & Shaver, 1999; Orloff, 2002). Yet, while women have become workers and earners, and sometimes breadwinners, they still remain as primary caregivers. Men, on the other hand, have moved from being primary breadwinners but have retained a secondary role in caregiving. Many commentators have argued that today's fathers are more involved in their children's lives than fathers of previous generations (O'Brien & Shemilt, 2003; E.H. Pleck & Pleck, 1997; J.H. Pleck & Mascaidrelli, 2004)[3] with significant increases in the time allotted to fathering (Gershuny, 2001; Yeung, Sandberg, Davis-Kean, & Hofferth, 2001) as well as in the gender balance of childcare tasks (Coltrane & Adams, 2001). Nevertheless, there remains an outstanding stability in mothers' *responsibility* for children and for domestic and community life. This pattern of gendered responsibilities has not shifted even where women have equal participation in paid employment (Beaujot, 2000; Coltrane, 2000; Coltrane & Adams, 2001; Doucet, 2000, 2001b; Robinson & Barret, 1986; Silver, 2000) .

Counter to these constantly reiterated social facts, the remarks of the fathers mentioned at the beginning of this chapter on giving up paid work, appreciating the subtle joys and struggles of caring, and their expressions of commitment to their children can indeed engender vertigo because they do not fit into the larger social landscapes of men's lives (see also Risman, 1998, and Connell, 1995, for a discussion of gender vertigo). Such vertiginous feelings may also be connected to what is well known about the gendered costs of caring and the social, political, and indeed 'revolutionary'[4] importance of the involvement of men in caring.

The Gendered Costs of Caring

A great deal of feminist ink has been spilled over this issue; ample scholarship has highlighted the economic, social, political, and personal costs to women of the gender imbalance in the 'costs of caring' (Folbre, 1994, 2001; Ruddick, 1995) for the very young, the very old, the elderly, the sick and the disabled in all societies. A consistent portrait has emerged, particularly in countries like Canada, the United States, and the United Kingdom where the responsibility for care has been largely market oriented and has fallen mainly on mothers' shoulders (See Epsing-Andersen, 1999; Korpi, 2000).[5] American journalist Ann Crittenden describes the gender disparity in care and the costs to women particularly well in her best-selling book, *The Price of Motherhood: Why the Most Important Job in the World Is Still the Least Valued*. She writes,

> Years ago Nobel prize winning economist Theodore W. Shultz observed that the development of human capabilities does not come free. There are always costs that someone has to pay. According to Shulz ... the basic questions about human capital are: Who will bear the costs? Who will reap the benefits? The answer to the first question is families, and mothers in particular. The answer to the second question is everyone. The entire society benefits from well raised children, without sharing more than a fraction of the costs of producing them. And that free ride on female labor is enforced by every major institution, starting with the workplace. (Crittenden, 2001, 86)

Although most of the scholarship on the gendered costs of care have focused on its effects for women, there has also been increasing attention to how *not* caring has had an impact on men. A position outlining such disadvantages for men actually goes back to several feminist classics, perhaps most notably Dorothy Dinnerstein's *The Mermaid and the Minotaur* (1977) and Nancy Chodorow's *The Reproduction of Mothering* (1978). Dinnerstein outlined the fundamental imbalances that occur in a society when *one* gender does the metaphoric rocking of the cradle while the *other* gender rules the world. She argued that the 'division of responsibility, opportunity, and privilege that prevails between male and female humans, and the patterns of psychological interdependence that are implicit in this division ... stems from a core fact that has so far been universal: the fact of primary female responsibility for the care of infants and young children' (Dinnerstein, 1977, 4). Chodorow's oft-cited work on mothering, written almost thirty years ago, considered the losses for men and for society more generally that female-dominated parenting engendered: 'the very fact of being mothered by a woman generates in men conflicts over masculinity, a psychology of male dominance, and a need to be superior to women' (Chodorow, 1978, 214).[6]

While feminists have been calling for men's involvement partly to ease the gendered costs of caregiving and as one of the routes towards greater gender equality,[7] men have also been busy documenting the personal and relational losses that they incur from not being fully involved in caring for children. Most of these claims are found in the burgeoning literature on fatherhood (Coltrane, 1996; Coltrane & Adams, 2001; Dienhart, 1998; Dowd, 2000; Hobson, 2002a; Lamb & Day, 2004; Marsiglio, Amato, Day, & Lamb, 2000).[8] Named as 'a hot topic in the 1990's' (Marsiglio, 1993, 88), research on fathering is now a well-established area of cross-disciplinary and international scholarship. This literature has drawn attention to the costs of stress and work-family conflict, the burden of being breadwinners, and the lack of opportunities to develop close emotional and relational attachments for men who are distant or absent fathers (Barnett, Marshall, & Pleck, 1992; Bumpus, Crouter, & McHale, 1999; Milkie & Peltola, 1999; Pruett, 2000). Being an involved father, on the other hand, has been argued to have significant benefits for fathers, mothers, and children. Scholars, for example, have pointed to the important generative effects for fathers who are highly involved with their children (Hawkins, Christiansen, Sargent, & Hill, 1993; Hawkins & Dollahite, 1996; Snarey, 1993b). As has been well summarized in a recent Canadian overview of fathering research, '[i]t is clear from the research that father involvement has enormous implications for men on their own path of adult development, for their wives and partners in the co-parenting relationship and, most importantly, for their children in terms of social, emotional and cognitive development' (Allen & Daly, 2002, 1).

The proliferation of interest and concurrent research on fathering has arisen partly out of the profound social changes in women's and men's lives over the past few decades. In North America and much of Europe, men's declining wages, increasing male unemployment, sustained growth in women's labour force participation, and changing ideologies associated with men and women's roles and identities as parents and as workers have all increased the emphasis on understanding the changing social institutions of mothering and fathering. At the same time, increased social alarm by certain sections of the population over issues of fatherless families (see Blankenhorn, 1995; Popenoe, 1993, 1996) combined with an interest in issues of generativity and enhanced personal development for involved fathers has led researchers of all political and theoretical stripes to turn their critical gaze to understanding the social worlds and perspectives of fathers.

In the burgeoning scholarship on fatherhood, there is a small but growing group of researchers who have studied shared-caregiving fathers (Coltrane, 1996; Dienhart, 1998; Doucet, 2000, 2001b; Ehrensaft, 1987; Risman, 1998; Risman & Johnson-Sumerford, 1997) and fathers who are primary caregivers (Barker, 1994; O'Brien, 1987; Pruett, 2000; Russell, 1983, 1987b; C.D. Smith, 1998; Wheelock, 1990). It is interesting to note that most of these studies have taken the position that these fathers *are mothering*. It is from this small group of studies that I arrived at the title for my book.

Do Men Mother?

This intriguing position that 'men can mother' or that 'fathers can be mothers' (Crittenden, 2001; Ehrensaft, 1987; Hrdy, 1999; Jackson, 1995; Risman, 1987, 1998, 2004; Ruddick, 1995)[9] has been constantly reconfirmed in the work of scholars who study fathers actively involved in caring for children. Gayle Kimball in her book *50-50 Parenting* has argued that men and women can 'co-mother' (Kimball, 1988), Diane Ehrensaft, author of *Parenting Together* has claimed that 'the word "mothering" is used specifically to refer to the day-to-day primary care of a child, the consciousness of being directly in charge of the child's upbringing' (Ehrensaft, 1984, 47), the authors Bryan Robinson and Robert Barret stated simply, 'Daddies are good mommies too' (Robinson & Barret, 1986, 31), while the feminist sociologist Barbara Risman has argued that 'I am indeed confident, then, that men can mother ...' (Risman, 1998, 71). More recently, Ann Crittenden in *The Price of Motherhood* defines a mother as 'anyone who is the primary caregiver of another person [and that although] women overwhelmingly fill the maternal, nurturing role, men certainly can' (Crittenden, 2001, 275).

The most frequently cited proponent of the men and mothering position is, however, the feminist philosopher Sara Ruddick. Most notably, in her book *Maternal Thinking*, she writes about mothering both in terms of its status as a noun (men are mothers) and as a verb (men can and do mother). In invoking mothering as both identity and as practice, she writes, 'Briefly, a mother is a person who takes on responsibility for children's lives and for whom providing child care is a significant part of her or his working life. I *mean* "her or his"' (1995, 40). Put differently, she says, 'A man or woman is a mother in my sense of the term, only if he or she acts upon a social commitment to nurture, protect and train children' (1995, 229–30).

In the second edition of her book, Ruddick does acknowledge that there exists a slight discomfort about men and mothering, both for men, 'who insist that they are not mothers' (1995, xiii) and for women, for whom 'a genderless mother trivializes both the distinctive costs of mothering to women as well as the effects, for worse or for better, of femininity on maternal practice and thought' (1995, xiii). Nevertheless, in rethinking her position six years after the first publishing of her acclaimed book, Ruddick maintains that men 'really can and often do in engage in mothering work' (1995, xiii; my emphasis).

At the centre of Ruddick's research is her argument that mothers 'are committed to meeting three demands that define maternal work' (Ruddick, 1995, 17–25, 65, 123).[10] These three 'demands' are 'preservation, growth and social acceptability' and 'to be a mother is to be committed to meeting these demands by works of preservative love, nurturance and training' (Ruddick, 1995, 17). Each of the maternal demands will be explored throughout this book, although I frame them as *responsibilities* rather than as demands (see chapters 4, 5, and 6). Moreover, as will be discussed in chapter 1, there are dissenting opinions on the 'Do men mother?' question. My own position, also laid out in that chapter, charts a path between the affirmative and negative responses to this question. The development of my answer to it has been evolving for well over a decade.

My Location in the 'Do Men Mother?' Question

Three particular instances sparked my interest in the 'Do men mother?' question. One was an observation at home, the second was a decade of academic inquiry, and the third was an inquisitiveness about embodied gender differences and parenting.

The challenges raised by the question first dawned on me when my husband and I were sharing the care of our first child. We were living in Cambridge, England, at the time, both graduate students taking turns at being the primary caregiver to our baby. She was eighteen months old when my husband decided that he would take her to some local playgroups so that she could socialize with other children. Thus, off they went, several mornings a week, to the moms and tots group that met in the basement of a local church. My husband was assured that *moms* was a generic term for *parents* and that, as a male mom he would certainly be welcomed. Yet the welcome he received was a cold one at best. To our surprise, each time he walked into the church basement with our daughter, he felt as if he was entering a very closed club reserved for mothers only and was viewed with a strange combination of suspicion, disdain, and at times congratulatory amazement. After a few weeks of trying to join the world of moms and tots, he stopped going, deciding that it was easier to care for our daughter on his own without the added stress of constant peer observation and judgement. Trying to blend in with a roomful of mothers was a harsh reminder that gender does matter, at least in some community sites, when it comes to just *who* is doing the mothering.

This incident resonated with the experiences of several fathers I interviewed for my doctoral research on shared parenting in Britain in the early 1990s (Doucet, 1995a). Many of the fathers who participated in that study also found themselves in playgroups, on the playgrounds, or at the school gates feeling like complete outsiders to the inner female worlds of parenting. A common lament of fathers who had left paid work to care for their children was not connected to the daily stresses and strains of caring for young children but to the loneliness, isolation, and the difficulties of entering into or creating their own parenting networks. Sentiments like 'loser,' 'outcast,' 'isolated,' and 'trying not to worry about what other blokes think' abounded in those narratives (see Doucet, 2000, 2001b).

The second impetus for my interest in men and mothering emerged, thus, out of my thinking around those fathers' narratives, collected during the early 1990s in Britain, and a decade of writing about men and women and parenting. During the 1990s and the early years of this new millennium, I wrote about theoretical challenges related to the study of men and women in domestic spaces (Doucet, 1995b, 1996, 2001b), the methodological and epistemological dilemmas posed by studying the private or the intimate (Doucet, 1998; Doucet & Mauthner, 2002; Mauthner & Doucet, 1998, 2003) and addressed the obstacles to men's greater involvement in parenting and caring (Doucet, 1995a, 2000, 2001a; Doucet & Dunne, 2000). In researching men's contributions to domestic life, I consistently noted that one puzzle has remained unsolved: why, in spite of men's growing participation in domestic *tasks* and their slowly increasing contributions to the *time* spent in childcare and housework, does the connection between women and *domestic responsibility* persist? Across time, ethnicities, social class, and culture, it is overwhelmingly mothers who organize, plan, orchestrate, and worry. What is it about domestic responsibility, then, that is so difficult for men? Although I engaged with this issue in my previous research, I strongly felt that it needed greater exploration. In particular, I wanted to talk to men who were taking on the primary care of children for significant periods of time because I thought that their reflections might hold part of the key to understanding why domestic responsibility has fallen to women.

Back at home, I kept mulling over the 'Do men mother?' question as I settled into a full-term twin pregnancy. My sense of inquisitiveness grew as I sat, feeling as if I was suspended in time, through the last ten weeks of a long and large phase of carrying two infants. I watched my husband care for our daughter who was then four years old. They played constantly while I sat in the window, full belly weighing me down, reading tomes of feminist theory on gender equality and gender differences. I watched him teach her to ride a bike, swing on the simple swing set he had made for her on our cherry tree, and constantly play together in our front yard on Queen Edith's Way in Cambridge. He cooked her meals, bathed her, comforted her, read to her, and lovingly tucked her into bed at night. I often asked myself, Was this father *mothering* this child?

I kept thinking about the men and mothering issue as I recovered slowly from an emergency caesarean, breastfed twin babies for ten months, and grieved each stage as they physically let go of me and the centrality of my maternal body in their little lives. In the years that followed, I spent a lot of time walking with the twins, pushing them in their double pram, and then stroller, first in Cambridge and then later in Halifax and Ottawa, Canada. With each passing season and with each year, I noticed how there were more and more fathers standing in schoolyards and walking with children in parks in the early morning hours. Who were these fathers? How did they come to be here? Why were there suddenly so many of them? Were they being warmly welcomed into the local versions of the moms and tots' group that had coldly excluded my husband a decade earlier? I constantly wondered, *Were these men mothering?*

An Ethnography of Fathering

I explored this question, and many others, through an ethnography of fathering (Burawoy et al., 1991; Hammersley, 1998; Hammersley & Atkinson, 1983). At the centre of this book is in-depth qualitative interview project conducted with 118 Canadian primary, caregiving fathers. As an ethnography, it draws on multiple sources from which I construct knowledge about fathers. These data sources include semi-structured interviews, focus groups, couple interviews, and Internet surveys, as well as a wide intellectual, academic, and personal immersion in mothering and fathering. The fathers who participated in the study self-identify as primary caregivers of their children (see chapter 3). Primary caregiver is further divided between stay-at-home fathers and single fathers. Within these categories, there is a fair bit of diversity: forty single fathers (twenty-five sole custody, twelve joint custody, and three widowers); fifty-three stay-at-home fathers (at home for at least one year); thirteen fathers who are both single and are/were stay-at-home fathers; and four fathers on parental leave when they were interviewed (including one father living in a same-sex partnership) (see appendix A, Tables A.1, A.2, and A.3). In the later stages of the study I broadened my categories to include eight shared-caregiving fathers, in an effort to include participants who did not necessarily fit into the categories of stay-at-home father or single father (see appendix A, table A.4). I was thus able to include gay fathers who did not have legal custody but were active caregivers in their children's lives and several immigrant fathers for whom stay-at-home fathering was not readily compatible with their cultural traditions. Moreover, the sample of fathers in this study is a very diverse representation of occupations, social class, and education levels and includes participation from fifteen fathers from visible ethnic minorities, four Aboriginal fathers, and nine gay fathers (see chapter 2 for greater detail). Finally, it is important to mention that fourteen women also participated in the study, taking part in couple interviews with stay-at-home fathers and their female partners/wives.

Surrounding this intensive research project was a process of informal participant observation for nearly fifteen years. As a parent of three daughters, I have constantly watched and conversed with fathers in parks and playgrounds, on the edges of soccer fields and basketball courts, on school field trips and at dinner parties. In researching the lives of fathers, I have felt like an anthropologist observing a culture that – though it is my own – I can know only partially because I was not raised a boy, do not have a male body, do not relate to men in the ways that men can and do, and I have never thought of myself as a father, nor have I been treated like one.

The Larger Relevance of the 'Do Men Mother?' Question

While the fathers interviewed for this study are Canadian, this book will have much resonance for readers in Western industrialized countries struggling to balance working and caregiving and the challenges of redistributing the caring work traditionally assumed by women. As in many other countries, the social terrain in Canada is characterized by rising labour force participation of mothers of young children,[11] a growing social institution of single fatherhood (either through joint or sole custody) and gradual increases in the numbers of stay-at-home fathers. As I complete the study, the most recent indicators from Statistics Canada suggest that stay-at-home fathers (about 111,000 of them in 2002)[12] have increased 25 per cent in the past ten years while stay-at-home mothers have decreased by approximately the same figure (Statistics Canada, 2002b).[13] Canadian fathers account for 10 per cent of all stay-at-home parents. Meanwhile, in Britain there are 189,000 men staying at home to look after the home and family (HomeDad.org.UK, 2005), while in the United States stay-at-home fathers make up nearly 18 per cent of all stay-at-home parents (98,000 of 5.5 million stay-at-home parents) (News, 2004).[14]

Also in 2001, there were approximately 96,000 male lone parents in Canada compared with approximately 480,000 single female parents (16 per cent of all lone parents) (Statistics Canada, 2002b), and joint custody decisions by courts have been rapidly rising, up from 10 per cent of all decisions in 1986 to 62 per cent in 2002 (Statistics Canada, 2003a).[15] One in six custodial parents in the United States are fathers (15.6 per cent), a proportion that has remained constant between 1994 and 2004 (Fathers Direct, 2004). In Britain, the number sits at approximately 10 per cent (Economic and Social Research Council, 2004). Even where fathers are not primary or shared primary caregivers, this work has relevance for a broad range of mothering and fathering patterns – and our understandings of such patterns. Such relevance is indicated in research that maintains that fathers' early and active involvement with children is one of the strongest predictors of sustained father-child connection over time, even after parental separation or divorce (Pruett, 2000), as well as scholarship that argues that the children of highly engaged fathers experience many positive social, emotional, and cognitive outcomes (Allen & Daly, 2002; Deutsch, Servis, & Payne, 2001).

Canada is also an interesting case study from which to conduct research on fathering and mothering because its approach to childcare has come under heavy scrutiny in the early years of this millennium. According to a study by the Organization for Economic Co-operation and Development, Canada's approach to childcare is one that provides 'basic babysitting, but not much else' for working parents, and disregards the importance of early education' (G. Doherty, Friendly, & Beach 2003; OECD, 2004).[16] Canada also invests less than half of what other developed nations devote to early-childhood education and has enough regulated childcare spaces for less than 20 per cent of children under six with working parents. This compares with the United Kingdom where 60 per cent of young children are in regulated care, while in Denmark the figure is 78 per cent. The decision of Canadian parents to have one parent stay at home is part of a strategy to balance work and home for both parents in a country where day care has never been seen as a viable option for many parents.[17] Such options are differently configured in countries with large investments in childcare such as Norway and Sweden, where parents have many choices for balancing work and home due to universal high-quality childcare, generous parental leave, and options to work part-time while children are young (Brandth & Kvande, 2001, 2002, 2005; Hobson, 2002a; Orloff, 2002, 2004). The decisions made by societies about how the care of others will be defined, evaluated, and supported (or not) has important symbolic, social, political, and economic consequences for all its citizens. Quite simply, the ways in which caring *gets done* has profound implications for the lives of women, men, and children and the societies that they inhabit.

Overview of the Book's Central Questions and Chapters

This book tells a story about fathers who are taking on the work that has been overwhelmingly in the hands and hearts of women for centuries. The book has three key aims. The first is to *describe, name, and understand the care that men take on*. More specifically, I have sought to carefully listen to, transcribe, and translate fathers' descriptions of how they care for their children. My second aim is to unpack the concept and issue of *responsibility/ies* for children. Given that many authors have argued that the essence of mothering is the responsibility for children (Fox, 1998, 2001; McMahon, 1995), it is important to know just *what* domestic responsibility is, *where* it is located, and to ask whether men who are primary caregivers take on these responsibilities or, alternatively, do they leave this work to their wives, female partners, or to other women? Furthermore, if men take on some or all of the responsibilities for children, does this shouldering of responsibility resemble maternal practice, or is it something of a completely different quality? I thus ask a series of questions around this issue of fathers and maternal practice, including, What kind of care is generated when male hands are metaphorically rocking the cradle? When men do the work that women have traditionally done, is it mothering, or is it something else? If we name men's active caregiving as mothering, are we using a maternal lens to frame our understandings and, if so, what are the theoretical gains and losses of such an approach?

Finally, my third aim in this book is to speculate on what happens to men, to masculinities, and to the relations between men and women when men are centrally involved in one of the most female-dominated and feminine-defined areas of work, practice and identity? Is it possible that men's increased involvement in caregiving could lead to a shift in political and cultural values and ultimately to an altering of the symbolic relation between, in Dinnerstein's terms, 'the rocking of the cradle and the ruling of the world?'

This book is organized into two parts and seven chapters. Part One (Coming to Know Fathers' Stories) consists of three chapters focused on unpacking the theoretical, methodological, epistemological, and conceptual issues that frame this study. Chapter 1 ('Studying Men, Mothering, and Fathering') details the theoretical influences, concepts, and contours of the book. Chapter 2 ('Knowing Fathers' Stories through Gossamer Walls') introduces an evocative metaphor from the novel *Fugitive Pieces* by the Canadian writer Anne Michaels as a way of configuring reflexive knowledge construction; this chapter is a detailed laying-out of the methodology and epistemology underpinning the study and the resulting stories from and about fathers' lives. Chapter 3 ('Understanding Fathers as Primary Caregivers') unpacks the complexity in the terms *primary caregiver* and *stay-at-home father*, the empirical categories of *gay father* and *ethnic minority father*, as well as theoretical understandings of *equal divisions of labour*.

Part Two ('Do Men Mother? Fathering and Responsibilities') provides the central working through of the question, 'Do men mother?' by focusing on Ruddick's three 'maternal demands' – the requirements for mothers to provide protection, growth, and social acceptability for their children. I frame and name these differently as captured in the titles of the next three chapters: 'Emotional Responsibility' (chapter 4), 'Community Responsibility' (chapter 5), and 'Moral Responsibility' (chapter 6).

Part Three consists of a concluding chapter and a postscript. Chapter 7, 'Conclusions: Men Reconstructing Fathering,' draws together the book's central arguments and identifies sites for future investigation. The postscript, 'Revisiting an Epistemology of Reception,' reflects on how I hope that the book will be received and read.

PART ONE

Coming to Know Fathers' Stories

1 Studying Men, Mothering, and Fathering

Introduction

The posing of a question such as 'Do men mother?' pulls together in one breath two seemingly opposed images, that of the male gender with its masculine connotations, and a feminine image of mothering. This pairing can provoke many diverse reactions. Indeed, in the four years that I have spent researching and writing this book, the strong responses to its title have always intrigued me. Whether they have been characterized by approval or disapproval, dismay or amusement, there has always been a distinct sense of its appropriateness or inappropriateness as a way of describing primary-caregiving fathers. Quite simply, the 'Do men mother?' question elicits considerable tension, both creative and abrasive.

Abrasive tension around this question crystallized most notably in the spring of 2003 when, deeply into the writing of this book, I was invited to give a public lecture on fathering and to do some media-related interviews. Like many academics, I was not accustomed to speaking outside the safe and resonant spaces of academic conferences, where one often finds shared understandings of theories, concepts, and issues. Rather, I found myself slightly uneasy speaking about my work (see also D. Mandell, 2002). The source of this discomfort was revealed when I realized that there were a few fathers' rights advocates in the audience who loudly applauded my work on encouraging active fathering. Several of my feminist colleagues looked at me with stony stares, clearly wondering how I could allow my work to be usurped by groups who are often anti-feminist or, more generally, anti-women. Days later I was shocked to find that a fathers' rights group as far away as Australia had made a link to a newspaper article about my public lecture (Tam, 2003).

This situation highlights how a positive view of fathers can suddenly be twisted to justify a different, possibly conflicting, set of claims, even exemplifying what the social theorist Tim May has termed 'the epistemology of reception,' which raises critical questions about 'how and under what circumstances social scientific knowledge is received, evaluated, and acted upon and under what circumstances' (May, 1998, 173; see also Grosz, 1995). Such an unexpected usurpation may await positive work on fathering in that some fathers' rights groups – particularly anti-feminist ones – could use the information to criticize particular mothers and mothering in general and, in some cases, to argue that men are better parents than mothers are (see Farrell, 2001). Intricately tied up with trying to understand and challenge a gendered division of domestic labour is the possibility of detracting from the struggles of mothers to have their own unpaid work valued (see Doucet, 2004). Thus, in spite of my intention as a researcher to simultaneously investigate the stubborn link between women and domestic responsibility and to encourage fathers' unpaid caregiving work, I was always vaguely aware of the alarming political and theoretical traps that may await feminist research on fathering.

Although such *abrasive* tension has accompanied my research on fathers, it has also represented *creative* potential in the requirement to think imaginatively about issues of gender equality and gender difference[1] and how they relate to parenting. Are women and men *different* in parenting? If so, how so? Can they be *equal*? If so, what does this mean and how do we define, measure, and evaluate equality and difference?

The question 'Do men mother?' also brings together a host of competing and conflicting views on how we should name, define, and speak about the love and labour invested by men in caring for children. Groups of thinkers and advocates of specific causes fall out on this question; moreover, diversity of approach within and between groups such as feminists, social scientists, and varied men's movements fragments even further on how to define and understand the issue of men's caregiving. Broadly speaking, there are two responses to the 'Do men mother?' question. The first is that *men do not mother* and second is that *men can and do mother*. My own position rests somewhere between the two and will be elaborated after I lay out the first two approaches.

Gender Differences: Men Don't Mother

The first position, that men do not mother, has been taken by writers and researchers whose work is based on the idea of gender differences or incompatibility. A position underlining irreconcilable oppositional positions of women and men is found in many popular television programs[2] as well as in the best-selling books and other media from the *Men Are from Mars, Women Are from Venus* series by John Gray. According to him, the modes of behaviour of women and men vary so greatly that the sexes seeem not to be from the same planet (Gray, 1992). And in the scholarly world of debate and disagreement, many authors and fields of study highlight differences between women and men. These include feminists working within a wide theoretical tradition of 'difference feminism.' In addition, particular manifestations of this position can be found in several movements such as historical and contemporary policy issue of wages for housework and the valuing of women's unpaid work; some fathers' rights movements, especially those asserting a more masculine kind of fathering; and, finally, feminists working on issues of child custody and divorce who accept and reinforce caregiving differences largely based on the unequal social and political positioning of women and men.

DIFFERENCE FEMINISM

In feminist theory, attention to *gender differences* has taken many guises, including what authors reviewing this body of work have titled 'difference feminism,' 'the difference category' (Scott, 1988), 'special treatment theorists' (Bacchi, 1990), 'those for whom sexual difference is a necessary and substantial divide' (Phillips, 1991), 'ethical feminism' (Braidotti, 1991), and 'relational feminism' (Rhode, 1989). Scholars such as Luce Irigaray (Irigaray, 1993, 1994) and Julia Kristeva (Kristeva, 1987; Oliver, 1993) and versions of Italian and French feminisms (Bock & James, 1992; Bono & Kemp, 1991; Fraser & Bartky, 1992) are often placed in this strand of feminist thinking. Most difference-oriented writers celebrate activities and work traditionally associated with women as well as challenge the value accorded to them by society. Three issues emphasized by difference feminism are explored below.

VALUING UNPAID WORK

A key area of importance to those espousing difference feminism has been the struggle for greater recognition of the value of unpaid domestic work. One theoretical articulation has been the long-running 'domestic labor debate' (see Fox, 1980) and a central policy expression has been the call for wages for housework (Landes, 1980; Malos, 1980). Attention to this issue has not waned in recent years, and feminists have developed a multiplicity of theoretical and policy approaches to it (Folbre 1994; Fraser 1997).[3] These have included the incorporation of unpaid work in census data as well as in national GDP accounting (Crittenden, 2001; Luxton & Vosko, 1998; Waring, 1998), the importance of universal high-quality childcare as a way of reconciling the valuing of care and parents' right to paid work (Mahon, 2002; Jenson, 2002), and the social and economic validation of mother work (Mandell & Sweet, 2004; Marks, 2004; Mink, 1995).[4]

FATHERS' RESPONSIBILITY MOVEMENT

Several fathers' rights groups affirm differences between women and men. As we will see later in this chapter, though some of these groups do offer an *equality* discourse, many embrace innate differences between women and men, mothering and fathering – for example, groups formed under the umbrella of the Christian Right such as the Promise Keepers and some sections of the Fatherhood Responsibility Movement that emphasize variance in both the practical *roles* and the divergent nurturing *natures* of women and men (for an overview of these movements, see Gavanas, 2002; Messner, 1997).

FEMINISM AND CHILD CUSTODY ISSUES

A third group of writers and policy advocates a focus on gender differences in issues of divorce and child custody (see Boyd, 2002; Mandell 2002) and holds that the high and low social status of men and women respectively has led to gender-related styles of parenting. According to Susan Boyd, this approach 'is not based on essential differences between men and women, but rather on social patterns of caring' (Boyd, 2002, 4). Feminists taking this position are, however, mindful that it remains caught in the 'perils and pitfalls' of accepting women as primary caregivers (Boyd, 2002) and that it 'seems to paint women into the very corner they have been trying to get out of' (Mandell, 2002, 230; see also Pulkingham, 1994). Nevertheless, this position is viewed by many feminists as the best possible strategy, given current economic and social conditions around caring and earning and the fact that child custody battles can lead to an erasure of women's investment in child rearing (see also Fineman, 1992, 1995; Smart, 1991).

Gender Equality: Men Do Mother

The position that men can and do mother is rooted in equality feminism and has developed mainly in the work of sociologists researching gender divisions of labour or primary-caregiving fathers, and more recently in the advocacy work of some fathers' rights groups. Framed by an overarching concern with gender equality and in minimizing, or explaining, the appearance or effects of differences, an investigation into the divergent life experiences of women and men is viewed as the systemic result of family and peer socialization and the ways that societies and their social institutions are structured. Theories variously describe such macro-level factors that create and sustain gender differences and can include, for example, 'the gender regime' or the 'gender order' (Connell, 1987), the 'relations of ruling' (D. Smith, 1987, 1999) or the 'gender structure' (Risman, 2004). The underlying argument is that if gender relations were altered at the level of social structure (i.e., in the social institutions of the family, workplace, state policies, the courts, and media), a more gender-free world would eventually lead to gender-free parenting. Several theoretical and empirical expressions include feminist theory focused primarily on gender equality, ongoing legal battles over women's equal wages for work of equal value, studies on gender divisions of domestic labour and on primary caregiving fathers, and finally, several fathers rights groups.

EQUALITY FEMINISM

The position that men can mother is rooted in broad theoretical principles of gender equality, much underpinned by liberal feminist assumptions. Many labels have been used to describe gender equality, including what some writers have named 'equal rights feminism' (Braidotti, 1991), 'equal treatment' (Bacchi, 1990), 'those who anticipate a genuinely gender-free theory' (Phillips, 1991), and the 'equality category' (Scott, 1988). This strand of feminist theory and related politics minimizes, or denies, differences between women and men because they represent obstacles to socio-economic equality. Moreover, there is a strong emphasis on facilitating women's participation in paid work on an equal footing, and indeed, the dominant areas of research informed by equality feminism are the investigation of gender divisions of paid labour, gender stratification, and the long-standing feminist struggle for equal wages for work of equal value.

STUDIES ON GENDER DIVISIONS OF DOMESTIC LABOUR

Most of the studies conducted on gender divisions of domestic labour are informed by the view that gender differences are to be avoided and gender equality is the gold standard that couples should strive for. Authors have employed various classifications to distinguish equal and unequal divisions of labour. For example, three well-known studies conducted in the mid to late 1980s in the United States (Hochschild, 1989), Britain (Brannen & Moss, 1991), and Wales (Morris, 1985) used relatively similar typologies to investigate equality between women and men in household life. These included 'traditional,' 'transitional,' 'egalitarian' (Hochschild, 1989); 'traditional,' 'traditional-rigid,' 'traditional-flexible,' and 'renegotiated' (Morris, 1985); and 'nearly equal sharing' or 'actual equal sharing' (Brannen & Moss, 1991, 180). Within such typologies, an 'egalitarian' household is one where the man and the woman do 'share[d] housework *equally*' (Hochschild, 1989) or 'whose contributions are roughly *equal* to one another' (Brannen & Moss, 1991) whether measured by minutes and hours, tasks, or overall responsibility. Whatever the terms used, the consensus by researchers is that something along the lines of fifty-fifty parenting or an equal division of labour is the ideal or most successful pattern (Brannen & Moss, 1991; Deutsch, 1999; Ehrensaft, 1984, 1987; Hochschild, 1989; Kimball, 1988). As Francine Deutsch recently put it, 'Equal sharers, of course, were the stars of this study' (Deutsch, 1999, 7).

STUDIES ON SHARED- OR PRIMARY-CAREGIVING FATHERS

The position that men can and do mother is also informed, at least implicitly, in equality frameworks that play down gender differences and assume that men and women are largely interchangeable as parents. Such is the argument made by most researchers who study equal parenting and shared- or primary-caregiving fathers (Coltrane, 1996; Crittenden, 2001; Deutsch, 1999; Ehrensaft, 1987; Hrdy, 1999; Jackson, 1995; Risman, 1987, 1998, 2004; Ruddick, 1995). This position is embraced, as mentioned in the introduction of this book, by authors from disciplines such as sociology (Coltrane, 1989, 1996; Risman, 1987, 1998, 2004; Ehrensaft, 1987), psychology (Kimball, 1988), philosophy (Ruddick, 1995, 1997), as well as by best-selling journalists (Crittenden, 2001; Jackson, 1995) all arguing that where men are doing the work of active caring, they are indeed mothering.

FATHERS' RIGHTS GROUPS

From the opposite end of the theoretical and political spectrum, a gender-equality argument is also made by some fathers' rights groups who have taken up discourses of equality and gender-neutral parenting to reinforce their claims in child custody cases for greater access to children (see Boyd, 2002; Mandell, 2002).

Clearly the positions on gender differences and equality in relation to parenting, and more specifically to the 'Do men mother?' question, are not uniform. Theorists and researchers have invoked varied versions of these approaches, depending on the empirical or theoretical issues under investigation. My own approach is to recognize the utility in each but to chart a third path down the middle. I now turn to the approach that underpins this book.

Charting a Path between Equality and Difference

Navigating the range of theoretical writing on gender differences and gender equality as well as the empirical research on gender divisions of domestic labour, I have been struck by how these two strands of thinking have not been more fully integrated. In reflecting on the Do men mother? question, I begin by considering how to obtain a richer understanding of the interactions of gender equality and gender differences in the domestic sphere. The seeds of my approach lie, first of all, in the growing consensus by feminist scholars that in certain theoretical and historical contexts, the concepts of gender equality and gender differences are highly interdependent, 'so that any adequate analysis must take account of the complex interplay between them' (Bock, 1992, 10; Bock & James, 1992; Offen, 1992).

Several key points recur in efforts to move out of the equality-difference gridlock, and these form some of the theoretical strands in this book. First, I shift my analytical lens from equality to *differences* and, moreover, from differences to *disadvantages* and to the *difference difference makes*. Second, I interrogate the terms on which equality is framed and then creatively envision the potential that arises from incorporating both the traditionally feminine and masculine in our understanding of what is valuable and significant in social life. The third tenet of my approach, which attempts to break down the difference-equality problem, is to focus on how to straddle both equality and difference through a version of 'strategic essentialism.' Fourth, I highlight the importance of considering differences *within* gender difference and ask, *Which men and which women are we speaking about?* That is, I incorporate insights from feminist intersectional theory (see below) in order to reflect on where and how social class, ethnicity, and sexuality can matter in caregiving.

Not Differences but Disadvantages

My first point in moving beyond the equality-difference dilemma has been well posited by the feminist legal scholar Deborah Rhode, who has maintained that rather than simply focusing on 'difference per se,' it is more useful to consider 'the disadvantages that follow from it' (Rhode, 1990, 204). She argues, 'The difference dilemma cannot be resolved; it can only be recast. The critical issue should not be difference, *but the difference difference makes*' (Rhode, 1989, 313; emphasis in original).[5] While it is an intriguing theoretical position, this issue of the *difference difference makes* has been given barely a mention in research on gender and domestic labour (but see Carrington, 1999; Doucet, 1995b). Rather, the overwhelming majority of studies on domestic life are framed by a search for equal parenting or equal divisions of labour.

It is important to note that it is understandable why gender *equality* has been the dominant framework for studying divisions of domestic labour. As mentioned in the introduction to this book, the weighting of the balance of household labour on the side of women has been very costly to many women (Adams & Coltrane, 2004; Bianchi, Milkie, Sayer, & Robinson, 2000; Cohen, 2004; Coltrane, 2000; Crittenden, 2001; Folbre, 2001). These costs can include occupational downgrading; loss of earnings, pensions, and benefits; economic vulnerability in cases of divorce; and long-term poverty for women (Arber & Ginn, 2004; Brannen & Moss, 1991; Folbre, 1994, 2001; Ginn & Arber, 2002; James, Edwards, & Wong, 2003). Yet while we know that women's experience in household life does often lead to disadvantages outside household life, this does not necessarily ease the challenges of delineating an equal division of labour. Janet Chafetz's assessment is one that informs research in this area: 'Undergirding all systems of gender stratification is a gender-based division of labour, by which women are chiefly responsible for different tasks than are men' (Chafetz, 1991, 77). Yet, does *different* always mean *unequal?* Can *differences* co-exist with *equality?*

The issue of the *difference difference makes* is the backdrop to my explorations of the complex interplay between equality and differences throughout this book. My approach is to examine what equality might actually mean in domestic life and parenting and to ultimately turn the focus from equality towards issues of gender differences and, moreover, towards considering how *differences* relate to *disadvantages*. Specifically, in chapter 3 ('Understanding Fathers as Primary Caregivers'), I unpack what it means to take on primary care of children, I reflect on what an equal division of labour might look like, and I accord attention to complexity, ambiguity, and the flow of differences and symmetries over time within households. Also, throughout chapters 4, 5, and 6, which focus on three key parental responsibilities (emotional, community, and moral), the question, What difference does difference make? is constantly at the forefront of my listening to fathers' narratives.

Equality on Whose Terms?

A second point in the difference-equality debate is the sombre realization that the *quality of equality* is often framed in male terms and thus needs to be constantly scrutinized. That is, although the equal rights tradition has been important as a theoretical tool and a political strategy for women's struggles to gain equal entry into and access to the rewards of the public world of work and politics, it nevertheless has its limitations as well. Many authors have concurred with Elizabeth Meehan and Selma Sevenhuijsen when they argue that 'the employment of equality as a concept and as a goal supposes a standard or a norm which, in practice, tends to be defined as what is characteristic of the most powerful groups in society' (Meehan & Sevenhuijsen, 1991; Rhode, 1989, 1990; Young, 1990a).

The importance of challenging the terms under which equality is pursued and the content of equality itself has been well expressed in the past decade in scholarship on work and caregiving. As reviewed in the introduction to this book, ample attention has been given to the politics of challenging the value of unpaid word and the conditions under which is it is performed. At the micro-level, the value of mothering has been deemed as 'socially necessary and praiseworthy' (Fraser & Gordon, 1997, 141). At the macro level, well-known scholars of caregiving have eloquently argued that its daily work should be integrated 'into a wide set of social practices, not only when it concerns the combination of paid labor and informal care in the life plans of individual citizens, but also when it comes to integrating care as a consideration in the social infrastructure and institutions of civil society' (Seven-huijsen, 2000, 21).

Questioning the terms on which equality is sought has a twofold significance in this book. First, the place of men – a group that, according to Connell (1987, 1995), reaps a 'patriarchal dividend' regardless of where they are placed in the social order – remains a complex issue. As mentioned in the introduction, when male voices articulate an 'ethic of care,' they can initially instill a sense of vertigo or tension.

Second, I continually turn the question of equality in whose terms? on its head in this book in the way that feminist theorists have done in reflecting on the problems with attempting to listen to women from male perspectives or with tools fashioned from the lives and perspectives of men. In this vein, the well-known American developmental psychologist Carol Gilligan wryly reflected on how models of human development were partly constructed from Levinson's *The Seasons of a Man's Life* (Gilligan, 1982). Similarly, the British sociologist Hilary Graham eloquently asked, 'Do her answers fit his questions?' (Graham, 1983b) when she observed that women's experiences were being measured in surveys designed using men's lives as the model. Still another decade later, also in Britain, the sociologist Rosalind Edwards wrote that the oft-repeated attempts to fit women's lives into male theories was much like trying to 'fit a round peg into a square hole' (Edwards, 1990, 479).

In the same way that feminists have exercised caution about the ways that we understand the voices of one gender against a landscape designed by the other, so too these cautions must be brought to bear when we study men in female-dominated domains of social life. In whose terms will we listen to them? Whether paid or unpaid, caregiving is undeniably a female-dominated profession that builds on what are considered traditionally feminine practices, and identities. In thus asking the question of equality on whose terms?, I am referring to the need to provide space for men's narratives of caregiving and to resist the impulse to measure, judge, and evaluate them through maternal standards (Hawkins & Dollahite, 1996; LaRossa, 1997; Richards, 1982). Adopting such a stance, with room for theoretical or empirical surprises, indeed offered innovative ways of describing and theorizing men's nurturing practices and ultimately novel ways of thinking about emotional responsibility (see chapter 4).

Straddling Equality and Difference: 'Both Horns of This Dilemma'

Many theorists have argued that the dilemma of both valuing care and challenging the conditions under which is it performed can best be addressed through a theoretical and political strategy that straddles *both* equality and difference. In relation to women's caregiving and the need to value as well as critique it, Allison Jaggar has referred to this position as 'having it both ways' and of embracing 'both horns of this dilemma' (Jaggar, 1990, 253). Deborah Rhode (1989, 1990) has called this 'taking a more contextual approach,' while Joan Tronto has argued for a disentangling of the 'feminine and feminist aspects of caring' (1989, 184). Referring to feminist struggles more widely, Luce Irigaray has invoked the metaphor of 'occupying two positions at once' (see Whitford, 1991), while Diana Fuss (1989) has employed 'strategic essentialism' as an approach and as a strategy.

How do I use such a theoretical approach in studying fathers? In the introduction to this book, I described my uncomfortable experience of speaking to an audience where several fathers' rights activists applauded my work, and my sudden and stark realization that fatherhood can be a politically sensitive area of research. To find a way to deal with this tension of encouraging men's participating in caregiving while not devaluing women's historical connection to caregiving, this book is underpinned by that approach devised by feminist theorists under the named of 'strategic essentialism,' that of taking a 'contextual position', or simultaneously holding 'two positions.' How, then, does this theoretical strategy actually work in practice?

Following Irigaray's metaphor of the two positions, the first position entails a close attentiveness to 'context and the complexity of women's interests' in concrete situations (Rhode 1990, 204). The second is to remain mindful of the fact that while in some contexts it is important to recognize gender differences, this should not translate into 'absolutist categorizations of difference' but rather a recognition that 'meanings are always relative to particular constructions in specified contexts' (Scott 1988, 175). Put differently, Diana Fuss argued that '... essentially speaking we need to theorize essentialist spaces from which to speak and, simultaneously, to deconstruct those spaces and keep them from solidifying' (1989, 118).

I begin by drawing on a first position, a 'contextual' or strategic essentialist approach, which looks widely to the social positioning of women and men in most societies and recognizes that while gender equality remains a lofty goal, profound gender differences still exist in regard to caregiving. Within this first position, I am mindful of several social facts: the invisibility of women's caregiving; the fathers described in this study are the exception rather than the norm; women still take on a disproportionate share of the responsibility for children; women's earnings are still less than those of men; and domestic violence and spousal abuse do exist in some families.

The second position is the larger terrain of the politics of challenging unpaid work, such as that described above in Selma Sevenhuijsen (see also Crittenden, 2001; Folbre, 2001; Luxton, 1997; Tronto, 1993), which highlights specific measures to assist mothers and fathers to achieve greater symmetry between employment and caregiving. Such measures would include income equity for women, greater acceptance by employers of fathers' use of parental leave, and work flexibility options for both men and women. It would also mean recognizing the possibility that men can nurture and care for children. This recognition is, however, not an unconditional one. Theoretically and politically, the feminist position that guides my work on fathers calls for the inclusion of men where it does not work to undermine women's own caregiving interests. That is, my feminist position on fathering is one that works towards challenging gendered asymmetries around care and employment, encouraging and embracing active fathering, while always remembering and valuing the long historical tradition of women's work, identities, and power in caregiving.

In adopting this two-part position, I look to the possibility of envisioning a future where men and women share fully and symmetrically in the joys and burdens of caregiving. While holding on to this hope, I remain cognizant of deeply ingrained gender differentials and power imbalances in the social conditions and life choices of women and men.

This perspective is implicitly, but not explicitly, addressed in this book. Rather, I mention it here as an imperceptible framing of both the conception and ultimate reception of this work. As meanings and messages take on a life of their own once they are free of their author's pen (Barthes, 1977; Foucault, 1977b), I am mindful of the need to be clear in my own mind about this book's underlying purpose and the tensions inherent in that purpose. As described earlier in this chapter, the epistemology of reception that will surround this book requires me to anticipate 'how and under what circumstances social scientific knowledge is received, evaluated, and acted upon and under what circumstances?' (May, 1998, 173). In taking a position that both works towards equality and recognizes gender differences in caregiving, I encourage active fathering while not diminishing a long and deep history of active mothering (see also postcript).

Intersectionality

A fourth point on moving beyond equality and differences relates to a wide array of differences *within* gender. Partly in response to the now central presence of post-modern, post-structural and post-colonial theories intersecting with feminism, recognition is constantly accorded to 'the multiple play of differences' (Scott, 1992, 174) among women's and men's experiences across culture, class, ethnicity, sexuality, and body. Arguing against additive models of identity (Spelman, 1988), which consider inequalities as separate from each other, feminists have articulated *intersecting*, or *interlocking*, forms of structure and agency (Cohambee River Collective 1983; hooks, 1981; Collins, 1994). The term in current use in feminist theory is *feminist intersectional theory.*

Studies on gender and household labour have been influenced by intersectional theory. While the initial focus of these studies was on predominantly middle-class white heterosexual couples, there has gradually been greater attention accorded to working-class or low-income households (Bolak, 1997; Luxton & Corman, 2001; Segura, 1994; Waller, 2002); ethnic diversity (Hofferth, 2003; Jain & Belsky, 1997; Mirande, 1988); and non-heterosexual couples (Bozett, 1988; Carrington, 1999; Doucet & Dunne, 2000; Dunne, 1999). In spite of this movement, however, studies on shared-caregiving couples or primary-caregiving fathers have continued to focus mainly on the narratives of middle-class white fathers and families (Deutsch, 1999; Dienhart, 1998; Ehrensaft, 1984; Gerson, 1993; Kimball, 1988; Pruett, 2000; Radin, 1982; Russell, 1987a). Part of the difficulty with qualitative research studies on these non-traditional families is the uneasy task of finding a sample of respondents and then encouraging them to open up their private lives to an inquiring researcher. Such obstacles to achieving diversity were clearly in evidence in my study, which took over three years and multiple strategies to gain a sample with a good level of diversity across social class, ethnicity, and sexual orientation (see chapter 2).

The importance of including diverse groups was thus a clear consideration in the selection of a research sample of fathers, but analyzing the interplay of differences between women and men still posed many challenges. That is, the ways in which multiple differences interact, and indeed *matter*, are hardly straightforward. In this vein, I draw on recent concerns in feminist literature on how contextual and empirical factors are important in considering how inequalities play out. Barbara Risman, for example has emphasized that '[t]here is a difference between an analysis of psychological, historical or sociological mechanisms that construct inequalities and the subjective experiences of the outcome of such mechanisms ... To focus all investigations into the complexity or subjective experiences of interlocking oppressions would have us lose access to how the mechanisms for different kinds of inequalities are produced' (Risman, 2004, 443).

In a similar vein, Jane Ward has argued that 'not all differences are created equally' (Ward, 2004, 83) and that at times 'counting and ranking' inequalities may be a sound political strategy. As demonstrated throughout this book, issues of intersectionality played out in varied ways with gender often being the main axis of differentiation in parenting. There were, however, diverse and unique intersections being mapped out between gender, class, ethnicity, and sexuality in relation to emotional, community, and moral responsibilities (see chapters 4, 5, and 6).

In addition to addressing these four points on gender differences and gender equality, I also incorporate critical contributions from current thinking in five other areas. Under the large umbrella of gender relations and divisions, these include the social construction of gender; gender and domestic responsibility; masculinities; embodiment; and spatial and situational contexts of gender relations.

Gender Relations and Divisions

Gender as Structure and Agency

Although there are now ample theoretical treatments of gender as a social structure (Ferree, Lorber, & Hess, 1999; Lorber, 1994; Martin, 2003; Risman, 2004), R.W. Connell's gender relations approach is a useful one to summarize my overall theoretical perspective on gender relations in that it seeks to 'understand the different dimensions of structures of gender, the relations between bodies and society and the patterning or configuration of gender' (Connell, 2000, 24-5). Like many other gender theorists, Connell maintains that gender exists as both structure and agency. His is a fluid notion of structure, broadly rooted in Giddens's structuration theory and the duality of structure (Giddens, 1984), which posits a constantly dialectical and recursive relationship between individuals and social structure so that, ultimately, they are constantly shaping and reshaping one another (see also Risman, 2004). Gender both structures social practice and occurs in the daily interactional social practices of women and men. In short, gender both constrains and enables action (Connell, 1987). While recognizing, as Pierre Bourdieu does (Bourdieu, 1977), 'the inventiveness and energy with which people pursue their lives' (Connell, 1987, 95), Connell also cautions that social structure is weighty: 'the gender order does not blow away at a breath' (Connell, 2000, 14).

Connell's is a fourfold model of gender relations that incorporates relations of power,[6] production,[7] emotions,[8] and symbolism[9] (Connell, 1987, 1995, 2000). It also focuses on gender as structure and agency, thus recognizing the gender inequities in the local and global structures within which households and families are located while also noting the potential for change by groups of individuals.

At the level of analysing everyday life, and at the level of what sociologists term collective and individual agency, my approach is one where women and men are active participants in the construction of gender. This approach is well captured by Scott Coltrane in his comprehensive overview of household labour; he writes, 'Perhaps the most popular approach to emerge in the last decade, gender construction theories, suggest that women and men perform different tasks because such practices affirm and reproduce gendered selves, thus producing a gendered interaction order. Drawing on symbolic interactionist, phenomenological, ethnomethodological, and feminist understandings of everyday life, the gender construction approach posits active subjects limited by situational exigencies, social structural constraints, and submerged power imbalances' (Coltrane, 2000, 1213).

My work has been especially informed by symbolic interactionism and its concept of the interactionist self as a basis for self-definition and action (see Barker, 1994; K. Daly, 1996, 2002; Finch & Mason, 1993; McMahon, 1995). As detailed at length in chapter 6, the ways in which men and women conduct themselves in their domestic and community lives are simultaneously informed by and form part of their moral identities, which are conceived as the shoulds and oughts of gendered social behaviours and norms. Furthermore, chapters 5 and 6 highlight how both women and men struggle with dominant 'moral' conceptions of how they should act as gendered household and community actors. More specifically, in relation to their identities and practices as caregivers and/or earners, men not only feel observed and judged, but they can also be subjected to varying degrees of suspicion, monitoring, and surveillance.

Gender and Domestic Responsibility

Throughout the past two decades, increasing attention has been directed at revising methodological and theoretical measurements of *time* (Davies 1990, 1994; Sullivan, 1996; Pleck & Mascaidrelli, 2004) with critical advances in conceptualizing household *tasks* so as to focus on the 'values, meanings and expressive goals with which women and men imbue their housework and understandings of gender' (Sanchez & Kane, 1996: 361; see also DeVault, 1991; Greenstein, 1996; Mederer, 1993). There has also been a focus on defining and theorizing the concept of *responsibility* in relation to the care of children (see Allen and Hawkins, 1999; DeVault, 1991; Doucet, 2000, 2001; Barnett & Baruch, 1987; Leslie et al., 1991; Mederer, 1993). With regard to the latter, several general impulses can be highlighted from this scholarship. First, as indicated in one of the most widely cited works on fathering and responsibility, there is a distinction between engagement (i.e., direct interaction with the child) and accessibility (i.e., availability to the child), and responsibility (i.e., planning and organizing around the child) (Lamb, Charnov, & Levine, 1987). Second, researchers have recognized that domestic responsibility involves 'remembering, planning and scheduling' (Barnett & Baruch, 1987, 33; see also DeVault, 1991, 56; Leslie, Anderson & Branson, 1991). Third, responsibility employs a range of responses, including '"feeling," "thinking" and "taking action"' (see Leslie, Anderson & Branson, 1991, 199). Finally, methodological complexity in measuring responsibility has been highlighted and, in light of such complexity, authors have lamented how responsibility is still rarely measured (see Coltrane, 2004; Leslie, Anderson, & Branson, 1991). For example, Leigh Leslie and colleagues have argued that 'the concept of "responsibility" itself involves complex methodological issues that may account, in part, for the lack of empirical attention'; they thus insist that '[t]o capture the complexity of the work of being responsible for a child, a multi-pronged approach is needed' (Leslie, Anderson & Branson, 1991, 199).

Throughout this book, I argue for a wide conceptualization of the responsibility for children that is simultaneously relational and interactional (chapter 4), both intra-household and inter-household (chapter 5), as well as both material and 'moral' (see chapter 6). While my arguments begin with the advances made by authors who specifically research issues of domestic labour, they are also rooted in two other sets of literature, as explored below.

DOING GENDER

My first theoretical underpinning for a wide concept of responsibility is rooted in a now well-established body of research in sociology and family studies; this theoretical approach 'focuses on individuals' construction of themselves through relational, interactional labours such as housework and childcare' (Sanchez & Kane, 1996, 361) (see also Backett, 1982; Thompson & Walker, 1989; West & Fenstermaker, 1993; West & Zimmerman, 1987). Originating in ethnomethodological analyses of gender relations, a relational or interactional approach to domestic labour concentrates on the way couples create and maintain gendered distinctions in domestic life and in gendered identities through their daily interactions. As stated by Linda Thompson and Alexis Walker a decade ago, 'Women and men participate together to construct the meaning of gender and distinguish themselves from each other *as* women or *as* men' (Thompson & Walker, 1989, 865). A relational and interactional approach to domestic responsibility builds on the already acknowledged recognition of the cognitive, emotional and activity dimensions of domestic responsibility (e.g., Leslie, Anderson, Branson, 1991). However, in addition to individuals' assessment of their 'being responsible' or 'feeling responsible' (see also Brannen & Moss, 1991; Hochschild, 1989), responsibility is viewed as not only as relationships between a person and particular domestic tasks but more important as relationships *between people*.

INTER-HOUSEHOLD RELATIONS AND DOMESTIC LABOUR

There is a wide body of feminist work that draws attention to the critical significance and role of work and relationships outside household life as key factors in sustaining gender divisions of labour within the home. For example, British sociologists, notably Lydia Morris (1985, 1990, 1995), recognize the importance of gender-segregated social networks in sustaining gender divisions of labour and gender ideologies about women's and men's appropriate employment and household roles (see also Bott, 1957; Gregson and Lowe, 1993, 1994; Finch and Mason, 1993).[10] The work of black feminist scholars widens this discussion in pointing to how community networks and inter-household relations are integral elements of black motherhood (see Collins, 1991, 1994). In addition, feminist research on 'kin work' (Di Leonardo, 1987; Stack, 1974), 'household service work' (Sharma, 1986), 'servicing work' (Balbo, 1987), and community work in low-income Third World urban settings (see Moser, 1993) also reveal the larger web of social relations within which domestic labour is enacted. Finally, a growing body of feminist work on women's friendships and the 'complex maternal worlds' built up around child rearing help to account for the gender-differentiated experiences of early parenting (see Bell & Ribbens, 1994). What *all* these studies have in common is an emphasis on looking out-side the household, at inter-household relations, in order to under-stand intra-household life and labour. These insights will be developed in this book through an argument that domestic responsibility is rela-tional in both intra-household and inter-household domains.

Masculinities

My approach to understanding gender relations and division in parent-ing and domestic life draws on the well-developed concept of mascu-linities.[11] While the literature on this topic, much like its sister field of gender studies, has proliferated over the past two decades, there has been some consensus by scholars on a number of key points. First, there is a plurality of masculinities (Brittan, 1989; Hearn & Morgan, 1990); that is, the meaning of masculinities differs across and within settings and there are, at the level of practice, several types of relations between kinds of masculinities (Connell, 2000; Lesko, 2000; O'Donnell & Sharpe, 2000; Pease, 2000). Second, masculinities are not essences that individ-uals have. Rather, they occur in social relations where issues of power and difference are at play and where masculinities exist at both the lev-els of agency and structure. As detailed by R.W. Connell, 'The patterns of conduct our society defines as masculine may be seen in the lives of individuals, but they also have an existence beyond the individual. Masculinities are defined in culture and sustained in institutions' (Con-nell, 2000, 11). A third point is that there is a distinction between men and masculinities in that 'sometimes masculine conduct or masculine identity goes together with a female body,' and similarly it is also 'very common for a [biological] man to have elements of "feminine" identity, desire and patterns of conduct' (Connell, 2000, 16). This latter observa-tion is particularly relevant when studying men who are engaging in female-dominated or feminine-identified work such as caregiving.

While all the above points inform my work on fathering, the most critical one relates to the much discussed concept of 'hegemonic masculinity' as adapted from the work of Antonio Gramsci and developed by Connell and colleagues (Carrigan, Connell & Lee, 1985; Coltrane, 1994; Connell, 1987, 1995, 2000; Kimmel, 1994; Messner, 1997). Hegemonic masculinity is defined as 'the most honored or desired' form of masculinity (Connell 2000, 10), one that usually aligns itself with traditional masculine qualities of 'being strong, successful, capable, reliable, in control. That is, [t]he hegemonic definition of manhood is a man *in* power, a man *with* power, and a man *of* power (Kimmel, 1994, 125; emphasis in original). Further, as Connell points out, hegemonic masculinity is perhaps most strongly identified '*as the opposite of femininity*' (Connell, 2000, 31; my emphasis). Other forms of masculinity, then, have come to be viewed as subordinated (especially gay masculinities), marginalized (exploited or oppressed groups such as ethnic minorities) and complicit masculinities (those organized around the complicit acceptance of what has come to be termed the 'patriarchal dividend') (Connell, 1995, 2000).

Increased empirical and ethnographic studies of men's lives have shed light on the diverse ways that hegemonic and other kinds of masculinities can play out in the same setting. In particular, the issue of where caregiving and fathering fit into this spectrum requires greater attention. Some authors have argued that fathers' caregiving practices are 'adopted by the hegemonic form of masculinity,' so that rather than challenge hegemonic masculinity, caregiving becomes incorporated into it (Brandth & Kvande, 1998; Dryden, 1999). Others have recently argued that fathering and caregiving can be seen as *complicit* in that fathers can express support for equal parenting while maintaining more traditional patterns of gender divisions of labour (see Plantin, Sven-Axel, & Kearney, 2003). Whatever the configuration of diverse masculinities, it is clear that 'the interplay between hegemonic and subordinate masculinities suggests the experience of masculinity is far from uniform and that new ways of theorizing these differences need to be developed' (Hearn & Morgan, 1990, 11). Moreover, as indicated by Connell, research on these varied combinations of masculinities 'is surely an empirical question, not one to be settled in advance by theory' (Connell, 2000, 23). Through this empirical study of fathers as primary caregivers, I pose questions about where hegemonic masculinity fits into the 'Do men mother?' question.

Specifically, I explore two key questions throughout this book. First,

I engage with David Morgan's compelling claim that 'one strategy of studying men and masculinities would be to study those situations where masculinity is, as it were, on the line' (Morgan, 1992, 99). Do fathers as primary caregivers put masculinity on the line, or do they reconfigure that same *line* according to what is defined as masculine or feminine? Second, do fathers' everyday caregiving practices confirm or challenge current theoretical understandings of masculinities? Specifically, given that hegemonic masculinity is largely associated with the devaluation of the feminine while caring is often equated with feminine practice, what is the relationship between hegemonic masculinity and care? That is, does fathers' caregiving disrupt the smooth surface of hegemonic masculinity? These questions are dealt with, in varied ways, in chapters 4, 5, and 6.

Embodiment

Like masculinities and fatherhood, the 'human body has in recent years become a "hot" topic in sociology' (Howson & Inglis, 2001a) and, as with the literatures on care and gender, there is indeed a 'whole industry of research and scholarship on the body' (Nettleton & Watson, 1998, 2; see also Shilling, 1993).

   In the expansive field of embodiment, I locate myself in the growing movement away from a largely theoretical sociology of the body to one that accords attention to 'concrete incorporating practices and sometimes messy empirical realities of actual flesh and blood bodies' (Monaghan, 2002, 335). As Lois Wacquant points out, 'One of the paradoxical features of recent social studies of the body is how rarely one encounters in there actual living bodies of flesh and blood' (Wacquant, 1995, 65). Where empirical studies of embodied aspects of men's lives *have* been conducted, they have focused mainly on hyper-masculine displays of bodies (Connell, 1995; Watson, 1998), male violence (Messerschmidt, 1999; Connell, 2000; Klein, 1983), body builders and boxing (Connell, 1995, 2000; Wacquant, 1995), men's health (Watson, 1998), and boys' embodiment in schools (Prendergast & Forrest, 1998). What is noticeable, however, is the scant attention given to these issues of 'messy empirical realities' within family life. According to David Morgan, '[D]espite these new explorations and developments around the sociology of the body it may be argued that there has still been relatively little systematic treatment of family and family issues under the heading of the sociology of the body' (Morgan, 1996, 113). This is a surprising omission, given that families are deeply imbued with embodied interactions and that practices of caring for others are so intrinsically embodied. Building mainly on the work of the philosopher Maurice Merleau-Ponty and the eminent sociologist Irving Goffman, as well as on feminist contributions to understandings of the body and space, my approach to embodiment, as discussed below, is fourfold.

EMBODIED SUBJECTS, EMBODIED AGENTS

For social scientists wishing to explore the 'lived experience' of embodied subjects, it is the phenomenological work of Maurice Merleau-Ponty (1962, 1964, 1965, 1968) and his concept of 'body subjects' that has become one of the most well cited work on bodies and embodiment (see, for example, Burkitt, 1999; Crossley, 1995a, 2001; Csordas, 1990; Howson & Inglis, 2001b; Nettleton & Watson, 1998).[12] The main tenor of his arguments as developed in *Phenomenology of Perception* (1962) and his unfinished last text, *The Visible and the Invisible* (1968), include the indivisibility of mind and body, the body subject as active and engaged with the world, human beings as embodied social agents, and human perception as intrinsically embodied. According to Charles Taylor, 'If one were to sum up Merleau-Ponty's philosophical legacy in a phrase, one might say more than any other that he taught us what it means to understand ourselves as embodied agents' (C. Taylor, 1990, 1). In his own own words, '[W]e are in the world through our body, and ... we perceive that world within our body' (Merleau-Ponty, 1962, 206).

A SHIFT FROM EMBODIED EXPERIENCES TO EMBODIED NARRATIVES

Unlike authors who emphasize that their 'concern is to examine how people experience their bodies and in particular how they articulate their experiences' (Nettleton & Watson, 1998, 3-4) or conduct 'social theorizing from lived bodies' (Williams & Bendelow, 1998b, 3), my interest is in *embodied narratives* or 'embodied ethnography' (Monaghan, 2002). As noted by many other theorists, attempts to grasp one's experience are contentious in that, epistemologically, this assumes a subject that is pre-social and beyond discursivity and representation (Burkitt, 1999; Scott & Morgan, 1993; Young, 1990b). Moreover, methodologically, to view subjects' words as transparent passageways into their experiences or selves is to get caught in what Wendy Hollway and Tony Jefferson refer to as the 'transparent self problem' or the 'transparent account problem' (Hollway & Jefferson,

2000, 3). Quite simply, processes of knowing others involve interpretation, translation, and ultimately transformation (see Mauthner & Doucet, 2003). My research thus investigates how men and women *talk* about the embodied aspects of parenting in direct and indirect ways. Rather than attempt to bring '"lived bodies" into sociology' (Nettleton & Watson, 1998, 3), I aim to make visible some of the embodied elements of fathers' and mothers' narratives and to bring those into sociology and into our larger theoretical and empirical understandings of mothering and fathering.

BODIES AS CONTINGENT AND VARIABLE

My third point about embodiment is that bodies, and their effects, vary across particular spaces and sites over time. This is very much in line with the work of many sociological and feminist writers who argue that while the body does have a biological and material base, it is nevertheless modified and variably enacted within different social contexts. That is, 'the socially contingent nature of the body, and how it is experienced, will vary according to how, where, and when it is located and the nature of the social situations which prevail' (Nettleton & Watson, 1998, 8). Moria Gatens has similarly argued that there is no 'true nature of the body but rather it is a process and its meanings and capacities will vary according to its context (Gatens, 1996, 57).[13] These contingent and variable meanings across different contexts further call for a greater appreciation of body and space.

BODY AND SPACE

In attempting to make sense of the relationship of a body to particular spaces, I first turned to the work of Goffman (Goffman, 1963, 1969, 1972, 1987) and the lenses through which he is read (see Burkitt, 1999; Crossley, 1995b; Mellor & Shilling, 1997; Williams & Bendelow, 1998a). From Goffman, I take several concepts that have relevance for my work on fathers and the ways in which they move with children through female-dominated public spaces.[14] The most relevant here is the 'moral' quality of bodily movement through public spaces (Doucet, 2005b).

Goffman argues that relations between people – inter-subjective relations – are both practical and moral. They are practical in that we learn how to move through spaces in ways that are acceptable, normal, and in concert with public expectations. These movements are also moral in the sense that embodied agents not only interact but make judgements about how people maintain or disrupt routine social and public interactions. 'The public order in which body techniques are exercised is not only a practical order ... [but] it is equally a *moral* character' (Crossley, 1995b, 139).[15] As Goffman puts it, 'Bodily norms not only enable individuals to recognize and label others ... but to grade them hierarchically, and stigmatize them in a manner which facilitates discrimination' (1963, 168). Thus, one's sense of self, her moral worth, and her understandings of herself as normal are at stake as she moves through public spaces and engages in public encounters (see Crossley, 1995b).

The image, as related in this book's Introduction, of my husband's attempting to push our daughter's stroller into the moms-and-tots public space in a church basement in Cambridge and his feeling like an abnormal embodied agent disrupting 'complex maternal worlds' (Bell & Ribbens, 1994) is one that constantly came to mind as I worked through Goffman's work on space and body. Throughout this book, fathers narrate similar social scenes of a perceived misfit between embodied gendered subjects as they move through what several men called 'estrogen-filled worlds,' especially in the early years of parenting infants and toddlers (see chapters 5 and 6).

If it is the case that 'bodies do matter' (Messerschmidt, 1999), how *do* they matter in my work on men, mothering, and fathering? Throughout this book, I attempt to make visible the embodied quality of mothers' and fathers' narratives. What will be revealed, in the chapters that follow, is that sometimes bodies *do not* matter. When a father is attending to children – by cuddling, feeding, reading, bathing, or talking to them – gendered embodiment can be largely negligible. But there are also times when embodiment *can* come to matter a great deal, both for the men in these situations as well as for those who are observing them. As detailed in chapters 5 and 6, this 'social gaze' at men's movements with children as they inhabit female-dominated community spaces is made all the more penetrating because it is tinged with suspicion and surveillance.

The sites where embodiment matters as disruption include recent versions of the moms-and-tots groups (community playgroups), schoolyards, classrooms, and other female-dominated venues. They also include instances of fathers caring for the children of others, or of single fathers hosting girls' sleepover parties (see chapter 6). It is in the latter two circumstances that many fathers speak about how they must tread carefully because of moral judgements about the fit between male bodies and other embodied subjects. At certain times and in certain sites, differently gendered bodies cannot simply be substituted for each other. Yet there are also sites and times where gendered embodiment seems inconsequential. With each passing year and with the increased presence of fathers on the social landscapes of parenting, this sense of disruptiveness has gradually eased, and at times it seems to have completely dissipated. Nevertheless, it can be ignited quickly. Indeed, the situations where gender does or does not matter are examples of 'borderwork' and 'border crossings.' As explored below, this is the final part of my theoretical approach.

Gender and Shifting Contexts: Borderwork and Border Crossing

An innovative way of thinking about gender in particular spatial sites and at particular times is offered in the work of the American sociologist Barrie Thorne. Her book *Gender Play: Girls and Boys in Schools* (1993) provides richly detailed observations of children and the varied contexts of boys' and girls' interactions in classrooms, schoolyards, lunch rooms, school line-ups, and neighbourhood streets and playgrounds. One of Thorne's main points is that in gendered interactions, *contexts do matter.* That is, particular spaces and moments have an impact on the way gender is experienced by people and perceived, in turn, by onlookers and observers. While Thorne's units of analysis are children's spatial sites, her reflections on extensive gender separation, the meanings of these gender divides, and, conversely, the cross-gender activity that breaks down the borders between genders have relevance for our understandings of mothering and fathering. The two key concepts from Thorne's work, which underpin my analysis in this book, are borderwork[16] and border crossings.

BORDERWORK
The concept of borderwork is used to describe spaces and times where intense gender differences are intensely perceived and experienced. Thorne reflects on how certain situations create the illusion of opposite sides between girls and boys. Using commonplace examples such as games of boys chasing girls or contests that pit girls against boys, she notes that there is 'a sense of the boys and the girls as separate and opposing sides' as well as 'the magnetism of gender-marked events for observers, participants and in the realms of memory' (Thorne, 1993, 64). She names these instances *borderwork* because they erect boundaries or borders between the genders, and their presence *works* at creating and maintaining gender borders. In

short, our minds and memories hold on to those instances through childhood and later in adulthood, where gender creates and reaffirms differences. As Thorne writes, 'The occasions of borderwork may carry extra perceptual weight because they are marked by conflict, intense emotions, and the expression of forbidden desires' (Thorne, 1993, 85).

Building on her observations of boys and girls play in classrooms, lunchrooms hallways, and schoolyards, Thorne makes several theoretical points. First, she argues that a constant emphasis placed on instances of borderwork has resulted in a 'hegemonic view of gender' that has serious consequences for how we conceptualize gender. Second, according too great an 'emphasis on gender as oppositional dualism' leads to an 'exaggeration of gender difference and disregard for the presence of crosscutting variation and sources of commonality' (Thorne, 1993, 86). Third, while borderwork is a concept that assists us in understanding how there are times and sites where gender boundaries are distinctly strong and oppositional, there are also times when the boundaries are relaxed to the point that they are barely noticeable. Thorne thus cautions that 'although the occasions of gender separation may seem more dramatic, the mixed-gender encounters are also theoretically and practically important' (Thorne, 1993, 36). To develop this point about relaxed gender borders and the less visible mixed-gender encounters that also occur in varied sites and at varied times, she offers her concept of 'crossing the gender divide' or the crossing of boundaries or borders.

BORDER CROSSINGS

By alluding to a concept of border crossing, Thorne shows that 'children sometimes successfully cross the gender divide' (Thorne, 1993, 61). She thus emphasizes not only the 'apart' but also the 'with' instances of gender mingling as a critical part of the contextual nature of gender, since frameworks that emphasize only gender differences 'cannot grasp the fluctuating significance of gender in the ongoing scenes of social life' (Thorne, 1993, 61). Thorne sees gender not as static unchanging interactions but rather as fluid relationships that are adaptive and contextual. She also highlights an important fact about gender research: the times that boys and girls are opposed to each other are more noticeable to observers, and, therefore, these occasions receive more attention in the literature. As a result, '[g]ender is often equated solely with dichotomous difference, but ... gender waxes and wanes in the organization and symbolism of group life, and that flux needs close attention' (Thorne, 1993, 64).

These concepts of borderwork and border crossings are utilized in my work on gender differences and gender equality in parenting because they provide useful metaphors for the ways in which space and time matter and how gender borders can be both 'quickly built and as quickly dismantled' (Thorne, 1993, 84). It is worth reflecting, then, on what activates or deactivates the boundaries between girls and boys, men and women, mothers and fathers. Who are the gatekeepers at these borders? In looking at how and when gender crossings occur, Thorne also lays out different tools and resources that facilitate such crossings. Particularly noteworthy are the instances where boys attempt to cross into girls' activities and the tensions that ensue due to being teased about being a sissy or a 'failed male' (Thorne, 1993, 116). The resources that assist boys in crossing over into female-dominated activities have relevance for our understandings of fathers moving into the similarly female-dominated terrain of parenting.

Throughout chapters 4, 5, and 6, my exploration of the question 'Do men mother?' intersperses key examples of borderwork where gender differences and borders are in play between women and men, the resources and factors that take down this same border, and instances where the border is invisible or muted. Moments and sites where borderwork are evident include postnatal massage classes, playgroups with infants and toddlers, men standing in schoolyards and volunteering in classrooms, men and women's friendship patterns around children, single fathers and teen daughters' sleepovers, as well as the range of beliefs about the exclusive social bond between mothers and children. Border crossings are also in evidence throughout the years of child rearing. As detailed in chapters 4, 5, and 6, several factors that encourage border crossing – or that confound gender binaries – include the passing of time within households and within communities; the lead that mothers take in influencing fathering patterns; particular biographical contexts where crisis or challenge force unexpected changes in mothers and fathers; and resources of masculinity such as social class, breadwinning, and demonstrated heterosexuality.

Conclusions

My work on men, mothering, and fathering is framed by several weighty bodies of academic literature. My intention in this chapter has been to sketch some of the elemental contours of my theoretical approach and to convey the ways that the stories of fathering as told here are rooted in such established scholarship and understandings of gender, men's lives, women's lives, mothering and fathering, masculinity and embodiment. I saw and heard fathers' narratives through these lenses and hearing aids, and at times I sought out new ones to make sense of unexpected currents in fathers' stories. In asking the 'Do men mother?' question, I indicate where gender similarities are in evidence, where gender differences ignite, like borderwork, and where gender is muted and fathers become parents in seemingly ungendered ways. In the next two chapters, I highlight the methodological and epistemological details and challenges involved in coming to know fathers' stories, and I unpack some of the key theoretical concepts that form an integral part of understanding fathers as primary caregivers.

2 Knowing Fathers' Stories through Gossamer Walls

Introduction

Gossamer (adj): Sheer, light, delicate, or tenuous.

(*Oxford English Dictionary*)

Awake at night, I'd hear her breathing or singing next to me in the dark, half comforted, half terrified that my ear was pressed against the wall between the living and the dead, that the vibrating membrane between them was so fragile. I felt her presence everywhere, in daylight, in rooms I knew weren't empty ... Watching with curiosity and sympathy from her side of the gossamer wall.

(Anne Michaels, *Fugitive Pieces*)

This chapter begins with an evocative image of a gossamer wall from Anne Michaels's novel *Fugitive Pieces*, about Jakob, a young Jewish-Polish boy who, at the age of seven, has a series of tragic and miraculous experiences; these include the murder of his parents and the apparent abduction of his older sister, Bella, by the Nazis, his own fortunate escape, and then his rescue by a Greek geologist who smuggles Jakob to his native island of Zakynthos. Weaving together two generations of men, the settings of Greece and Canada, loss and healing, geology and poetry, the book is also framed by the haunting relationship between Jakob and Bella, who is always present and painfully absent throughout the days of his life. The sense of separation and connection is beautifully captured in the image of a gossamer wall as a metaphor for the delicate space between him and his lost sister. Perceiving only a 'vibrating membrane between them [that] was so fragile,' Jakob is never quite sure which thoughts and experiences are his and which are Bella's.

The image of ghosts and gossamer is also present in the work of the sociologist Martha McMahon in a similar manner but specifically in relation to social science research. She reflects on the way 'shadow others' of her childhood, especially her Irish aunts, came to haunt her and to dramatically influence her analysis of her interviews with Canadian mothers. McMahon confesses that 'hidden selves and shadow others are present in our stories,' and they 'draw us into the research in unforeseen and disturbing ways' (McMahon, 1996); '"absent others" or "shadow others" ... can include characters from the researcher's past and even the people the subjects are *trying* to become' (McMahon 1996, 320–1; see also McMahon 1995).

These poignant examples of how shadow subjects slip through gossamer walls to influence our hearing, interpretation, and telling of life stories are emblematic of a key dilemma in social research: how can we come to know others when our subjectivity is so entangled with our own multiple subjectivities – selves and shadow selves – and those of others? All qualitative researchers are faced with this issue. In the process of interviewing others and coming to know their stories, we confront the difficulty of determining where our own stories end and theirs begin, and where our listening is careful enough to hear what people are trying to tell us (Ribbens & Edwards, 1998). This is even more acute in research projects that focus on the personal, intimate, and private such as the fathering and mothering narratives that inform this book. While this problem of trying to know others cannot be overcome, there has been much grappling with it, particularly in the burgeoning literature on the concept of reflexivity.

Reflexivity, broadly defined, means reflecting on and understanding our own personal, political, and intellectual biographies as researchers and making explicit our location in relation to our research respondents. It also means acknowledging the critical roles we play in creating, interpreting, and theorizing research data. While reflexivity has certainly been an issue on social science research agendas for thirty years, and in anthropological studies for much longer (see Mauthner & Doucet, 2003), there has been an explosion of interest in it in the past decade. This is partly due to the enhanced recognition – as fostered by postmodern, poststructural, feminist, hermeneutic, interpretive, and critical discourses – that the knowledges we create are grounded in specific historical, cultural, and linguistic contexts. Within methodological discussions, however, most authors have focused on reflexivity's use in data collection and the interaction between researchers and research respondents during the interview process. Building on my jointly written work with Natasha Mauthner, the concept of reflexivity that informs this book is a very wide one that incorporates reflections on the personal, interpersonal, institutional, pragmatic, emotional, theoretical, epistemological, and ontological influences that shape our research (see Mauthner & Doucet, 1998, 2003; Doucet & Mauthner, 2002).

In considering the varied levels of reflexivity that occur in research practice, I have begun to think that Anne Michaels's evocative image of the gossamer wall is a useful one for theorizing the diverse sets of reflexive relationships that occur in research. In particular, I want to argue here that there are at least three gossamer walls that illustrate the thin and tenuous lines that exist in research relationships. The first is between researcher and her/his self. Here, I will draw on McMahon's 'shadow others,' 'absent others' and 'ghosts' from our past.

A second gossamer wall that exists between researchers and readers is an area of reflexivity that has been given minimal attention in the methodology literature (but see Mauthner & Doucet, 2003; Doucet & Mauthner, 2002). This one refers to issues of accountability and transparency in knowledge production, to what Loraine Code has referred to as the creation of 'responsible knowledge' (Code, 1988, 187–8), or the laying-down of what Clive Seale has called an 'audit trail' (Seale, 1999; 2002, 105) of methodological procedures. Thus, in this chapter, I detail for the reader not only the methods employed in my project for sampling, data collection, and data analysis, but I also outline a methodological and epistemological shift that occurred in my research and the implications that this shift had for the knowledge produced.

The third gossamer wall described in this chapter is between the researcher and the research respondents. While most work in this area has focused on the processes of intersubjectivity between researcher and researched during data collection, my particular interest is in the way this plays out during data analysis when the researcher has the power to selectively shape and reshape the respondents' stories into larger social science narratives (see also Mauthner & Doucet, 1998, 2003; Doucet, 1998).

Framed by these three gossamer walls, what follows below is a three-part discussion of the methodology and epistemology that underpin the research on which this book is based. I begin with the first gossamer wall, that of my own reflexive positioning, through an elaboration of significant aspects of my biographical and theoretical location within the project. Second, I discuss the gossamer wall between my readers and me by highlighting the methods employed in the project for sampling, data collection, and interviewing as well as a critical epistemological shift that occurred in my work and subsequently affected the analysis of my data and ultimately my findings. Third and finally, I briefly peel back the gossamer wall between me – the researcher – and my research respondents as I describe my data analysis processes and how I translated fathers' narratives into social science knowledge.

The Gossamer Wall between Researcher and Shadow Others

At varied points throughout the process of selecting research participants for this study, many fathers asked me how it was that I – as a woman, as a mother – came to be interested in the study of fathers and men's lives. I told a simple story, a true story. The initial impulse came from my own first experiences of parenting and my observations of my husband as he took on the primary care of our eldest daughter at varied points in her early years. As detailed in the introduction to this book, his recounting of the excruciatingly painful details of sitting sidelined in a moms and tots' group in Cambridge over several cold winter months in 1992, and the similar stories from fathers that I interviewed for my doctoral thesis on shared parenting (Doucet, 1995a), awakened my curiosity about the lives of fathers who challenge conventional gender norms. As my research progressed, however, I became increasingly aware of the many autobiographical ghosts on the other side of my gossamer wall.

Characters from the Researcher's Past

As I began to interview fathers and analyse their narratives, I entered the stage of immersion that most qualitative researchers know. It was here that the words of fathers filled my waking and sleeping hours and rolled through my conscious and unconscious mind. Their faces and their fathering stories mixed inextricably with the ghosts of fathers I had known throughout my life, particularly in the seventeen years when I was growing up in northern New Brunswick on the eastern coast of Canada. Throughout those years, I lived in a green wooden house on the Baie de Chaleur, a small bay that empties into the Atlantic Ocean. My house, which both my grandfather and father grew up in, sat on Main Street in the working-class, Catholic side of town. That house, my neighbourhood, and the whole town moved slowly and unquestionably along gender-divided lines. In our house, my father rose early six days a week, went to work at the paper mill, called by the screeching 8 a.m. whistle signalling the start of the men's morning shift. We heard him shuffle out the door while we gradually crawled out of bed to be fed and cared for by our mother. My father earned a wage that my mother ingeniously stretched to feed, house, and clothe six children. This is a familiar story, with some variations and mutations, that echoes repeatedly in the work of many scholars who have taken similar experiences and crunched them into numbers and social science narratives about the primary breadwinner male and the primary homemaker female.

But there is more. I was three years into this research project, and my life felt completely taken over with analysing fathers' interview transcripts when I awoke suddenly one night to a long-buried memory. I remembered a house, also on the bay, directly across the street from my childhood home. It was a duplex that belonged to Ozzie Aubie, a lobster fisherman.[1] In the upstairs apartment was a family led by my mother's second cousin, Penny Melanson, and her five daughters. The story was that her husband had lost all his money gambling, and he just up and left one day, leaving Penny to scrape together a living for her daughters. There was welfare, there was charity from the Catholic Women's League and the local nuns, and there was part-time work when she could get it. The town talked. More specifically, my grandmother, my mother, and my aunts talked. Penny was pitied for not having a man to provide a family wage. Yet, as they sat on our front veranda drinking coffee and looking across the street to Penny's house, they did acknowledge that she was a good mother. Her children were lacking nothing.

Meanwhile, in the downstairs apartment of that duplex was a family of four – Ozzie Aubie and his three sons – Billy, Johnny, and Harry. Other than the famous Canadian prime minister Pierre Trudeau taking on custody of his three sons, we had never seen a family living in a house without a mother. Again, the town talked. My grandmother, my mother, and my aunts talked. Where was their mother? How could she leave? Those poor Aubie boys. How would they ever turn out without a mother to raise them?

Billy was in my grade at school. Everything that went wrong with him was blamed on the fact that he wore the stain of being a motherless boy. In Grade 2 when he called me names, in Grade 3 when he chased me home from school, lifting up my skirt, in Grade 4 when he threw my newly knitted winter hat so high into our maple tree that it could never be recovered – each of these incidents was met with the same lamenting sigh and response from my mother and my aunts. 'Well, what do you expect? He has no mother.'

I grew up with the mystery of Billy's missing mother and the wonder of how it was that the town pitied the motherless family of Ozzie Aubie that lived downstairs, yet embraced Penny Melanson's fatherless family living upstairs. Moreover, my memory of Ozzie Aubie and his three sons is as much about *them* as it is about the *town* that defined them and how they in turn defined themselves in relation to this small and powerful place that watched and judged. Indeed, my attraction to symbolic interactionism, and its central concepts of self-other relations, as one of the key theoretical frameworks for my study on primary-caregiving fathers must have begun there in my constant watching of Ozzie Aubie's family and our community. When I think back to Billy through all my school years until we graduated together from high school, it was not just Billy I came to know but also the collective interpretations of him and his family by the town that talked – the town that watched with curiosity and sympathy, the town that still lives on the other side of my gossamer wall.[2]

These memories and assorted collages of reflections sprouted an interest, at times a passion and obsession, in me to investigate issues of how gender differences are constructed and enacted in domestic and community spaces. From the story of Ozzie Aubie and his three sons, I developed a deep personal and academic curiosity about the relationship between a primary-caregiving father and the community in which he lives, is defined, and judged. On the other side of this gossamer wall, there are many 'complex contexts and locationally variable aspects of cognitive practice' usually 'excluded from epistemological analysis' (Code, 1993, 20) that can be the rationale for our interest in a topic, the structure of our questions, and ultimately the knowledge created.

Shadow Selves

In addition to the ghosts and memories that haunt us as we make sense of narratives, there is also our social positioning and its effects on us, particularly when we analyze data and translate it into knowledge. My reflexive positioning as a white middle-class woman who was raised in a working-class family, an assimilated Acadian, an academic, a mother of three, a sister to three brothers meant that I had the emotional, biographical, and common-sense tools to understand some narratives more than others. I particularly felt myself drawn into the narratives of fathers from difficult working-class backgrounds. Admittedly my own background was not an economically or socially harsh one, largely because of extended family networks and two grandmothers who provided ample social resources. Nevertheless, my memories of our house on Main Street – on the working-class, Catholic side of town, near the paper mill and the low rental houses – translated into my identification with narratives from low-income backgrounds or ones from small towns where tolerance for diversity was largely stifled. I read such narratives with a tacit understanding as they brought me back to a place of familiar stories and rhythms.

In addition to peeling back some of the gossamer wall between me and the shadow others and biographical ghosts that came to matter in my research, a second gossamer wall between me, as researcher, and you, the reader, comes into play. In what follows, I offer the nitty-gritty details of how I came to construct knowledge from and about fathers.

The Gossamer Wall between Researcher and Reader

The knowledge that I constructed from and about fathers is part of what I have termed an ethnography of fathering. Here I am using 'a broad interpretation of ethnography as a research process based on fieldwork using a variety of (mainly qualitative) research techniques but including engagement in the lives of those being studied over an extended period of time' (Davies, 1999, 4–5).[3] This research process included a range of qualitative methods: semi-structured face-to-face interviews, telephone interviews, focus groups, Internet surveys, and couple interviews. While this ethnography is rooted in my own process of becoming a parent fifteen years ago, my constant interactions and observations of other mothers and fathers, as well as in a previous study on shared-caregiving couples (Doucet, 1995a), the process effectively began with my search for a sample of fathers who would participate in the study.

Finding the Fathers

My search for fathers to participate in my study began in the summer of 1999, when I placed several ads in community newspapers in the city of Ottawa. The caption read, 'Attention, Fathers: Are you a primary caregiver of your children?' The response was overwhelming. Within days, over fifty fathers left messages on my voice mail at Carleton University. I was astounded. The study had clearly hit a nerve with fathers who felt a strong desire or need to speak about their experiences. Having read that men are often reluctant participants in research studies (Daly, 1993), I had expected that it would take months or years to amass a reasonable sample of fathers. In that first round, after phoning each father back and speaking with him to gain a sense of his status as a primary caregiver, I sent each father a background form to fill in. The number dwindled to about half the original response. Some of the fathers chose not to participate, perhaps unwilling to sit through an interview. At that point, I decided to offer fathers several ways of participating in the interview, including an in-depth interview, a focus group, a telephone interview, or an Internet survey. The latter would allow fathers to participate but with less interaction and in a way that they could organize around their schedules. Also at this stage, it became clear that a few single fathers who had answered my newspapers ads clearly had a political or personal vendetta against their ex-wives, and I feared that they saw the interview as a forum to vent their frustrations. I thus chose not to interview these men, or they decided not to follow through by not sending in their background forms.

The three years that followed this initial phase of enthusiastic response included intensive and sporadic recruitment, which was long and arduous, even with the assistance of varied community centres and research assistants. The chief difficulty I faced was in locating a reasonable number of fathers who represented diverse segments of the Canadian population, including fathers of ethnic minorities, fathers from lower social income brackets, and gay fathers. To gain the participation of diverse groups, I contacted over twenty agencies and organizations throughout Canada, including community and health centres, programs working with ethnic minority groups, fathers' organizations, and gay fathers' groups. I was able to recruit twenty-four fathers through this method of target sampling.

Over a three-year recruitment period, fifty-one fathers responded to ads in national and local newspapers, small community papers, school newsletters, a university publication and ads in newsletters of varied ethnic organizations. Furthermore, twenty-four fathers were found through snowball sampling, whereby one father, or an acquaintance, would provide me with the name of somebody he knew who was a primary caregiver (Miles & Huberman, 1994). Four fathers were found by simply approaching them in public settings,[4] and fifteen fathers discovered the study on my Web site and contacted me.

Who Are the Fathers?

The research sample for my study consists of 118 Canadian fathers who self-define as primary caregivers of their children.[5] Most of the fathers (60 per cent or 70 of 118) were found in Canada's capital city, Ottawa, while the geographical locations of the other 48 are as follows: 13 from cities and 13 from rural areas in the province of Ontario, 5 from the province of Quebec, and a further 13 from six other Canadian provinces; thus fathers participated from eight of Canada's ten provinces and three territories. In addition to the fathers, fourteen couples (with a stay-at-home father and with some diversity along the lines of income, social class, and ethnicity) were interviewed in order to include some mothers' (and couple) views in the study.

The study includes a wide diversity of caregiving experiences: forty single fathers (twenty-five sole custody, twelve joint custody, and three widowers); fifty-three stay-at-home fathers (at home for at least one year); thirteen fathers who are single and are/were at home; and four fathers on parental leave when they were interviewed (including one father living in a same-sex partnership) (see appendix A, tables A.1, A.2 and A.3). In the later stages of the study, I broadened my categories to include eight sharedcaregiving fathers – in an effort to include participants who did not necessarily fit into the categories of stay-at-home or single fathers (see appendix A.4). I was thus able to include gay fathers who did not have legal custody but were active caregivers in their children's lives and several immigrant fathers for whom stay-at-home fathering was not readily compatible with their cultural traditions.

As further expressions of diversity, there are nine gay fathers with considerable variation in the parenting arrangements. The sample has a fairly high degree of ethnic diversity, with four fathers of Aboriginal origin and fifteen fathers from visible minorities (with all but one being first-generation immigrants). In addition, there were fourteen first- or second-generation immigrants of varied white ethnicities. Finally, the social class, income levels, and education levels of the respondents were richly varied and diverse.[6]

Interviewing: 'Coaxing' Fathers' Stories

Of the 118 fathers who participated in the study, nearly two-thirds of the fathers (62) were interviewed through in-depth face-to-face individual interviews, 27 through telephone interviews, 12 in one of three focus groups; and 17 through Internet correspondence. It is important to point out that 17 fathers participated through Web-based correspondence only, while 101 were interviewed in person through the varied methods described above or by telephone. As the project's lead researcher with a strong belief in the epistemological significance and importance of data collection sites and interactions (Doucet & Mauthner, 2002), I personally interviewed all the fathers, except for 3 (i.e., 59 of the 62 individual interviews, and all the telephone interviews, the focus groups and the couple interviews). Of the 118 fathers in the study, 28 were interviewed two or three times using different methods.[7]

FOCUS GROUPS
Three focus groups were held at Carleton University early on in the project (see appendix B.1). These were used as both data collection venues as well as a place to try out ideas with fathers and to allow their responses to shape the next phase of research, the individual interviews. The interaction among the fathers was interesting to observe, and I was humbled by the opportunity to sit and chat about matters of everyday life and caring with fathers. Four fathers who articulated issues that we felt required greater discussion were later interviewed on their own.

There were a few early mishaps. One father arrived slightly inebriated to one of the sessions, dominated the group, and had to be politely hushed so that others could also speak. One focus group with single fathers was set to run on a cold winter evening, but only one man showed up. As I sat waiting with my research assistant, surrounded by ample supplies of Tim Hortons doughnuts and coffee, we were reminded that it was likely difficult for fathers to get into their cars and drive to an academic institution to be interviewed about their private family life by a female researcher.

In addition to the three groups held at Carleton University at the beginning of the project, a fourth focus group was conducted, two years after the project began, with a Somali men's group. This group interview occurred in a small community centre in Ottawa with the assistance of a female community worker, also a Somali, and the male leader of the men's group (see appendix B.2).

INDIVIDUAL IN-DEPTH INTERVIEWS
Individual in-depth interviews with fathers took place over a period of three years (between 2000 and 2003). These sixty-two interviews were held face-to-face in venues that the fathers chose, most in coffee shops (twenty-eight), and the remainder in their homes (twenty-three), in my office (eight), their offices (three) or at a community centre (one). Nearly three-quarters of the individual interviews were conducted by a pair of researchers (a research assistant and I) while all twenty-seven telephone interviews were conducted by me. The individual interviews were structured around five themes in an interview aide-memoire. These themes included how fathers came to be in their situation of primary caregiver, daily and weekly parenting routines, relationships with others (community organizations, other parents, kin, health, and educational institutions), role models, and views on mothering and fathering as practices and identities (see appendix B.3).

COUPLE INTERVIEWS AND THE HOUSEHOLD PORTRAIT TECHNIQUE
Couple interviews were held in families' homes and provided an opportunity to speak to mothers and fathers together about their domestic division of labour as well as to glean mothers' views on mothering and fathering. The joint interview with fourteen couples revolved largely around the Household Portrait technique, a participatory/visual method for collecting data on the division of household labour.[8] It encourages both partners to reflect on and discuss together how their household is run, currently and in the past, with respect to a broad range of tasks and responsibilities. Mirroring the five-point scales used by researchers to assess the division of domestic labour (see Mederer, 1993, 138; Leslie, Anderson, & Branson, 1991, 203), the Household Portrait organizes responses according to who performs the bulk of particular domestic tasks from the jointly constructed point of view of the couples.

The strengths of the Household Portrait as a participatory research tool for collecting data on domestic divisions of labour are twofold: first, it is visual, and second, it is interactional. The visual quality is found in the fact that the technique involves sorting through different sets of coloured papers that represent a broad range of household tasks and responsibilities.[9] Tasks are colour coded according to the following general categories: (1) Housework; (2) Caring work; (3) 'Kin Work' (Di Leonardo, 1987); (4) General household repair and maintenance work; (5) Financial management; (6) Household subsistence activities (Pahl, 1984); and (7) Overall responsibility for housework and childcare. The couples sort through, discuss, and ultimately place these coloured slips of paper in one of five columns on a large sheet of paper. Each of the five columns represents the person who takes on that particular household task or responsibility as indicated by (1) Woman; (2) Woman with man helping; (3) Shared equally; (4) Man with woman helping; and (5) Man.[10] Some couples added an extra column to include the work of others who assisted with household work while others pencilled in their own categories of household work that were particular to their household (i.e. renovations; snow blowing; cleaning cat litter; making baby food; see appendix B.3).

The Household Portrait technique provides a visual portrayal of how household work is divided and enacted. The technique thus illuminates some of the elusive, invisible, and the taken-for-grantedness of domestic labour and responsibility. Research respondents seem to 'see' their household routines and rhythms for the first time. The technique assisted the couples in my study to remember, conceptualize, and articulate how they arranged and carried out their domestic work, how each household's particular division of labour had changed over the years, and how women and men's own views differed as to *why* changes did or did not occur. Indeed, some couples wanted a copy of their Portrait to keep, surprised at how it looked and how much or how little each partner did.

In addition to being a visual aid in research, the Household Portrait technique is also interactional. Rather than asking each partner who does a particular task or takes on the responsibility for it, the technique encourages discussion and analysis of the definition of each task as well as of determining who does it (see Doucet, 1996, 2001). Indeed, the negotiations that underpin domestic labour, both silent and overt, were partially revealed through discussion around who does each task and disparate perceptions about who does what and how often. In the case of Nina and Mitchell, for example, the differing understandings of how much ironing is done in the household is apparent via their discussion of the little piece of paper that connotes this task. While Mitchell claims he does it, quickly placing the task into his column and stressing that indeed he 'love[s] ironing,' Nina wonders aloud about

Figure 2.1. Household Portrait: Peter and Linda

Peter	Mainly Peter (with Linda helping)	Shared equally	Mainly Linda (with Peter helping)	Linda
Making breakfast	Cooking evening meal (weekdays)	Changing beds	Household cleaning – bathroom	Watering plants
Taking out garbage	Cooking evening meal (weekends)	Cleaning stove	Washing floors	Ironing
Vacuuming	Cooking for guests	Laundry – doing it	Organizing social events with friends (setting up)	Creative play
Shopping for groceries	Tidying	Household cleaning – kitchen	Library	Repairing clothes
Physical play	Laundry – putting it away	Washing dishes	Reading childcare books/magazines for parenting ideas	Knitting
Taking children to doctor's appointments	Indoor painting	Household cleaning – bedrooms	Buying furniture	Garden – flowers
Car maintenance	Children turn mainly to ... when upset	Family contacts (letters, phone calls)	Decorating house	
Minor repairs – plumbing, electrical		Organizing holidays and special family times	Washing windows	
Household bills		Remembering birthdays and sending cards	Setting up babysitting when required	
Making children's doctor's appointments		Organizing extended family gatherings		
Overall planning and management of children's day-to-day activities		Sending Christmas cards		
Planning meals		Buying Christmas presents		
		Taking photos		
		Attending to children at night if they awaken		
		Putting children to bed		
		Promoting children's independence		

Figure 2.1. *Concluded*

Peter	Mainly Peter (with Linda helping)	Shared equally	Mainly Linda (with Peter helping)	Linda
		Evening play		
		Homework		
		Reading		
		Bath-time routine		
		Sports		
		Outdoor activities		
		Setting discipline and following through		
		Worry		
		Buying children's clothes		
		Making decisions about children's behaviour		
		Outdoor painting		
		Deciding what needs doing re housework		
		Mowing lawn		
		Long-term planning of children's activities		
		Buying major household appliances		
		Baking		
		Outdoor yard work		
		Overall budgeting and financial management		
		Parent-teacher meetings		
		Organizing children's birthday parties		

his judgement, given how rarely he does it. Mitchell likes the satisfaction of ironing as it constitutes a completed task in a busy household with three young children where so many tasks are mundanely repetitive and endless. He seems to equate his pleasure with completing the task, however infrequently, with the view that he does it frequently:

MITCHELL I love ironing
NINA But ...
MITCHELL *When* I iron.
NINA How often do you iron?
MITCHELL Well, I iron some of Nicole's stuff and some of the boys'
      stuff. And I iron for you.
NINA But usually it goes three or four months and ...
MITCHELL A couple of months. Then I'll iron for hours. I like ironing.
      You can see it and then it's done. That's what I really like about it.'

The Household Portrait with its interactional quality kept both partners 'on their toes' as they saw the technique as something resembling a game or competition. Many respondents would say things like, 'Oh good, I get one in my column' or 'Give me that piece of paper – it goes in my column!' When Manuel puts 'makes clothes' in his column, he defends this by saying, 'Well, I tried making dresses for Lyse.' His wife, Julia, interjects bluntly as she removes the paper from his column: 'It doesn't say *tried*.'

A final example of the interactive quality of this methodological technique is Joe and Monique's discussion over the task *worry*. The word itself sparks discussion over what constitutes worry and whether *quiet worry* is as salient as *vocal worry*. Monique feels strongly that she is the one who worries about the children, but their discussion allows Joe to enlighten her on how he is also concerned, although he does not show it in the same way. When they come to the little piece of paper that denotes who worries, Monique immediately puts the paper into her column. A revealing conversation ensues:

MONIQUE Worries – that's mainly me. I'm the one who worries. Would
      you say that's fair, Joe? I'm the one who worries about the kids
      more? [Monique turns to me.] Joe worries. But not like I do. He's
      more laid-back.
JOE I'm not as *vocal* about it as you are.

MONIQUE I do worry a lot. I'll say, 'Joe, I'm worried about this. I'm worrying how thin Jess is or the fact that she eats like a bird' ... [She turns
to Joe.] You do worry too, Joe, but you don't worry as much, like he'll
say –

JOE No, no, no. I don't *talk* about it as much as you do.

MONIQUE Do you think you worry just as much?

JOE I think so but I'm not as vocal about it as you are. That's the only
difference. I sort of internalize it and I hold it in and I convince
myself that things will work out. You know, vocalizing and stressing
myself and other people around me about it doesn't help the problem at all.

Overall, the Household Portrait technique highlighted the taken-for-
grantedness of domestic tasks and responsibilities, the relational processes underpinning their being carried out, and the ways in which the
duties were conceived, undertaken, and perceived differently within
and between couples. More specifically, my analysis of the discussions
that emerged from the joint interview with couples, as facilitated by
the Household Portrait, led to several key findings from the research.
These included tremendous variation in the meaning and structure of
sharing domestic labour as well as diverse ways of speaking about the
three parental responsibilities addressed in this book: the emotional,
community, and moral components.

INTERNET SURVEY

My research study also used an Internet survey in a marginal way. I
developed this technique partly because of its efficiency in saving time
and financial costs involved with transcription and partly because it
allows for greater participation by people who live a considerable distance away from the lead researcher (Mann & Stewart, 2000) (see
appendix B.4). In the end, the Internet survey was used as a vehicle to
attract more research participants who found out about the project by
searching the Internet for support groups or for information on single
and stay-at-home fathers. The Internet survey also proved helpful in
encouraging gay fathers to participate, as they initially filled out the
survey and then I followed up with a telephone call to all those who
indicated in their form that they wanted a follow-up interview. Fifty
men filled in the Web-based survey, and all but seventeen were contacted for an individual interview.[11]

Epistemological Shifts: From Subjects to Narratives

As I conducted the interviews, and especially as I began to analyse them, I became acutely aware of tensions lurking beneath some of the accounts. When I struggled to get at the experience behind the narratives, it gradually dawned on me that the fathers, the subjects behind and within these stories, were largely inaccessible. This was partly due the difficulties for men with disclosing vulnerability (K. Daly, 1993) and partly because of the highly political context in which fathering, particularly single fathering, occurs (Doucet, 2004). In light of these combined forces at work in the production of their stories, several men gave accounts that I came to name as *heroic narratives*. An example is given here through selections from my interview with Mick.

Mick, a forty-five-year-old transport truck driver provides a good example of a heroic narrative. The father of a sixteen-year-old daughter, Mary Kate, he found out about the study through an ad in *The Toronto Sun* classified ads and phoned my office three times to say that he wanted to participate. I interviewed him in April 2000. According to Mick, his wife had a history of substance abuse and left the home when Mary Kate was three years old. She lives in another province and has seen the child only a few times over the past thirteen years, although she does telephone often. He has had sole custody of his daughter for about twelve years.

Mick was jolted into becoming a primary caregiving father when Mary Kate's mother left. He tells the story of how he learned of this state of affairs when he was on the road and received a distressed phone call from his father, who lived with Mick's family. Mick then drove his transport truck back to Toronto to find his pre-kindergarten daughter standing on the street. In his words:

> Mary Kate came home from school. She was in pre-kindergarten, and her mother was not home. She was supposed to be there. My father called me. So I went to Windsor, I dropped the truck's trailer, and I came from Windsor with no trailer, just my own truck. I came as fast as I could. When I came down the street she was in her little summer dress with the flowers. And she was standing there holding on to the street sign on our lawn. And my dad was on the veranda, sitting there watching. I promised Mary Kate that never would I let this happen again. I parked my truck and ended up eventually selling it. I never went back on the road again. I promised her that I would do that. That's when it started.

Mick's narrative is filled with heroic statements about how he 'had to do it' and his determination to stick with his commitment: 'There is no way that I would have said, Go to Children's Aid, or something like that. Her mother is not going to look after her. Well, damn, I'm going to do it. I'm not going to let someone else do it. It's my job. It was a choice that I had to make. I knew that I had to do it. It was never a question. There were days when I used to sit there and cry when Mary Kate was sleeping and wonder. It wasn't a case of 'am I doing it right or wrong?' It was, I *had* to do it. I made a commitment and I'm going to stick with my commitment, my damn commitment.'

It was the enthusiastic, seemingly scripted, and heroic narratives such as that of Mick and several other fathers that propelled my thinking on the issues of research subjects onto new terrain. Specifically, one epistemological implication and two methodological ones emerge from this discussion. First, while initially interested in gaining access to research subjects and their stories (see Mauthner & Doucet, 2003, Doucet, 1998; Doucet & Mauthner, 2002), I began to realize that certain projects and certain sites of research do not lend themselves to knowing subjects but rather to *knowing only their narratives*. I thus made an epistemological and methodological shift from subjects to narratives.[12] In paying attention to stories and narratives, I drew particularly on the work of the British sociologist Ken Plummer who, in researching accounts of sexual identity and 'personal narratives of the intimate,' has developed 'a sociology of stories,' which includes 'the social processes of producing stories,' and 'the social role that stories play,' and 'the wider political and social frameworks within which stories are told and heard' (Plummer 1995a, 15–18). Using this wide and intrinsically social framework for understanding stories, I deliberately refer, throughout this book, to fathers' and mothers' *narratives* rather than to fathers and mothers' *experiences or selves*.

A second point, a methodological one, that emerged from my grappling with heroic narratives is that diverse sampling strategies are required in order to invite both enthusiastic and reluctant participants into research projects. In my research, the participants who were recruited through third parties, such as community associations and the fathers approached in schoolyards and public parks, often provided more reserved stories, less scripted, less heroic narratives. I thus brought greater scrutiny to the narratives of fathers who volunteered to participate as opposed to the ones who entered the study after being recruited. Plummer urges us to consider what it means to 'coax or coerce stories out of story tellers' (research respondents) and compels us to consider questions such as 'what brings people to the brink of telling?' and 'how do stories get produced?' (Plummer, 1995a, 1995b).

A further methodological issue is that rehearsed stories and heroic narratives may be more likely to occur in response to topics that are politically or personally sensitive. For example, fathers who stay at home with their children, particularly those who have not had the opportunity to establish a career identity for themselves, can face insecurities over how others perceive them as men when they are primary caregivers and not earners. Divorced fathers, particularly those with sole custody or those fighting for custody, live in a social world that often pits fathers' rights against mothers' historical commitment to caregiving and, thus, fathers' stories are often tinged with anger, bitterness, and hostility (Mandell, 2002). The hidden or explicit emotions that can accompany the processes whereby fathers come to be primary caregivers (i.e., domestic role reversal, loss, custody negotiation, or court battles) are inextricably entwined with what Plummer refers to as that which 'brings people to the brink of telling' and 'how people come to construct their stories.'

As a result of this epistemological shift that occurred in my work on the concepts of research subjects and subjectivities, my interest in narrative analysis grew. This was somewhat consistent with my previous work on analysing transcripts informed by the use and further development of an analytic strategy titled the Listening Guide. As detailed below, the multilayered readings provided by the Listening Guide approach to transcript analysis does include a reading for narrative or central story line (see Mauthner & Doucet, 1998, 2003). However, given my concerns about heroic narratives that surfaced in my interviews on a topic that can be highly political or sensitive, I gave much greater emphasis to narratives than I had in my earlier work. My approach to analysing interview transcripts and the description of this approach is part of my 'audit trail' (Seale, 1999, 2002) and the gossamer wall between me as researcher and my readers. It is also part of the gossamer wall between me and my research respondents in that analyzing interview transcripts illuminates the thin line between the point where our research respondents end and we begin, and vice versa. These processes will be briefly described below.

The Gossamer Wall between Researcher and Researched

A third gossamer wall exists between the researcher and the research subjects. This image is much like the one invoked by Anne Michaels in that the research respondent, like Bella, is 'watching with curiosity (perhaps sympathy) from her side of the gossamer wall.' Like Jakob, the researcher is never quite sure which thoughts are hers and which thoughts are those expressed by the research respondent. This image of research respondents perhaps looking back through this gossamer wall at the researcher is a powerful one, invoked by several researchers who remind us of the 'respondents' integrity' and how 'a researcher should imagine that she will be sitting beside her respondents as they read what is written about them' (Andrews, 1991, 49).

My analysis of research interviews took place via a lengthy and multifaceted process of transcript analysis. First, research assistants carried out in-depth readings of verbatim interview transcripts on their own and then in conjunction with me, using the Listening Guide (Brown & Gilligan, 1992; Mauthner & Doucet, 1998, 2003). My layered theoretical approach, moving heuristically from individuals to social relationships to wider social structures was reflected in the four readings employed within this analytic strategy. Group-based analysis of common themes and issues were then conducted, followed by a labour-intensive process of coding (conducted mainly by me) using the data analysis computer program Atlas.ti. As the Listening Guide was the centre of my interpretive strategy, a brief explanation of its workings will be presented here.

The Listening Guide

The Listening Guide is an approach to data analysis that combines reflexivity and subjectivity while also focusing on narratives and storytelling. It was first developed over several years by Lyn Mikel Brown, Carol Gilligan, and their colleagues at the Harvard Project on Women's Psychology and Girls' Development at the Harvard Graduate School of Education (see Lyn Mikel Brown, 1998; Brown & Gilligan, 1992; Gilligan, Brown, & Rogers, 1990). It was subsequently extended and modified by researchers at Harvard (e.g., Taylor, Gilligan, & Sullivan, 1997; Tolman, 2002; Way, 1998), as well as by other researchers (see Mauthner & Doucet, 1998, 2003). Since I first used it as a doctoral researcher under the careful guidance of Gilligan, I have further refined it with each subsequent research project that I have taken on, drawing on other methodological approaches that complement it – such as narrative analysis (Mishler, 1986; Reissman, 1993, 2003), institutional ethnography (DeVault & McCoy, 2003; D. Smith, 1987, 1999) and a 'sociology of stories' (Plummer, 1995a, 1995b).

Reliant on at least four readings of interview transcripts, 'each time listening in a different way' (Brown 1998, 33), the Listening Guide data analysis method is best used within the context of an interpretive group. Although I advocate a flexible approach to the number and types of readings, depending on the nature of the topic under investigation, it is the first three readings that I have remained committed to because they provide a practical way to *do* 'strong reflexivity' while also emphasizing research subjects, their narratives, and the broader social contexts within which these narratives are told and heard. The Listening Guide urges researchers to attend to the 'harmonics of relationship' in interview settings and to pose the following questions about the multilayered social and structural relations underpinning a particular story. In the words of Brown, 'In order to understand and interpret the meanings of a person's words, one has to ask (and answer) two interrelated questions: "Who precisely is speaking, and under what concrete circumstances?" In addition ... one must also ask: "who is listening and what is the nature of her relationship with the speaker – especially with respect to power?"[12] Such questions acknowledge the complicated social landscape in which discourse occurs and the various forces, personal and political that move one to speak and act in certain ways' (Brown, 1998, 32; Brown & Gilligan, 1992; see also Plummer, 1995a, 1995b).

The first reading with the use of the Listening Guide entails a reader-response reflexive strategy; the second reading traces the 'I' or central protagonist within the narrative; and the third reading follows the narrative or central story line.[13] Subsequent readings draw the analysis out from the research subjects and their narratives to their nexus of social relationships. In conjunction with several colleagues and research assistants, I conducted a fourth reading, which mapped social relations at the micro level (family, friends, kin, community members). A fifth reading was similar to aspects of an institutional ethnographic reading (Campbell & Gregor, 2002) in that I explored larger structural (macro level) relations of gender, race, class, sexuality, space, and body as well as social institutions (work, family, education, community, health care, and childcare institutions). This fifth reading recognizes that knowing fathers entails a layering of theory and data and that it is impossible to separate, to use Adrienne Rich's terms, the 'experience' from the 'institutions' of mothering and fathering (Rich, 1986). These readings are described in further detail in appendix C.

Other Analytic Strategies

In addition to using the Listening Guide to construct knowledge from the interview transcripts for this study, I employed two other analytic strategies: the first included working on particular case studies in the context of a small interpretive groups, and the second was a computer software program (Atlas.ti) for analysing qualitative research.

As part of the processes of opening up my analytical lenses, I widened my interpretive community and brought colleagues, research assistants, and friends with varied social locations who could help me to make sense of areas of experience that I was less familiar with. For example, throughout the process of interviewing and group-based analysis, colleagues who had a familiarity with alcoholic family backgrounds helped me to interpret the narratives of fathers whose family patterns were rooted in alcoholism or substance abuse. To assist me with interpreting the narratives of fathers of ethnic minorities and those of gay fathers, I involved several research assistants in analysis of transcripts, or in conversation, to gain understandings of area of experience and social identity that I was less familiar with.[14] In addition, four men (one single father, two fathers who had spent time at home, and a male research assistant) acted as a pilot focus group interview and gave valuable feedback on issues that they felt would matter for men and for fathers. Finally, a Somali couple (a community social worker and a university instructor) assisted me with conducting, and making sense of, the Somali father focus group. As Natasha Mauthner and I note, 'Working within the context of a group was useful because, having read extracts from our transcripts, others were able to point out where we might have missed or glossed over what they regarded as key aspects of the interview narrative. This made us acutely aware of our own role and power in choosing the particular issues we emphasize and pick up on, and which we ignore or minimize. Working with other colleagues highlighted the fact "that people have more than one way to tell a story and see a situation through different lenses and in different lights"' (Gilligan, Brown, Rogers, 1990, 95 cited in Mauthner & Doucet, 1998, 320).

One of the drawbacks of the Listening Guide is that ideally it requires a great deal of time to conduct four to five separate readings of interview transcripts. It is important to emphasize that with large data sets, such as the one used in this study of over a hundred interviews, it is not necessary to spend the same amount of time reading each and every one of the transcripts. After conducting the interviews, transcribing and/or reading all of them, I systematically conducted all four readings in a group-based context with twenty-five of the in-depth face-to-face interviews. Of the fourteen couple interviews, I conducted the four readings and wrote up brief case studies for ten of these couples. In effect, these intensive and lengthy readings of interview transcripts 'tuned my ear' (Mauthner & Doucet, 1998, 324) for dominant or critical themes within the narratives. I then tracked similar themes in the remaining transcripts.

After the in-depth and interactive analyses of my large data set, I expanded this process across the entire data set through the creative and visual computer coding program Atlas.ti. Designed to closely resemble the in-depth and manual process of working closely with qualitative data, Atlas.ti is a tool for the management, evaluation, and visualization of qualitative data. It also assists in drawing intimate and powerful connections between disparate aspects of the data and, ultimately, with theory building.

Methodological Limitations

Like all research studies, this study on fathering was faced with several methodological limitations. Most notable was the absence of mothers' perspectives in the single-father interviews, the absence of some fathers, and the limits of retelling 'sensuous' stories.

The Absence of Mothers

Research studies are guided by limitations of time and money and decisions about whom to interview and when. While fourteen women were interviewed in couple interviews, the absence of mother's perspectives, particularly in the case of divorced fathers, was a heavy weight in this study. Paradoxically, mothers were both conspicuously present and absent in the fathers' narratives, and yet this dual position was still told only via men's voices and not those of the mothers. While stay-at-home fathers living with female partners sometimes spoke about their wives as though they were with them in the room, thus signalling a degree of consensus on some issues, the views of the female ex-partners of divorced fathers were given short shrift and often negative coverage. With only one side of the parenting story, the interpretation of their narratives was especially challenging. I was sometimes at a loss to know what to think. The more bitter the divorce or separation, the more I worried about the story being told.

As described earlier in this chapter, the highly political and sensitive nature of the topic of primary-caregiving fathers came to be seen as something that would frame and limit the study. Although the voices of most mothers were largely absent, one strategy for grappling with this challenge was to invite others to assist me in group-based analysis of the transcripts. Fresh ears and eyes, as well as diverse backgrounds and experiences, brought more rigorous analysis to the project and uncovered multiple storylines, which enriched my understandings and ultimately the larger story being told in this book.

The Absence of Some Fathers

There are, of course, voices missing from this study. Notably, there were fathers who refused to participate. This absence was well typified by the man introduced to me by another father on the edge of a children's soccer field; he readily agreed in front of his friend but later wrote me a thin e-mail saying, 'I just do not feel comfortable telling my story at this time.' There was also the single unemployed father living on social assistance who made excuses each time I called that it was 'not a good time to talk.' After four phone calls in four different seasons, I decided that there was likely never going to be a good time for this low-income father of a four-year-old girl. There were fathers approached by my research assistants who agreed when first asked but then would not answer our phone calls or numerous letters. In the end, it took over three years to amass what I considered to be a reasonable sample in terms of size and diversity. Nevertheless, no matter how much, in the words of Ken Plummer, one coaxes, coerces, or attempts to pull research respondents into a study, there are always missing stories. The author Sean French expresses this silence particularly well when he writes in the preface to his book, *Fatherhood*, 'I trust that somewhere in a parallel dimension there is shadow version of this book ... [in which appears] the public figure and the pundit who could not write because he felt he has been a failure as a father' (French, 1993, 5).

Limits of Retelling 'Sensuous' Stories

Within the 'social production of stories' (Plummer, 1983) there are limitations on how we hear and retell the stories told by the people who participate in our research. In this vein, I have been drawn to Joy Parr's call for more 'sensuous' and 'tacit' (Parr, 2001) stories as she imaginatively reflects on the limited quality of what we know because, as academics, we rely mainly on textual analysis and dissemination of knowledge. In one particular article, Parr works from the narratives of elderly residents on the changing quality of their beloved town and the loss of a central river that had run through the geographical and emotional heart of that town. Struggling to convey the texture, richness, and sadness of the town and its resident narratives, Parr writes, 'How did the river change? Here I have only a printed page in a scholarly journal, no audio, or video tape with which to invoke the sensations more directly. *We can go only part of the way*' (Parr, 2001, 726; my emphasis).

Parr reminds us to go beyond the textual, such as the commonly used interview transcript, and to recall the sensuous and visual images that occur during the production of these stories: the sounds of language, the silences and uncomfortable pauses, the relational dynamics when two or more people are interviewed together. She urges us to draw on our own tacit knowledge and asks us to consider the implications of what we are missing when we rely only on text. She writes,

> By preference we have been wordsmiths. We value written words most as sources; use the skills of the word-smart to appraise the provenance, integrity, and reliability of the evidence we privilege; and use sentences and paragraphs to tell what we know. Our orientation has been empirical and social scientific. We rank the rational over the intuitive, the distinctly cerebral over the otherwise embodied. Our practice marginalizes any fleshly perceptions about physical landscape and material circumstances. These we take as more subjective evocations, suspect until they are distilled into written words. The written word thus stilled we more readily consider to be objective. The written word becomes attached to the mind, *the spoken word to the body*, and all the sainted and benighted philosophical history of the mind/body distinction comes muscling in. (Parr 2001, 731; my emphasis)

The weight of these words came 'muscling in' when I found a disjunction between confident accounts of fathering as revealed in interview transcripts and my detailed field notes that surrounded the production of those stories. My insistence on interviewing all the fathers, an unconventional strategy in most research projects, helped me to make somewhat assured judgements on how to interpret and present fathers' accounts. My judgements were bolstered by post-interview debriefings with my research assistants. Nevertheless, I have also struggled hard to convey even some of the richness and texture of these interviews. These are the challenges for us as researchers as we *attempt to know* and to *transmit our knowing* of others. How do we relay these wider and fuller stories that hold the uncertainties, fluidities, and sensuousness of people's lives? How do we describe men and women living in their domestic spaces, the tacit and tonal feeling of being in their homes amid the relics and paraphernalia of their family lives, the ways they relate to and with their children, and the manner in which they speak with all their gestures, silences, and awkward pauses? Like Parr, I am cognizant of how the stories presented throughout this book 'only go part of the way.'

Conclusions

All the years I felt Bella entreating me, filled with her loneliness, I was mistaken. I have misunderstood her signals. Like other ghosts, she whispers; not for me to join her, but so that, when I'm close enough, she can push me back into the world.

(Anne Michaels, *Fugitive Pieces*)

At the end of Michaels's novel, the central character, Jakob, realizes that it was not his lost sister, Bella, on the other side of the gossamer wall; rather, it was her 'whispers' and 'her signals.' Moreover, Jakob 'misunderstood her signals' and misinterpreted 'her loneliness' for his own feelings of longing and grief. In the end, he recognizes that what Bella was trying to tell him, through whispers and signals, was an amalgamation of his own thoughts and dreams and his memory of his different shadow selves and those of Bella. As researchers grappling with the challenges of knowing others, we also work through gossamer walls. Here sheer and tenuous barriers exist between our research aims, ourselves as researchers (with our many shadow and absent others) and a complex myriad of social, emotional, theoretical, epistemological, institutional, political, and interpersonal attributes and conceptions.

In this chapter I have exposed some of the ghosts that live behind the thin gossamer walls of our knowledge construction processes. Knowing others requires both strong reflexivity as well as concrete ways of *doing* reflexivity. This entails more than simply situating ourselves in terms of our gender, class, ethnicity, sexuality, and geographical location. It means going beyond the ways that social locations are 'deployed as badges' (Patai 1991, 149) and being more cognizant of and accountable for the epistemological, ontological, theoretical, and political assumptions that inform our work (Mauthner & Doucet, 2003). I recognize that we cannot always know or name the multiple influences on our research at the time of conducting it (see Mauthner & Doucet, 1998) or the ways that people will interpret and use our work (Bordo, 1997); we can, nevertheless, be as reflexive as possible in the very wide sense that I have outlined in this chapter.

The ethnography that informs this book aims to build on existing theoretical and empirical work done in the rapidly developing areas of gender, domestic labour, fathering, masculinities, and embodiment. Rather than focusing on processes of discovery or working from the ground up or discovering theory (Glaser & Strauss, 1967), I concur with Michael Buraway in his collaborative work on global ethnography that what we do as researchers involves an '*extension of theory.*' He writes, 'Rather than being "induced" from the data, discovered "de novo" from the ground, existing theory is extended to accommodate observed lacuna or anomalies. We try to reconstitute the field as a challenge to some theory we want to improve' (Burawoy, 2000; see also Campbell & Gregor, 2002; Hammersley, 1998; Hammersley & Atkinson, 1983). In this vein, my work focuses on the co-construction of accounts or narratives produced in particular places at specific times, where a research respondent speaks and the researcher listens as widely as possible and interprets from within a framework of understanding and analysis. While the latter tries to be as open as possible to hearing new strands of thinking and knowing, the listening always occurs within particular personal, political, theoretical, and institutional settings (see Mauthner & Doucet, 2003). 'We cannot see the field, however, without a lens, and we can only improve the lens by experimenting with it in the world' (Burawoy, 2000, 28). The task facing researchers is to be as reflexive and as openly accountable about what these influences might be, while also recognizing that we cannot always know all that influences us during our processes of knowledge construction. With Elisabeth Grosz, I hold that as researchers come to write about the worlds they study, it may well be that case that 'the author's intentions, emotions, psyche, and interiority are not only inaccessible to readers, they are likely to be inaccessible to the author herself' (Grosz, 1995, 13).

In the chapters that follow, I provide a partial and humble retelling of some of the stories that fathers offered me. Although, as mentioned above, these retellings go only 'part of the way' toward recapturing some of what I heard and how it was told, my hope is that these snippets of long narratives given by fathers will contribute to our current understandings of the shifting personal experiences and social institutions of mothering and fathering.

3 Understanding Fathers as Primary Caregivers

Introduction

What comes to mind when we think about fathers as primary caregivers? Readers' imaginations may go back to movies such as *Mr. Mom* where Michael Keaton let the house turn into a metaphoric pigsty while his wife went out to work and brought home the bacon; or perhaps to the Academy Award–winning *Kramer versus Kramer*, with Dustin Hoffman in the role of a man who learned to be the primary caregiver to his son while the rest of his life crumbled around him. More recent versions are depicted by Hollywood's leading men acting as primary caregiving dads, most dramatically depicting Dad left literally holding the baby while Mom bolts out the door.[1] Predictably there are always funny or sentimental scenes of fathers shopping for diapers and baby formula and awkwardly navigating the aisles of grocery stores as well as through venues populated overwhelmingly by mothers. Several recent novels have picked up on the joys and challenges of being a primary caregiver[2] while several well-known celebrities have called themselves Mr. Mom, including actors Michael Douglas, Billy Crystal, and the late John Lennon.

Outside of these glossy, fictional, or rather distant portrayals of fathers as primary caregivers, there is still a lingering question of what it actually means to be a primary-caregiving father. Do these fathers take on the primary role in caring for children as well as for the housework? Do they do all or most of the cooking, cleaning, mopping, vacuuming, and the clothes laundering (including folding it and putting it away)? Do they chauffeur kids to soccer practices and dance classes, oversee homework, and keep track of doctor and dentist appointments?

Do they help daughters through the angst-ridden phases of adolescence, or do they turn to women in their lives to do this? Does Arlie Hochschild's description of mothers' responsibilities apply to fathers who are primary caregivers? That is, can we say that these particular fathers 'kept track of doctors' appointments and arranged for children's playmates to come over,' that fathers 'worried about the tail on a child's Halloween costume or a birthday present for a school friend,' that they were 'more likely to think about the children while at work and to check in by phone with the baby-sitter' (Hochschild, 1989, 7–8)?

How do we define the primary-caregiving father? By his efforts to attend to the daily routines and dramas of domestic life, by the number of hours he devotes to childcare compared with the number of hours he devotes to paid work or by his self-definition only? If we look to existing studies for clues, we find that researchers have used varied definitions. Some have used a measure of time allocated to parental and household activities, with the primary-caregiving father being solely responsible for the care of their child(ren) for twenty-six hours a week (Russell, 1983) or for that of the youngest child (zero to six years of age) for at least thirty hours a week (Frank, 1999) or 'assumed primary caregiving duties for at least half of the infant's waking hours' (Geiger, 1996, 17). Others have focused on time at home; for example, the study by Michael Lamb and colleagues of seventeen infants of primary-caregiving fathers chose an average of three months (Lamb, 1981, 1987). Norma Radin's American longitudinal study of twenty primary-caregiving fathers used self-definition of their role by both fathers and their spouses (Radin, 1982, 1988).

My study employed fathers' self-definition (see also Ehrensaft, 1987) as the criterion for selection, combined with a minimal length of time as primary caregiver of at least one year so as to gain a sense of changes over time.[3] As detailed in chapter 2, I used a three-pronged recruitment strategy that allowed for varied dimensions of self-definition. First, I recruited fathers by approaching them in community settings; second, I included fathers who responded to ads placed in newspapers, school and community newsletters, and on bulletin boards at community centres; and third, I chose fathers identified by others as good candidates for the study. I did not choose exact hours spent in childcare. This assumes that during the specified number of hours as primary caregivers, fathers are devoting themselves exclusively to childcare and housework, whereas the quality and character of this time depends very much on the ages of the children, social networks, family resources, and whether fathers are balancing flexible paid work with childcare responsibilities. A more global indicator for me in recruiting fathers was that they claimed to be *responsible* for the primary care of their children for significant periods of time. For the two categories of fathers that fit under the umbrella of 'father as primary caregiver' (i.e., stay-at-home fathers and single fathers), the term had even more specific meanings. For stay-at-home fathers, this implied being the primary caregiver during regular working days (i.e., his partner worked in a full-time job), while for sole and joint custody fathers, this meant time on their own without a resident mother to share or take on most of this work.

Early on in my study, I realized that the category of fathers as primary caregivers was excessively complex and riddled with contradiction. This was first revealed to me when I telephoned Jimmy, a stay-at-home father and self-employed car mechanic, who had responded to my ad in a local newspaper. The conversation went as follows:

'Hello. May I please speak to Jimmy? '
    At the other end of the phone, a woman's voice said, 'He's under the car right now. Can I take a message?'
'Are you his wife?'
'Yes.'
'It's Andrea Doucet from Carleton University. He phoned me to participate in my study of fathers as primary caregivers.'
'Fathers as primary caregivers?' she asked.
'Yes,' I replied.
A long silence followed. 'Oh. So *that's* what he calls himself.'

What became clear to me at that moment was that fathers' self-identification as primary caregivers might be differently interpreted by mothers and, furthermore, that fathers' claims in this regard might have implications for mothering. Further confusion over terminology began to arise, and six points reflect this sense of ambiguity. First, some men had overlapping periods of time when they were both single fathers and stay-at-home fathers. Second, some single fathers had girlfriends, mothers, or sisters who played important mothering roles in the children's lives. Third, stay-at-home fathers were not necessarily *at home*, and most were doing some kind of paid work. Fourth, the question of housework would also have to be considered in that it had implications for what being at home meant to stay-at-home fathers.

Fifth, there was considerable diversity under the label of ethnic minority fathers. Finally, an area of further conceptual and empirical diversity was found in the term *gay father*; while the image that comes to mind is of two men raising children together, in fact the household configurations that gay fathers form are tremendously diverse.

In order to paint the background for this story of men and mothering, it is important to have a clear idea of *who* the fathers in the study are. Since the research concentrated on fathers self-identifying as one or all of the following – primary caregiver, stay-at-home father, or single father – it is important to clarify what these terms actually mean within the context of men's lives. Although I started out with what I thought were fairly straightforward terms, I gradually came to see that they were malleable and open to multiple interpretations. In the following sections, the concepts of primary caregivers and stay-at-home dads will be explored by noting the internal diversity within each of these terms. Furthermore, I also explore 'diversity within diversity' by breaking down the categories even further, examining the concepts of gay father and ethnic minority father. Finally, following up on some of the issues raised in chapter 1 on the difficulties of arriving at a definition of an 'equal' or 'egalitarian' division of labour, I dissect some of the empirical and theoretical complexity of this puzzle.

Fathers as Primary Caregivers

In this first section of this chapter, several facets of primary caregiving will be reviewed. Do households with a stay-at-home father and a female primary breadwinner constitute a role reversal? Or, alternatively, are they enacting shared parenting? Are single fathers shared or primary caregivers? While the practical enactment of fathers' caregiving was partly revealed in the individual interviews with fathers, the most telling insights, while limited to only a select group of fathers, were gleaned from the fourteen couple interviews. Such an interview was the one I conducted with Manuel, a Latino stay-at-home father for seven years, and his wife, Julie.

Fathers as Primary Caregivers: Role Reversal?

For the first five years of Manuel and Julie's parenting, Julie worked the midnight shift at the Canadian National Railway. She recalls that 'this was hard on Manuel because we had two young kids and I had to sleep during the day. I would go to bed from ten till six.' Then she was able to switch to the evening shift for ten years while the children were in their school years. 'I wouldn't see the kids very much ... But I would communicate with them in different ways. I would write them letters and they would write back to me. It was definitely *a role reversal*.'

Manuel was home with the two children for seven years until both started school and he went back to work as a special education consultant for the local school board. Yet residual effects of Manuel's being at home remained, and both Julie and he started off their interview by saying that he was definitely the primary caregiver of the children. Julie noted that he was 'like a mother' and that he was 'the one who was always there' for the children. When their eldest son left home to attend university, Manuel said that he 'felt like the umbilical cord had been cut.' As Julie put it, 'The way I see it, Manuel really was, and still is, the stable point, the stable piece in this family, and I did more swinging in and swinging out.' Some of this 'swinging in and swinging out' was due to her shift work as well as to her completing her undergraduate and her master's degrees over the years.

Not only was Manuel a primary caregiver but he also set the routine and the pattern of care, while Julie fitted into his structured pattern. As Julie said, 'I kept the routine the same when I came in and took over; I didn't change any of the infrastructure that was already here.' Moreover, when the children were younger, he was the person who took on most of the networking with other parents as Julie was less social and he 'knew the neighbourhood really well, who was talking to whom, who was mean; he knew the playground, set up playdates, and had a very good sense of the relationships with the kids.' While they both volunteered at school, Julie admits that 'Manuel was more active; he knew the teachers and the politics more than I did.' As revealed in their Household Portrait, there are also points of traditional masculine task definition in that he does minor household repairs, car maintenance, mowing the lawn, and washing windows. Manuel has always taken on the lion's share of the cooking and laundry, a pattern that began when he was at home and has persisted despite his now working full-time, with Julie working regular day shifts and their children's ages currently twenty and eighteen.

At the end of their couple interview, Julie and Manuel look at their Household Portrait and reflect on how it has changed over time. Julie notes that they have both played constantly changing and *different* roles, but ones that are *equally* important in terms of the care of their

Figure 3.1. Household Portrait: Manuel and Julie

Manuel	Mainly Manuel (with Julie helping)	Shared equally	Mainly Julie (with Manuel helping)	Julie
Minor repairs – plumbing, electrical	Organizing social events with friends (setting up)	Sending Christmas cards	Remembering birthdays and sending cards	Reading childcare books/magazines for parenting ideas
Buying major household appliances	Mowing lawn	Family contacts: letters or phone calls	Overall budgeting and financial management	Buying Christmas presents
Making beer, wine, or other	Laundry – putting it away	Organizing extended family gatherings	Making breakfast	Making photo album
Making (sewing) clothes	Taking out the garbage	Organizing holidays and special family times	Worry about children now	Washing windows
Laundry – doing it	Outdoor activities with children	Buying furniture		Indoor painting
Cooking evening meal (weekdays)	Attending to children at night if they awoke	Decorating house		Household bills
Washing dishes	Taking children to doctor and dentist	Repairing clothes		Garden – vegetables
Tidying	Sports with children	Outdoor yard work		Garden – flowers
Changing beds	Physical play with children	Shopping for groceries		Baking
Putting children to bed	Daughter turned mainly to ... when upset	Household cleaning – bedrooms		Watering plants
Setting discipline and following through	Son turned mainly to ... when upset	Vacuuming		Cooking evening meal (weekends)
Bed-time routine		Promoting children's independence		Laundry – hanging it out
Family contacts: e-mail		Creative play with children		Washing floors
Outdoor painting		Worry about children when they were small		Cleaning stove
Car maintenance		Buying children's clothes		Household cleaning – bathroom
		Daughter is more emotionally connected to		Ironing
		Son is more emotionally connected to		Helping with homework
		Taking photos		Household cleaning – Kitchen
		Cooking for guests		Reading to children
				Library

children (see figure 3.1). Julie sees Manuel as the 'protector,' whereas she provides guidance a different way. In her words,

> I think they go more to me now than they did before. Certainly in terms of the outside world, they know really clearly that Manuel is their protector and that he would fight the world on their behalf. But I think that I give a little bit more of that now too. I suppose their needs are different now. Before, their needs were protection, food, love, comfort, warmth, stability. And now their needs are 'help me think out my life! Where would I go to talk about this?' I think that I am of the world a little bit more like that. Whereas they think of Manuel as the stable rock. I think that the sustenance that they draw from this is just a real honest-to-goodness [feeling of] *'home is still where it is, and nothing has changed.'*

Manuel, like several other fathers interviewed with their female partners, could be called his children's primary caregiver during his time at home,[4] but it is also the case that households, relationships, individuals, couples, and children are not static entities. As will be explored in this book, there is a great deal of ebb and flow in parental care. Over time and in a global sense, most fathers were actually in situations of *sharing* care rather than providing primary or secondary care. This will be more fully discussed in the next section.

*Couples as Shared Caregivers: 'I Didn't Just Come In,
I Came in Full-fledged'*

While admitting by the time she came to the end of their two-hour couple interview that Manuel was 'like a mother,' Julie was more certain that their situation was in fact *not* a role reversal but rather one of shared caregiving overall for two reasons – first, because she was always 'not that far away' and she was constantly 'making conscious connections with them' and indeed that she was 'paranoid aware.' She says, 'I was really intimately aware of where they were in terms of their development. I read countless books. I was intimately aware of their homework and their mental states. But I wasn't moulding it. I wasn't there moulding and comforting, but I was very aware. You know, paranoid aware [laughs].'

Second, the situation of Manuel and Julie was not, in her view, a role reversal simply because she is a woman and not a man: 'It was not like the man who goes off to work and then comes home and says good-night to them. I think what happened is that I was *physically* gone. But the truth is the minute I set foot in this house at any time of a day, whether it was for two hours or five hours or a day, I took over. I did that consciously so that Manuel could get a break. Because I knew that this busy and important work was draining. I didn't just come in. I came in full-fledged, even though I wasn't there very often.'

Coming in 'full-fledged' was a pattern among *all* of the female partners of stay-at-home fathers. There were variations over time, depending on women's work patterns, but the consensus among the fourteen couples interviewed as well as the individual fathers was that having a stay-at-home father led to a situation of *shared* caregiving because, as detailed more fully in chapters 4, 5, and 6, the social, historical, ideological, and moral conditions of parenting meant that most women felt a strong pull towards mothering. As Sam, stay-at-home father of two children for five years, put it, 'I have to say it's a shared thing. Being a stay-at-home dad is really more shared parenting than where there is a stay-at-home mom and a working dad. [...] My daughter mixes up our names. She says, "Mom, oh no, I mean Dad!" It's more joint parenting.'

Single Fathers as Shared Caregivers: 'Backpacks Here, Backpacks There'

For the joint custody households, most could be characterized as shared caregiving with the father being *a* primary caregiver but not *the* primary caregiver. There was a sense of shared but separate caregiving with fathers having to take on the primary care when the children were at Dad's house, and they partially relinquished this when the front door closed and they were off to Mom's house. In Logan's narrative, for example, the children have separate lives between his house and that of their mother, which is 'a kilometre from here, on the other side of the bridge.' The image of the children's two sets of backpacks is an apt metaphor for the shared but separate division of care and responsibility for most joint custody fathers:

Fridays at 4:30 p.m. is the transition time ... Because of the way the rotation started, they come from their mom's obviously wearing clothes and they go back to their mom's in the clothes that they wear when they came to me. That's the only thing that travels back and forth, if you will, that and OHIP (health) cards. They have their complete set-up here. Toys don't come. Nothing. The odd time they have a personal book or something from school that they're working on. But that's it. They don't even bring backpacks. Backpacks here. Backpacks there.

Single Fathers as Primary Caregivers: 'I Can't Do It All on My Own'

In the cases of sole-custody fathers, the fathers are indeed primary caregivers. Most, however, draw heavily on *another woman* to assist them: a caregiver, a sister, their mother, a neighbour, or an older daughter. Several examples can be given here in the circumstances of Burt, Bruno, and Kofi.

Burt, a sole-custody father of a twelve-year-old girl, has spent many years piecing together part-time work as a computer consultant. Now working full time, he pays a woman who lives in his apartment building, the mother of his daughter's best friend, to cook evening meals and to do housework. He has had this housekeeper for a year and a half. Although he did try to cook good meals for his daughter, it was usually hit and miss. He says,

> Well, this year has been basically abnormal because I have a nine-to-five job ... Now I have a housekeeper. Originally I got her just to look after Anastasia between three-thirty and five-thirty, when she got out of school and I came home. She's Anastasia's best friend's mother. They were always together anyway, and Lizzy's a single mother, so the money helped her. And, 'Well, you're there, I'll give you a couple of extra bucks if you make dinner.' She said okay. Then I said, 'I'll give you a couple of extra bucks if you want to do some laundry while you're at it.' So basically right now every couple of weeks I give her food and household money, and I pay her, and she washes and she cooks and she cleans and she does the groceries ... So there is always a good hot meal for supper and things like that because it doesn't depend on me.

Bruno, a fifty-year-old Italian Canadian, has lived down the street from his mother for most of the fourteen years that he has been the primary caregiver of his two sons. 'The boys' mother left when my youngest was six months old,' and they are now sixteen and fourteen. The boys see their mother 'every other Wednesday and every other weekend,' and Bruno says, 'My mother cared for my children like they were hers ... They call my mother Mom.' He describes his situation as a primary caregiver, and the central role his mother plays, as follows: 'For most of these years, my mom has lived up the street from me. So the boys would spend the nights there because I worked nights. I would get off at six-thirty in the morning, go home, and get an hour's sleep – hour and a half. We had a toy and book-lending co-op, and I would go and pick the kids up, and we would be there at the co-op from eight-thirty till noon ... In the afternoon, we'd eat at my mom's. They would have lunch there, and they would go to sleep. They have bunk beds there. I'd have a little nap, supper, and I would go home to sleep until ten. Then I would go to work. It was super.'

Kofi, a forty-four-year-old African Canadian living in Quebec City, found that the community day care was his lifeline when his wife left; the youngest of his two sons was not quite two years old. That was nine years ago. Also he spoke a great deal about one of his son's English godmother who lives about five minutes away who would care for his children when he was away on business. 'This provides a female component in their lives, a mother figure for the kids, which I think is important.'

Many single fathers start off with sparse social networks, having relied heavily on their female partners to provide the necessary social support around parenting. Yet these fathers gradually learn to rely on others to assist them with parenting. As Ryan, sole-custody father of two, repeatedly said, 'I can't do it all on my own.'

Diversity within Diversity: Other Fathering Groups in the Study

While the study that informs this book is based on the narratives of fathers who self-identify as primary caregivers, and while there is, as described above, considerable diversity within this category, there was also diversity within diversity. Most notably, the categories of ethnic-minority fathers and gay fathers are worth addressing.

Ethnic-Minority Fathers

There are fifteen fathers from visible ethnic minorities and four Aboriginal fathers, in the sample, and also considerable internal differentiation *within* ethnicity (see table 3.1). Differentiation occurs largely at the intersections of ethnicity, immigration status, and social class. For example, Maurice, a black father who immigrated to Canada from the United States, is culturally fluent in Canadian child-rearing practices, while other black fathers who had recently emigrated from African countries face cultural, economic, and linguistic barriers.

The degree of assimilation into Canadian society also makes a difference to fathers experiences. While Gilbert, Dennis, Joe, and Jude are Aboriginal fathers, the first three have lived much of their adult lives

Table 3.1 Fathers of Ethnic Minorities and Aboriginal fathers

Names	Age	Ethnicity	No. of children	Ages of children	Relationship and fathering status	Income	Occupation
1. Shahin	40	Iranian (20 years in Canada)	1	6	Married; at home since his son was born; wife (French Canadian) is a lawyer	90,000	Self-employed carpenter
2. Ahmed	52	Iranian (12 years in Canada)	3 (triplets)	10	Was at home for three years, now shares custody; wife (also Iranian) works in a restaurant	24,000	Freelance journalist, part-time student
3. Ayan	50	Somali (12 years in Canada)	1	13	Married; he is raising his cousin's son	N/A	Previously a teacher, now student
4. Dalmar	52	Somali (10 years in Canada)	4	24 21 18 13	Married; highly involved father	50,000	University lecturer
5. Samatar	67	Somali (12 years in Canada)	11	3–39	Third wife; wife is studying, so he is caring for their 3-year-old	N/A	Retired businessman
6. Jarabee	35	Somali (10 years in Canada)	2	3 1	Married; wife is younger (26), a newly arrived immigrant; she is studying English	Under 20,000	Polling researcher
7. Ghedi	49	Somali (10 years in Canada)	3	10 7 4	Married; wife (also Somali) is studying to be a nurse; he shares the care of the children	40,000	Previously a doctor in Somalia, now administrative assistant (government)
8. Eduardo	37	Latino (6 years in Canada)	1	3 (and wife is pregnant)	Married; stayed home for over a year when his son was an infant	50,000	MA student; previously worked in international development
9. Pedro	50	Latino (10 years in Canada)	2	17 12	Married; highly involved father	50,000	Social worker
10. Dennis	28	Half Aboriginal (grew up partly on a reserve) and half Chinese	1	10	Sole-custody father; child's mother lives in another province	Under 20,000	Chef

Table 3.1 (*Concluded*)

Names	Age	Ethnicity	No. of children	Ages of children	Relationship and fathering status	Income	Occupation
11. Joe	55	Aboriginal (grew up on a reserve)	2	4 2	Married; wife is lawyer; at home since she ended maternity leave (3 mos)	60,000	Previously varied unskilled jobs
12. Gilbert	46	Aboriginal (grew up on a reserve)	1	11	Sole-custody father	30,000	Salesclerk
13. Jude	44	Aboriginal (grew up on a reserve)	2	13 11	Sole-custody father	25,000	Teacher's aid
14. Golin	42	African Canadian (20 years in Canada)	4	13 10 9 6	Sole-custody father	50,0000	Information technology in government
15. Kofi	44	African Canadian (20 years in Canada)	2	13 11	Sole-custody father	70,000	University professor
16. Robert	33	African Canadian (20 years in Canada)	3	14 12 10	Joint-custody father	Under 20,000	Dancer and dance teacher
17. Osie	47	African Canadian (20 years in Canada)	2	15 12	Joint custody for 10 years; sole custody for 3 years	50,000	Self-employed software traning
18. Maurice	30	African American (born and raised in the United States; immigrated to Canada)	2	4 1	Married; was home for one year while waiting for his immigrant papers to process	70,000	Was in American army; now a restaurant manager
19. Hubert	35	Chinese (in Canada 20 years)	3	9 5 1½	Married; wife is seamstress; was home for six months in between jobs; his mother-in-law is now living with them; he notes that Chinese men typically do not stay at home	40,000	Chef

outside Aboriginal communities, while Jude still lives on a reserve in Saskatchewan, which means that he parents within a distinct set of cultural ideas and economic conditions. Further differences are in evidence between Dennis, a Chinese-Aboriginal Canadian and single father who lives in a lower income-housing unit, and Joe, an Aboriginal father married to a lawyer and living in a middle-class suburb. Nevertheless, for Joe, his upbringing in a different school system and having not completed high school puts him at a considerable disadvantage in dealing with his children's schooling.

Immigrant fathers coming from distinct cultural traditions commented on the difficulties of reconciling their traditional cultures with that of mainstream Canadian society. For the six Somali fathers who participated in the study, the role of involved father required them to step outside their traditional cultural conceptions of mothering and fathering. On the other hand, for second- and third-generation black fathers who had been raised in Canada, these were not central issues. Finally, the intersections of ethnicity with immigrant status and class need to be mentioned. In particular, recent immigrants to Canada, according to recent research, continue to experience significant difficulties in successfully integrating into Canadian society; this is partly owing to changes in social policy such as cuts in social welfare, waning support for resettlement services, and changes in the labour market toward greater flexibility, which has translated into immigrants filling low-paid and inscure jobs (Palamet, 2004; Shields, 2003; Vosko, 2000). All this leads to a lowering of the social and economic conditions faced by immigrant fathers, many of whom arrive in Canada with high levels of education from their countries of origin.

Gay Fathers

The complexity and diversity of gay fatherhood is perhaps best illustrated in the categories of gay fatherhood employed in the work of Gillian Dunne: those in a heterosexual marriage, divorced, or parenting in a non-heterosexual context (Dunne, 1999). My study had one gay father in a heterosexual marriage; six divorced gay fathers (one with sole custody, two with legal joint custody, two with informal joint custody, and one involved after initially being shut out of child rearing), and two fathers parenting in a non-heterosexual context[5] (see table 3.2). One divorced gay man was a stay-at-home father for four years and remains the children's shared primary caregiver. The two fathers

Table 3.2. Gay Fathers

Names	Age	No. of children	Ages of children	Status of gay father
1. Morris	57	2	27 23	*Married* Openly gay within his heterosexual marriage; stayed with his wife initially for the children's sake and remains now for companionship
2. Aidan	51	1	20	*Divorced* Was married; now separated and openly gay; left the family home when his daughter was 15 but still went back three times a week to help with homework and spend time with his daughter, who now lives with him as she attends university
3. Edward	46	2	19 16	*Divorced* Joint custody; lives a few blocks from his ex-wife
4. James	33	1	3½	*Divorced* Was a stay-at-home father for 18 months after his ex-wife's maternity leave; shared custody (not legal yet)
5. Jean Marc	43	2 (twins)	7	*Divorced* Does not have joint custody because he was shunned by his ex-wife's family (after he came out); has gradually become more involved in the family and now takes the twins on his own at his home, on holidays, and participates in decision making
6. Leslie	33	3	9 7 5	*Divorced* Was a stay-at-home father for 5 years; now has joint custody
7. Harrison	54	1	2	*Divorced* Has had sole custody since his daughter was an infant
8. Bernard	42	1	4	*Parenting in a non-heterosexual context* His male partner died a few years ago. He participated in his son's conception through artificial insemination ('The building of Jake took about 15 to 20 minutes') and shared custody of the boy with two lesbian mothers
9. Ray	36	1	6 mo.	*Parenting in a non-heterosexual context* He and his partner have adopted a baby in an open adoption; he has taken unpaid parental leave to be at home with her

parenting in a non-heterosexual context include one gay man who fathered a child (through artificial insemination) and is sharing custody with two lesbian mothers, and a gay couple who have adopted a baby girl.

As described above and as indicated in tables 3.1 and 3.2, there is considerable differentiation in the sample of fathers in the commonly employed social science categories of ethnic minority fathers and gay fathers. Perhaps the most ambiguous term in the study, however, is stay-at-home father.

The Stay-at-Home Father

Although there were sixty-six stay-at-home fathers in my study, the meanings of the term *at home* require clarification. Were these fathers at home full time? Had they relinquished their connection to the labour market? What struck me as particularly fascinating about these allegedly at-home fathers were the diverse relationships that they carved out between their unpaid and paid work.

Specifically, three patterns, with varying degrees of overlap, characterized the balance between work-home and between paid-unpaid work for these stay-at-home fathers. First, there were eleven fathers who had achieved financial and professional success and wanted to take a break from working and/or were seeking to move into another line of work once their children were in school. The overarching commonality with this group was that they seemed to have achieved their career goals and were looking for other forms of fulfilment, one of which was caring for their children as well as alternative work or leisure interests (e.g., travel, sports, writing). Second, twenty-five fathers were taking a break from working (as was the case with the two fathers on extended parental leave), were in a clear transition between jobs, were planning to go back to college or university for further education or training, or were currently taking evening courses along this path. Third, there were thirty fathers working part-time, flexibly from a home office, or as an employee in their wife/partner's business; of these thirty, ten (one-third) were both working part-time *and* in transition between jobs or careers.

For all of these stay-at-home fathers, the decision to relinquish full-time employment was a result of a complex mix of factors that included variations on the following themes: his wife/partner having the higher income with employment benefits and a stronger career interest (at this stage of their lives); strong views on the importance of home care; the opinion that there is a paucity of good childcare facilities in Canada; the cost of childcare; and, in some cases, a child with particular developmental, physical, or health needs came to play a role in the decision.[6] Each of these patterns will be illustrated in several brief case studies.

Fathers with Work Success: 'It's Not like I'm Saying 'This Kid Is Holding Me Back'

The first pattern among the stay-at-home fathers is well represented in the narrative of fifty-three-year-old Rory. Living in Calgary, Alberta, Rory gave up his consulting business as a quality control expert on gas pipelines to stay at home with Tristan, who is now seven years old. His wife is a high-level civil servant with the provincial government. At home for four years, Rory has been president of the local school's parent council, takes language courses to assist with French immersion schooling, and cooks a daily special diet for his son, who has debilitating food allergies. He also renovates the home and takes on community work that relates to his son's interests. In his words, 'If my son is really interested in something, I am really interested in it. If he's not, I don't have the time.' Rory describes his decision to leave work: 'He had been having problems with a stutter and he had been in a home day care. We were both working. The kids in the day care all had colds, so I kept him home. Things were pretty slow at work that week. So we decided I would stay home with him that week. His stutter started to get better. The next week he stayed home because he had the cold. Then his stutter got even better. And so I said to my wife, "If this is what it is going to take to get him better, then this is what I will do."'

Unlike many of the stay-at-home fathers, Rory seems to have a particular sense of ease about his time at home. At the end of the interview, he adds that they have no debt, the house has been paid off, that his wife is younger than he is, that it was her turn for her career to take off, and that his age is definitely a factor in his sense of ease. 'If I had been twenty years old with a son with stutter and food allergies, I would have responded completely differently. How I would have, I don't know, but I would have responded differently ... I mean, I have travelled; I've worked in many different places. It's not like I'm saying that this kid is holding me back.'

Two other fathers serve as good illustrations of this pattern of fathers who had achieved work success. Martin, a forty-two-year-old second-generation Czech Canadian and father of a preschool boy, worked as an insurance adjuster for twenty years and says, 'I don't have a huge stigma about not being out there earning the money. Again, it's probably because Denise and I just worked it in a way. I worked the first twenty years. We joke about it once in a while. I worked to help pay off her student loan and that was all on my back. I worked since I was seventeen.'

Richard, a French-Canadian stay-at-home father of three who was a car mechanic for many years, is quite blunt about his aspirations for a career: 'I've done it. I did it before. I made money. I went to work. I used to have expectations and dreams. And I don't want to work anymore.'

Fathers like Rory, Martin, and Richard who identified themselves as having met their own standards of employment success were a small part of the study. It was more likely that most of the stay-at-home fathers, as described in the next section, are in transition between jobs or between careers.

Fathers in transition: 'This Is Not the Kind of Thing I Want to Do for the Rest of My Life'

Approximately 37 per cent of the stay-at-home fathers (twenty-five of them) were in transition between jobs or careers. Craig, a forty-year-old stay-at-home father to four-year-old twins Michael and Zachary,[7] typifies the in-transition father. While he identifies himself as a musician, his paid job for many years was as a mechanic. Craig now works at a hardware store for two evenings a week and Saturdays; he plans to eventually 'go back to school in computers.' When I asked him how he came to be at home with his sons, he responded this way:

My wife is a psychiatric nurse; she has a career. I am a musician from a long time ago, and that's what I like to do primarily. My job was just that, it was not a career, so it was a very easy choice. We looked at it and I was working in auto parts, mostly car dealerships, and before that I was in forklifts and things like that, parts for these machines. But when we found out that it was going to be more than one baby and without even thinking that there would be anything aside other than happy normal bouncing kids, running around, my salary would have been eaten up by daycare and I figured, well, what the heck, we're going to be in the same boat financially, so I'll stay home until they go to school. That's how we came to the decision; it took us not even a minute to come to that decision.

Andrew, a water-supply engineer whose wife has a demanding job that involves international travel, has a similar story. He says, 'I was also thinking about getting out of the business anyway. This is not the kind of thing I want to do for the rest of my life. We thought two years, ideally three.' In the end, Andrew stayed home for two years and then went back to teachers' college when his children were both in school.

Within this group of in-transition fathers, some had lost their jobs, others went through a serious illness that forced them to rethink their career paths at the same time as they were juggling expensive childcare arrangements, and still others found that their jobs were dead-end ones offering little satisfaction and did not justify two stressful jobs and the high cost of childcare. Some men took a break to concentrate on their children and to simultaneously prepare for a new career, while others, as described in the next section, took on part-time jobs or moved their work into a more home-based setting.

Fathers Balancing Paid Work and Caregiving: 'My Shop Is in the Garage'

Of the sixty-six stay-at-home fathers in the study, thirty were employed in part-time jobs or were working flexible hours from a home-based workplace. Within this group, one-third of the fathers were also in transition between careers but were working part-time to supplement the family income. Shahin, a forty-three-year-old Iranian Canadian, provides a good example of the home-working father. Shahin began staying at home with his son, now six years old, when his wife, a lawyer, went back to work after a four-month maternity leave. A self-employed cabinetmaker, he has a workshop in his garage. Reflecting on how he and his wife decided that he stay at home, he says, 'Well, the decision was rather simple because my wife makes more money than I do, and I did not want my son to be raised without at least one parent at home ... So the decision was made on that basis, based on economical feasibility. It just seemed more logical for me to stay home, especially since I have my own business. I could do at least part-time work.'

In his long descriptions about his routine when his son was an infant, he frequently referred to the way he balanced work at home and care: 'My shop is in my garage. It's rather practical. So I had the monitor in the shop ... He had this rocking chair – you know, you put the baby in there and it goes back and forth. He loved to sleep in it, and it was forty-five minutes, I think, a cycle. So I used to run in every half an hour and crank it up.'

Shahin and twenty-nine other fathers kept their hand in paid work through part-time or home-based employment.[8] The range of occupations and creative flexibility within this group was astounding. Of the thirty stay-at-home fathers who work part-time, several diverse examples can be provided. Sam is a driving instructor two evenings a week and Saturdays. Jamal, a Somali immigrant father, takes care of his two sons during the day while his wife studies English, and he works nights conducting surveys by phone. Brandon, a sole-custody father, balances the raising of his three sons with running his organic farm. Jerome, at home for the past eleven years, works about eight hours a week as a paid office manager in his wife's pediatrics practice in a small Nova Scotia town. Cameron and his wife have taken in a foster son, which 'allows me to stay at home and look after the kids; otherwise, we couldn't survive on the one salary.' Finally, Harry, at home for the past nine years in rural Ontario, has always taken on an assortment of jobs: 'I've helped the neighbours with the hay and, well, ... I do cleaning for two hours a week at the church in Griffith ... I have my chickens and the garden ... And last year I looked after a couple of other kids in the morning. I got paid for putting them all on the bus.'

The complexity and diversity of home-work patterns for these fathers raises the question of whether the term *stay-at-home dad* is a useful one. What is worth noting is that the patterns described above can be viewed as similar to those of mothers who have long been challenged to find creative ways of combining working and caregiving (Bradbury, 1984, 1993). In her book *Weaving Work and Motherhood* Anita Garey, for example, details a wide array of patterns for working mothers, including varied kinds of 'sequencing' and the 'midlife switch,' which have parallels with the narratives of the fathers in this study (Garey, 1999, 165–90). One large difference, however, is that the majority of fathers in my study felt compelled to talk about paid work in relation to caring, whereas mothers, as described by Garey, were more likely to focus on how their caregiving responsibilities were not hindered by working. As explored more fully in chapter 6, a slight difference exists in emphasis, with fathers feeling the weight of a moral responsibility to earn while mothers feel pulled by a moral responsibility to care (see also Townsend, 2002).

The Stay-at-Home Father and 'Equal' Divisions of Labour?

Having explored above the question of what it means to be a stay-at-home father in relation to paid work outside the home, I now investigate the issue of fathers' unpaid work inside the home. Is the stay-at-home father responsible for running the home? Moreover, do primary-caregiving fathers take primary responsibility for the home? Is it shared labour, or perhaps even an equal division of work and responsibility? Is there a possibility of equal divisions of domestic labour? Two examples will be presented to help grapple with these issues. The first example, using snippets from the narrative of Jimmy, makes the case for considering the issue of housework for stay-at-home fathers. The second example, Gary and Kathy, illustrates the continuing perplexities of working between equality and differences within the division of domestic labour.

Jimmy: 'Leaving Dishes and Laundry for Her Is My Way of Making Her Feel Wanted ...'

Jimmy is a self-employed car mechanic and a stay-at-home father of a four-year-old girl for the past three years; his narrative illustrates the need to distinguish between the stay-at-home dad who is running the home in a primary sense and the stay-at-home dad who leaves the housework to his partner. Jimmy takes the latter approach, and he does this so that his partner 'feels wanted and needed.' Two hours into the interview at his home in rural Ontario, an opportune moment arrived, and I broached the topic of housework. While initially he evaded my question on the issue of cooking, he then presented a clear picture of his domestic contributions as a stay-at-home dad:

ANDREA So who makes supper?
JIMMY I get real sick of it. I can easily see how being a person at home cooking meals ... it's like you kind of lose your appetite after a while and you really don't know what you like to eat anymore. You're just so sick of cooking. It gets routine-ish. You know what I mean? Nothing fancy anymore.
ANDREA Well, who plans the meals?
JIMMY You mean people actually plan meals? [laughs] I used to.
ANDREA Do you do the shopping?
JIMMY No.

ANDREA Okay, so she does ...

JIMMY I don't shop, I don't do dishes. I don't do laundry.

ANDREA Okay.

JIMMY And I don't take care of the finances. Those are her duties and I've got my duties. I'll do a little bit of housecleaning. I'll make sure that things don't get out of control.

ANDREA Yes ...

JIMMY I don't usually vacuum or wash floors or do dishes, but, like, when I cook, I'll rinse off dishes and I'll stack them up. It's not a big mess for her to do – you know, scraping things off plates for five or ten minutes. You know what I mean?

ANDREA Yes. And what about the nighttime routine with (your daughter) Valerie?

JIMMY That's hers because she's been away.

ANDREA Oh yeah ...

JIMMY Like, I put the garbage out and I keep the cars running and do all the general maintenance. I think it's a matter of role-playing. It's like whatever roles that you're good at.

ANDREA Yes, yes.

JIMMY Like, if she was doing good at fixing cars. If the cars broke down, she'd be out there doing that and maybe I'd be washing dishes ...

JIMMY You have to have a sense of fair play because, honestly, you don't want to hog all the duties.

ANDREA Yes.

JIMMY Because if you hog all the duties, and you're a little meany about it, then the other person's going to think, Why am I here? Know what I mean ...?

ANDREA Yeah.

JIMMY Like, you have to give people something to do, to make them feel wanted.

ANDREA Yes.

JIMMY Like, it might sound a little bit funny, but to a certain degree leaving dishes and laundry for her is my way of making her feel wanted.

ANDREA Mmm.

JIMMY And *needed*. You know what I mean?

It is important to add that this conversation was atypical among the stay-at-home fathers in this study and certainly stood out as the rare case of the stay-at-home father who did very little domestic work. Indeed, it closely resembled the traditional fathering model of the breadwinner male who takes infrequent turns at domestic labour and concentrates mainly on tasks such as fixing the car and taking out the garbage.

As discussed in chapter 1, most researchers of domestic life strongly advocate equality while remaining cognizant of the fact that women still, on average, spend more time doing domestic work than men.[9] Yet just what an egalitarian household should look like remains something of a puzzle. One of the underlying conceptual problems with assessing an equal household is that it is tremendously difficult to define and measure domestic life and labour. Marjorie Devault's lament is still a relevant one when she write that 'researchers lack an adequate language for the work of everyday caring' (Devault, 1991, 228). We also lack categories that can capture the daily, weekly, and temporal flow of family life. Whereas equality in employment is more easily measured and tested against factors such as pay, promotions, and the relative status of women and men, the issue of equality within the home is not so straightforward. Does equality in housework mean that women and men perform the same household tasks, and/or do they spend an equal amount of time performing such tasks? Does it imply doing *everything*, even if that suggests that the woman may learn how to do plumbing and electrical chores for the first time, whereas her male partner may have been doing such tasks since he was a boy? Moreover, in terms of parenting, does equality imply that women and men share all childcare tasks from the first day of their first child's life or, alternatively, do they have periods where one parent does more than the other? Should, for example, a father go to the toddler groups or playgroup sessions where he might be the only man in the room, and should women spend as much time coaching soccer or baseball as fathers typically do?

Most of the couples in my study had divisions of labour that were certainly *different*, but that could also be described as *symmetrical* and *complementary*. Gary and Kathy's division of labour is typical of couples with a stay-at-home father and a full-time working mother. A snapshot of this couple in the next section of this chapter provides a concrete example of the challenges of defining equality, and the greater utility of reflecting on differences within domestic life and the possibility of integrating differences *and* symmetry within domestic life.

Gary and Kathy: Traditional or Non-Traditional Divisions of Labour?

When I arrived on a Monday morning in October 2002 at the home of

Gary, Kathy, and their three sons, it was Kathy's day off from the hair-dressing salon that she owns and manages. She was carrying her infant son, Oscar, on her hip and stirring a large pot of tomato sauce for the lasagna that she was making for the week ahead. In his individual interview, held a few months earlier, Gary had already told me about Kathy's cooking sessions: 'Kathy has Mondays off. So she will some-times go out and get a large family pack of chicken legs and then she will cook that and then we can just nuke everything in the microwave over the week. Or she'll make a large lasagna and we'll have that over the week.'

Kathy confirmed Gary's description of her family cooking sessions. She had been up early that morning buying the necessary groceries. She admitted that she *did* try to pass the cooking over to Gary at one point, but she was not satisfied with the result: 'I came home every night and they were eating hot dogs, chicken fingers, hot dogs, chicken fingers. That's not food!' Thus, Kathy took the cooking back. As she stood in the kitchen ladling the tomato sauce into the large lasagna pan, she effused: 'I like to nurture. You know it's funny what you learn about yourself as you get older. I love to have ten people over and cook a huge meal and stuff them silly.'

As I analysed Gary and Kathy's interview and their Household Portrait, I wondered, Is Gary and Kathy's division of labour traditional or non-traditional? Their Household Portrait (figure 3.2), constructed as part of their couple interview, reveals areas of what might be called a traditional division of labour with Gary doing more stereotypically masculine tasks such as yard work, recycling and garbage, plumbing and electrical, car maintenance; in addition, they recently put in a backyard pool, and he cleans and maintains it. Yet there are also areas of domestic distribution that are non-traditional. For example, he does most of the laundry, and he is one of the few men in the study who enjoys shopping for birthday and special-occasion greeting cards. Kathy says he will even go into a shop to browse for cards. Certainly much of their housework is shared and could be seen as equally dis-tributed. Two large jobs – laundry and cooking – are divided between them, with Kathy doing most of the cooking and Gary doing most of the laundry.

If we were to return to the terms used by most studies in this field, we would also ask, Is this an equal division of labour? In the first instance, it is not possible to give percentages because Gary and Kathy themselves are not sure about how much time they spent on any particular area of household work. When Kathy is home she multitasks and does, as Gary points out, 'about ten things at once.' He, on the other hand, moves more slowly and methodically through the home, asking each child to wait his or her turn as he does one thing at a time. As Kathy puts it, 'Gary knows how to enjoy a moment. He can sit here and enjoy a good joke, a good game with the boys, while the whole place is in distraction or whatever, while he's got five million things to do. I can't do that. I've got to do the forty million things.' Moreover, the division of labour has changed constantly with the addition of each child and how much extended family support is available. In the summer, for example, teenage cousins come in and help with babysitting, which allows Gary to attend to the maintenance work in the building that he owns.

Gary and Kathy's household is similar to that of many others in my study. There is great diversity, but it is the case that in most households (with the exception of three of the fourteen joint couple interviews) men still take on traditional masculine tasks of maintenance, construction, plumbing and electrical and issues dealing with their car. Women do more of the laundry – especially folding it and putting it away – and men do more of the weekday cooking while women do more weekend cooking. Women do more of the reading to children, homework help, creative play, and board games, and men do more physical play, outdoor activities, and sports. With the exception of Gary, who 'loves buying greeting cards,' the card and gift buying falls mainly to women because, in general, women seem to place greater value on birthdays and anniversaries. Denise, for example, reminds Martin that his mother's birthday is coming up: 'I think I have a better memory than he does for those things.' Women almost exclusively buy children's clothes, while men buy more of their footwear (shoes and boots). Women do more of the vocal or expressed worry (see also Ehrensaft, 1987).

My analysis of all fourteen households, and their Household Portraits detailing their divisions of labour, reveals that it is tremendously difficult to fit individuals and couples into the categories and classifications typically employed by authors in this subject area – for example, 'traditional,' 'transitional,' or 'egalitarian' (Hochschild, 1989). When I tried to characterize individuals and couples as egalitarian or traditional, another aspect of their narrative saw them quickly slipping out of these same categories. Each couple's story represents a wide range of distinct patterns of sharing related to differing ideas on

Figure 3.2. Household Portrait: Gary and Kathy

Gary	Mainly Gary (with Kathy helping)	Shared equally	Mainly Kathy (with Gary helping)	Kathy	Others
Cleaning stove	Shopping for groceries	Household cleaning – kitchen	Taking children to doctor's appointments	Cooking evening meal (weekends)	Outdoor painting
Changing beds	Household cleaning – bathrooms	Laundry – doing it	Cooking for guests	Cooking evening meal (weekdays)	Indoor painting
Watering plants	Household cleaning – bedrooms	Library	Organizing extended family gatherings	Laundry – hanging it out	Making jams / preserves
Taking out garbage	Laundry – putting away	Boys turns mainly to … when upset	Deciding what needs doing re housework	Making breakfast	Making photo albums
Making daily lunches	Washing floors	Physical play		Reading childcare books / magazines for parenting ideas	
Vacuuming	Setting discipline and following through	Putting older boys to bed		Attending to older boys at night if they awaken	
Sports (in future or now)	Outdoor activities	Promoting children's independence		Putting baby to bed	
Minor repairs – plumbing, electrical	Mowing lawn	Homework		Attending to baby at night if he awakens	
Setting disciple and following through	Making decisions about children's behaviour	Reading childcare books/magazines for parenting ideas		Bath-time routine	
Sports	Parent-teacher meetings	Evening play			
Washing windows		Creative play			
Garden – flowers		Buying Christmas presents			
Car maintenance		Reading			
Buying furniture		Buying children's clothes			
Outdoor yard work					
Pool maintenance					
Decorating house					

Figure 3.2. (*Concluded*)

Gary	Mainly Gary (with Kathy helping)	Shared equally	Mainly Kathy (with Gary helping)	Kathy	Others
Buying major household appliances Remembering birthdays and sending cards Sending Christmas cards Garden – vegetable Organizing social events with friends (setting up) Household bills Overall budgeting and financial management		Organizing holidays and special family times Family contacts (letters, phone calls) Taking photos Organizing children's birthday parties Planning meals Setting up babysitting when required Feels they have the overall responsibility for the children's lives Overall planning and management of children's day-to-day activities Long-term planning of children's activities		Baking Repairing clothes Knitting Making (sewing) clothes Making children's doctor's appointments	

both the *meaning* and appropriate *structure* for sharing the household work.

If equality cannot be gauged or measured, can we be certain about the differences that matter in household life? That is, what is the utility of my approach, as described in chapter 1, which shifts the focus from equality to differences and the *difference difference makes*? Is it clear when differences turn into disadvantages? Alternatively, is it readily apparent when differences are simply *differences per se* that arise from individual or couple choices and preferences? What does become clear is that attempts to arrive at any solid judgements are hampered by problems of definition and measurement.

Equality and Differences: Problems of Definition and Measurement

Problems of definition and measurement plague attempts to categorize couples and their divisions of labour. Several issues can be mentioned here. First, fathers did not speak much about housework, and in their individual interviews, it was nearly impossible to get a clear picture of what was being done and how often. Certainly the Household Portrait technique and the relational context of a couple interview assisted with some of these problems since couples conversed and came to mutual decisions on who did what and why. Nevertheless, what emerged for me were three issues around the collection of data on housework that have implications for the way we think about differences and equality in households.[10] First, housework is a sensitive issue; the second point relates to housework standards; and finally, women's overwhelming propensity to take over the domestic sphere when they arrive home from work clouds attempts to evaluate difference and disadvantage in the division of domestic labour.

Housework as a Sensitive Issue: 'The House Has Really Been an Issue'

Fathers were forthcoming about what they did with their children and their parenting personas and activities but much quieter about housework. Jimmy's apparent honesty and forthrightness about how little housework he did was certainly the exception, and it was the opposite tendency that was more in play where many men attempted to give the impression that they did it all. More often, however, fathers gave scant detail on their housework routines or they gave the impression that housework is a sensitive issue. Alistair remembers that when the house was untidy over a long period of time, his wife, Claire, would get up in the middle of the night and vacuum, partly as a coping mechanism, partly as a bit of a protest. Tom says, 'Actually the house has really been an issue because stuff gets really dirty.'

There were also some contradictions between fathers' individual interviews and the couple interviews and, thus, as far as housework is concerned, most of my analysis is drawn from the couple interviews where there was an opportunity to discuss together what the pair did and why. As discussed in chapter 2, the Household Portrait technique was very useful in bringing forth discussion about the definitions and enactments of tasks. As a visual and interactional methodological tool, it allowed couples to discuss an area of their lives that was intangible, invisible, taken for granted, and at times heavily laden with tension and resentment. A few examples will be given here to illustrate this point.

While Theo told me, in his individual interview, that he did all the laundry, his wife, Lisa, laughed when she heard this and insisted it was shared. 'Excuse me, but we share the laundry, dear.' Theo, in fact, agreed with her after they had discussed the different aspects of laundry (doing it, folding it, putting it away) and how it *did* count that she did it on the weekend whereas he did it more during the week. Martin told me that as far as the housework was concerned, 'I basically do it all,' whereas in their joint interview, it was clear that Denise did her fair share of housework.

Difficulties with accurate reporting by individuals on a relational set of tasks and the need for joint discussion was also made apparent in the interactive couple interviews. With Martin and Denise, for example, he does more of the cooking for guests because, as he says, 'I enjoy it more than Denise does.' She contests this and says that this task should be seen as one that is 'shared equally' because she makes the pancakes for the annual maple feast. Their dialogue goes as follows:

DENISE Mind you, I do the pancakes for the maple feast cooking.
MARTIN Hold on, I make the maple syrup. I tap the maple trees. We have an annual maple feast. Just over a hundred people come. Friends and families. Yes, Denise makes the pancakes. It takes me four weekends in a row to make the maple syrup, and it takes her four hours, and she thinks that evens it out [laughs].

Mitchell and Nina disagree about laundry and how it gets done. Nina contests Mitchell's claim that he does it all:

NINA   Laundry, that's yours.

ANDREA   He does the laundry?

NINA   He does all the washing.

ANDREA   Okay, so there's doing it and there's also putting it away.

MITCHELL   That's also mine.

NINA   Excuse me?

MITCHELL   Okay. Half and half.

ANDREA   Do you take it out and fold it and put it in the laundry baskets?

MITCHELL   No, I don't fold it and put it in the laundry baskets. I separate it and put it into laundry baskets ... Nicole's, the boys', ours. And I then just put them in the room. And then Nina will come along, take it all out, fold it all, and put it away.

The above conversation between Nina and Mitchell also draws attention to the difference in standards that can matter in domestic labour. Not only is this a possible source of tension but also an issue in determining equal divisions of labour because 'equal' can mean struggling over meeting higher standards or reluctantly accepting lower standards.

Housework Standards: 'My Wife Sees Things That I Don't'

There was some gendered variation in household standards. Certainly some fathers were, as Kyle put it, 'fanatical about cleaning' and a few fathers, as confirmed in the couple interviews, had higher standards than their wives or partners (e.g., Peter and Martin). Yet overall there was a strong sense that housework was a secondary concern for most fathers. This is expressed by Aaron, Jacob, and Andy, who speak about how playing with the kids or homework always takes priority over housework. Aaron, a stay-at-home father of two says, 'I hate it. If I never see a broom or mop in my life I'd be happy [laughing]. Irene and I always had different standards with respect to that. My priority was the kids' play, and if the room didn't get dusted that week, that's part of my personality.'

Jacob, a sole-custody father of three, says that 'homework is a priority, housework is not and if the house is a shambles I don't care.' Andy thinks it is a general pattern with stay-at-home dads to put the kids' play ahead of the housework, but he also acknowledges that it can cause tension in his relationship with his wife: 'All the men I meet at the playground and all the stay-at-home dads I've talked to are not as concerned, well, with [pause] neatness. We've had discussions about parenting styles and housework. She says, "I wouldn't do it that way." I'll say, "I'll vacuum it later. Let him play." She has learned how to relax, how to trust me. I've learned that there are some things I have to attend to right away. And I have learned that Danny has to learn good habits because my wife has good habits.'

Victor, a stay-at-home father for over a decade says that 'my children grew up in a house that looked like a bush camp' while Robert, a Québécois stay-at-home father of two, is a bit defensive about how much housework he accomplishes and rationalizes this by saying, 'My wife sees things that I don't.'

Differing standards in domestic labour can cause tension in a relationship. It can also lead to women taking on more of the work and possible resentment coming from this. As Deutsch put it in her work on shared parenting, 'Most commonly ... the difference in standards becomes a driving force behind an unequal division. The person who cares more takes the responsibility and does the work' (Deutsch, 1999, 48). In addition, this issue of housework standards also points to difficulties with coming to a clear judgement on what constitutes an equal or symmetrical division of labour. A final point on the difficulties of measuring the division of domestic labour relates to women's tendency to take over the domestic realm when they come home from work.

Mothers Coming in 'Full-Fledged': 'When I Come Home, I'm a Mother'

A final issue that further confounds the challenge of determining domestic equality is that of women's large contribution to the household, particularly to the care of the children. As detailed earlier in this chapter, through the example of Manuel and Julie and her description of how she came in 'full-fledged,' what was intriguing was that despite the presence of primary-caregiving fathers, mothers did not let go of their role as caregivers and usually took over when they came home at the end of the working day. Many mothers and fathers indicated that this was one of the key differences between a household with a stay-at-home mom and one with a stay-at-home dad. Julie, for example, says, 'It was not like the man who goes off work and then comes home and says good-night to them.' Rather, what happened was that 'the minute I set foot in this house at any time of a day, whether for two hours or five hours or a day, I took over.'

All the women interviewed in the joint couple interviews expressed variations on this same theme. Linda, for example, says that as a working mother she has much more empathy than a working father coming home to a stay-at-home mother: 'I think it is different for women whose husbands are at home than for the man who has a stay-at-home wife. When I come home, I'm a *mother*. I'm not just the working person coming home. I am very much the *engaged* mother. So I sort of shift the responsibility from him to me in terms of the parenting. We do a lot of things together in the evening, but in those hours after work before dinner, I take on a lot of the active parenting ... For me it is a priority to get home to be with my kids and take the pressure off Peter.'

Monique makes a similar comment about the difference between being the partner of a stay-at-home mom or a stay-at-home dad: 'I find with my friends who stay home and then the fathers come home from work, their biggest complaint is that the fathers come home and say, "I've had a hard day." And they go to the TV or the newspaper. Whereas I come home and I take over the girls. I do the bath and I do the bedtime. My girlfriends are still doing the bath and bedtime even when they're there all day. That's the difference.'

It is also the case that many of the men confirm the statements given above from Julie, Linda, and Monique. Sam, for example, says, 'I'm very lucky. My wife comes home and does everything. She comes home and takes over.'

How, then, do we make sense of this? Is this unequal because women are coming home from a long day of work and putting in, as Arlie Hochschild (1989), so famously called 'a second shift'? The answer to this question rests on our understandings of women's and men's lives more widely. As detailed in the next part of this book in chapters 4, 5, and 6, there are deeply ingrained social, emotional, community, moral, and embodied differences in parenting. To assume equality or even shared caregiving can imply overlooking the profound differences in the social worlds of women and men, including the ways they express, and are expected to express, emotional connections to their children and significant others, the ways they create and maintain social networks around their children, and the gendered moral norms of parenting. Moreover, assumptions of equal parenting downplay issue of hegemonic masculinities in men's lives and how embodiment can, in certain sites and at certain time, matter greatly. These are some of the issues that will be highlighted in the remainder of this book.

Conclusions

This chapter has laid out some of the complexities and challenges involved in working with concepts such as *fathers as primary caregivers, stay-at-home fathers, fathers of ethnic minorities* and *gay fathers*. Furthermore, I explored the tensions in defining an equal division of household labour. Coming up with clear definitions of equality is confounded by methodological difficulties in getting information about who does what, the ways in which housework standards are tied up with what it means to be a good mother or father, and how women may come in 'full-fledged' at the end of their working day and take over domestic labour from their male partners. In Part Two of this book (chapters 4, 5, and 6), I explore more fully the complex interplay between equality and differences for mothers and fathers and the constant flow of these concepts, theoretically and empirically, within households and communities over time.

PART TWO

Do Men Mother?
Fathering and Responsibilities

Maternal practice begins in a response to the reality of a biological child in a particular social world ... But in my discussion of maternal practice, I mean by 'demands' those requirements that are imposed on anyone doing maternal work, in the way respect for experiment is imposed on scientists and racing past the finish line is imposed on jockeys. In this sense of demand, children 'demand' that their lives be preserved and their growth fostered. In addition, the primary social groups with which a mother is identified, whether by force, kinship, or choice, demand that she raise her children in a manner acceptable to them. These three demands – for *preservation, growth* and *social acceptability* – constitute maternal work; to be a mother is to be committed to meeting these demands by works of preservative love nurturance, and training ...

To describe mothering as a work out of which a distinctive thinking arises, I develop a somewhat eccentric way of identifying 'mothers.' Briefly, a mother is a person who takes on responsibility for children's lives and for whom providing childcare is a significant part of her or his working life. I *mean* 'her or his.'

(Sara Ruddick, *Maternal Thinking*)

4 Fathers and Emotional Responsibility

A mother's attachment to her baby is beyond the universe. You know yourself. I mean you'd rip your body apart if it was to save your children. I'm sure a father would, but the fear isn't there as much. When Gary mentioned how he worries, that's a very learned thing. When you become a new mother, you can either spend your life worrying about whether they're going to outlive you, or you can just push that aside and realize you have very little control over it, that it's a waste of energy ... So, you have to push that away. But sometimes if it creeps in, you can get a little crazy. A man wouldn't worry because he knows he will survive if something happens to his kids. I don't know if I would. *I would survive, but I would be a different person. It would scar me for life. I would never hit a happy plateau like I hit every day now. There would always be this hole as big as the house.* Just hearing about it – I heard someone lost their child, just a few weeks younger than Oliver, to crib death. I mean, I go through a half an hour of 'Oh my God! How are those people surviving?'

(Kathy, interviewed with her husband, Gary,
stay-at-home father of three children, October 2002)

I think that mothers care for their children differently. When my son has something going wrong emotionally, [my wife] has the emotional reaction that stems from the first moment that he was born. And I know that she has that connection with the physical act of childbirth and it is kind of a continuum. And I think that is a unique thing. I was there at the birth. I was there for all three of them. And I had a connection with them. But she had her body transformed. I don't think we can undermine the fact that women are connected to their children in that very physical, that very primordial sense. Then every time he cries or she gets upset – and especially him, because it was a very difficult birth – she'll think about that, and I think that *she's more inclined to go the extra mile to be emotionally connected to him*, whereas my response, in contrast, is to look at it for what it is.

(Tom, stay-at-home father of three, speaking about
his wife, Natasha, July 2002)

Introduction

It was the end of summer in 2002 and Denise's ten-month maternity leave was coming to an end. She found herself sleepless in Ottawa, filled with worry. She wasn't concerned about leaving her son, Nathan, but rather about the fact that her son's daytime caregiver would be Martin, her husband. Denise was especially anxious about the bond being formed between Martin and Nathan, a deep bond that would intensify as the two spent days together while she was at work. Night after night, she wrestled with several recurring qualms: would Nathan become closer to his father than to her? Who would he go to for comfort? Perhaps the most vexing question for her was, Who would Nathan call out for in the middle of the night? As she explained to me in the joint couple interview I conducted with them in October of that year, 'I felt threatened when we first decided that Martin would stay home ... If he had wanted Daddy in the night instead of me, I would probably have fallen apart ... *I wanted to be the mommy.* I wanted to be the one he calls in the middle of the night.'

While Denise lay awake worrying about whose name Nathan would call in the dark of night, fathers in other households throughout the city were waking to their children's cries while their wives lay undisturbed beside them. In Richard and Aileen's home, seven-year-old Sarah would walk around to the far side of the bed where her father lay sleeping. Greg, a joint-custody father of a five-year-old girl explained to me, 'I've always said I have mother's ears. My ex would have never heard that baby cry in a hundred years.' Archie, who used to be the one who slept soundly through the nighttime cries, found that after a few months of being at home he was getting up with their infant son, Jordan: 'A really interesting thing happened when I started staying home. Up until that point, I would ... do the night feeding and then go to bed. If the baby woke up after that point, Jean would hear it and would get up with Jordan. After two months of me staying home, she no longer heard when he woke up. It was *me* getting up. It was really bizarre and I still can't account for it.'

There is something about responding to a child's tearful cries in the middle of the night that cuts to the heart of parental protection and care. The parent who wakens and lovingly responds to the child's cries – or the parent whose embrace is sought by the sleepy child – is a metaphoric encapsulation of *nurturing*. As beautifully rendered in a traditional lullaby, 'Hush, my darling, don't fear, my darling, the lion sleeps tonight,' the parent who brings 'hush' and calm to the 'darling' child embodies emotional bonds and connection.

Denise's profound worry and Archie's noting of a 'bizarre'and unaccountable shift in his behaviour exemplify what Sara Ruddick, in *Maternal Thinking*, has termed 'preservation' or 'protective care': 'it simply means to see vulnerability and to respond to it with care, rather than ... indifference, or flight' (1995, 19). This state of mind and the sets of practices associated with it are also well captured in several decades of feminist scholarship on 'care' and the 'ethic of care'[1] as including qualities of attentiveness, competence and responsiveness (Fisher & Tronto, 1990; Gilligan, 1982; Graham, 1983; Noddings, 2003; Tronto, 1989, 1993, 1995). As evinced by the political theorist Joan Tronto in her description of caring, emotional responsibility involves skills that include '*knowledge* about others' needs' which the caregiver acquires through 'an *attentiveness* to the needs of others' (Tronto, 1989, 176–8; my emphasis). In wanting to denote both the tasks of caring and the responsibility for caring, I have used the term *emotional responsibility* to capture the essence and work of protective care and the responsibility for its enactment (that is, the 'response-ability')[2] (Doucet, 2000, 2001b, 2004).

Fathers and Emotional Responsibility

While there has been some debate on the character, quality, and enactment of care with distinctions drawn between levels and kinds of caregiving (Tronto, 1993), between care as *love* ('caring about') or *labour* ('caring for') (Graham, 1983; Ungerson, 1990, Tronto, 1993), and whether care is a feminine or feminist practice (Larabee, 1993; Tronto, 1993; Noddings, 2003), the issue of the *gendered* quality of care is less a matter of debate. International research has demonstrated that most of the work and responsibility for protective care and emotional responsibility for children rests with women. Nevertheless, it has also been shown that men can and do take on the work of care. In this vein, Sara Ruddick's assertion that 'men can mother' is supported by a large body of research attesting to men's successful efforts with the maternal tasks of 'preservation' and 'protective care.' That is, many studies on fathering have argued that fathers have the desire and the capacity to be protective, nurturing, affectionate, and responsive with their children (Coltrane, 1996; Dienhart, 1998; Doucet, 2004; Dowd, 2000; Lamb, 1981, 1987; Lupton & Barclay, 1997; Parke, 1996; Pleck, 1985; Pruett, 2000; Snarey, 1993).

Given that my research is on self-defined primary-caregiving fathers, it is not surprising that these findings about fathers' capable nurturing are strongly confirmed in my research. Cameron, a stay-at-home father of two preschool children as well as a foster parent of a mentally challenged teenager, tells me, *'I often find myself even ahead of them. I know what they want before they even express it.'* When asked to describe his fathering, Jerome, a stay-at-home father for ten years of two school-age children in rural Nova Scotia, chooses only the following words: *'Kind and gentle. Lots of hugs, Protective.'* A final example is with Manuel, the comment of his wife, Julie, that he is so tremendously in tune with the children:

> There was a little thing on the radio the other day. Some engineer has decided there are five different kinds of cries from a baby – you know, tired, hungry, uncomfortable ... And he has found that most babies fall into the categories of those five cries. He's developed a monitor that will tell you what that cry is. We were listening to this on the CBC, and I said to [our daughter] Lyn, 'You know what? Your dad was like that. Just wonderful. Well, I have never seen anybody who just knew [for instance] that that baby needed a sweater taken off. That this little squirm meant that.' I tell them things like this and they go, 'Oh he is so wonderful!'

All these statements by and about fathers hint at connection, hugging and holding the child, and knowing intuitively what the child wants. But do fathers' stories about caregiving add anything *new* to our understanding of nurturing and emotional responsibility?

In addition to confirming that fathers are indeed nurturing, my research confirms that fathers shed a light on *other* kinds of protective care. While preservation and protective care are usually related to closely holding and looking after children, fathers also specialize in the following kinds of nurturing: fun and playfulness; a physical and outdoors approach; promoting children's considered risk taking; and encouraging children's independence. These findings emerge from fathers' descriptions of their typical daily and weekly routines with their children, their reflections on differences between mothers' and fathers' care, as well as from the fourteen couple interviews, where mothers' views on the differences and similarities between the parents' care were directly discussed. Findings on recurrent patterns of fatherly nurturing are discussed below.

Fun and Playful: 'A Bouncing, Rollicking Time'

Many cross-cultural longitudinal studies have demonstrated that fathers use play to connect with their children (Coltrane, 1996; Lamb, 1987; Parke, 1996; Pruett, 2000; Yogman, Cooley, & Kindlon, 1988). This finding is also evident in the fathers' narratives in this study and is repeated across social class and ethnicity and for both heterosexual and gay fathers.

The women in my study also concur with this view. In the couple interviews, where couples place little pieces of paper on their co-constructed Household Portrait, the response is overwhelmingly consistent along distinct gendered lines when they come across the piece of paper that denotes play. Craig, a stay-at-home father of twins says, 'My immaturity has come into this in a big way. I can get on the floor and find myself watching their TV programs with them.' Kathy places the 'play' task slip in Gary's column, indicating this as his domain: 'They like playing with their dad. To say I play with them would be a gross exaggeration. I do games and that sort of thing, but Gary's a lot of fun. He's all of about ten years old.'

Several fathers use the example of cooking to contrast their approach with their female partners.' Kyle says, 'I teach the kids more about cooking than Carol does. Probably because I take the approach that cooking should be fun, and Carol takes the approach that cooking should be perfect.' William, who has run fathering groups, offers a similar view: 'It is less the practices and more the style. Feeding a kid is feeding your kid. With fathers, there is more fun associated with cooking, more adventure, flexibility, and getting the kids involved in doing it themselves.'

Bernard, a forty-two-year-old father who shares custody of a son with two lesbian mothers, notes that the style of parenting that four-year-old Jake receives is different between the moms' house and Dad's house. He evokes an approach to fathering similar to that of most heterosexual fathers:

When Jake and I are at my house, it's a different pace. They do more domestic stuff at the moms' house. I say, to heck with all that. We are out there doing things, spending time together. Moms' place is domesticated: There are books, photos, a computer, a playroom. He see that his moms work and that they spend time with female friends – some guys but mainly female friends. He doesn't see them do much outside of that. At my place he sees photos of himself and my family. He sees books. Sports trophies. My golf clubs, my bowling ball. He comes to my bowling group. He sees all this guy stuff. When I go out into the community, he sees a lot of males. It's a *testosterone world here, an estrogen world there*.'

This does not mean that mothers don't use fun and play as a way of responding to their children but rather that fathers and mothers high-light this as a dominant *paternal* pattern in relating to infants and young children. Carl, for example, mentions that though they both take turns putting their two preschool daughters to bed, there is a slight difference, with his style being more a 'big, bouncing, rollicking time,' whereas hers is 'very much a cuddle kind of time.'

Physical Activities and the Outdoors: 'I Get Them Out as Much as Possible'

The majority of fathers in my study talk about making it a point to get their children outdoors as much as possible, to do lots of physical activities with them, and to be very involved with their children's sports (Brandth & Kvande, 1998; Doucet, 2004; Plantin, Sven-Axel, & Kearney, 2003). Three examples illuminate this theme in the fathers' narratives. Robert, a former sign maker who lives in rural Quebec and is home with two boys, talks about his typical daily routine: 'I like to spend time outside with them. Spring, summer, winter, fall, if the weather is nice, we're gallivanting outside all over the countryside. I get them out as much as possible ... to get them away from the routine in the house. It re-energizes me.'

Peter, a part-time graphic designer and stay-at-home father of two boys for the past six years, speaks about preferring being outside with his sons to going to community playgroups: 'If we have a choice between going to playgroups or going to the river to throw rocks, we will always go down to the river. We like to go to the parks that are wilder so we can be out in nature.'

James, a gay divorced father who took a four-month paternity leave with his son, sums up his time at home this way: 'We got out every day. We'd be out of the house by ten. He had an afternoon nap, so we would get back at about one-thirty ... I saw it as an eighteen-month adventure. People used to comment on how adventurous we were. I would put him on the back of the bike and we would bike to museums, to the island, everywhere.'[3]

Mitchell, a former naval officer and a stay-at-home father of three children under the age of six (including twins), reflects that it may be personality and not gender that leads him to be out with the kids. Nevertheless, he adds, concurring with most of the other men's narratives, that he prefers to be outside with them: 'I think it has more to do with personality than whether you're male or female. I think if I enjoyed something like painting or more arts and crafts type thing, I'd probably spend more time doing that with the children. But I prefer being outside running around and going to the park.'

Can the valuing of physical and outdoor activities be part of nurturing and emotional responsibility? I would argue that, indeed, they represent ways of responding to the physical and developmental needs of children. Fathers reason that being outdoors and engaging in physical exertion is good for children; they get fresh air and exercise, sleep better, and have the opportunity to explore parks and nature trails. Indeed, fathers' encouragement of activity and exercise with young children and recreational sports for school-age children can be seen as having positive physical and mental developmental outcomes (Beauvais, 2001; Kremarik, 2000).[4]

Measured, Practical Reactions: 'My First Response Is to Fix the Problem'

Many fathers also remark that their response to emotionally charged situations is to fall back into what is often viewed as masculine ways of being. When Peter's youngest son was severely ill in the hospital, he found himself acting with what would be considered stereotypical masculine responses focused on *doing* rather than on *being*: 'My typical male characteristics are lack of emotion or the deferring of emotion, which I found out when we had a very sick child. My first reaction would be action rather than an emotional response.'

In a joint interview, Alistair, a writer, and his wife, Claire, a researcher and doctoral student, reflect on how they respond to the children. Her approach is to 'make her feel better' and to 'get her to tell me,' whereas his response is more 'measured' and more oriented to trying 'to fix the problem.' Alistair says, 'I think if [our daughter] Georgia is upset, my first response is to try to identify and fix the problem.

Whereas your initial response [turns to Claire] is, How can I make you feel better?'

In response to Alistair, Claire notes that at certain times, his more measured and patient response is what is required, particularly as the children grow older and may not always be willing to open up quickly to their parents. She says, 'With Georgia, I can see that she's sad. I'll get her to tell me. It won't come pouring out of her. If she's ready to talk, he's there to listen. And he gives an even, measured response. So they will draw on that too.' Claire's noting that 'they will draw on that too' reminds us that *connection*, strategically disguised here as *distance* or strategic *indifference*, can nevertheless act as a form of protective care in certain contexts.

Promoting Risk Taking: 'I Am Quite Willing to Let These Kids Fail'

Fathers' narratives are also replete with evidence that they encourage risk taking. Whether it is on the play structure in the park, exploring, or learning through physically falling or intellectually failing, most fathers claim to be more likely to facilitate their child's trying things out on his or her own. A couple of examples illustrate fathers' comfort with judicious risk taking.

Bernard, mentioned earlier as a gay father who shares custody of his son with two lesbian mothers, talks about his approach to his son's outdoor play, which contrasts to the child's two mothers. His relaxed attitude resonates with many fathers in the study: 'I do consider his safety. I help him to make a decision. If he was climbing a tree, the mothers would be sitting back and watching him and then yelling that that was far enough ... They would be more careful. I would be close by him helping him to make the decision about how far he can go; I would guide him through that decision.'

A different kind of risk taking comes from Kyle, an Italian-Canadian father of two daughters who is married to Carol, a German Canadian. They live in a rural area and both work part-time, Kyle as a local city counsellor and Carol as a librarian. In speaking about their daughter Emma, a gifted child who is home-schooled and who often has difficulties adjusting to social situations, Kyle refers to his wife's approach as 'setting up structures, lectures, long heart-to-heart talks late at night,' while his is best characterized as 'more sink or swim. Push her into a situation and then talk to her later about it. I am quite willing to let these kids fail.'

Encouraging Children's Independence: 'You Guys Can Make Your Own Lunches'

The issue of risk taking and letting children learn in an independent manner is a more narrow articulation of the wider issue of promoting their independence. This fourth aspect of fathers' emotional *connection* with children is, ironically, their role in facilitating processes of *autonomy* in children. That is, most fathers in this study indicate that they play a strong role in promoting the children's physical, emotional, and intellectual independence. Recurring examples in fathers' accounts include strongly encouraging the kids to be involved in housework, to make their own lunches, engage in independent play, tie their own laces (shoes or skates), and carry their own backpacks to school. As Alistair says, 'I might be less likely to go out of my way to help the kids if it's something they can do themselves.'

Jacob, a sole custodial father of three young children, also captures this particularly well in noting that 'I have always had them help out with chores' and that all three children (eleven, nine, and seven) make their own lunches: 'This year I said, "you guys can make your own lunches." I lay the ground rules: "You need a sandwich, or sometimes soup, then fruit and vegetables and a snack." They can do it with a little guidance – even Pippa [the youngest].'

Versions of this story were repeated by the majority of men interviewed. Initially, this telling of events puzzled me. Is the promotion of children's independence the opposite of protective care, or a fundamental part of it? As I worked laboriously through the reams of interview transcripts, my first interpretation was that this was an example of the father letting go of the child, in contrast to dominant understandings of nurturing and protective care that suggest that the parent is connected to (or holds on to) the child. Gradually, however, I came to view this behaviour as an integral part of nurturing. That is, the protective care of children with its qualities of attentiveness, responsiveness, and competence, involves both holding on and letting go – and it is the careful letting-go that fathers demonstrate particularly well.

Understanding Fathers' Narratives of Emotional Responsibility

In examining fathers' caregiving, my research reveals several dominant paternal patterns. What are the sources of such differences? Why do they appear so prominently in fathers' narratives? Drawing from both fathers' and mothers' narratives, I have developed six points to assist us in making sense of gendered differences in approaches to, and the enactment of, the emotional responsibility for children. First, both mothers and fathers remark on the residue of gendered upbringing as key factors accounting for differences in caring. Second, there are the strong beliefs by fathers – as well as many mothers – that mothering and fathering are inherently different – as identities and as *embodied* experiences. Third, many fathers speak further about embodiment issues, specifically the social taboos around men and physical touching, both with boys and girls in the preteen and teen years. Fourth, fathers note the leading role played by mothers in determining the balance of emotional responsibility within households. Fifth, fathers' narratives are marked by hegemonic masculinity, evidenced mainly in their devaluation and concurrent distancing from the feminine. Finally, I consider what we learn more broadly about nurturing and parenting by looking at differences in fathering narratives on emotional responsibility. Is it possible that fathers develop a concept of nurturing that incorporates both traditionally feminine and masculine qualities and, indeed, exists *between* maternal *equality* and paternal *difference*?

Growing Up Male: 'I Grew Up as a Guy'

It should not be surprising that most fathers exhibit more traditionally masculine qualities in their caregiving, given that most boys grow up in cultures that encourage sport,[5] physical and emotional independence, and risk taking (see Connell 1995, Mac an Ghaill, 1994; Seidler, 1997).[6] Alistair says he learned on the playing fields (and arenas) of boyhood that the rules of the sports take precedence over attention to somebody getting hurt: 'We were out playing ball hockey and Vanessa got hurt. It's the kind of accident that happens in ball hockey. Someone gets hurt, and you kind of stand around like a bunch of male apes and you kick them gently and say, "Well, can you play or not?" We're not a great nurturing bunch. Because you're learning certain things when you're playing ball hockey. There was my daughter and she was hurt in the face, and, you know, I was concerned. But also *this is ball hockey,* and you learn certain things when you do that.'

Devon, a technician and a sole-custody father of a seven-year-old son notes that danger is just part of 'what little boys do': 'I grew up as a guy. We did dangerous things, That's what little boys do. A father thing is, should I let him go up the tree? Yeah, but then a little scepticism is there.'

In contrast to Devon, as well as to her own husband, Peter, Linda takes a more cautious parenting approach, rooted partly in 'having grown up as a girl': 'I don't know if boys take more physical risks than girls. I suspect that they do. Having grown up as a girl, I saw boys on the highest bars at the park, or riding their bikes on one wheel. I think that has some bearing on it.'

Most sociologists view statements like ones given above as evidence of socialization. Yet it is more than this. As Patricia Yancey Martin has recently written, gendering processes are deeply ingrained so that they 'become almost automatic': 'Gendered practices are learned and enacted in childhood and in every major site of social behavior over the life course, including in school, intimate relationships, families, workplaces, houses of worship, and social movements. In time, like riding a bicycle, gendering practices become almost automatic' (Martin, 2003, 352).

Within such automatic gendering processes, there remains the question of how active fathering affects their daughters. That is, will fathers' daughters who 'are learning certain things when ... playing ball hockey' or 'riding a bike on one wheel' also grow up to exhibit these traditional masculine qualities? The long-term impact of fathers actively caring for their daughters will, however, only be revealed if and when the daughters become parents.

Embodied Differences between Mothers and Fathers:
'A Longer and Tighter Hug'

A second factor that underlies gendered differences in fathers' narratives is their profound belief in distinct differences between mothering and fathering as identities and as embodied experiences. Even where fathers are left literally holding the baby as their ex-wives or ex-partners leave home, or where they express little feelings towards their ex-wives or partners, the majority of fathers still noted that mothers are more protective, nurturing, and emotionally connected. While admitting that his ex-wife is not nurturing, Jack, a sole-custody father living in New Brunswick, nevertheless says, 'I still think in general that the most common situation is that women feel that attachment to the children ... because she's the mother, right?'

Fathers express great confusion over the origins of this special bond.

Is it based in biology (hormones, birthing, and breastfeeding), or is it a result of culture and socialization? Some fathers did implicate the latter. For example, Lorne, a papermill foreman and sole-custody father of three in a northern Ontario town, says, 'It's the way we programmed ourselves,' especially the fact that 'boys are not allowed to get emotional in public.' A few fathers reiterate these sentiments, but most suggest an embodied basis for the differences between mothers and fathers. Alistair, who stayed home for over a year with his first infant daughter, is aware of the physical connections associated with pregnancy, birth, and breastfeeding, and also of women's overall emotional involvement, especially with young children: 'I think you are *so physically* involved as a mother, from the beginning. Nine months of pregnancy – such a commitment – and then into the breastfeeding. And then normally mothers are much more involved with taking care of very small babies. There is a tremendous bond right there. Even when I was taking care of Georgia at home, I didn't have the same physical bond as Claire did with this baby. I think women are more sensitive and more inclined to be emotionally involved.'

Gary, a carpenter and stay-at-home father of three boys, succinctly captures many of the fathers' views on this matter when he speaks about how his wife, Kathy, relates to the kids: 'Well, like I said, men do nurture. We do give them a hug, tell them it's okay, sit them on our knee. But I just find with the mother they do it more or longer. They give a tighter hug.'

Embodiment: 'I Am Very Nervous about That Kind of Thing'

It may be that a mother's hug is longer and tighter because there are different social perceptions of fathers' and mothers' acceptable physicality with children. Although the early years – with infants and pre-school children – provide fathers with ample opportunity to hug and hold their children, many fathers of preteen and teenage boys and girls noted that they were more closely scrutinized by society in general. Brandan, a self-employed sole-custodial father of four, draws links between hegemonic masculinity and homophobia (Connell, 1987, 1995; Kaufman, 1999; Kimmel, 1994) when he says, 'I hug and kiss them, but it's not the same. And frankly I'm not as comfortable hugging the big guys as the little guys, Like, the older guys go, "Hey, man ..." I mean, we're not homophobic, but it's something you're raised with.'

Similarly, most of the single fathers of preteen and teenage girls say that, in some way, public displays of close physical affection can easily be misinterpreted. Henry, a sole-custodial father of two, currently unemployed, says he is always aware that his actions may be misinterpreted:

> As a single dad, all I have to do is breathe at the wrong time, or say the wrong thing in front of the wrong person. I am very conscious of that. For example, one of my daughter's favourite rants is 'You can't touch me! You can't hit me!' because she has been taught at school about violence and stuff like that. I don't use that against her any more at twelve years old. A couple of years ago, she would get a smack if she needed one. But I am very conscious of the fact that if she screamed that out in public it's like 'whoh!' They could be taken away on a moment's notice. Just on suspicion. So I am very nervous about that kind of thing.

Even several fathers living with female partners relay a subtle sense of unease in embodied father-daughter relations. Alexander, a university professor who took parental leave to be with two of his three daughters and is now a joint-custody father, reflects on how things changed when his daughter reached puberty: 'When puberty arrives, the entire dynamic changes. You don't think much of the physical thing that goes on with your kids until then. Embracing and hugging. I am trying to think about the parallel with a mother and son. Obviously the same thing happens to a degree, yet far less starkly.'

Fathers Rely on Mothers: 'You Can Never Replace the Mother'

References to gender differences in parenting also appear throughout fathers' narratives partly because fathers *rely* on mothers to take on the overall primary care of children (see also Daly, 2002; Stueve & Pleck, 2003). That is, the role and influence of mothers on the processes of fathers *becoming* and *enacting* their caregiving is highly significant within these narratives. In two-parent households, or even in joint-custody households where parents live apart, the father *expects* that the mother will take on the emotional responsibility for the children. Sasha, an African Canadian, a dance instructor, and a joint-custody father, says, 'I think it is a spiritual thing. They were with their mom before they came to earth. That is what men do not have, that extra, extra-special thing with the children.'

Luke, a stay-at-home father of two girls for twelve years who now works night shifts in a home for mentally challenged adults, says, 'You have to recognize that [even] as a stay-at-home father you can never replace the mother. Don't even think about it.'

Narratives of Hegemonic Masculinity and Difference: 'We're Still Men, Aren't We?'

Fathers also explicitly and deliberately draw attention to differences in mothering and fathering because they want to distance their fathering from mothering and indeed from any feminine associations attached to it. Archie says that fathers in general respond to children 'in a less feminine way. If a kid falls and hurts himself, women would probably rush over more than men. I say, "Come on, toughen up." I think there are more differences there. I am not sure how to characterize it.'

Indeed, many fathers express confusion about this issue because they simply do not want to equate what they do with the work that women do. As Maurice says when I ask him about housework, 'I like to cook. But I wouldn't want to call this women's work.'

Theoretical assumptions that can initially assist us in making sense of these processes are those that highlight the way men distance themselves from and devalue the feminine (Bird, 1996; Chodorow, 1978; Connell, 1987, 1995, 2000; Johnson, 1988; Thorne, 1993) as well as theoretical work related to the concept of hegemonic masculinity (Coltrane, 1994; Connell, 1987, 1995, 2000; Kimmel, 1994; Messner, 1997). Although there have been varied discussions of the meaning and relevance of the concept hegemonic masculinity, one of the authors who coined it, Connell, has recently boiled it down 'the opposite of femininity' (Connell, 2000, 31). The fathers' narratives touched on in this chapter are filled with inchoate contradictions that illuminate how fathers distance themselves from the feminine. Yet, as explained below, some also admit that being a primary-caregiving father allows them the opportunity to find, as one father, Roy, put it, the 'feminine in me.'

Between Equality and Difference, between Masculine and Feminine

What seems to occur for fathers entering into female-dominated terrain is that by crossing into an area where they have not been traditionally equal to women, they move both between equality and difference and between the stereotypically feminine and masculine. In seeking to find ways of becoming equal or symmetrical to women in their caregiving efforts, men also have hegemonic masculinity at their backs, reminding them that they are men operating in traditional female worlds. Most men, even sole-custody fathers, thus cling to the view that in spite of their most ardent efforts, they can never be mothers or replace the *mothering* done by women. Rather than *duplicate* the maternal terrain travelled, fathers *alter* it to incorporate differences, which could be viewed as more traditionally masculine traits such as independence, autonomy, and sporting interests.

It is notable that most of the gay fathers in this study recognize the need to consider both masculine and feminine in mothering and fathering and to emphasize the importance of traditionally feminine qualities in fathering, particularly in the raising of sons. A good example of these qualities is found in Bernard's narrative. While drawing borders between the moms' house and his own and between 'an estrogen world there' and 'a testosterone world here,' he also points out that he is aware of the need to demonstrate some traditionally feminine qualities in his parenting and to allow Jake to develop his own feminine qualities:

> I do some things that are typical of fathering. I throw a ball and play catch, mini golf, take him on the roller coaster, watch movies, play sports. But I also do non-typical things. I let him cry; I am physically demonstrative. I want to break that generational cycle. I let him play with dolls, watch women superheroes like the Power Puff Girls. He plays with girls and boys. I want him to experience things that he is interested in ... If boys were allowed to be whatever they are, I think that would mean they would become fathers who are extremely close to their children. More expression. Less inhibiting ... There is male and female in all of us, but the female is pressured out of boys more. The inhibiting of the feminine. Like the censoring of boys emotions.'

Bernard is in fact remarking on the setting-up of borders between girls' and boys' activities and identities and the potential for breaking down some of these borders through the recognition of the 'male and female in all of us.' This provides a good entry point into using the lenses of *borderwork* and *border crossings* to assist us in seeing and theorizing men's caring work and the 'Do men mother?' question. In the final two sections of this chapter, I intersperse men's narratives of care through the metaphors of borderwork as the setting-up of boundaries between men and women and the simultaneous crossing of these same borders through the recognition of 'the fluctuating significance of gender in the on-going scenes of social life' (Thorne, 1993, 16).

Borderwork

As I've outlined in chapter 1, my work draws on the concept of *border-work* as developed in the work of Barrie Thorne, sociologist and ethnographer of children in schools. The concept draws attention to the way context matters greatly in gendered interactions. It also provides a way of describing spaces and times where gender boundaries or borders are instigated between the genders. Like the childhood games that pit girls against boys and create the illusion of irreconcilable and permanent opposite sides, there are parallel moments and sites where gender borders divide mothers and fathers.

There are many instances of borderwork in the narratives collected on mothering and fathering, two of which will be highlighted here. The first one is the overwhelmingly different reactions from mothers and fathers to an anecdote discussed in the individual interviews with fathers as well as in the couple interviews, that of how each parent responds when their child is hurt or has fallen down. Second, there is the constantly reiterated belief in the close embodied connection between mother and child, a connection that most fathers believe they cannot replace or duplicate.

Gendered Responses to the Child's Falling Down: 'Oh, Get On with It'

When they speak about their daily routine with children, the most recurrent example that fathers give as a difference between mothering and fathering is the promotion of children's independence and, more specifically, how parents react to the child's falling down or hurting himself in physical play or solo exploration. This example came up on its own in so many of the first interviews that I started using it as an anecdote and having fathers as well as mothers comment on it. Denise gives the example without being asked: 'If Nathan falls down and hurts himself, I am more likely to go and pick him up right away.'

Shahin, an Iranian-Canadian cabinetmaker and a stay-at-home father of one son, says, 'My wife would be much gentler with my son about how you throw a basketball into a hoop and is willing to put up with mistakes, whereas if my son misses once, I would say, "Oh get on with it" or "Get off your tush!" If my son falls, my wife immediately hugs him – whereas I would immediately go there and say, "No cut, no bruises, you're okay."'

I ask Harry, a rural poultry farmer and stay-at-home father of two sons, whether he thinks mothering and fathering are different. After a long silence, he responds: 'I don't know how to describe it. It's like when they fall and get hurt, we both tell them that everything is going to be all right. But the boys get a different feeling about it from me than from my wife, I'm sure. She is all over them, and from me, well, "You're all right; let's get on with it."'

The articulation of a 'different feeling' of mothers is related, in turn, to the way fathers narrate a larger story of another emotional connection of mothers and fathers to children.

The Connection between Mother and Child: 'It's Something I Will Never Understand'

As described earlier in this chapter, fathers' narratives are marked by a strong belief in fundamental differences between mothering and fathering. These beliefs are so consistent across the study that I came to view them as a second form of borderwork in emotional responsibility. Although there is considerable confusion over just where these differences come from, the majority of women and men nevertheless take the position that mothering and fathering differ in relation to the propensity for connection with their children. As Matthew, an electronics technician on parental leave, says, 'It's not the same. She holds the baby more to her body; she rocks the baby more. I love her and everything, but I don't hug her as much. She's not part of me as much.'

Shahin's narrative includes many of the explanations that fathers offer for mothers' greater connection with their children. In one fell swoop, referring to birthing, psychological factors, hormones, and Mother Nature's way of 'making sure that the child is protected,' he says, 'In my opinion, women have an edge in parenting, whether you say psychological or hormonal or whatever, in terms of being able to cope with certain things. I think the bond is vaster in women. Whether it's Mother Nature's way of making sure that the child is protected or not, I think they're willing to put up with a lot more. I think in general that society has made women better workers, or at least those expectations are there. I could never be a woman – I would die of exhaustion!'

Similarly, in a joint interview Nina and Mitchell concur that there is a different connection between the mother and the child, that it may be a spiritual one and of another 'nature,' as well as something that, as Mitchell says, he may 'never understand':

NINA I think there is more to being a mother than just being a stay-at-home
parent. I think there is a difference in terms of what it means to be a mother,
what it means to be a father ... I think part of it has to do with certain early
connections with the child. I think the mother is connected just by being the
vessel that the child is carried in. You're much more connected.

MITCHELL I'm sure there's a spiritual connection there. It's something I will
never understand.

NINA You know, talking to the child, feeling the child move around inside of
you, I always found an incredible experience. I mean, I didn't have great
pregnancies, but I just thought it was so neat ... I think it makes a difference. I don't think that means that fathers can't be connected to their children, but I think that it starts earlier on for the mother. And it changes the
nature of the connection.

Like heterosexual fathers, the majority of the gay fathers (seven out
of nine) also espouse fundamental differences between mothering and
fathering and a belief in the greater significance to the role of the
mother, even though they are admittedly uncertain about it. Jean Marc
expresses this well. A forty-three-year-old gay and divorced father of
seven-year-old twin boys, he took a four-month parental leave when
his twins were infants. He says, 'Frankly I am perplexed about the
fathering role. I think there is a mothering instinct that goes way
beyond what a father feels for his children.'

These articulated instances – reacting to a child's falling down and
parental reflections on the close bond between mother and child –
demonstrate remarkably consistent gendered responses in both mothers' and fathers' narratives and, indeed, 'a magnetism of gender-
marked events for observers and participants in the realms of memory'
(Thorne, 1993, 64). Borderwork thus occurs in specific times, usually
the early months and years of parenting when children require a great
deal of physical and emotional nurturing. It is also articulated in particular spaces, notably the embodied space between parent and child
as most often expressed through the metaphor and empirical reality
of the hug. In these moments and sites, gender borders are drawn
through the expressed belief that mothering and fathering are oppositional sets of practices and identities (see also chapter 6).

Crossing Borders

In spite of such borderwork sites and moments, there are also spaces and times in the flow of mothers' and fathers' lives when gender boundaries are relaxed to the point that they are barely noticeable. Then mothers and fathers are side by side and difference in roles is largely indistinguishable. That is, 'although the occasions of gender separation may seem more dramatic, the mixed-gender encounters are also theoretically and practically important' (Thorne, 1993, 36). Several such moments are highlighted below as examples of the dismantling or crossing of gender borders.

While fathers acknowledge deep-seated differences between mothers and fathers in their caregiving styles and their perception that mothers have a greater propensity for emotional connection, what emerges in the daily practice of care and emotional responsibility is not so stark. While working through the interview transcripts generated from my interviews with fathers and mothers, I repeatedly attempted to group couples into tidy categories of various kinds of emotional responsibility according to, for example, their protectiveness or the promotion of independence. Yet these efforts were confounded by the way, for each person, and especially in the couple interviews, individuals and couples move back and forth in their views as to *who* was more nurturing, in which contexts, and at which times. That is, these shifts in emotional responsibility are deeply rooted in the changing ages of the children, specific spatial and time-bound contexts, cultural contexts, and what is occurring in these complex balancing acts between working and caring at particular points in time. Metaphorically, the back-and-forth movements resemble something of a dance (see also Dienhart, 1998), or the ebb and flow of moving water (Hamilton, 2005; Hekman, 1999). As one mother, Claire, expresses it, '*Looking back over all these years, there is movement and flow.*' Six factors are flagged here as important generators of an increased sense of connection and protectiveness on the part of men and the breaking-down of gender borders between mothers and fathers in relation to emotional responsibility.

The Impact of Passing Time and Children's Changing Ages: 'Movement and Flow'

Examples of movement and flow over time for two-parent mother/father households is well illustrated by Richard, a stay-at-home father of three young children, and his wife, Aileen. Initially, they point out that their two-year-old son, Jean-Philippe, goes mainly to Aileen when he is upset or tired. When considering why this is the case, Richard notes that Jean-Philippe 'gets more sympathy' from his mother, which, in turn, generates a discussion of the changes over time as the children mature:

> AILEEN I think it has changed. It changes through the child's life because when Elizabeth was born, the first – what, two years ...?
> RICHARD Two – three years ...
> AILEEN For two years she didn't want to have anything to do with Richard ...
> RICHARD Not to that point ... but if she got hurt she would go to her mother.
> AILEEN She wanted me. And then when she was about two, she changed. And it had to be Richard.

Later in their interview, however, they reverse this view and argue that 'Mommy's not as sympathetic.' They both agree that Aileen now encourages greater separation from the children while Richard feels more connected to them. Aileen's words have resonances of a traditional fathering model seeking more time and space from his children. When I ask them to whom seven-year-old Elizabeth turns to when she is upset, their joint interview elicits the following responses:

> RICHARD She will come to me.
> AILEEN Mommy's not as sympathetic.
> RICHARD She'll walk right by her and even ask her where I am. Come and find me... in the garage or wherever.
> AILEEN That's because you let her come out of her room two or three times every night – me, that's it!
> RICHARD I don't let her, I mean ...
> ANDREA Are you fine with that, Aileen? You know, the fact that Elizabeth goes to him?
> AILEEN Oh, yeah [laughs]. The more they go to him, the more time I have for myself.

Mother Moving Over: 'Oh Wow, I Get to Try This'

A second factor that helps to account for changes in the movement and flow of emotional responsibility between men and women is the shifting presence of mothers into and out of the emotional domain of parenting. In spite of the reliance on mothers for emotional responsibility as well as mothers holding on to this as their domain, what is also particularly striking in fathers' narratives is that when mothers are not available or they let go of caring for brief or long periods, fathers do come to take on emotional responsibility for children. When Denise went away for a business trip, for example, Martin came to take a bit more of an emotional role with four-year-old Nathan. In his joint interview with his wife, Denise, he says, 'I don't know how to describe it. He is certainly more emotional with Denise, whereas with me, we get out, we wrestle. We still read and cuddle. But not as much. When Denise was away, he got into our bed in the middle of the night, and he was surprised that she wasn't there. But he had a cuddle with me.'

William, who set up one of the first series of father-only playgroups in Ottawa over fifteen years ago, illustrates that the absence of women in father-centred spaces increased fathers' confidence in their ability to respond to children: 'I thought it was very interesting that men learned from other dads. When the wives are there, the men may step aside and let the woman take over.'

Dean, who used to be a stay-at-home dad and is now a joint-custody father, 'discovered' that he 'got to function in areas that [his ex-wife] Carly wouldn't allow [him] to function in before.' In his words, 'She used to be the listening ear for the girls, sitting with them at night before they went to bed. She would go in and tell a story. Suddenly I got to do some of that. But mostly I would go in and listen to the radio. Get my little earplugs. They just needed a body in the room. I would be there. And they would chat, you know, and ask, "Are you still there?" "Yeah, I'm still here." And they would fall asleep. This was a ritual that we did with all the children. When she left, it was like, oh wow, I get to try this.'

Fathering without a Mother: 'I Get Lost in the Nurturing'

Perhaps what is most revealing about the permeability of the line between motherly and fatherly nurturing is at the time that mothers have effectively moved out of parenting. This is the case for the twenty-five sole-custody fathers in my study who were parenting with only minimal participation by the mother (and the two widowers). In their interviews with me, many of these fathers visibly and audibly struggle with the way to express these thoughts but find themselves admitting that they have become different kinds of father as a result of being on their own with their children. Roy, a military technician and sole-custodial father of a four-year-old boy, speaks about how, when he has a difficult time raising his son, he cannot rely on the child's mother to take care of things. Thus, he grapples with his own inner struggles and reasons that he has become a 'soft father' because he is fathering without a mother: 'And because he doesn't have that mother side in the house, a mother to turn to me and say, "Would you just go away?" And for her to turn around and take care of things. I'm like, Now what do I do now? If I had to try and fit myself somewhere into the equation, I probably would try to give him more of a soft father than anything else. But a soft father who wants him to learn not just have fun.'

Golin, an African-Canadian sole-custody father of four school-age children, find that nurturing can become all-encompassing: 'There is this big cultural background, which does not escape me, so I draw on that a lot, partly Nigerian, but partly my own family where I grew up. So the nurturing comes from there. I always have to remind myself to set boundaries because I get lost in the nurturing.'

Particular Cultural Contexts: 'There Are Very Different Expectations'

Ethnicity and gender intersect to create even more issues for fathers to deal with, ones that do not play out in straightforward ways, however. For example, the experience of being a Latino father is related to the length of time he has spent in Canada, his level of education, and the social networks that surround and affect his parenting. That is, a university education in Canada and living among friends and colleagues who espouse symmetrical parenting can greatly mute the effect of ethnic tradition on parenting approaches and beliefs. This is the case with two Latino fathers in the study, Eduardo and Manuel, whose university education and marriages to feminists have led them to shed some ideas on fundamental gender differences that they had absorbed from their Latin-American upbringing. A similar situation occurs for Shahin and Mohammed, two Muslim fathers from Iran whose education levels and marriages to working mothers have encouraged them to question deeply rooted beliefs in gender difference in parenting. As Shahin puts it, 'If anything, my background probably would have told me that I shouldn't be doing this [being a stay-at-home father] because I come from a rather chauvinistic country. And then on top of that I was raised with a very strict, very disciplined and harsh father. I never saw a father who raised the kids practically in my life. It was always a mother.'

While particular cultural ideas might promote a very specific parenting style and affect gender roles more generally, these influences can be mediated by social networks, choice of marriage partner, or education. What is notable is that for immigrant fathers who remain embedded in their particular cultural community in the larger Canadian society, parenting ideas are more likely to change slowly. Thus, the five Somali immigrant fathers in this study hold to the view that mothering and fathering are different because these are strong cultural ideas retained by both men and women in their community and neighbourhood. Dalmar, for example, is clear that his opinion on the importance of the mother's role with younger children comes from his Somali background. A fifty-two-year-old father of four children and a part-time university lecturer, he finds that neither his high level of education nor his marriage to a social worker have transformed his deeply held cultural views. In a focus group with other Somali fathers, he says, 'In Somali culture, the perception is that the mother is important, especially with young children. Just as boys and girls are raised differently, fathers and mothers are not the same. Boys and girls are still treated differently in Somali families. There are very different expectations.'

Moments of Crisis and Challenge: 'I Guess Because We Lost John ...'

The crossing of gendered borders in emotional responsibility can also occur as a result of emotional crises that enable, or force, men to shift emotionally. Such severe crises can include one's own childhood traumas, a child's serious illness, losing a child, or the responses to a child with developmental delays or difficulties. Craig speaks about becoming more protective after the death of one of their infant triplets: 'I guess because we lost John, I'm an overprotective parent. When I have Zachary in my arms, I am on Michael all the time to stay with me and not to move. The thing is that, if he is going to take off, I've got Zachary in my arms, and I am not going to be able to catch him as fast as I want do. That is always in the back of my mind.'

Some fathers mention moments of crisis or challenge that occurred in their family of origin and that marked the way they cared for others. Kyle, for example, says that his caring for his ill mother was a formative experience in the development of his 'female side' and of himself as a shared caregiver of two children: 'I think I'm more in touch with my female side than most men are. That may have to do with my upbringing. I had to deal with caring for, in a palliative kind of way, an aging and dying mother for a very long period of time.'

Similarly, Luke's vivid story of becoming a caregiver early begins with a traumatic incident that marked him. When I asked him about his own parents, he stumbled with his words as he worked around the edges of the question: 'There was not real nurturing from my father, but my mother was a really nurturing person.' As I probe to learn more, he admits that 'both my parents were alcoholics.' Luke describes an accident that marked the beginning of his own emotional and caring capacity: 'I had two sisters that were older than I am, but when I was three they died tragically in a bus accident. It was in 1963. They got out of the bus and there was a big steep grade. This transport that was behind the bus tried to stop and let them cross, but he jackknifed, and my two sisters, six and nine years old, and this other girl were killed ... I don't remember them ... I don't remember anything in that era. But I do remember I was given the caring role after that.

Being There: 'Because of What Has Transpired in My Life ...'

Gender borders are also taken down by shifts in feelings and behaviour that occur for fathers caring for a child on their own for long periods without having a female partner to rely on. This occurs for fathers parenting alone and for stay-at-home fathers who have had long periods of time alone with their children. Two examples can be provided here.

After his wife left, Ron, a sole-custody father of two school-age children, moved his computer business into his home so that he could balance work and caring for his children. He reflects on how having this 'forced on me' led to remarkable changes in his emotional life with his children. In his words, 'Because of what has transpired in my life, I have a paternal feeling. And I have a maternal feeling, whatever that means. All I know is that you totally love them to the best of your ability. You protect them ... There are differences in men and women, but as a parent, the same heart chord can be struck.'

Frank, a stay-at-home father of two young children, says that he is now the more protective parent as a result of being at home and that his experience has generated the awareness of his nurturing side: 'I have changed from being at home ... I see this at the park. The kids are running all over the equipment and they're having fun, but I think they're going to fall ... From my own experience, it's brought out some nurturing side of me. I mean, I knew it was there, but I didn't know to what extent.'

Conclusions

In this chapter I have explored, in Sara Ruddick's terms, the first maternal demand of preservation or protective care, which is at its core an ability to know and attentively respond to the needs of one's children. My own naming of this maternal, or parental, responsibility is that of *emotional responsibility*. The question 'Do men mother?' can be answered, at least partially, by asking, Do fathers take on the preservation and protective care of children? Do they resemble mothers in their approach to emotional responsibility?

At first glance, the answer is an affirmative one. My research on primary caregiving fathers joins a large body of scholarship produced over the past two decades that argues that fathers can be just as nurturing and responsive with their children as mothers are. It is well documented that fathers who are actively involved with their children can develop skills that enable them to partake in this task of preservation.

On second glance, the answer to the question, Do men assume emotional responsibility and partake in the task of preservation? is also negative, in the sense that fathers widen our current understandings of protective care, preservation, and ultimately that of emotional responsibility. My research also uncovers some unique dimensions that fathers bring to our understandings of protective care. In examining fathers' caregiving, my work highlights their emphasis on fun and playfulness, especially with infants and young children, physical activities, an outdoors approach, an emphasis on the practical sides of nurturing, and the promotion of independence and risk taking with older children. This occurs for the majority of father across social class, income levels, occupations, ethnicity, and sexuality. While all these dimensions of caring are not normally part of what we consider nurturing behaviour, my argument is that all these elements are important aspects of the emotional responsibility for children. For example, physical and outdoor activities can lead to positive physical and mental developmental outcomes (Beauvais, 2001), which represent, in turn, unique ways of responding to children's needs. Similarly, while the promotion of independence and of risk taking are rarely included in discussions of nurturing, encouraging autonomy in children can be seen as a form of long-term protection and ultimately of connection.

The roots of these strong patterns in fathers' narratives of nurturing can be traced to several key elements in men's lives. This chapter went back to their boyhood, to the embodied experiences of fathers as they move on female-dominated terrains of parenting, to the reliance on mothers, and to the role of hegemonic masculinity. The latter was evident in men's apparent need to emphasize gender differences through the distancing of themselves from the feminine connotations tied up with the work and identities of caring for children.

This chapter has also detailed where and how embodiment figures into the ways that both fathers and mothers accord greater significance to women's emotional connection to children whether symbolically or in practice. In particular, fathers and mothers draw on embodied aspects of early parenting by reference to the physical, emotional, and symbolic experiences of pregnancy, birth, breastfeeding, and post-childbirth recovery. Men and women refer to all the 'messy empirical realities of actual flesh and blood bodies' (Monaghan, 2002, 335) and the differing gendered locations of women and men in relation to the passage of children into the world. What remains striking is the belief in the mysterious and symbolic power of *mothering* as something that the majority of men and women inexplicably uphold. Many are perplexed by the strength of this belief, and indeed most are at a complete loss to explain it, but it nevertheless emerges as a dominant theme from fathers' and mothers' narratives. Fathers also draw attention to the way bodies can matter in the physical touching between fathers and preteen/teen daughters, as well as in noting the tensions of men kissing and touching boys in a society where homophobia thrives.

This chapter has also highlighted that though fathers' and mothers' narratives indicate strong beliefs in gender differences in emotional responsibility, there is a fair degree of ebb and flow within households and ultimately some disjunction between beliefs and practices. Following the work of Barrie Thorne, I have named this ebb and flow as the crossing of gender borders and the breaking-down of some of the binary distinctions between mothering and fathering. Notably, the passage of time and children's maturing affect the ebb and flow, as do particular cultural contexts, men's previous experiences of caring, and the effects that family crises have on fathers' beliefs in their nurturing capacities. Perhaps more than anything else, the movement and flow within daily domestic practice is very much led by mothers. That is, the role of the mother is a key factor in determining the ways in which fathers take on the care and emotional responsibility of children. While some theorists within the sociology of the family (i.e., Allen & Hawkins, 1999) have called this 'maternal gatekeeping,' implying that women exclude men and do not want to give up this area of power and expertise, my research suggests that many fathers also expect mothers to take this on (see also chapter 7).

Yet, though men do rely on women to take on emotional responsibility, what happens in everyday practice can contradict such expectations. When mothers are not available, or have let go of caring for brief or long periods, fathers do fill the powerful and protective space where emotional responsibility is taken on. There are times when women are unavailable, involved in other activities, or simply need to let go. The mother moves over and the father nudges gently into this space. They will, as Julie says of Manuel, 'father like a mother.' If the mother leaves or is a fleeting presence in the daily lives of the children, the father will sometimes take on emotional responsibility in a manner that combines both protection and promotion of independence. As Golin says, 'I get lost in the nurturing,' and as Roy says, 'I'll be a soft father.'

To conclude this chapter, the comments of two fathers are apt descriptions of perceived gender difference in emotional responsibility. Ed, a stay-at-home father of two living in rural Ontario comments, 'We certainly do look at things differently – housework and activities for the children. I tend to be more concerned about *doing things* with the children rather than making sure the house is perfect. Instead of play-groups, we'll go to the park and walk through the forest.'

Archie remarks that in the everyday practical care of children 'the broad strokes' remain somewhat different: 'Some of the stuff by definition is the same. When you have smaller children, the getting through the day is by definition the same – the feeding, the changing have to be the same. Once you start getting into the non-physical, non-life-sustaining, you do get different practices between women and women. Men are going to be outside more, and more physical. But not always. I think in broad strokes, you will find that women tend to be more emotional and supportive.'

As explored in this chapter, these 'broad strokes' of parenting where fathering is linked with being 'outside more and more physical' while mothering is linked with being 'more emotional and supportive' are also related to the larger gendered worlds of women and men. This includes growing up male, issues of embodiment around mothering and fathering, relational narratives of 'doing gender' and hegemonic masculinity as revealed mainly in the devaluation of the feminine. In the next chapter, the everyday work of fathers and the question 'Do men mother?' will be explored by investigating a second area of parental responsibility that is more widely located within the community. This is the area of community responsibility, or what Sara Ruddick calls 'growth.'

5 Fathers and Community Responsibility

There's a lot of networks for moms and yet there isn't a network for guys, and I think a huge part of that is it isn't as easy for a guy. I've been out to the library and I've seen a guy pushing a baby carriage. But it's just not so easy for a guy to go up to another guy and say, 'Hey, how old is she? Do you want to be friends?'

(Martin, stay-at-home-father of one son)

It was never said. But for some parents, it was there. Some children would get invited three times and there was always some excuse. 'Oh, she doesn't like sleepovers', or 'It's not a good weekend,' or whatever. Parents who knew me, well, there was no problem. Their kids would come. But some of them, I just knew.'

(Dean, joint-custody father of three daughters, formerly a stay-at-home father)

Introduction

We sort of always talked about it in a half-serious, half-joking way prior to having kids. In a lot of ways I think it came down to a common-sense decision. At the time my wife was working in the finance minister's office and travelled a lot on short notice and worked a lot of hours, and I was working shifts for Imperial Gas from four to midnight. The logistics of trying to arrange daycare seemed impossible. She was making two to three times what I was making. I stayed home when Jordan was three months old. I took the ten weeks of parental leave, and when that came due, I just resigned.'

(Archie, stay-at-home father)

Nearly ten years ago, Archie left his job as a natural gas serviceman in Ottawa to stay home with his infant son while his wife, Jean, worked long hours in a high-pressure job on Parliament Hill. When Jordan was a few months old, Jean suggested that Archie should take him to the well baby clinic at their local community centre. He still remembers the steely stares that came his way: 'The first day I go trotting in there, there are three women breastfeeding and they are staring daggers at me. "Who is this pervert coming in, checking us out 'cause he is going to catch sight of my breast?" It was so incredibly uncomfortable. I never went back – it was just that look.'

The stares persisted when Archie walked down the street pushing his son in the baby stroller: 'On more than one occasion when I would be walking the stroller home, women would actually cross the street to avoid passing me. It was bizarre. I don't know why. There are so many stories that men are the bad guys. It's not clear what is going through their minds. They are pushing the stroller, I'm pushing a stroller. For the most part, there is a sense that if a man stays home there is something wrong with him, he's lost his job, or he's a little off kilter. It's not his job. He shouldn't be there.'

Four years later, Archie was still at home with their second child, a toddler, while Jordan was in half-day kindergarten at the local school. He distinctly remembers being dismayed that after four years on the parenting scene, he was still regarded with suspicion as he stood in the schoolyard waiting for his son to appear: 'This woman comes up and introduces herself and says, "I am a little embarrassed but I'm coming to check you out. My daughter came home and told me about this man hanging around the schoolyard reading stories to the kids. I hope you're not offended." At this point I'm used to it. I said, "Isn't it interesting that if a kid came home and said a mom is reading to kids in the yard, you would say, 'Isn't that nice?' and wouldn't give it another thought." She admitted that was true.'

Across town in an Ottawa suburb, a decade after Archie's pioneering move into this 'bizarre' world of the suspicious-looking man hanging around the schoolyard, Martin and his wife, Denise, inadvertently caused a minor crisis in their local playgroup when he replaced her when she went back to work full time. While the mothers in the group had always joked about it, a few had assured Martin that it would be no problem that he continue bringing eight-month-old Ethan to the group. As Martin later explained it to me in his joint interview with Denise, his intention to continue with the playgroup was 'more for

Ethan; he's starting to know those kids and they're learning how to play together.' Thus, when Martin went to his first group, he noted that although he 'felt really awkward going in,' he nevertheless thought that 'it went okay' except that he 'noticed that there was one woman who didn't came out into the living room where we all were the whole time, but I didn't think much of it at the time.' Martin relays the events that brought to light his disruptive presence as a male:

> I thought it went pretty good, other than that he wet his diaper and sort of peed all over. I was quite proud of myself. And then the next morning, Denise was checking the e-mails and when she came into the living room she was crying. She said, 'You better come and see this.' So I went in, and there was an e-mail from a woman who had stayed in the kitchen, and on behalf of the group she basically wrote how did I dare come out to their group and that she was very embarrassed and she thought it was horrible for me to just show up and they didn't want me to come anymore. So we put a letter together basically saying that we apologized. It was our understanding that it was okay to come; we're sorry; we didn't mean to create a problem for anybody or make anyone feel uncomfortable.

What ensued was a flurry of e-mails and a very open discussion among the twelve playgroup members over what kind of group they wanted to have. After much debate, a core of nine mothers came to a consensus, as described by Martin: 'Nine members of the group agreed that if anyone feels uncomfortable about Martin coming out, that's not the sort of group we want to run. They can either live with it or leave. So three members of the group dropped out, and they haven't been heard from since.'

Such awkward moments of feeling like a misfit or a threat to what Archie calls 'estrogen-filled worlds' are commonplace in the narratives of stay-at-home fathers. With few exceptions, every stay-at-home father described an uncomfortable or downright painful experience in playgroups or, more generally, in the parenting community. Some fathers glanced into the windows of the culture and quickly made the decision to avoid mother-dominated settings; they cited lack of time, fears that their child would catch a cold or flu, or the kids' schedules. Sometimes these reasons seemed justified. Other times it was clear that they are just avoiding one of the most female-dominated areas of early parenthood.

The state of affairs has, however, improved for fathers with each passing year. Peter, a part-time Web designer and a stay-at-home father of two young boys, captures this increasing social acceptance of fathers: 'It has gotten easier. I can walk into our community centre and I can say hi to them and inquire after their kids and they after mine. But they're still around at the table at their regular coffee session that they have. And it wouldn't occur to them to invite a man. And I can kind of understand that. They wouldn't invite a man to their reading group or whatever social experience they had a common bond with. I have eventually made individual friendships with people. I haven't been included in any small groups. To me as a man, that was a pretty alien environment, and it continues to be.'

Fathers in the position of primary or shared caregiver do, as Martin pointed out earlier, make efforts to connect with others because they recognize that there is a social component to child rearing. As Peter puts it, 'I did find those things difficult. But when you have a child, you feel some responsibility to take him out when he's beyond that baby phase.' Looking back to his awkward experience of being the only male in a community playgroup, Burt, a sole-custody father, says bluntly, 'I wasn't at playgroup for *me*. I was there for Anastasia.' Although some fathers do indeed make the decision and do not go to community groups, it remains the case that relations between parents, and the facilitation of networks for children are integral parts of the social raising of children. In Sara Ruddick's terms, social networks are a critical part of the social development of children.

Growth and Community Responsibility

Growth

According to Ruddick, a second characteristic of mothering is 'growth.' She writes, 'The demand to preserve a child's life is quickly supplemented by the second demand, to nurture its emotional and intellectual growth. Children grow in complex ways, undergoing radical qualitative as well as quantitative changes from childhood to adulthood' (Ruddick, 1995, 19). She also recognizes that others are interested in these growth processes:

> In the urban middle class cultures I know best, mothers who believe that children's development is sufficiently complex to require nurturance shoulder a considerable burden. Many people other than mothers are interested in children's growth – fathers, lovers, teachers, doctors, thera-

pists, coaches. But typically a mother assumes the primary task of maintaining conditions of growth; it is a mother who considers herself and is
considered by others to be primarily responsible for arrested or defective
growth. (Ruddick, 1995, 20)

Although Ruddick recognizes that others are *interested* in children's
growth, I would go further to emphasize that others *partake* in ensuring
children's growth, and mothering involves coordinating, balancing,
negotiating, and orchestrating these others who are drawn into children's lives. Drawing on Ruddick's indentifying the demand on mothers to foster growth, I posit that mothering entails taking on community
responsibility, and to answer the 'Do men mother?' question, we need to
gain a sense of how fathers engage with this maternal responsibility.

Community Responsibility

By community responsibility, I am referring to the extra-domestic,
community-based quality of the work of being responsible for children. That is, the responsibility for domestic life and for children
involves a variety of relationships *between* households as well as
between the social institutions of families/households, schools, the
state, and the workplace. Within and between households and other
social institutions, parents share responsibility for their children with
others who take on caring practices – caregivers, other parents, neighbours, kin, child care experts, nurses and doctors, teachers, librarians,
music teachers, soccer coaches, and so on. Each stage of child rearing
introduces its own issues, according to the particular needs and
demands of each child. For all these issues and decision-making processes – from a child's preschool to university years – other people are
often consulted and relationships are thus built on the basis of a shared
interest in particular children. This level of responsibility builds on the
attentiveness and knowledge involved in emotional responsibility, but
then somebody works to satisfy the needs by piecing together limited
resources of time, energy, and money (see Balbo, 1987). Community
responsibility is beautifully captured by the political theorist Selma
Sevenhuijsen who writes that caring implies 'not just the meeting of
children's needs but also the *ability to "see" or "hear" needs, to take
responsibility for them, negotiate if and how they should be met and by whom'*
(Sevenhuijsen, 1998, 15; my emphasis).

Mothering thus involves not only domestically based tasks and
responsibilities but also community-based, inter-household and inter-

institutional responsibilities. This work of mothers and others appears in varied guises in a wide body of feminist research. Concepts such as 'kin work' (Di Leonardo, 1987; Stack, 1974), 'servicing work' (Balbo, 1987) 'motherwork' (Collins, 1994), 'household service work' (Sharma, 1986), 'relationship work' (Dollahite, Hawkins, & Brotherson, 1997), 'inter-household responsibility' (Doucet, 2001) as well as 'community-based responsibility' (Doucet, 2000) each describe domestic work as much broader – spatially, theoretically, and practically – than simply housework and childcare.

The idea of community responsibility is also explored by scholars working in Third World settings who refer to complex webs of social relations within which domestic labour and mothering are enacted (Goetz, 1995, 1997; Moser, 1993; Scheper-Hughes, 1992). Moreover, black feminist scholars have shown that community networks and inter-household relations are integral elements of black motherhood (see Collins, 1991, 1994). Patricia Hill Collins, for example, writes, '[T]he institution of black motherhood consists of a series of constantly nego-tiated relationships that African American women experience with one another, with black children and with the larger African-American com-munity' (Collins, 1994, 180). Finally, Micaela Di Leonardo provides one of the most colourful descriptions of community responsibility in her definition of kin work as 'the conception, maintenance, and ritual cele-bration of cross-household ties, including visits, letters, telephone calls, presents and cards to kin; the organisation of holiday gatherings; the creation and maintenance of quasi-kin relations; decisions to neglect or to intensify particular ties; the mental work of reflection about all these activities ...' (Di Leonardo, 1987, 442–3).

Fathers and Community Responsibility

Do fathers take on community responsibility for children? Much inter-national research has confirmed that the responsibility for children's growth as well as the broader work of building bridges and social sup-port between families and households is – while enacted and experi-enced in varied ways across class, ethnic, sexual, and cultural lines – still overwhelmingly taken on by women. Put differently, much of the plan-ning, orchestrating, organizing, managing, worrying, and decision making related to children is predominantly handled by women (Balbo, 1987; Bell & Ribbens, 1994; Doucet, 2000, 2001b; Hertz & Ferguson, 1998; Hessing, 1993; McMahon, 1995; Mederer, 1993; Walzer, 1998).

But what about fathers who take on the primary care of children? The overarching issue that will be explored in this chapter relates to the way fathers promote children's growth and social development through the creation and maintenance of social networks around their children.[1] Are there gender differences in these stories of social growth? Do fathers meet the maternal demand of facilitating children's social growth, or are their efforts to be viewed as parallel and complementary to those of women and mothers?

As mentioned above, it is amply documented in international studies on mothering and fathering that mothers overwhelmingly take the lead in creating and maintaining networks for and around children's social growth. Fathers are helpers in this process. Overall, this study on fathers and primary caregivers confirms that role. There are, however, some variations and shifts in the central storyline. Four patterns of community responsibility can be highlighted. First is the dominant story of men as helpers to women. Second are patterns of shared responsibility, different but symmetrical, between women and men. Third is a small proportion of fathers who take on the community responsibility for children when mothers relinquish it; they do so by filling a gap left open, by 'letting things slip,' or by soliciting help from friends. Fourth, and finally, fathers also create fathering networks that enable them to take on particular aspects of community responsibility. The four styles are described below under the shorter titles Assistants, Partners, and Managers (who manage this responsibility in varied ways: filling a gap, cutting back, or delegating/seeking help). Most men also fall into the subcategory of Network Builder, although the networks formed differ somewhat from traditional female-dominated networks.

Assistants: 'She Does the Higher Care'

Most (just over one-half)[2] of fathers in the sample of stay-at-home and joint-custody group have established a pattern whereby women take on most of the community responsibility, which is named in varied and eloquent ways. For the fathers who confirm the dominant pattern identified in other international studies, varied phrases and terminology are used, such as *the higher care*, *administration* versus *maintenance* and *seeing the need* versus *filling the need*.

It is Luke who coins the phrase *higher care* to describe community responsibility. At home for twelve years balancing part-time shift work in a residential home for the physically and mentally challenged while his wife, Robyn, works full time as an urban planner, Luke says,

> Robyn is really a bigger part in what I would call the higher care. We definitely have areas that are preferred. I don't care to do the planning of summer programs, for example. Robyn is really into that. She is a planner. Whereas I had a really strong sense in me that I wanted Alyssa to be musically inclined, Robyn took that and went further with it. She made sure that Alyssa was in music programs. She was always finding different things – like Kinder Tots and Music for Young Children. I would take Alyssa to all these things during the day. But it was Robyn who orchestrated it.

The notion of higher care is also invoked by Ghedi, a Somali father and government administrator, who shares the care of three school-age children with his wife, who is studying to be a nurse. In their joint interview they concur that she is the one who organizes and plans the children's social activities and their social growth because in Somali culture 'it is the mother who is responsible for passing on the culture and the religion.'

Joe, a fifty-year-old Aboriginal stay-at-home father of two preschool girls, employs another term for community responsibility. In a joint interview with his wife, he half jokingly refers to the different 'departments' in dealing with issues of organizing the children's schooling, making decisions about the children's friends, and their enrolment in community activities: 'I think about them, but I don't focus on them because that's *your* department. That's "administration." Down here at "maintenance" we don't deal with that sort of thing. That's *up* there at "administration" [laughs].'

Other fathers refer to who identifies the need and who fills it. For example, Mitchell, a stay-at-home father of three for seven years and his wife, Nina, tell me how they came to have the help of a teenager for infrequent babysitting. They concur on how this need was filled. In Nina's words, 'I was the instigator for Melissa because she was just playing with the boys after school, and when she got of age I asked her if she'd be interested and she said yes. Often what will happen is, I'll realize that we need a babysitter so I'll call Mitchell from work, and say, "Mitchell, next Wednesday we need a babysitter. Call Melissa or Naomi." Then he calls them after school. So I'll identify the need and then he fills it.'

The words of Mitchell and Nina are reminiscent of those of a couple who participated in my doctoral research on shared-caregiving couples, about a decade earlier in Britain, and their poignant discussion of community responsibility as they looked back over twenty-three years of shared child rearing. In drawing on the same idea of identifying and filling the need, Saxon chose words about his wife, Elizabeth, that have remained with me as a succinct encapsulation of community responsibility: 'Elizabeth has been very good at saying we should do this and getting it organized and making it happen and finding people to do this, that or the other.'

The organizing of birthday parties is a good symbol of how community responsibility is enacted in most households. The majority of mothers take on the work of planning, while fathers fill in. Doug, for example, who shares custody of his daughter with his ex-wife, says in relation to the organizing of birthday parties, 'For birthdays, her party will be at her mom's place and I will be there. Organizing falls mostly to her mom. She likes to do that, and I will just fill in where I need to.' William, who is married to an Iraqi woman and has been a stay-at-home father of three for the past five years, says, 'I would say that my wife does more of the birthday party type of thing. I will do the shopping and heavy lifting [laughs].'

Most stay-at-home fathers and some of the joint-custodial fathers rely on these traditionally gendered patterns. Despite the expectation that fathers might take on more, it is clear that mothers keep areas of responsibility because a habit has been established, because they are not willing to let go, or because their standards are different.

Partners: 'It Just Works Out That We Have Different Circles'

For about one-quarter of the stay-at-home and joint-custody fathers, community responsibility is shared by mothers and fathers, with each taking on different but symmetrical roles. An example of shared community responsibility is well illustrated in the couple narrative of Richard and Aileen. In their busy household of three children, Richard does more of the long-term planning, partly because he is at home and partly because the school and community are predominantly French and he is a francophone. Aileen works a long day as a government manager and is 'fairly anti-social.' He organizes the birthday parties, decides on the theme, and makes elabourate cakes. Nevertheless, the task of kin work – maintaining contact with family and friends – falls mainly to Aileen, who organizes family gatherings and arranges to have friends over. Referring to the issue of keeping in contact and organizing extended family events, she says to Richard in their joint interview, 'I organize that, but I have to have your help to contact your family. I need you to tell me what to write to your relatives.' Richard replies, 'You bring me the card and you say, "What do I write on here?" And I say, "I don't know – whatever you like."'

For other couples in which the woman either has a demanding work schedule or she is admittedly less social than her male partner, she does some of the long-term planning around their children, but lets her partner make the necessary community connections. When Manuel and Julie's children were younger, he took on most of the networking with other parents as she was less social and he 'knew the neighbour-hood really well, who was talking to whom, who was mean. He knew the playground, set up play dates, and he had a very good sense of the relationships with the kids.' They both volunteered at school, but Julie admits that 'Manuel was more active. He knew the teachers and the politics more than I did.' Nevertheless, Julie took a large role in helping her two children make connections and decisions about their education as they grew up.

In the case of Craig and Mary Claire, they have each taken on different aspects of community responsibility for their children. Having twins as well as a special-needs child has meant that there are two net-works to maintain. Mary Claire says, 'The special-needs' parents are his connection and that's his support kind of thing. I did the Twins' Moms' thing, and you can only go to so much. It just works out that we have different circles.' They reflect, in turn, on how Mary Claire does more 'social things – the Twin Picnic or the Halloween party,' whereas Craig 'really hooked in to special-needs end of it.'

Managers – Women Moving Over and Fathers Taking on Community Responsibility: 'I Have to Pick Up the Slack'

A final manifestation of family engagement in community responsibility is fathers coming, readily or reluctantly, to take it on themselves. Approximately one-quarter of fathers fall into this pattern. What is notable is that, as with emotional responsibility described in chapter 4, fathers' involvement is often led by mothers and may show up in one of three ways. First, men take on the planning and organization of their children's lives and fill the gap left by wives or ex-wives. Second, men scale back on the social activities that their kids are involved in. Third, fathers invite others to assist them with this aspect of child rearing.

FILLING THE GAP

In cases where women are working long days in demanding jobs, some fathers take on aspects of community responsibility that usually rest with women. Howard, for seven years a stay-at-home father of two children, tells me that he has assumed responsibility for the 'the endless cycle of birthday presents and a card to make.' He also organizes the children's extracurricular activities: 'I call instructors. I talk to people. I end up doing a lot of that. It just makes it less stressful because she has the classic busy high-tech job. It's a lot of hours, so I have to pick up the slack.'

Ryan, a sole-custody father of two, including a learning-disabled teenage son, says, 'Well, I'm sure that if I was still together with my wife, I would be helping out with a lot of the chores around the house. But when it would come to things like these kinds of activities – planning and organizing – I would probably leave it up to her.' After nearly three years on his own with his kids, Ryan says, 'I just do it all now. I carry this book everywhere. I got the *Ottawa City Magazine* in the mail yesterday, and I go, "I wonder what's going on in June and July?" The RCMP Musical Ride is the twenty-eighth of June. Free activities – I just write that kind of stuff down.'

'LETTING THINGS SLIP'

A second possibility is that men may scale back on wha.   iildren do. It is difficult to know how much this occurs. In households with a stay-at-home father, there were a few moments of tension in some of the interviews. Andrew, for example, reflects on his planning and organizing of the children's activities: 'In terms of planning and deciding what the kids are doing, it's still very much a mutual decision. But now that I'm home, Bev thinks I should get all the details. Do the research, plan it out. She expects me to do that. I let a lot slip. There's no doubt about that. And she doesn't let go of it. I will hear about it forever!'

Harry, who has been at home for the past nine years and has taken over almost all the running of the household, says, 'Usually it's fifty-fifty. It depends. Sally likes to have all that stuff organized, so it drives her nuts when I'm a little more casual about it. But it all gets done eventually.'

There were also silences about certain activities for sole-custody fathers. Paul, for example, who sometimes feels like an outsider at his son's school, both as a single father and as a low-income artist, claims that he has not attended parent-teacher meetings because he has been unable to get a babysitter. Further, he chooses not to be involved in the school because, as he explains it, 'As far as being in the community here, like school and stuff, because I'm a single father and an artist, it just feels too eccentric, whereas lots of parents at the school are middle-class people. I can't really relate to them that well.'

Similarly, Dennis, a restaurant chef and a sole-custody father, has regrets about how little he has done with his nine-year-old daughter's schooling and gives a recent example of how he let his daughter down by not going to her art show at school: 'It's a little tough sometimes. She's been disappointed twice. They had meetings at school that I had to miss because of work. The last one she was quite upset about, because she was doing her artwork and I missed that. I came home and told her I was going to take a nap and to come and get me when it was time to go. It started at six o'clock and she woke me up at ten after six, and only half an hour was left. I said, "You should have woken me up earlier. There's no point in going now." She was all upset and crying. I was like, oh, God. Later she brought everything home, and we just sat here one afternoon and looked at it all.'

It is difficult to know whether it is being a single *father* or being a single *parent* that is the issue. Osie, for example, an African-Canadian father of two, says that there were things that they 'had to give up' when his wife moved out. 'The negative side of being a single parent is that there is only so much you can do. It's a balancing act.' While facing similar challenges of time and resources that single mothers face, fathers' balancing acts are often supported by more fragile social networks combined with less experience in forming them. Some fathers, however, work hard to build up their own social networks.

GETTING BY WITH A LITTLE HELP FROM MY FRIENDS
The third example of fathers taking on community responsibility is men's deliberately drawing on the help of others, particularly mothers, to assist them in planning and organizing their children's activities. Golin, also an African Canadian, relies on a female neighbour to help him with his second daughter, whom he feels needs more female role models and activities with girls of her age. Greg, who does shift work, arranges some of his four-year-old daughter's activities with her care-giver's help. Ryan admits that he cannot 'do it all on my own' and thus he turned to organizations to help. Some sole-custody fathers also rely on new female partners. Devon is very involved with his son's school, particularly because his son has Attention Deficit Hyperactivity Disor-

der (ADHD) and is on medication, but he says that his new girlfriend, Leanne, 'is my memory on anything going on with Zachary.'

In taking on varied aspects of community responsibility, fathers are finding ways of navigating what British sociologists have termed 'complex maternal worlds' (Bell & Ribbens, 1994). Moreover, fathers also develop parallel paternal worlds and areas where they have a particular interest, skill, and legitimacy.

Network Builders: Fathers' Unique Contributions to Community Responsibility

Across the three types of responsibility patterns described above, it is important to note that fathers form networks as they meet others in sites where children cluster – schoolyards, playgrounds, in the places children's extra-curricular activities occur – and through increasing acceptance in community playgroups. There are also several other interesting ways that fathers are currently forming networks relating to their children: community involvement; outdoor activities and sports; and friendships with other dads and fathers' groups. While some of these position men alongside women on the social terrain of parenting, others distinguish fathering from mothering and show the distinctive ways that fathers provide social venues for their children.

COMMUNITY INVOLVEMENT

Increasing numbers of fathers, stay-at-home as well as part-time, full time, or flexi working, are taking leadership roles on school councils, in community organizations, as well as by volunteering in classrooms. One good example from my study is Rory, who lives in Calgary and previously worked as a consultant in the oil and gas industry. At home with his son for four years, he uses his work skills and channels them into community involvement, and this also provides him with a way of connecting with other parents. He says, 'We did a lot of playground inspection. I was involved on a neighbourhood committee that was building new playgrounds, and I took him out to a zillion playgrounds and he played there. I've been on the school council for several years. I am now chair of the council, and I write proposals for the school. The way I see it, if my son is really interested or involved in something, I am really interested in it.'

The acceptance of fathers in a school context varies from rural to urban areas as well as over time. Lester, a police officer and a joint-custody father of nine-year-old Amy, admits that 'old gender roles still have a big effect in small communities' and that it is 'very rare to see a father helping out while there were quite a number of mothers.' Nevertheless, he remains involved in the school: 'My primary interest in being on council initially was to follow through on stuff happening at the school with Amy.'

OUTDOOR ACTIVITIES AND SPORTS

Fathers are also forming networks via children's physical activities and sports. Building on traditional areas of male connection with other men, such as sports, fathers are creating networks based on their involvement and interest in their children's sports. An excellent example of this kind of networking is soccer, a popular sport for boys and girls (ages four to eighteen) in Canada. The fathers' narratives in this study, combined with years of participant observation from the sidelines of children's soccer fields, and a review of the coaching staff of recreational and competitive soccer in the city of Ottawa, show that the majority of volunteer coaches, assistant coaches, organizers, and managers of children's soccer are fathers. Even though sports is typically not included in studies that consider parents and networking for children's benefit (but see Messner, 2000), I would argue that it provides an opportunity for fathers to connect with other fathers and link dominant masculine activities with networking and facilitating children's social and physical growth.

OTHER DADS AND FATHERS' GROUPS

For the stay-at-home fathers of the past, the discomfort with mother-dominated playgroups led a few to create their own. Dean is one of three fathers in the study who began his own group:

> When Chloe was born in 1990, and I started going to the little playgroup, I also had a number of men friends who were too far away to go to the playgroup in Wakefield [Quebec]. So I phoned them up and said, 'Listen we all have babies. Do you want to get together? Just for fun, let's have a picnic at Balmoral Park.' They agreed. We had a great time, so we did it another time at another park. And then the guys said that we should just do this on a regular basis. So me and another person organized a rotation where we went from guy's house to guy's house, and it was the first Sunday of every month and there was a big long list of people who could come.

The playgroup went on for four years under the name Fathers with

Young Children's Group. Dean laughs as he remembers the name: 'Really poetic, eh?'

In more recent years, fathers have also begun to connect with each other in community programs that increasingly focus on dads. Frank, a stay-at-home father of two preschoolers, is on the board of an Early Years Program, which operates government-funded centres set up for the exchange of information and resources, as well as providing a meeting place for parents. In the small city of Guelph, Ontario, Frank organizes parenting courses aimed specifically at dads, and a fathers' playgroup on Saturday mornings. According to Frank, 'I am the only male on staff [laughs], but they have been really open to what I've wanted to do. They found that there was a need for some kind of program for dads.'

Understanding Fathers' Narratives of Community Responsibility

Given that community responsibility is about the formation and main-tenance of social networks and relationships for children, there are sev-eral aspects of men's propensity to form and maintain relationships that figure into understanding their narratives of community responsi-bility. The majority of fathers in my study comment that the friend-ships and connection necessitated by the daily work of care are often beyond what they have known from their own experiences, having grown up as boys, engaging in traditional male friendships or believ-ing that men and women simply form friendships differently (see also Walker, 1994). Men refer to several issues connected with friendships, including men's sparse social networks; that talking about the kids is not an easy way for men to relate to other men; and that the appear-ance of self-reliance is important to many men. Other theoretical and empirical understandings that assist us in making sense of men's approaches to forming networks and taking on community responsi-bility include hegemonic masculinity and its relation to men's friend-ships, the limits of cross-gender friendships, issues of male embodiment, and the links between hegemonic masculinity and mas-culine conceptions of care.

Networking as a Father: 'It's Just Not Easy for a Guy to Go Up to Another Guy'

Martin points to the potential misfit between traditional avenues for male friendships and newly evolving male practices of caregiving. His simple rendering of this difficulty is well captured in his snapshot of himself and another father entering a library to participate in a children's program. Martin says, 'I've been out to the library and I've seen a guy pushing a baby carriage. But it's just not so easy for a guy to go up to another guy and say, "Hey, how old is she? Do you want to be friends?"'

Vincent, a joint-custody father of a six-year-old boy, says that he is more likely to speak with women about child-rearing issues than with men, even with single fathers with whom he shares a 'single-parent mantle': 'Since Zach has started getting into school, I have met a lot of other fathers who are primary caregivers. Do I share a lot of information with these fathers? No! Because the fact that we are both single fathers is not sufficient to give us something to talk about. I think with women, this would be different.'

Peter, who has been at home for five years, also makes this point about men milling about on the social scenes of parenting but never really connecting with one another in a meaningful way: 'There are men around that I see but I have not struck up a bunch of close friendships. Men don't network in the same way [as women do]. We're all just acquaintances. We know each other from the schoolyard. But we have not formed a support group of men in a minority doing this job.'

Men Networking with Other Men: 'It Really Is a Guy Thing'

Several fathers drew a connection between men's general reluctance to make the kids a central discussion point and the pressure on men to appear autonomous and self-reliant. At the end of his interview, Cameron, a stay-at-home father of two preschoolers, offered his reflections on the differences between women and men as parents: 'I was thinking about the way in which women bond versus how men bond, about how strength for men was the absence of weaknesses, whereas for women perhaps it is the disclosure of weaknesses, the willingness to share. Women have that willingness to share that men don't necessarily have.' When I ask Cameron where women's 'willingness to share' comes from, he answers while looking intently at his infant daughter, Olivia, who sits with us through the interview: 'It could be coming from this survival, dealing with children. In order to survive we need to share you [to baby Olivia]. Feeding and caring for children, women are more clued in to that. Whereas for men, it's "If I'm going to disclose that information, I will appear weak."'

Related to the issue of being 'closed' and not having many friends to 'open up to' is the strong belief espoused by many of the men that they must be self-reliant and autonomous. Eduardo, for example, a Latino father who works in international development and was home with his infant son for one year, cites the awkwardness exhibited by men when they go to parent-toddler groups; he reflects that this has something to do with internalized male notions of self-reliance and independence: 'Perhaps men in this society have been taught to be independent, to be self-reliant, to be Oh, I can do this by myself. I think mothers are more open. In the playgroup, there was immediately a connection between women. It happened naturally.' Martin suggests that men's fear of being seen as inferior is one of the reasons they do not make the effort to form networks with other men. He says, 'It really is a guy thing. Men make friendships in a different way. I think it takes a lot more time, and it usually has to be the right circumstances. It almost lets you look inferior if you're out there looking for a friend.'

These fathers' statements resonate with some of the research on men's friendships (Oliker, 1989; Rubin, 1985; Seidler, 1992, 1997; Walker, 1994). Such research suggests that men's friendships are relatively sparse compared with women's, and are built largely around sports, employment, or hobbies. In the main, these primary-caregiving fathers do not challenge some of the key research findings on men's friendships from the past few decades that have argued that men have significantly fewer friends than women, especially close friendships or best friends. What is notable in these fathers' narratives is that children are not readily regarded as an obvious basis on which to form friendships with other men. Moreover, the literature on men and friendships also underlines that men's friendships are framed by a fear of intimacy with other men and by homophobia (Kaufman, 1999; Nardi, 1992). In speaking about their social networks with other fathers, the men in my study are narrating, in clear and articulate voices, some of the dimensions of hegemonic masculinity.

Hegemonic Masculinity and Men's Friendships:
'One-liners' and 'Zingers'

As discussed in chapter 1 of this book, hegemonic masculinity plays out in fathers' relations with other fathers. Defined as different and superior to cultural symbols and practices of femininity, this concept can illuminate how men are keen to differentiate their friendships from those of women, which are often viewed as more open and intimate. Moreover, in relation to the discussion here on men's friendships, hegemonic masculinity includes qualities of exclusive heterosexuality, homophobia, emotional detachment, and competitiveness (Connell, 1987, 1995; Kane & Disch, 1993).

What characterizes fathers' narratives as they speak both about community responsibility and friendships with other fathers is a combination of needing to be autonomous and self-reliant and to avoid intimacy with other men. While some men only hint at these issues, Dean talks about them eloquently and at length. Formerly a stay-at-home father and now a joint-custody father of three daughters, he was in a men's group for several years. He provides an analysis of men's friendships that comes out of his years of speaking about these issues with other men.

> It has got to do with intimacy. Men equate intimacy with sex, so if I'm getting close to this guy, sex must be just around the corner, and no thank you. With men, we've got the homophobic line, so it's like where you could be good buddies with somebody in high school. We've got a motorbike, chess club, sports, whatever. This is what keeps us together. Good music, whatever it was. But it never got down to how you were really feeling 'cause that's what you said to your girlfriend. With women, intimacy and sex are independent and it's lovely when it's combined, but men can have one without the other quite easily. Both of those things mean that once you left your high school years, few men have any close friends. I've talked to so many men who said, 'Yeah, I had so many close friends back then and they're gone now.' I remember this one guy I met who had a really close friend, and all they did was get together and make one-liners. It was a morning of one-liners, and it after an hour I was weary 'cause I couldn't keep up and I just wanted to talk about life. How's your child? How's your relationship? How are your children? Have you read any good books? Zingers – that was what kept them together. They had this respectful distance that they maintained. They entertained each other. And there was never any danger of closeness.'

While avoiding the danger of closeness with men, heterosexual fathers also find themselves equally wary of the danger of closeness with women.

Cross-Gender Friendships: 'There Always Is a Bit of a Limit'

The female-dominated character of parenting networks can cause some tension for men and may further reinforce men's feelings of isolation within these same networks. Many fathers make a point of saying that they have to tread carefully into, and through, this world. While Archie, Theo, and Vincent referred to 'estrogen-rich' or 'high-estrogen' environments, Aaron acknowledged the challenges involved in the fact that 'I work in a female world.' Owen, at home for ten years, says, 'I would go to other women's houses. But I was always conscious of how it would be read.'

Alexander, who took two parental leaves and is now a joint-custody father, says, 'I am more connected with the mothers. But cross-gender friendships always have a complicated dimension.'

Many stay-at-home fathers readily offer their own observations on the possible tensions involved with meeting in other women's homes; they see this as a strain both for themselves and their mothering friends as well for each of the spouses involved. Aaron, a stay-at-home father of two boys, brings up such worries without being prodded by a specific question: 'You had to make friends with two people – them and the husbands. Their husbands were not comfortable with it. It's one thing to say, "I'm having Liz over for coffee this morning, and the kids will play." It is another thing to say, "Hey, I am having Aaron over for breakfast." So it's a different reaction.'

Archie notes that the community cast a suspicious eye when he went on kids' outings or socialized with one other mother, Petra: 'I think some people raised their eyebrows and wondered, and quite frankly are still wondering. And for the record, nothing happened!'

In their joint interview, Linda and Peter both acknowledge the difficulties for Peter's being at home. He says that although he is 'sort of plugged in for the practical purposes, making the playdates or arrangements or whatever,' his situation as a male parent is still 'not the same as it would be for the mothers.' He admits that while he does 'know a lot of people because it's been several years' that he has been home with the kids, nevertheless 'that's it, I just *know* them.' Linda agrees with his assessment of the situation but says to him, 'You do get along with some of the moms, but there is always a bit of a limit.'

Related to the issue of cross-gender friendships is a fairly well established body of academic literature arguing that from early childhood throughout adolescence and into adulthood, girls and boys form mainly same-sex friendships (Beneson, 1990; Cairns, Perrin, & Cairns, 1985). Thus it should not be surprising that parents seek out parents of the same gender, which makes it difficult for fathers since there are smaller numbers of male parents at home during the day. Peter and Linda make this point about the importance of numbers. Peter says, 'It could also be numbers. Just because they are guys at home with kids, it doesn't mean that we'll hit it off. It's not a requirement that we have to become buddies.' Linda concurs, 'With the women there are so many more of them. I'm sure they're not all friends with each other. But there are enough that you can make a couple of friends.'

Thus, with women heavily outnumbering men in parental society, many men expressed a sense of unease there, particularly in the years of parenting infants and toddlers. Indeed, men's presence seems to take on the quality of a disruption. This is well articulated by Archie, Martin, and Peter at the beginning of this chapter, with Archie saying, 'You shouldn't be there,' Martin noting that he 'felt really awkward going in,' and Peter lamenting that 'it continues to be a pretty alien environment.' The issue has parallels with that of women entering masculine-dominated venues and women in non-traditional occupations (Hughes, 2000; Williams, 1989). Yet it is more than this. Luke put it bluntly when he first filled out a brief background form for my study. In identifying key issues for him as a primary caregiver, he wrote just two sentences: 'Uneasiness of neighbourhood women (when they don't know you well) to allow their children to play with those cared for by a man, Women are initially wary of male caregivers.' This wariness of male caregivers is further explored below.

Male Embodiment: 'This Group of Girls, the Fence, and Then Me'

Listening to fathers narrate their excursions into female-dominated areas, makes clear that it is not any one thing that any one father is doing to elicit the wariness. Rather, it is the larger social backdrop as one of abstract but actual suspicion of fathers and children, particularly fathers and the children of others. Taking on community responsibility means networking to enhance the social growth of one's own children but also facilitating relations between parents, between children, and, less visibly, between parents and the children of others. Setting up playdates, inviting children for sleepovers or birthday parties, organizing babysitting, carpooling for extra-curricular activities, and volunteering for children's events can all imply an active role for fathers. Yet many fathers speak about feeling that they have to initially · watch their footing because there can be something potentially disturbing about their presence compared with mothers. This will be explored more fully in chapter 6, but it warrants some mention here.

Dean speaks about his difficulties juggling a household of three busy daughters when he first became a joint-custody parent because, as a man, he felt less able to rely on his neighbours. Surprisingly, this was the case even though he has lived in the same small town since his children were babies and had been a stay-at-home father for several years the community:

> Normally in a two-person family or an extended family, there is a mother nearby or even good neighbours. But I found much less of that. I think part of that is because I'm a man. If I was a woman, I probably would have made connections in the neighbourhood where they would trust me with their children, and I would trust them with mine. I don't know of any male in the neighbourhood that I would leave my daughter with, or that she would consent to be left with. Some of the women I have that type of relationship with, but it would only be one-sided.

In a similar manner, Jesse, a stay-at-home father of one daughter, speaks about how he can only babysit the children of a very small group of friends and that this barrier to caring for other children arises solely based on his gender: 'It's kind of bad for men to be interested in other children.'

Looking back fifteen years, Adam notes that it was very difficult for him to be involved with his children's school: 'I tried to get involved with the school from time to time but I didn't feel extremely welcome. I know I sound defensive. But I really did get that feeling. You're in among young children in the classroom. You're a male. There's a female teacher. As a volunteer I got that. Field trips were a bit better.'

Doug describes going to his daughter's school at lunchtime and being made painfully aware that gender does matter. The example he uses is that of speaking to a group of girls in the schoolyard while he stood on the other side of the school fence. He says,

> She had this Grade 3 testing thing and she was so stressed out about it. So the day she had her first test I dropped her off at school and I could tell that she was kind of worried. At lunchtime I took off from work and went to the school 'cause I knew they'd get out right after lunch. I walked up and caught her eye and asked her how it went. It was kind of cute because they all saw me coming and they all kind of ran over to the fence. And there is this group of girls, the fence, and then me. So I asked them

how it went and what was it like and then I see the teacher running across the schoolyard, asking, 'What are you doing here?' I said, 'Really, I am her father.' Still, I was glad that she came over.

When I ask Doug why he was glad that the teacher came rushed over, he replies, 'I think it was probably about being a man, which is okay – I'm glad that they picked up on [someone unfamiliar being around]. I didn't recognize this teacher. She didn't know me, so she came over.

While men speak about feeling different about themselves as em-bodied beings in the parental community, they also, as described in the next section of this chapter, emphasize differences in the way they take on community responsibility.

Hegemonic Masculinity and 'Masculine' Care

To find a comfortable place in what are still female-dominated or 'com-plex maternal worlds' (Bell & Ribbens, 1994), stay-at-home fathers choose particular areas of community work and volunteering, such as assisting with children's sports, working in classrooms on tasks that require renovation, construction or manual labour, or leadership posi-tions. While it is certainly the case that men do help with classroom reading, go on field trips, participate in school or community com-mittees, the fathers in my study nevertheless stress certain kinds of involvement for several reasons.

First, fathers' community involvement that builds on traditional male interests and connection like sports provides for the possibility of con-structing their own community (Messner, 1987, 1990). A second related point is that fathers, particularly stay-at-home dads, view coaching and assisting in children's sports at school and in the community as both enjoyable for themselves and a way to ease scrutiny of their decision to give up full-time paid work. Third, this involvement reflects how fathers seek to distinguish their caring from mothering and to recon-struct particular kinds of masculine care that retain some relationship to dominant or hegemonic masculinity (see also Brandth and Kvande, 1998). While fathers seem keen to emphasize gender differences in the ways that they take on community responsibility, there are particular ways that community responsibility encapsulates borderwork.

Borderwork

There are many instances of borderwork in mothers' and fathers' narratives of community responsibility. These include moments and contexts where gender seems to matter greatly with regard to fathers creating and maintaining community relations and networks around their children. Three notable examples of occasions when men and women are set up on opposite sides of what appears to be an uncrossable border include men's participation in female-dominated playgroups; fathers as the sole parenting presence for girls' sleepovers; and men's networking and friendship patterns related to children.

Playgroups: 'Girls on One Side, Boys on the Other'

If there is a 'worst moment' in their parenting tales, fathers' experiences in playgroups would certainly win the prize. Playgroup attendance as a point of tension, awkwardness, or excruciating discomfort was described so often by men that I came to see it as one of the key areas where men and women are on opposing sides of a parenting divide. It seems to be the perfect encapsulation of what Barrie Thorne calls borderwork, resembling her caricature of the instances in schoolyards where girls and boys are pitted against each as boys versus girls. Bruno, an Italian-Canadian sole-custodial father looks back fifteen years to the time when, after working night shifts, he would sleep until about ten and then take his two preschool boys to his community's playgroup: 'Me and another guy were the only two dads in the group. It was really awkward. It was like being at a high school dance all over again. Girls on one side, boys on the other. It took them a long time to accept us.'

Burt, a sole-custody father, reflects that twelve years ago, his entry into a community playgroup stunned the room into silence: 'As soon as I walked in the door there was utter silence; nobody said a word.' He reasons that it could have been partly because he was 'grubby looking,' but nevertheless it was because he was a grubby-looking *male*: 'Talking to some of the girls since, I heard that half of them thought I was a child molester because it was pretty obvious that there was no way that this cute little blond girl could have come from someone that looked like me. The other half figured that I probably kidnapped her from her real parents and that I'd only be there a day or two to keep one step ahead of the law. They never told me this until years later.'

After a couple of weeks, however, Burt became, as he puts it, 'one of the girls.' In the same breath, however, he acknowledges that this was not *really* possible, given his embodied differences as a heterosexual male in a group of women. Burt exemplifies Thorne's point about how borderwork invokes an image 'of many short fences that are quickly built and as quickly dismantled' (Thorne, 1993, 84). In his words, 'That went on for about two weeks or so, until everyone started to relax. The first couple of weeks nobody would talk to me. I'd walk by and they would sort of grab their kids protectively. After that I was just basically one of the girls, which was not necessarily a good thing because I was so completely one of the girls that when they wanted to breastfeed they would just whip it out, stick junior on it, and keep talking. In the meantime, I'm sitting there – I hadn't even thought about dating a girl in about three years at this point – and going, oh my God!'

The issue of men's discomfort in playgroups is accentuated by ethnicity and culture. Jarabee, for example, a Somali stay-at-home father of two, comments that he never goes to playgroups because 'in Muslim culture, it is not acceptable for a man to be mingling with the women like that.' Eduardo, a Latino father who was home for a year says that 'it was difficult to relate to the other women in the playgroup. It could have been culture or gender. Or both.'

While a father entering a playgroup in the 1980s and early 1990s was more likely to feel the pressure of this gendered divide, the border has gradually eased with each passing year. Perhaps the issue that matters most in borderwork in community settings is, as Burt made clear, that of male bodies disrupting female spaces. That is, there are places and times when gendered bodies matter. This point is particularly relevant in my second example of borderwork, that of fathers being the parent supervising girls' sleepovers.

Fathers and Girls' Sleepovers: 'It Was Never Said ... but I Just Knew'

Many fathers of daughters know the tensions that can arise for an adult male organizing commonplace events for girls. The one repeatedly mentioned is the sleepover. For stay-at-home fathers whose partner is away on a particular evening, sleepovers are a carefully scrutinized issue, and fathers willingly accept this state of affairs. Adam says, 'When my wife, Kara, was away and I was the only one home, it was only the kids of people I was really comfortable with that I would have over. I read it as parents being cautious. I think I'd be a little cautious myself.'

Dean is also aware of this issue: 'It was never said, but for some parents, it was there. Some children would get invited three times and there was always some excuse. "Oh, she doesn't like sleepovers," or "It's not a good weekend," or whatever. Parents who knew me, well, there was no problem. Their kids would come. But some of them, I just knew.'

Finally, Burt ties together the issue of men being in domestic spaces with teenage girls and the important issue of male embodiment, both in finding babysitters and with his daughter's sleepovers: 'Even today, I have a big problem getting babysitters because, you know, babysitters are usually fifteen-, sixteen-, seventeen-year-old girls, and their parents are not willing to have their child spend the evening at the house of a forty-one-year-old single male. It's as simple as that. It also affects Anastasia having a lot of sleepovers for the same reason.'

Whereas male embodiment is present in the first two examples of borderwork between men and women in relation to creating and maintaining community networks, a third kind of borderwork can be discerned from women's and men's frequently reiterated views on gendered divisions in friendship patterns.

Gendered Friendships: 'What Do You Guys Talk About?'

The ways that most men and women speak about gendered friendships is a further example of borderwork. Many invoke a 'Venus and Mars' metaphor for men and women's seemingly oppositional approaches to friendships. Three tales are repeatedly told in this study. First, many men have only a few friends. Indeed, when asked to talk about their friendships, several fathers are hard-pressed to mention even one close friend. Asked about his friendships, Luke, for example, answers, 'Not a lot. I've got some real close friends that I've had for a long time, but they all seem to move away. I must have some. None come to mind.'

In a similar way, Ryan says, 'I'm not a person to get close. That's not my nature. Because I'm in the military, I've moved all the time. I've never really had close, close friends. But I've had people that, you know, I talk to and I'm friendly with. But if I was to move away, would I keep in touch with them? Maybe, maybe not.'

A second theme in fathers' and mothers' friendship narratives is one of constant gender comparison. Men often note that women make friends more easily, are more 'open,' that their conversations are 'deeper,' and that they often speak about themselves and their children. Andrew puts it well when he says of his wife, 'I would be inclined to say that she goes more deeply.' Similarly, Maurice, an African American, reflects on his year at home and says that one obstacle in his experience was that he was not as open as his wife: 'I'm not as open. I'm more reserved, I guess. She'll talk to anybody, and she doesn't care if she just met you a minute ago or ten seconds or thirty years ago for that matter. She's just like that.'

Further interesting commentary is provided by Gary, a stay-at-home father of three, whose wife, Kathy, is a hairdresser.

> I think men tend to be less social. My wife actually put it well. We were renovating Kathy's shop and I was working nights. There was another guy helping me who was the husband of one of Kathy's hairdressers. Kathy said, 'Well, what do you guys talk about?' I said, 'We're working, we're not talking.' What do we talk about – 'Can you hand me the square?' That's about it. Girls in the shop talk about everything and everybody. With us it's, you know, we don't talk about ourselves at all. We don't talk about the kids. We're talking about the job at hand.

A third theme in the narratives is that 'talking about the kids' represents a disjunction with traditional male ways of relating and forming friendships. In this vein, Andrew, a stay-at-home father for two years, says that when he was sitting in the playgroups with his three-year-old daughter and the other women, 'I was never sure what to talk about.'

Yet is it the case that a firm and unchanging border divides women and men in their friendship propensities and patterns? This is a question that has generated a tremendous amount of academic scholarship over the past few decades. On the one hand, there is a large body of literature that emphasizes the close, self-revealing, and intimate quality of women's relations while men usually shy away from intimacy and closeness and form friendships largely around sports and work-related interests, or 'activity friends' (Maccoby, 1990; Miller, 1983; Rubin, 1985). On the other hand, Ray Pahl's recent work on friendships points out that sociologists have made wide-ranging *generalizations* about men's and women's friendship patterns: 'Men were held to be emotionally reticent – fearful perhaps of homoerotic overtones, while women were held to be more articulate and emotionally accomplished'(2000, 111–12). Pahl, however, also cites survey evidence that 'demonstrate(s) that [women's] regular contact with family and friends declined from the mid-1980s to the mid-1990s. This was attributed partly to the pressure consequent upon the successful juggling of family and work responsibilities' (Pahl, 2000, 116).

Could it be the case that women's traditional role in managing family and community relationships has translated into relational ways of being and communicating? In this sense, it remains difficult to hold on to long-standing stereotypes in light of shifting education and employment trends for women and men, changes in the use of leisure time, the development of electronic communications, changing responsibilities of women and men at work and at home, as well as the increasing involvement of girls and women in sports and in activity-based friendships. In recognition of altering social relations, there has thus been a move from easy explanations to a greater sense of nuance, diversity, and complexity in scholarship on gender and friendships. Such accounts highlight, for example, that heterosexual males may yearn for greater connection and relationships with other males (Way, 1998a, 1998b), may have higher levels of self-disclosure than often reported in both historical and contemporary men's friendships (Hansen, 1992; Reid & Fine, 1992; Wright, 1982), and that women may engage in relational aggression and take on stereotypically male qualities of autonomy and independence (Brown, 1998; Simmons, 2002; Spence, 2002).

Context and setting play an enormous role in the issue of gender and friendship and in breaking down gender differences between women and men in this regard. While gendered patterns in friendships may remain due to stereotypical, historical, and ideological issues, there are nevertheless contexts where gender has less salience. What emerges from this study is that because women and men are placed in working and caregiving contexts where gender is stretched and tested, they begin to hint at changes in themselves along typically non-gendered lines. As detailed below, these can be viewed as examples of border crossings.

Border Crossings

I have carefully chosen the word 'crossing' to allude to the process through which a girl or boy may seek access to groups and activities of the other gender ... The process of crossing is complex and often contradictory, affected by matters of definition, activity, and the extent to which an individual has developed a regular place in social networks of the other gender.

(Thorne, 1993, 121)

Fathers' and mothers' narratives also draw attention to instances of gender symmetry. That is, particular contexts demonstrate greater variability and a loosening of the gender border around these friend-ship patterns. It is notable that of the fourteen couples interviewed, most of the women mention friendships that might be identified as more stereotypically male; these included activity-based and work-based friendships, as well as isolationist tendencies at times. All the women, and some of the stay-at-home fathers speaking about their wives/partners, hint at this, while five women claim explicitly that they are antisocial in many settings. Aileen, for instance, says, 'I'm antisocial. I like doing my own things in my own time.' She also points out that 'I wouldn't say that I have close friends. I have friends. That's it. Richard [her husband] is my best friend.' Similarly, Julie admits that 'I actively don't talk to my neighbours.' Referring to herself and to Manuel, her husband, she adds, ' Manuel is definitely more social. For a long long time I would stay home, and he would go out and meet with his Latino friends. I am just more a home loner type. No, I don't really have many close friends. Since my thirties, when I finally figured out that I like to be alone, that made a difference.'

Cameron, a stay-at-home father of two, reflects on the role reversal in sociability that has occurred as a result of his being at home: 'There's a real role reversal going on. I say to her, "I want to go dancing. I can't believe that you don't want to go out dancing! I've been cooped up in this house all day" [laughs].'

Manuel also loves to dance. He says, 'If I could go every week or every two weeks to a place where I could dance for a bit, it would relax me.' His wife, Julie, emphasizing again that she is the antisocial one, quickly adds, 'Whereas it would be painful for me.'

Rather than avoiding all talk about children, men do find themselves encouraged by certain social settings to talk about their kids. Andrew, who admitted that he was 'was never sure what to talk about' in female-dominated contexts such as the playgroups, is much more com-fortable sitting in the coffee shop across from the school discussing the kids. Part of this is the gender-neutral setting provided by the environ-ment. As Andrew put it, in a coffee shop, 'as a father, you don't stand out there.' 'I can certainly carry on that conversation about the kids. I did when I went for coffee with the mothers from Elena's class. We'd talk about the kids and what they're doing, and making plans about what is important in the next little while. Maybe try and line up stuff. Those Monday mornings tended to be not gripe sessions but people talking about what's going on at school. And what needed to be addressed. And different problems we might be having with kids. And part of it is was finding out what people were doing in their lives around the kids.'

Men initially resist admitting that they form friendships related to their children, but this was, in fact, happening slowly for them, particularly in neutral or masculine venues such as sports and outdoor activities. Vincent, for example, a speech writer and a joint-custody father of a six-year-old son, starts off by saying, 'We will talk more about kids than I would have guessed a couple of years ago. With the guys after hockey last night – there were eight of us – every one of them is an involved parent. Every one of them would have something to say in this study of yours. Did we talk about child-rearing issues? Yes. But in the course of an hour and a half, this took up five minutes.'

When I ask Vincent what they *did* talk about at the bar after playing hockey, his reply is revealing to both of us: 'What do guys talk about [laughs]? We were debating whether Avril Lavigne was fourteen or eighteen, we were talking about Gordon Campbell's drunk driving conviction.[3] We talked about hockey. Actually, we talked a lot about our sons and sports.'

While clinging to the view that men and women are from different planets when it comes to friendships and in their propensity to talk about the kids, fathers – at certain sites and moments – *do* talk about their children. In addition to the effects of various contexts, particular resources assist men to make connections with others. I am drawing again on the work of Thorne, who highlights the resources that assist boys and girls to make successful gender crossings. She pays special attention to boys, since they are more likely to be teased about being sissies if they participate in female-dominated activities. Specifically, there are six resources that assist men in developing and maintaining community networks around children. First, women move over to create space for men; second, having a 'crossing partner' (Thorne, 1993, 126) or a woman who acts as a bridge for men entering into female-dominated venues; third, connecting with others in extra-domestic spaces; and fourth, being well-known in a community. A fifth issue is what Thorne calls 'skill,' noting that some are 'successful at crossing the gender divide not because of persistence but also because of skill' (Thorne, 1993, 131). Referring to children, she writes, 'They were adept at negotiating the junctures of social interaction – initiating activities, forming new groups, and securing access to groups already formed' (Thorne, 1993, 131). This skill in social interaction can be seen in fathers' high level of community involvement, which facilitates their 'crossing the gender divide' in parenting. Sixth, and finally, there are the effects of passing time on community norms related to fathers' involvement.

Women Moving Over: 'But Then I Shoved It All Over to You'

When women move over to create space for men in community responsibility, gender borders begin to come down. Like emotional responsibility described in the previous chapter, community responsibility is not set in stone but fluid and constantly changing. The interviews employing the Household Portrait technique allowed couples to reflect on such areas of change and movement. I was often reminded of one particular research respondent, Laura, from my doctoral research in Britain a decade earlier; she explained, in reference to a Household Portrait that she had completed with her husband, that every five years 'she went on strike' (see Doucet, 1995a, 2000, 2001b).

While there is no explicit mention of going on strike by the mothers I interviewed for this study, there is certainly a sense of deliberate movement by mothers out of spaces, which leaves room for men to enter. For example, the way Claire and Alistair make plans for their children to attend summer camp has altered over time.

> CLAIRE I'm thinking of the camp programs that I set up. Finding if they
>   have friends going, talking to their friends' parents, finding out about the
>   Shakespeare camp –
> ALISTAIR But I've done a fair amount of camp organizing too.
> CLAIRE Yes, you did too. Last summer –
> ALISTAIR Discussing it with the parents? Well, I wouldn't do it formally, but
>   I would talk to parents when I'm dropping the kids off –
> CLAIRE I'm talking about in the next few months, making arrangements for
>   the summer camps now. This is January and I'm already planning the
>   summer camps! [laughs]
> ALISTAIR Claire finds more programs –
> CLAIRE There are friends that Vanessa goes to camp with and they make
>   arrangements for agriculture camp. And so soon after her birthday, I start
>   arranging of these camps.
> ALISTAIR [Sigh] She does more of the long-term planning.

At the end of their discussion, however, Claire notes that when she was completing her doctorate, she gave up much of the organizing and

Alistair began to take on more of it: 'But last summer when I was finishing my thesis, I was useless, so you took more on. And I used to do all the choir stuff for Georgia, but then I shoved it all over to you ... Everything changes as kids change. We move back and forth, and it depends on our work and their activities.'

The shifting quality of community responsibility is also revealed in the narratives of the twenty-eight fathers who were interviewed more than once. Moreover, the couple interviews provide points of further elabouration, contradiction, and discussion. Thus, while some men had, in their individual interviews, indicated one interpretation of how community responsibility was enacted, their conversation with their female partners sometimes brought forth another version. Tom, a stay-at-home father of three young children, insists that he is a 'lazy slob' when it comes to organizing, and that his wife, Natasha, a physician, 'sees the bigger picture.' Nevertheless, in their joint interview, Natasha maintains that Tom is on top of what the children are doing on a daily, weekly, and monthly basis and that he is undoubtedly in charge of the overall planning and organizing of the children's activities.

A Woman as a Bridge: 'She'd Say, "This Guy's Okay"'

In her work on boys and girls in school, Thorne identifies the importance of a 'crossing partner in helping boys to cross into girls activities or vice versa' (Thorne, 1993, 133). While this can be a person of the same gender who accompanies the person crossing into the activities of the other gender, it can, as was the case in my work, be of the opposite gender. Thus, a second factor that assists men in gaining access to female-dominated community spaces, particularly when fathers are new arrivals, is having a woman who acts as a bridge for them. Such a bridge may be his own partner/wife, a female neighbour, a sister, the wife of a friend, or a caregiver. As mentioned earlier in this chapter, Martin's participation in the local playgroup, although marked by a rocky beginning, was facilitated by the fact that his wife had previously been a member. Indeed, Denise is still involved in the group in a different way. Martin says, 'They have a once-a-month Girls Night Out. I don't want to be involved in that [laughs], so Denise goes. And they all go out – just the women, the moms – to dinner. So Denise keeps in touch with them.'

For Luke, there was one woman who kept him informed of the groups and eased his entry: 'I met Bonnie at the library. She was the instrumental one. She was the liberal one of the group. She'd say, "This guy's okay. You don't have to worry about him. You can trust him." She would call me up and let me know where the group was meeting.'

Connecting in Extra-Domestic Spaces: 'It Just Doesn't Look Good for Me to Be in Private with One Other Mom'

In addition to having women assist them with crossing into female-dominated community sites, fathers also meet with women in particular sites where they feel more comfortable as men to be mingling with women. Many stay-at-home fathers readily offer their own observations that the possible tension associated with cross-gender friendship is greater when they visit other women's homes and dissipates in public settings. Theo, a computer engineer who left work to stay at home with four preschool children, astutely points to the advantages for stay-at-home fathers in busy urban settings or enclaves rather than those in mainly residential suburbs:

> We are very lucky in this community. Because it has a rich infrastructure, lots of public places you can go, with kid-centred activities, and parks, playgrounds, coffee shops. Where there isn't that infrastructure, you would have to go to people's houses more. And that's tough. I make play-dates regularly [for the boys]. Sometimes we will go as a group, sometimes alone. But probably lots of moms wouldn't do that, because it just doesn't look good for me to be in private with one other mom. I don't like to do it either. Unless I know them really well and their husband and it's all okay all around, it's just not worth the impression that it gives. So if I was in a community where I had less options, it would be a lot more difficult.

Fathers also stress that the spatial contexts of these friendships do matter, confirming one of Barrie Thorne's central points that 'heterosexual meanings [act] as a barrier to crossing' (Thorne, 1993, 132). In this vein, she writes that a component of successfully crossing to the groups and activities of the other gender means that 'they have in effect avoided the meanings that accompany borderwork situations. Gender remains relatively low in salience [...] This can only be achieved if gender marking is minimized and heterosexual meanings are avoided' (Thorne, 1993, 132). Connecting with mothers in extra-domestic spaces (in coffee shops, in the schoolyard, in other public settings) minimizes 'gender meanings,' and helps to decrease the complicated and potentially threatening quality of the heterosexual meanings attached to cross-gender mingling.

Being 'Tightly Embraced by the Community'

Ray, a gay father of five-month-old Ruby, says that being known and 'tightly embraced by the community' is an asset in creating parenting connections and networks.[4] He and his partner, Carson, are co-owners of a local shop and their adoption of Ruby was embraced by many in their supportive network of friends, neighbours, and community members. He says, 'Once the word was out that Ruby had arrived, every day a gift arrived at the store or at the house. We are very connected in this community.'

Jack, who lives in the same eastern Canadian city that he grew up in, offers a similar story. When his wife moved to another province and he was left to care for the three children, the adjustment issues were minimal for him. What especially assists Jack is that his mother, who lives in an apartment above his family home, was the school librarian for twenty-five years and has just recently retired. His sister is a teacher in the school that his children attend. Moreover, he says, 'The kids have friends in the immediate neighbourhood. And I have known many of the parents since I was a kid. I grew up in this community, about one mile away. There is a comfort level with these kids, I knew their parents when I was young. I know the parents and my mom knows the parents.'

Community Involvement: 'Otherwise You'll Be Sitting at Home Watching Oprah All Day'

High involvement in the community allows gender borders to become less visible while easing suspicions towards men in caring roles. It gives fathers status and replaces the social and normative expectations that they should have a job. Archie, mentioned at the opening of this chapter, made a conscious effort to get out of the house, to get involved in community activities and the council of his children's school. He reasons that being a stay-at-home parent is like any other job: 'You have to get more ties. I was the soccer coordinator, a pretty typical thing for a dad to do. Otherwise, you'll be sitting at home watching *Oprah*. It's the same when you start a new job. If you sit at your desk all day, you won't be making those connections. This is your workplace. You need to know who your kids are playing with, and if you are not going to get involved, how are you going to do that?'

Archie then went on to chair the school council, led a campaign to save his children's small inner-city school, and won a prestigious community award for his efforts. He reflects on how his acceptance in the social arena of parenting is largely related to his community work, which earned him respect and increased his credibility in the eyes of other parents. He says, 'I think the acceptance is there on the whole. A lot of it has to do with my work on the school council. Part of this is because the school closure issue was so high profile and it was such a huge success.'

Another father, Vincent, who lives in the same neighbourhood as Archie, echoes this view. Vincent first notes that 'people look at these guys differently because being a stay-at-home father is not considered a worthy vocation in this culture.' He then points out that community involvement cushions fathers from such social stigma and scrutiny, mentioning the example of Archie: 'Do you know Archie? Now there is a fascinating exception to what I'm saying. He has enormous stature in the community as a stay-at-home dad, and he parlays that into intense community activism. Now if he wasn't such a powerhouse on the school board and school councils, would people look at him in the same way?'

Changes within Communities Over Time: 'Now I Go to
Three Playgroups a Week Plus the Library'

The passing of time also helps to ease gender borders. There have been remarkable changes in the way men's presence is experienced and perceived in many Canadian communities. The situation has progressed from Archie's walking into a community centre and feeling like the women 'were staring daggers at me' to Theo's experience a decade later when he and another man, at *the same community centre*, took on the coordination of a community playgroup. Theo notes that although the group is still composed mainly of mothers, several men now drop in on a regular basis. Indeed, it was the mothers in the playgroup who urged Theo to take on the job. This signals something of a revolutionary change in fathering. In his words, 'The more you're around, the more you start volunteering for things. Everybody was asking us, so I said I would do it. But I said I would do it with somebody I could work with. So Brian put his hand up. The last thing I expected was another guy!'

Aileen and Richard sum up the changes that have occurred in the two years that Richard has been at home with the children:

AILEEN When he first started going to playgroups, nobody would talk to
   him.
RICHARD But now I go to three playgroups a week plus the library.

Several social changes have occurred in the past few years in Canada
that will likely lead to a continued increase in the comfort level of
fathers in the parenting society. As mentioned earlier, Canadian men
are forming child-related networks in traditional areas of male connection such as sports. Also, there has been a dramatic increase by
Canadian parenting resource centres on programs directed towards
assisting fathers in making connections with other fathers (Bader &
Doucet, 2005).[5] Finally, the recent extension of parental leave in Canada (from six months to one year) and the increased use of parental
leave by fathers to care for infants in Canada is likely to increase
fathers' creation of community networks. In a recent study by Statistics
Canada, the main government statistical agency, it was reported that in
2002 parental benefits taken up by fathers increased by five times more
than it was just two years earlier (Marshall, 2003; Pérusse, 2003).[6]
Greater numbers of fathers walking around with strollers, this can't
help changing community norms on gender and caregiving.

Conclusions

Returning to my central question, 'Do men mother?' we can now ask,
Do fathers meet the maternal demand of facilitating children's growth?
Do they take on community responsibility? The answer to the questions is a mixed one. Overall, fathers remain helpers in the process,
leaving women to take on what one father, Luke, called the 'higher
care' of orchestrating, coordinating, managing, organizing, and planning for children's social and developmental needs. Yet there are also
households where community responsibility is shared by mothers and
fathers taking on different, but symmetrical, responsibilities. Furthermore, in about one-quarter of mother-father households (both joint-
custody and stay-at-home-father families), fathers do take on most of
the community responsibilities as they devise varied ways to 'pick up
the slack' and 'fill the gap' left by women who are more engaged in
paid work or have opted out of such responsibilities.

   This research thus does not dispute the already large library of international research that makes the case that the majority of unpaid work
in communities, and the overwhelming bulk of community responsi-

bility, remains in the hands of women. Nor does it counter Anita Garey's astute claim that 'homework, volunteer work and extracurricular activities are ways in which mothers link their children to the public world – and are symbolic arenas in their strategies of being mothers' (Garey, 1999, 40). Nevertheless, this research demonstrates that fathers also 'link their children to the public world' through their central role in extra-curricular activities such as sports and recreational activities.

As established in this chapter, community responsibility builds on emotional responsibility with its *attentiveness* to the needs of others' (Tronto, 1989, 176–8), and it links this recognition of children's needs to the wider relationships within which caring work is planned and negotiated. Thus, if men are to take on, or share in, community-based responsibility, the ways in which they create and maintain relationships and friendships with other men and women become particularly significant. The tendency for men to have – or to believe in men's propensity to have – sparse social networks, to form friendships mainly through sports and paid work, and the homophobic tendencies that tinge men's relations with one another come to the fore in fathers' reluctance to connect with other fathers.

This chapter has also illuminated moments of heightened gender distinction – or borderwork – in fathers' and mothers' narratives. Fathers feeling sidelined in mother-dominated playgroups in the early years of child rearing, the awkwardness for some fathers around chaperoning girls' sleepovers in the preteen and teenage years, and the beliefs in the pervasiveness of gendered friendship patterns seem to put men and women on opposing sides of the gender divide with regard to community responsibility.

Yet fathers can and do cross into the groups and activities associated with community responsibility. In doing so, they take on some aspects that have been traditionally defined and done by women, and they also alter the meanings of these responsibilities. With community responsibility, having 'a regular place in social networks of the other gender' (Thorne, 1993, 121) is critically important for men. Yet they also develop their own networks, which adhere to the areas of community responsibility that fathers assume. Gender borders in community responsibilities are traversed, particularly when women move over to create room for men. Furthermore, issues of time and space matter in gender crossings. Fathers connect more easily with mothers in gender-neutral settings such as coffee shops or parks and less well in female-dominated playgroups or in women's homes. Community involvement, and concurrent community acceptance, also act to minimize the effects of gender differences mattering in men's attempts to create and maintain community networks. Finally, the passage of time has lessened the perception that there are irreconcilable differences between fathers and mothers on community terrain. Efforts at the greater inclusion of fathers in the early years of child rearing is evident in more father-focused and father-inclusive programming by community, health, and parenting centres in Canada as well as in the government's recent doubling of parental leave, combined with official documentation indicating that both fathers and mothers are encouraged to take leave. In sum, the overall social portrait of Canadian fathers has gradually changed with each passing year so that the initial discomfort for men of joining the 'complex maternal worlds' (Bell & Ribbens, 1994) of early child rearing has given way to a slow increase in the visibility of fathers, and in their comfort level, in these settings.

Some of the difficulties that men face as they move through community settings relate, however, to how they are viewed and judged in their role as primary or shared primary caregivers of children. As discussed in the next chapter, it is moral assumptions that mark fathering and mothering as distinct identities and practices.

6 Fathering, Mothering, and 'Moral' Responsibility

NINA I do think being a mom is different from being a dad. I get irate when people say, 'But really Mitchell is the children's mom. He's the one that's staying home and therefore he's the mother.' You want to get my dander up, that is one of the fastest ways to do it.

ANDREA Why is that?

NINA Because I'm the mother. I carried them, I bore them, delivered them, nursed them. I'm perfectly comfortable with saying he's their primary caregiver. I have no problem with doing that, but don't say that he's their mother. I'm their mother!

MITCHELL Yeah, I was there. She is their mother!

> (Nina, psychotherapist, and Mitchell, a retired naval officer and
> stay-at-home father of three children, October 2002)

Introduction

'It's funny,' says Adam. 'There were lots of pros and cons about being home ... One of the things I missed was that you lose a sense of stature, a sense of common ground between myself and other men, a sense of being able to say, *"Hey, I'm a man too!"* I think a lot of that revolved around not having employment. Not working and being at home. For me *not working* was the bigger issue than being at home ... I liked the domestic stuff, cooking and all that, a lot, but I missed work. As a man, you have no status at all if you don't work.'

Adam, forty-two and living in rural Ontario, was a stay-at-home father of three children for a decade. Adam's children are older now (seventeen, fifteen, and eleven), and he works full time as an economist for the government. He still remembers the difficulties he faced when he was not employed outside the home.

A similar stigma has affected Paul, whose narrative is framed by his feeling that he has 'failed as a man.' A twenty-six-year-old visual artist, he has struggled with shedding sources of low self-esteem: being poor; trying to build a career for himself; a lack of success at finding another partner; and the raising of his seven-year-old son, Josh, on his own for the past three years. In spite of having taken almost exclusive responsibility for his son in Ottawa while his ex-girlfriend, Josh's mother, has been studying for her law degree in Vancouver, he feels as if his parenting status is low ('I'm just the father') while also noting that 'mothers fear me.'

Paul explains the discrepant treatment of primary caregiving fathers using the example of an accident that occurred one Saturday morning when he and Josh were at the local community centre. While Paul was talking to a group of people in his tae kwan do class, Josh was 'looking through the window and running his hand up and down the crack in these metal doors.' What occurred in an instant was that somebody opened the door and Josh got his finger caught in the door, an episode that left his son crying inconsolably while people rushed around screaming, 'Where is his mother?' Looking back, Paul remembers: 'I kind of felt at that point everyone in the centre was looking for his mother or his family. There was even this one lady who tried to take him out of my arms into hers to try to comfort him. I keep hearing again and again, "Where's his mother?" I tell them, "I'm his father." They're like "Oh!" Suddenly, there's three people looking very embarrassed and they say, "We're sorry." They walk off and leave us alone at that point.'

Worlds apart in terms of the social conditions in which they father, Adam and Paul describe fathers' struggles with what Sara Ruddick has called 'social acceptability.'

SOCIAL ACCEPTABILITY/'MORAL' RESPONSIBILITY

'The third demand on which maternal practice is based is made not by children's needs but by the social groups of which a mother is a member,' writes Sara Ruddick. Social groups require that mothers shape their children's growth in acceptable ways ... [T]he criteria of acceptability consists of the group values that a mother has internalised as well of the values of group members whom she feels she must please' (Ruddick, 1995, 21).

This criterion for mothering raises the question of just who these 'group members' are and how a mother will 'please' them. First and foremost, the majority of the group members are women. Second, they often hold very fixed ideas about appropriate masculinity, femininity, mothering, and fathering. More specifically, the social acceptability of fathers *as mothers* relates to how they act in concurrence with deeply ingrained moral responsibilities and with wider societal expectations of them as men, as fathers, as earners and caregivers.

By moral responsibility, I am not using *moral* in the sense of right or wrong but rather in the sense of people's identities as moral beings and how they feel they should act in society. That is, *moral* is used here not in reference to issues of ethics but, rather, draws on symbolic interactionism and its concept of interactionist subjectivity as a basis for self-definition (see also Barker, 1994; Daly, 1996, 2002; Finch & Mason, 1993; McMahon, 1995). Moreover, my conception of *moral* is informed by Janet Finch and Jennifer Mason's (1993) work on negotiating elder care responsibilities, particularly in their discussion of the interwoven material and *moral* dimensions of family responsibilities.

Drawing on symbolic interactionist ideas (Finch, 1989; Mead, 1962), they argue that it is 'through human interaction that people develop a common understanding of what a particular course of action will mean: for example, if I offer financial help to my mother in her old age, will it seem generous, or demeaning, or whatever?' (Finch & Mason, 1993, 61). In other words, taking on caregiving within households is intricately connected to 'people's identities as moral beings,' which 'are being constructed, confirmed and reconstructed – identities as a reliable son, a generous mother, a caring sister or whatever it might be' (Finch & Mason, 1993, 170). According to Finch and Mason, any individual is always 'actively working out his or her own course of action' from within a social and cultural location and 'with reference to other people' (Finch & Mason, 1993, 61). To add a 'moral dimension' to the picture is to bring in an understanding of how fathers and mothers feel they should act, and how they think others will view these actions.[1] Furthermore, the intersection between symbolic interactionist understanding of selves and a moral dimension to responsibility highlights how couples 'do gender'; as outlined in chapter 1, women and men co-create and maintain gendered distinctions in domestic life and in gendered identities.

These insights are useful for a discussion of domestic responsibility in that they illustrate the importance of considering, as discussed in chapter 5, the wider social relations in which households are located. They also refer to the ways that men may feel observed and judged as they take on primary or shared caregiving. In specific terms, moral dimensions played out in relation to fathers as earners , men as carers, and the multiple ways that fathers wrestle with and engage with moral assumptions. Each of these aspects will be dealt with below, briefly for mothers and then, in greater depth, for fathers.

Mothers' Moral Responsibilities

Martha McMahon (1995) beautifully illuminates the idea of moral responsibility by pulling together concepts of social class and mother-hood. Drawing on symbolic interactionist and ethnomethodological (Goffman, 1963) precepts, she uses the concept of moral in the sense of the 'self or self conceptions' (McMahon, 1995, 15). McMahon argues that motherhood can be seen in terms of moral transformation and reform. For middle-class women, this transformation is articulated in statements about personal growth, while for working-class women, McMahon highlights their narratives about responsibility and settling down as symbolizing moral reform. Moreover, she indicates that 'moral transformations' represent a synchronicity between women's mothering and dominant cultural images of what mothers ought to be. In her words, 'The cultural meanings of motherhood and female morality ... provided, for the women in this study, metaphors through which individual biography and personal identity could be organized. In this sense, becoming a mother can become an essence-making process that produces and sustains meaningful distinctions between mothers and nonmothers, proper and improper motherhood, and reflects not what people "truly" are, but idealized social representa-tions ...' (McMahon, 1995, 272).

McMahon was at a loss to describe sociologically what she heard in the women's narratives. She writes, 'What I didn't know, and still find difficult to put into words, is how becoming a mother can provide some women with symbolic and relational opportunities for human experi-ences, that, when experienced by men have been called heroic: that is, transformative of self and potentially redemptive of society' (265).

Other sociologists and social psychologists have written about issues of social acceptability of mothers, or their moral responsibility to-wards their children (Duncan, 2003; Maushart, 1999; Ribbens-McCar-thy, Edwards, & Gillies, 2000). Over twenty years ago, Sara Fenstermaker Berk wrote about the moral weight of domestic labour and childcare that weighs on women in her discussion of the 'interwoven structures of the material and the symbolic' and how 'the way household labour is brought into line with an image of how it *should* be divided' (Berk, 1985, 206). More recently, in her work on mothers and post-natal depression, Natasha Mauthner writes that for mothers, 'being responsible for her child is about being moral as a person' (Mauthner, 2002, 59).

These ideas of sociologists and social psychologists on idealized social representations and the distinctions between 'proper' and 'improper' mothers are also explored, in a humorous tone, in the bestselling novel by Allison Pearson titled *I Don't Know How She Does It* (Pearson, 2002). While the book is somewhat trite, with unchallenged stereotypical assumptions about mothering, Pearson's recurrent image of 'the Court of Motherhood' evinces the social and interactive world of meaning, identity, and image-making that many women may feel pulled into. Pearson's book opens with Kate, a British mother of two, exhausted from a business trip, preparing store-bought mince pies for the Christmas party at her five-year-old daughter's school. Kate is 'distressing' mince pies in the middle of the night, trying in vain to hide their manufactured perfection. In her upper-middle-class community, store-bought is a sign of imperfection, and thus Kate endeavours to make them look homemade to avoid the censure of 'the Muffia' (her phrase for stay-at-home mothers) and the 'Court of Motherhood.' These are the women in her community who will judge whether she is a 'proper mother.' Pearson writes at length about the thoughts of Kate Reddy:

'How did I get here? Can someone please tell me that? Not in this kitchen, I mean in this life. It is the morning of the school carol concert and I am hitting mince pies. No, let us be quite clear about this, I am distressing mince pies, an altogether more demanding and subtle process.

Discarding the ... luxury packaging, I winkle the pies out of their pleated foil cups, place them on a chopping board and bring down a rolling pin on their blameless floury faces. This is not as easy as it sounds, believe me. Hit the pies too hard and they drop a kind of fat-lady curtsy, skirts of pastry bulging out at the sides, and the fruit starts to ooze. But with a firm downward motion – imagine enough pressure to crush a small beetle – you can start a crumbly little landslide, giving the pastry a pleasing homemade appearance. And homemade is what I'm after here.

Home is where the heart is. Home is where the good mother is, baking for her children ...

[B]efore I was really old enough to understand what being a woman meant, I already understood that the world of women was divided in two: there were proper mothers, self-sacrificing bakers of apple pies and well-scrubbed invigilators of the washtub, and there were the other sort. At the age of thirty-five, I know precisely which kind I am, and I suppose that's what I'm doing here in the small hours of the thirteenth of December, hitting mince pies with a rolling pin till they look like something mother-made. Women used to have time to make mince pies and had to fake orgasms. Now we can manage the orgasms, but we have to fake the mince pies. And they call this progress.' (Pearson, 2002, 3–4)

A first reading of this compelled me to ask an obvious question: Do women *actually* get up in the middle of the night and rework store-bought pies to make them look homemade? Moreover, do they wake in the middle of the night to worry about how they will be perceived by other mothers? In spite of presenting a far-fetched and unflattering view of mothers, Pearson nevertheless strikes a chord when she writes about women feeling watched and observed by 'proper mothers,' both in the community as well as in mirrors of symbolic idealized images of mothers. In referring to the Court of Motherhood, Pearson's protagonist implicitly refers to women's moral responsibilities as mothers. Kate Reddy is meant to symbolize the way mothers are forever standing in this metaphorical courtroom being judged on their ability to combine work and family life. Are they 'proper' mothers – or 'the other sort'? Are their houses neat enough? Are their children holding up?

It is important to pause here to note that the Kate Reddy character is a white middle-class woman. She is likely demonstrating what the British sociologists Simon Duncan and Rosalind Edwards have referred to as a *'primarily mother* gendered moral rationality,' which was exhibited mainly by the white middle-class and white working-class mothers in their study (Duncan & Edwards, 1999; my emphasis). Duncan and Edwards contrast this with the ways that lone mothers, especially those influenced by feminism and 'alternative views of family and gender roles' held a *'primarily worker* gendered moral rationality' while working-class black lone mothers tended towards a *'mother/worker integral* gendered moral rationality. Overall, these authors argue that both ethnicity and distinctions between conventional and alternative families are the chief lines of differentiation in mothers' moral identities in Britain in the late 1990s and early years of this century.

In my study, the female partners of stay-at-home fathers exhibit a clear *mother/worker-integral*-gendered morality in that they value both paid employment and mothering and devote considerable time and identity resources in both of these. However, the women note that they are still judged differently from men and that their decision to work while their partners stayed at home did initially raise questions. Thus, a distinction might be drawn here between the gendered moral rationality that women hold and, alternatively, the ways that they reflect on this issue when *compared with their male partners*.

Four points can be made here as examples of women's sense of moral responsibility as mothers. The first is that mothers can initially feel judged in their decision to return to work while their male partner is at home. The second is the role of mothers planning their children's birthday parties as a way of exhibiting their moral responsibilities as mothers. Third, I refer to gendered shoulds and oughts regarding housekeeping and the social presentation of one's domestic space.

Mothers as Primary Breadwinners: 'I Felt Like a Bad Mother'

The vertigo image employed in the introduction to this book can be invoked once again in relation to mothers and breadwinning in that, in two-parent heterosexual households, some mothers and fathers refer to the uneasy transition that can occur as the male partner stays at home while the female goes out to work. In spite of women's holding on to the view that they are both mothers and workers, gendered judgements on what they *ought* to be doing still surfaced from time to time. Richard and Aileen, for example, both comment on a sense of dislocation engendered by their role reversal; in their couple interview, Aileen says, 'It was actually when Richard started staying home that my nose was really out of joint. Not because I didn't want him to stay home but because I felt like a bad mother.' Richard adds, 'She felt it was *expected*.'

Rory, a former oil consultant in Alberta, makes similar comments about his wife's feelings when he started staying at home more than four years ago, partly because his son had debilitating allergies and needed a constant carer. He says, 'She took a lot of flak at work. It was more related to, "I'm working and I've got a son with problems. Should I be quitting work to look after my son?"'

A very telling description of mothers' moral responsibilities in relation to work and home can be extrapolated from a study that I completed in Britain about a decade earlier than this Canadian one (Doucet, 1995a). The relevant example is embedded in an interview with Monica and Joshua, both managers in departments of the British government. Monica beautifully captured the processes whereby women internalize an ideal of what a mother ought to do and ought to know. Because of her extensive travelling, Joshua had taken over the daily and weekly running of the household and the activities of their two young daughters. Yet Monica still felt, as 'their mother,' that she *'ought* to know' exactly what they were doing on any particular night: 'I hate it when I don't actually know what they're doing. I rang home yesterday evening, and I'd got the nights wrong, and I was thinking Pippa would be going to guides and she wasn't. It was choir. And I hate that feeling. Because I'm their *mother* and I *ought* to know.'

Monica also found it difficult to accept the idea that Joshua was planning to reduce his working hours so that he was, in his words, 'able to give a bit more to house and family, *home* interests.' She alluded to a moral dimension in her recognition of the source of her unease: 'I can't quite work out whether it's because I'm much more materialistic than Joshua, and I think, Oh God, we won't have as much money or whether it's all wrapped up in the norms and roles and it's, you know, it shouldn't be Joshua who's working part-time. If anybody, it should be me! Although I don't wish to work part-time, and I'm far more ambitious and career oriented and career minded ... There's an *unease* about it. I still haven't worked it out.'

These decade-old sentiments of unease are remarkably similar to those expressed by several of the women in this study. Claire conveys unease well when she remembers how she felt when her first daughter went to her husband, Alistair, more than to her:

> It's quite interesting because Georgia would always go to Daddy when she slipped and fell and hurt herself. She would always go to her dad. And this upset my very conservative attitude. When a child is hurt, they don't go to their father. They go to their mother. It's interesting. This funny little shoot from the past. I was so happy to have Alistair there to take care of her, but when I heard the words, I suddenly realized that there was this special bond between Alistair and Georgia that was not there for Georgia and me. So I thought, well, for baby number two [Vanessa], I'll stay home. So I did. Before Vanessa came, I took the summer off for Georgia and me.

Linda articulates a similar sense of discomfort when she realized that her infant son, Blake, had a special language with her husband, Peter: 'I remember feeling left out when Blake was a baby and when he started to talk. Daddy and Blake – do you remember that? Daddy and Blake, Daddy and Blake. It was like an entity. Daddy and Blake were doing this, and Daddy and Blake were doing that. He would have been less than two because Charlie was not born yet. I remember feeling a little left out. There was Daddy and Blake, and then there was me.'

Two different kinds of scenarios wherein women feel pulled by their moral responsibilities and identities as mothers are explored below.

Birthday Parties: 'That's Her Domain'

While the physical work of running children's birthday parties is mostly shared between mothers and fathers, it is overwhelmingly mothers (in two-parent and joint-custody households) who take on the organizing, the choice of the theme, the guest lists and invitations, and any follow-up thank-you cards for gifts sent from friends, relatives, or grandparents. Kyle, a stay-at-home father for over a year says, 'That's her domain because she enjoys *creating* events.' Shane, stay-at-home father of a four-year-old, admits that he often is not even on hand for the parties: 'In fact, I chose to leave during the first few years.' In their joint interview, Craig says that organizing birthday parties 'is a very big Mom thing.' His wife, Mary Claire, concurs but also points out how much he does contribute: 'He's the one who helps out, and he's the one who will call the people since they are still young and we are still inviting parents to the parties. So he'll call the parents, but I make up all the lists. I do the theme, the cake, the planning it all out, making the actual lists, doing the little loot bags, wrapping the presents. But he does the grunt work, like phoning the people, putting a big banner outside and putting up the streamers and blowing up the balloons, and he'll clean the house while I'm decorating the cake.'

Children's birthday parties are both a way of celebrating the child's birth and of connecting children to the communities where they live. Although, as discussed in chapter 5, this is a part of community responsibility, a moral dimension enters in that women feel that they ought to do it in a certain way and may feel judged adversely if they do not. Thus, their feelings of social acceptability as proper mothers are confirmed – or denied – by this and other public presentations of their good mothering to their communities. Similar, although more mundane, processes come to the fore with the issue of housework.

Mothers and Housekeeping: 'Carol Was Absolutely in a Tizzy over That'

Kyle makes it a point to let me know that his wife, Carole, 'did the vac-uuming before she left for work today because she knew you were coming to interview me.' While Kyle is also admittedly 'fanatical' about cleaning as well as a 'neat freak,' he does not worry about the presentation of their home to others to the extent that his wife does. He does confess that he likes to keep the kitchen clean because he is the one who does most of the cooking: 'If I'm going to cook, I have to do the shopping. If I'm going to cook, I have to make sure the counters are clean. I suffered many years ago from two bouts of salmonella. I don't intend to do that again.' In contrast, Carol is more concerned about the house being clean, especially when it is seen by others. He gives the example of people coming to assess the house: 'I was in the home show, met up with one of the real estate agents who offered to do an assessment. I said, "Oh, yeah, sure, come on over at such and such a time." Carol was absolutely in a tizzy over that because could she guarantee that the house would be perfectly clean when someone comes in to deliberately look in every corner? And I said, *"So what?"'*

In their joint interview, Carl says to Penny that having a dirty house 'affects your mood, whereas it won't affect my mood. You actually get really stressed about it, and it makes you more ornery, dare I say so.' He also points out that, given that I was coming to interview them, 'we blitzed this morning.' Jacob, a sole custodial father of three puts the point bluntly when he says, 'Housework is not a priority; homework is.'

Sam reflects on some of the differences between him and his wife, while commenting on 'other moms' more generally: 'My wife would want to make sure everything was done in the house and to get things done at the same time. There's the difference. I'd let things lapse totally. Generally if I go to visit other moms I notice the house would be clean. They'd be already cooking dinner at two o'clock in the after-noon, or making lunches for the next day. Very structured. They must learn it from their moms or something.'

There is tremendous variation in all the households in this study, particularly as revealed in the Household Portraits conducted in the fourteen couple interviews. Fathers are adept and involved in virtually all aspects of housework. There are certainly women who do not con-sider housework a priority. Nevertheless, there is a slight difference in emphasis between mothers and fathers in relation to social judgments of the upkeep of the home (see also Deutsch, 1999). Natasha expresses this point very well. As a busy family physician, she admits that she has changed many fewer diapers than her husband, Tom, who stays at home with their three young children. Moreover, she admits, while constructing their Household Portrait, that her contribution to routine housework is so much less than Tom's that, as she tells me, 'You should have a bigger page for Tom!' In spite of this role reversal, Natasha still feels social pressure as a woman and sees this as a key difference between herself as a mother and Tom as a father: 'If things aren't cleaned he doesn't get worked up. He figures, Who cares? But if somebody is coming over at night, I *do* care. He'll be, "It's a nice day, let's go to the beach." And I'm like, "I can't. The house is a mess." He's like, "*What?*"'

Fathers and Moral Responsibilities

Moral responsibilities work differently for fathers. Overall, stay-at-home fathers do not feel judged on the cleanliness of the house, and they seem to worry less about how their children or they, as fathers, are judged by others. Theo's blunt statement about housework exemplifies this well: 'It's not that I just don't know how, it's that I don't care,' an attitude that he carries over into how he feels about one child's taste in clothes: 'I'm letting Adam pick out his own clothes. He picks out the wildest things, but that's what he likes. I don't care, and people know I don't care. I guess I'm not sensitive to criticism.'

Theo, like many fathers, is 'not sensitive to criticism,' partly because he is not judged in the same way that women are. Nevertheless, there is certainly a parallel version of the Court of Motherhood in the form of a Court of Fatherhood. For stay-at-home fathers, in particular, it contains a unique group of people. As invoked in diverse ways in different fathers' narratives, it includes the people milling about at dinner parties who question what stay-at-home fathers *do* all day; the fathers and fathers-in-law who are perplexed at the thought of a man leaving work to care for children; the elderly man across the street; a brother, a cousin, a workmate, or a male friend from childhood who responds with a mixture of admiration and disbelief; finally, it almost always holds the metaphoric 'lady at the grocery store' who queries fathers each time they step into the store with children in tow – 'Oh, you have the day off from work today?' This Court of Fatherhood judges fathers both for *not* 'working' *and* for caring for children. Fathers respond, in turn, to these judgements by emphasizing particular kinds of domestic and community work. Each of these themes is addressed below.

Stay-at-Home Fathers and Earning: 'I Felt I Wasn't Being a Good Man'

The sentiments expressed at the beginning of this chapter by both Adam and Paul on how 'not working' made them each feel like 'a failed man' are present in the narratives of the majority of stay-at-home fathers. Each and every father interviewed referred in some way to the weight of social scrutiny and the pressure to be earning. Some claim that they are unaffected by this pressure but nevertheless admit that they feel this social gaze on them. Peter, a stay-at-home-father of two young sons for the past five years, describes this quite well. His previous job in desktop publishing was gradually phased out, but he was able to maintain his connection with his former employer and take on contract work for about twelve hours a week from a home office. He very much identifies with the stay-at-home-father label, but he nevertheless feels compelled to tell people, especially other men, about his status as a working and earning father: 'I've always – in social occasions, dinner parties, talking with other people or whatever, with other men I guess especially – been able to talk about something I do in the 'real world.' And this has been kind of important socially. This doesn't make me sound limited or stuck. I can show that I am able to work, although I have chosen to be a stay-at-home father.'

Marc, a father who began staying at home fifteen years ago with his two young sons, also talks about how important it was to be able to say that he was working: 'It was hard at times, and quite honestly I'm not sure that I would have done it full time for as long as I did if I had not been working part-time, if I didn't have some sense of worth.' He further indicates that different moral expectations weigh on women and men and that both he and his wife felt the pressure to fulfil their traditional gendered roles: 'Back then, I think there were times when I felt I wasn't being a good man, by not providing more money for the family. And that I wasn't doing something more masculine. And there were times when my wife felt that she wasn't filling her traditional role as a wife and a mother.'

Marc's words reflect those of Scott Coltrane a decade ago when he observed that 'the underlying equation for men with work and women with home has been surprisingly impervious to the labour market changes that have occurred over the past few decades' (Coltrane, 1996:

26; see also Potuchek, 1997). And while Marc mentions that he felt
judged for not 'being a good man,' Archie goes further, suggesting that
communities cast a suspicious gaze on men at home. Having looked
after his children for seven years, he says, 'For the most part, there is a
sense that if a man stays home there is something wrong with him, he's
lost his job, or he's a little off kilter. It's not men's job. They shouldn't
be there.'

Fathers and Unpaid Self-Provisioning Work:
'We Get Together and Talk Tools, and That's Great'

Where stay-at-home fathers have given up a formal investment in the
labour force, many replace employment with 'self-provisioning' work
(Gershuny & Pahl, 1979; Pahl, 1984; Wallace, 2002; Wallace & Pahl,
1985), which allows them to contribute economically to the household
economy as well as to display masculine practices both to themselves
and to their wider community. As discussed in chapter 3, most of the
stay-at-home fathers are working in some capacity or are preparing to
return to work. Yet they also remain connected to traditional sources of
masculine identity such as paid work as well as self-provisioning at
home and in the community.

Richard, a thirty-nine-year-old French-Canadian father, draws attention to this issue without even being asked about it. He left his work as
an electronic technician two years ago to be at home with his three children. In his joint interview with his wife, Richard takes out a photo
album and shows me before and after pictures of his household renovation, saying, 'Now you can see how much I've done.' He enjoys the
domestic routine and has made award-winning birthday cakes for the
kids (he proudly shows photos of his cakes); he also makes homemade
baby food and does a batch of jams and jellies every fall. When I ask him
about the long-term plans, he says, 'I'm not going back to work. I'll be
doing work on the house. Renovations. Cooking, cleaning. They're only
gone for six hours. I'll probably be more involved in the school. I'll do
these things I've been wanting to do for years. Simple things like organizing my recipes. Organizing my tapes and music ... I have a lot of
projects that I want to do in woodworking, but I don't have the time.'

Most of the stay-at-home fathers speak about work they are doing
on the house, landscaping, carpentry, woodworking, or repairing cars.
Adam, mentioned in the opening of this chapter, provides a good
example of how masculine self-provisioning replaced paid work. In

speaking about his typical weekly and daily routine when his first two children, Jeffrey and Bryn, were pre-kindergarten age, he quickly lets me know that he also fixed cars while he cared for his younger son and daughter: 'Jeffrey and I, those first two years, were joined at the hip. And then Bryn and I were joined at the hip for the next while. We did a lot of stuff whereby they would come along with me to do things. Jeffrey would hang around when I was doing things. We had a series of old cars. He would hang around while I fixed the cars.'

Like Richard and Adam, many of the stay-at-home fathers in this study reconstruct the meanings of work and home to include unpaid self-provisioning work (Pahl, 1984; Wallace & Pahl, 1985), specifically 'male self-provisioning activities' (Mingione, 1988b, 560) which include 'building, renovation ... carpentry, electrical repairs and plumbing, furniture making, decorating, constructing doors and window frames, agricultural cultivation for own use, repairing vehicles' (Mingione, 1988, 560–1). While some of these can be viewed as masculine hobbies, which these men would have likely picked up from their fathers or male peers, these are also activities that display or justify masculinity and that seem to alleviate some of the discomfort men feel with giving up breadwinning.

Fathers' narratives are replete with references to masculine self-provisioning activities. For example, Howard, a stay-at-home father for five years of two school-age children, says he likes renovations but not cleaning: 'I do a lot of work around the house. I do the renovation, the house repairs and a lot of construction ... I don't like cleaning. I like renovations and home repair work.' Luke, who works with mentally challenged adults and has been a stay-at-home parent for twelve years while working nights at a group home says, 'I'm always building something. I'm a renovator. I've renovated the whole house, all on my own.' Martin, who often takes his four-year-old son to the Home Depot store, describes his typical day with Nathan and then notes how the day comes to an end: 'And then as soon as Denise gets in, I'm gone! I go down to the basement and work on renovations for an hour, an hour and a half.' Finally, Tom shows me his woodworking shed at the end of our interview. In talking about his typical week, he also adds that in addition to caring for the kids, 'I'll call my neighbours whom I do woodworking with, and we'll talk woodworking. That's a guy thing. We get together and talk tools and that's great.'

For many men in my study, the impulse to take on self-provisioning is partly financial, but it is also part of an effort to justify being at home

by emphasizing more masculine work and hobbies that involve traditional male qualities, such as building, construction, and physical
strength. This very much carries over into the community work that
men take on, where, as discussed below, the emphasis is often on
sports and occasionally on traditional masculine roles of physical
labour and leadership/management.

Community Work and Fathers' Moral Identities:
'They Call Me Bob the Builder'

In addition to unpaid self-provisioning work, men also take on unpaid
community work, particularly involvement in school and extra-curricular activities. This unpaid community work has gender-neutral tones
such as volunteering in the classroom or on school trips, but fathers
also tend to emphasize work that has masculine qualities. Building on
traditional male interests such as sports (Messner, 1987, 1990) and
physical labour, men translate the skills into assets in their caregiving
and become involved in recreational sports as organizers and coaches,
and taking on more physical tasks in the classroom. Some fathers
assume leadership positions on school councils and community organizations. Archie, for example, says his position as president of the
parent-teacher council became 'a full-time job.'

Making community work a central part of stay-at-home fathers' daily
routines is well illustrated by Robert, a former sign maker who lives in
rural Quebec. Caring for three years for two sons (aged six and four), he
left work because of a back injury that affected his ability to keep running his own company. He speaks about having done a lot of 'hard
physical labour and often outside' for the past twenty-five years. While
at home, he is slowly building up a workshop in the garage and is starting to do renovation jobs for himself and his neighbours. He also has a
particular involvement at his sons' school: 'I'm head of maintenance at
my son's kindergarten ... They call me Bob the Builder – "fix this, fix
that." Every time I go in, they're always asking me to do things ... It takes
up my morning, so I can't get back to do my renovation work.'

Stay-at-Home Fathers and Caregiving: 'The Incompetent Father
Needing a Woman's Help to Get the Job Done'

When fathers feel judged by the metaphorical Court of Fatherhood, it
is often based on perceptions of their incompetence as caregivers.
Craig, one of whose twin sons has physical disabilities, reflects on how

a recurring issue for himself as a father is that 'the incompetence thing comes into play' and how social onlookers 'very much want to make sure that the babies are okay.' He points out that in situations where people know him, such as in his weekly visits to the physiotherapy clinic, his competence is not questioned. He says, 'I used to carry them in car seats with a diaper bag over my shoulder. I got known pretty quickly, and there seemed to be a lot of other dads there as well.' It was a different story, however, when he entered other places where he was less well known. He remembers when he first went to these sites, he was often 'approached with offers of help. It was very much like the incompetent father needing a woman's help to get the job done.'

Peter says that sentiments of assumed incompetence are particularly strong when a man has in his charge young or pre-verbal children because onlookers may worry about the baby's care, while also assuming that the father is a secondary, and less competent, caregiver:

> When I had a little tiny baby, there was always that sense that I was babysitting rather than taking care of my child like I do every day – when I have to understand his wants and needs because he can't speak. That's where I felt it was very different from women. There was a bit of an assumption that I felt like I was just tiding things over until the real mother or the person who really knew what they were doing would show up. Maybe I just felt like I was under the microscope more. I don't continue to have that sensation. Because now that the kids are older, the way we speak and interact shows that I know what I'm doing.

At the end of his interview, Peter gives a frank assessment of the social acceptability of fathers as caregivers: 'Even in a society where people believe that men and women are equal and can do just about everything, they don't really believe that men can do this with a baby, especially a really tiny baby.'

Alexander, a law professor who took two parental leaves and is now a joint-custody father, reflects on the *other* side of this incompetence coin and that he was always offered support in ways that would likely not occur for women. When the children were younger and he was travelling on an airplane or visiting the local grocery store with his three children, he comments on the amount of attention and support he would often get from others: 'I know that a woman travelling in the same situation is seen as ordinary and not needing support. I think it was the same kind of thing in the grocery store. [A father] is definitely a slight oddity.'

Fathers caring for their children are not only viewed as a 'slight odd-ity' but in some cases, as explored in the next section of this chapter, as downright suspect.

Scrutiny of Fathers in Public Places

In addition to being judged on their earning capacity and caregiving ability, many fathers face a covert level of surveillance as they care for their children. Most interviewed for this study speak about having felt a watchful eye on them at least once. Examples occur in fathers' descriptions of different parenting sites; the most frequently men-tioned, as indicated previously, are women-centred postnatal venues, parks and schoolyards, and girls' sleepovers.

BABY MASSAGE CLASSES: 'SHE KEPT HER EYES ON ME'
Craig speaks about his discomfort in a baby massage class when the female instructor quietly singled him out. In his view, she seemed to fear that as a man, he would equate touch with sexual touch: 'When she started getting into how she'd be doing the massage, she said you have to be careful that nothing is perceived as sexual touching, and with that she turned and looked right at me. She kept her eyes on me when she went around this whole subject. Being the only guy in the room, I felt self-conscious. I didn't say anything, and then I looked at Marcia (the woman next to me), and she said, "Did you see that?" And I said, "Oh yeah, I just wasn't sure if everybody else did."'

MEN IN SCHOOLS: 'A MAN WANDERING THROUGH THE
SCHOOL IS UNUSUAL'
In chapter 5, I used the example of Archie, who describes his discom-fort years ago when he was in a schoolyard reading to his child and other kids and was confronted by a woman who wanted to check out the man her daughter had said was hanging around the schoolyard.
    Many other fathers make a similar point. Burt, the sole-custody par-ent of a daughter, summarizes the dominant sentiment about a decade ago: 'A lot of parents were nervous because a man wandering through the school is unusual.' In spite of these feelings about their place on school premises, most fathers admitted that it is getting easier as more dads volunteer to help out in classroom and to go on field trips. Harry notes that men are needed on field trips to, among other things, help with chaperoning the boys into their washroom: 'I work at the library

with the Grade 1 class. I go on all the field trips. They need a male to go on field trips. They need help with the washrooms. You know the school is half boys and half girls.'

MEN IN PARKS: 'WHO ARE THESE GUYS?'

Jesse, a young artist and a stay-at-home father of one daughter, finds that in spite of his attempts to be open about men and children, he still harbours suspicions about men lingering around children in public places, such as parks: 'I think it's hard, I mean, even with me. There was a couple of guys who used to come to the park and were hanging out, and I would think, whoh, who are these guys? Why are they hanging around? A woman could do this and it would be just the opposite. A woman in the park and reading a book and looking at the kids and you would think the opposite: Isn't that nice; she has positive feelings towards the children and she wants kids of her own. You put it in a different way. I try to fight that but it's hard.'

FATHERS AND DAUGHTERS' SLEEPOVER PARTIES: 'I'M REALLY LEERY ...'

As discussed in chapter 5, several fathers describe some of the challenges they face in raising girls. While many note the gender boundaries they cross as they learn to braid hair, tastefully clip on barrettes, and understand the intricacies of girls' shopping, makeup, and nail polish, the dominant father-daughter narratives revolve around the hidden, unspoken sense of unease that fathers face at one time or another, particularly as their daughters reach the pre-teen or teen years. Girls' sleepovers are the window through which many men see the need to be very careful around their daughters and her friends. As Ryan, a sole-custody father of a son and a twelve-year-old girl, puts it, 'I have purposefully not had anybody to sleep over, especially girls, because I'm really leery of the possibility that somebody might think something bad.'

Understanding Fathers and Moral Responsibility

Men's and women's lives as caregivers and earners are affected by deeply felt moral and social scripts about what they *should* do within and outside of household life (Berk, 1985; Coltrane, 1989; Hochschild, 1989; Mauthner, 2002; McMahon, 1995). How are we to make sense of these differently framed, and differently narrated, moral responsibilities? Five issues will be highlighted here. First, women's and men's lives are rooted in structured gender relations that exist beyond couples, household, and communities. Second, while there are many ways to describe gendered expectations, many commentators remark on gender ideologies, discourses, or what Nikolas Rose terms *psy complexes* (N. Rose, 1991, 1996) as ways of explaining how women and men come to hold socially sanctioned beliefs about differing gendered positions. Third, links can be made between hegemonic masculinity and men's earning power. Fourth, connections can also be made between hegemonic masculinity and the devaluation of the traditionally feminine. Finally, issues of embodiment come to matter in mothers' and fathers' moral responsibilities.

Gender as Social Structure and Agency

A first factor that assists in understanding gender differences in moral responsibilities in parenting is the way that gender acts as a social structure in work and family lives. As described earlier in chapter 1, R.W. Connell's gender relations approach is a useful one to summarize my overall theoretical perspective on this issue in that it seeks to 'understand the different dimensions of structures of gender, the relations between bodies and society and the patterning or configuration of gender' (Connell, 2000, 24–5). Focusing on gender as structure and agency thus recognizes the local and global structures within which individuals, families and communities are embedded while also recognizing that women and men create and re-create gender behaviour through their daily interactional practices. This occurs not only in the household, as has been amply demonstrated by others (Berk, 1985; Coltrane, 1989; DeVault, 1991; Rissman, 1998), but also in the community.

Framed within this gender relations perspective, this study on fathers and mothers began with a clear understanding of the gendered power relations that exist in a society like Canada where women and men still face different opportunities and where gender divisions of labour, responsibility and expectation persist both in home life and employment. Thus in examining the choices and actions of women and men as they negotiate who stays home and who works, how housework is divided, and who takes on varied aspects of domestic life and child rearing, we are reminded that such actions, decisions, and strategies[2] must be situated in a wide set of social relations where women's and men's lives are structured differently. Glass ceilings still exist for women, glass escalators for men (C.L. Williams, 1992); women generally earn less than men do, and assumptions about women, mothering, and care abound in and between social institutions. Gender relations matter profoundly in social institutions (work, family, state policies, communities, the courts, education, the media), and all these social institutions are implicated in thinking through how to change current gender relations (Hochschild, 1997; J. Williams, 2000).[3] As well stated by the American sociologist Barbara Risman, 'We cannot simply attend to socializing children differently, nor creating moral accountability for men to share family work, nor fighting for flexible, family-friendly workplaces. We must attend to all simultaneously' (Risman, 2004, 441).

Gendered Expectations Related to Earning and Care:
'She Is More Inclined to Want to Please the Kids'

In fathers' and mothers' narratives, gender ideologies are best expressed as deeply felt gendered expectation related to care and earning. While *ideology* may be viewed as 'one of the most troublesome words in the sociological lexicon' (Morgan, 1992, drawing on Williams, 1983), *gender ideologies* may be loosely defined as a set of social beliefs about men's and women's roles and relationships in varied social institutions (Boyd, 2002; Hochschild, 1989; Coltrane, 1996).[4]

The deeply felt shoulds are transmitted and reinforced through a complex amalgam of historical and social traditions. These include not only ideologies but also discourses, peer relations and judgements, and psy complexes. The latter refer to knowledges produced in bastions of accepted expertise and social authority such as medicine, pedagogy, psychology, and psychiatry, which increasingly inform the self-perceptions of many individuals in Western industrialized nations.[5] Perhaps more important, such knowledges are not only restricted to professional practice but also permeate other professional and information venues (i.e., social work, education, health care, counselling, self-help, and specialized magazines and courses). These knowledges are thus reiterated in the mundane workings of everyday life as people read magazines, watch talk shows and reality TV, go the movies, and engage in conversations with neighbours. All the daily processes inform the way people define and understand their sense of self as men and women, and – in the case of this particular study – as mothers and fathers. As Rose claims, 'It has become impossible to conceive of personhood, to experience one's own or another's personhood, or to govern oneself or others without "psy"' (N. Rose, 1996, 139).

While it is impossible to determine just how moral conceptions get transmitted, my work is informed by the view that people conduct their daily lives within a broad range of ideologies, discourses and psy complexes, which generate particular ideas about how women and men should act, particularly in relation to working and caring. Women, for example, act and are viewed and judged according to a long tradition that defines women as caregivers. Tom expresses this point well when he says that mothers' responsibilities are framed in terms of a long history of societal expectations.

> I'd like to think I'm a little less inclined to come into my kids' whimsies as much as my wife is. They'll say, 'Can we go swimming? Can we go fishing?' And I'll say, 'No, we'll go at a different time.' Whereas my wife would kind of think about it, and say, 'Let's not do that, but let's think of an alternative. Let's do this or that.' I think she is more inclined to want to please the kids. And I think I've learned that I have to take care of myself as a guy, as a dad, as a person, that I have to look out for my own limits, and my own state and not really feel guilty about that. And I think that is partially probably a trend that men and women are different in the sense that women might feel a little more responsible as mothers. You can't ignore the fact that you've got a much bigger history of women doing this kind of job than men. And so you have to contend with that fact, and this is an issue that she has struggled with. It is, Am I shirking my God-given responsibilities, the thing that my mother did and my mother's mother and everything that has been expected of me? *Women are expected to raise their kids.*

Fathers who are primary caregivers still feel governed by the social dictates that, as men, they should be earning. What is remarkable in my study is that fathers, whether home for one year or twelve years, still feel profoundly that they should be earning. Tom speaks at length:

> It is actually a big struggle for me. But each time I think of working full time, I get a little bit of a heavy stomach because I think about being away that much from the house. So I have this overwhelming – probably from my own background – sense that men are supposed to go out and work, supposed to be generating income, supposed to be at parties answering questions like 'What do you do for a living' with something other than 'I am at home, I sweep floors and squeeze blueberry shit out of diapers.' That is a very big struggle, and I don't think being a man at home you can ignore that ... There is a traditional feeling like, Gee, shouldn't I be earn-

ing a living? Shouldn't I make money doing something sitting around the water cooler with people talking shop or something like that?

Jesse speaks in a similar way, noting a gendered quality to some feelings: 'These things are so ingrained in us. It can weigh on you, those kind of things. Sometimes I do wonder if people have that sort of perception of me as a stay-at-home father. I'm still not sure if there's a widespread acceptance of it. I think some people still wonder, Why is the father at home? Like, he can't earn as much as his partner or something? I struggle with that, and it is my own internalized kind of conditioning too that I have this struggle. You know, my background, working class, a strong work ethic. And it's a guy thing.'

Hegemonic Masculinity and Earning: 'A Certain Male Imperative'

In mentioning the 'guy thing,' these fathers are implicitly referring to the connections between hegemonic masculinity (Connell, 1987, 1995) and paid work and the associated sense of unease that they feel when they relinquish earning as a primary part of their identity (LaBier, 1986; Pahl, 1995; Waddington, Chritcher, & Dicks, 1998). In the case of stay-at-home fathers, as detailed in chapter 3 of this book, most remain connected to paid work. This is partly from financial necessity but also from a need to maintain a link with masculine conceptions of identity and to respond to deeply felt moral precepts. As one father, Kyle, put it, 'There's a certain male imperative to be bringing in money, to feel like you are actually caring for your family, a sense of providing.'

As explored above in the discussion of unpaid self-provisioning work, one of the ways that men deal with these losses is to take on unpaid work that has masculine qualities – household renovation, woodworking, repairing cars. In this vein, the majority of stay-at-home fathers' narratives are peppered with references to varied configurations of paid and unpaid work. That is, while fathers are at home, they are also establishing complex relationships with home, paid and unpaid work, community work, and their own sense of masculinity.

Hegemonic Masculinity and Devaluation of the Feminine: 'I Was Still Needing the Men Thing'

Even if they replace paid work with masculine self-provisioning and/ or community work that sometimes involves traditional masculine qualities, what seems very clear in most fathers' narratives is their determination to distinguish themselves *as men*, as heterosexual males, and as fathers, *not* as mothers. There are several notable interjections by fathers throughout the interview process making clear that they want to convey such thoughts. For example, in my first focus group with fathers, Sam, stay-at-home father of two for five years, said several times, half jokingly, 'Well, we're still *men*, aren't we?' Another stay-at-home father, Mitchell, made pointed references to often working out at a gym and enjoying 'seeing the women in Lycra.' These men's words add further support to what theorists of work have emphasized about men working in non-traditional or female-dominated occupations (such as nursing or elementary school teaching) and that they must actively work to dispel the idea that they might be gay, un-masculine, or not men (Fisher & Connell, 2002; Sargent, 2000; C.L. Williams, 1992). These processes of masculine identification and distancing from the feminine occurred in at least three ways.

First, as discussed in chapter 4, most fathers emphasize masculine qualities of their caregiving such as promoting their children's physical and outdoor activities, independence, risk taking, and the fun and playful aspects of care (see Brandth & Kvande, 1998; Doucet, 2004). While it would seem to be the case that these are dominant patterns in paternal care, it is also interesting to note that fathers seek to draw attention to these to distinguish their caring from maternal caring. Second, given that domestic space, the *home*, is historically and meta-phorically configured as a maternal space with feminine connotations of comfort and care (Grosz, 1995; Walker, 2002), many fathers more readily identify with the *house* as something to build and rebuild, thus attempting to carve out their own paternal and masculine identities within spaces traditionally considered maternal and feminine. Finally, men also find ways of reinforcing their masculinity – such as engaging in sports or physical labour – to maintain masculine affiliations and to publicly exhibit displays of masculinity (see Bird, 1996). In this vein, many men asserted that they had to 'hang out with the guys' by play-ing traditionally male sports such as hockey or baseball or by working with men on activities involving physical labour. Owen, a stay-at-home father of two children for ten years, says that this helps to bal-ance the time that he is doing caring work: 'At the same time I was still needing the men thing. I needed a break from the kids ... I would build sets for the theatre. I would hang out with the guys.'

Embodied Parenting

When we think about fathers moving as embodied subjects in female-defined settings, the work of the sociologist Irving Goffman on space and body is helpful to remind us that relations between people are both practical and moral. The movements of fathers are *practical* in the sense that men learn how to involve themselves in ways that are acceptable, normal, and in concert with public expectations. Furthermore, these movements are *moral* in that, as embodied subjects, fathers and mothers not only interact but also judgements are made about whether, and how, people maintain or disrupt routine social and public engagement. Goffman argues that one's sense of self and moral worth and whether one can sustain a definition of oneself as normal, are at stake as one moves through public spaces and engages in public encounters (see Crossley, 1995b).

Goffman's theoretical points are useful to show those occasions where father's movements can sometimes be viewed as disruptive; such occasions occur throughout the years of child rearing – from baby massage classes, playgroups, schoolyards and classrooms to teen sleep-overs. As discussed in this chapter and in chapter 5, there are many haunting images of men and children in relationships that stretch public expectations of what is viewed as normal and within the range of 'social acceptability'; these include Archie standing in the schoolyard and a woman 'coming to check [him] out'; Doug looking through the school fence talking to 'this group of girls' as the teacher runs towards him; Burt's comments about how parents were 'nervous because a man wandering through the school is unusual'; and the worries of Jesse about 'a couple of guys who used to come to the park and were hanging out' around children.

With each passing year and the increased presence of fathers in parents' social venues, the perception of men's presence as disruptive has gradually eased or even dissipated. Nevertheless, suspicion can be ignited quickly, most notably when unknown men linger in sites where children gather (parks, playgrounds, schoolyards), when fathers care for the children of others, or when single fathers host girls' sleep-over parties. The fit between male embodiment and other embodied subjects is commonly the issue (see also Williams, 1992).

As described in chapter 2, bodies matter in certain times and contexts, while in others they do not. Theoretically speaking, bodies are regarded as contingent and their effects vary across particular spaces, and over time. That is, there is no 'true nature of the body but rather it is a process and its meanings and capacities will vary according to its context' (Gatens, 1996, 57). Contingent and variable meanings in different contexts and the sites and times where gender does or does not matter are examples of borderwork and border crossing. I turn to this discussion again in the next section.

Borderwork: Mothering and Fathering as Moral Identities

The concept of borderwork shines a spotlight on spaces and times where gender boundaries or borders are instigated. Fathers' sense of themselves as moral beings – how they define themselves as and act as interactive subjects in public settings and how they are judged in turn by others – are integral parts of their daily experiences in parenting society. Their movements, in Goffman's terms, are both practical and moral. Thinking about mothers and fathers as moral beings entails a recognition that their decisions and courses of action are made in interactive contexts with 'reference to other people' (Finch & Mason, 1993, 61). They are also made in relation to the way they think and feel they should be acting as women and men, and as mothers and fathers. Could it be that mothering and fathering as separate moral identities are one of the best examples of borderwork in adult life? Parallel to prevalent childhood memories of schoolyard interactions that pit girls against boys in the schoolyard, or boys chasing girls (or vice versa), mothering and fathering, particularly in the early years, may constitute an equally powerful and memorable gender divide in adult life. In this instance, men are neither pitted against women, nor indeed chasing them, but men and women are positioned on opposite sides of a symbolic gender divide.

All fourteen mothers interviewed express the view that mothering and fathering are dissimilar identities and states of being. There is much reflective stumbling over this issue and a great deal of discussion, but all the women at some point in their interview articulate that mothering and fathering are fundamentally different as moral identities.[6] Such difference plays out in several ways, three of which are explored below. First is the confirmation of the issue, as explored partially in chapter 4, that both fathers and mothers believe in a distinctive and profoundly deeper connection between mothers and children; second is the issue of *worry* as women's way of expressing their moral responsibility; and third is the view that the experience of a primary breadwinning mother is unlike that of a primary breadwinner father.

Keeping in Touch Emotionally

In their interviews, mothers move back and forth from the view that mothering and fathering are the same to the view that in spite of some overlap there are differences between mothers and fathers. Linda, a high school teacher married to Peter, expresses this shifting position particularly well: 'I think we are different parents. We have a lot of common elements. As a *mother*, I am very concerned with keeping in touch with them emotionally. I think Peter is too. Like talking to Blake – he is very sensitive and so on. But I want to connect with him on that very emotional level. He's at school all day now, but I still want to maintain that connection. That is very important to me.'

Peter adds to the conversation that if the roles were reversed and he was out at work all day, he 'may not recognize the importance' of the emotional connection between parent and child and thus 'wouldn't give it the importance that I've learned to give it.'

Nina, a psychotherapist, summarizes the view of all fourteen mothers in the study in recognizing shifts in 'socialized expectations' and that there is not 'necessarily anything intrinsic about being a female that makes you a good parent.' Nevertheless, in her joint interview with Mitchell, she spends a long time reflecting on mothering and fathering and reasons that 'being a mom is different from being a dad.'

When I ask Nina where she thinks this comes from, she again echoes the views of other mothers as well as fathers in making the link to how embodiment matters: 'I think part of it has to do with certainly early connection with the child. I think the mother is connected just by being the vessel that the child is carried in. I don't think that means that fathers can't be connected to their children. But I think that it starts earlier on with the mother and it changes the nature of the connection.'

Worry: 'The Influence That I'm Having on Them'

In households, mothers are the main worriers. Fathers *do* worry, and fathers who spend ample time with children find themselves worrying more than they ever thought possible. Moreover, as expressed in chapter 2, Joe and Cheryl speak about the differences between *vocal worry* and *quiet worry* and perhaps it is the case that men may internalize the worry and let it remain unspoken. As Joe puts it in his joint interview with Cheryl, 'I'm not as vocal about it as you are. That's the only difference. I sort of internalize it and I hold it in and I convince myself that things will work out.' Nevertheless, even when mothers are at work all day or when mothers have joint custody, both mothers and fathers say that mothers are the primary worriers. Mothers worry about their children's emotional, academic, social, and physical well-being and development. It may well be that worry is a vessel for holding on to the moral weight of raising children. In this vein, Kathy's words are worth repeating: 'A man wouldn't worry because he knows he will survive if something happens to his kids. I don't know if I would. I would survive, but I would be a different person. It would scar me for life.'

Mothers also seem to worry more about their influence on their children and whether, reiterating the concern of Kate Reddy in the Pearson novel *I Don't Know How She Does It*, they are being 'proper mothers' or 'the other sort.' Natasha and Tom express this well:

> TOM I think men are less concerned with transmitting whatever influences they have on the kids. I find that you're really preoccupied with what you're giving the kids ...
>
> NATASHA And the influence that I'm having on them. You know, if I give them this or do that, will that screw them up?

The Perceived Difference between Mothers and Fathers as Primary Breadwinners: 'As a Woman ... I Understand the Work That He Does'

Linda emphasizes that whether the primary breadwinner is a mother or a father is the key difference between mothering and fathering. 'If I was a man with a stay-at-home mother, I think I would have a different view of his work than what I have as a woman with a husband who stays at home. As a woman I appreciate and don't take for granted and understand the work that he does in a way that maybe many working dads don't feel about their stay-at-home wives. So I think I have more insight and more empathy for him and his role than a man would have in my situation.' Most of the mothers concur with this. As discussed in chapters 3 and 4, female partners of stay-at-home husbands come in at the end of the day 'full-fledged' to take over the domestic labour.

In sum, borderwork in mothering and fathering is expressed first for fathers in terms of the separate but relational identities of mothers and fathers and second for both women and men in the belief that there is a gender divide in emotional connection, with that of mothers being more profound. In spite of these instances of separate moral identities for mother and fathers, it is also the case that there is flexibility and fluidity in border constructions around mothering and fathering.

Border Crossings

When girls and boys cross into groups and activities of the other gender... they challenge the oppositional structure of traditional gender arrangements [...] [I]ncidents of crossing may chip away at traditional ideologies and hold out new possibilities.

(Thorne, 1993, 133)

Fathers can and do cross into the 'groups and activities' associated with emotional responsibility and community responsibility, and in doing so, 'they challenge the oppositional structure of traditional gender arrangements' around parenting. It is the identities and activities associated with moral responsibility, however, that are particularly difficult to change. Moral responsibilities hold the crux of what it means to be a mother or to be a father. As Martha McMahon argues, 'Motherhood ... has much to do with moral identities' (McMahon, 1995, 264).

Motherhood and fatherhood cut to the core who we are, as men and women, in relation to others and in our communities and larger social worlds. Thus, the question 'Do men mother?' meets its greatest challenge here. We must ask, then, What resources help fathers to cross the gender divide in moral responsibilities and identities? What helps them to break down the binary distinctions between the moral identities of mothering and fathering? Moreover, do such crossings indeed 'chip away at traditional ideologies and hold out new possibilities?' (Thorne, 1993, 133). That is, do fathers take on new moral identities as a result of crossing into the female-dominated and feminine-defined terrain of caregiving?

It is worth drawing again on Barrie Thorne's discussion of the resources that assist boys and girls to make successful gender crossings. In particular, she highlights how certain resources, most notably 'resources of masculinity' (Thorne, 1993, 123), assist with boys' border crossings. The concept of resources of masculinity is akin to hegemonic masculinity with its emphasis on being part of the dominant male group – white, middle class, and heterosexual. It is thus interesting to examine how having such resources assists them with ensuring that their sense of masculinity is not threatened, or, when immersed in feminine-defined activities, that their masculinity is not 'on the line' (Morgan, 1992, 99). We have seen examples in this study where the intersections, first, between masculinity and social class and, second, masculinity and heterosexuality are reinforced for fathers caring for children. Third, we have noted that border crossings exist in the changes in the moral identities of fathers actively parenting without the presence of mothers. That is, the men take on qualities that resemble everyday understandings of mothering. Finally, moral transformations in fathers provides evidence of more fluid, less binary, practices and ideologies of mothering and fathering.

Resources of Masculinity – Social Class:
'It Might Be Different If I Was a Plumber'

To be placed in a position of primary caregiver without having achieved success as a breadwinner signals something out of sync with what many communities consider a socially acceptable moral identity for a male and for a father. Fathers without jobs or those in low-income jobs, particularly single fathers, can be viewed with particular suspicion in communities, as were the thirteen single fathers in the study in low-income or low-status occupations or between jobs. Stay-at-home fathers fare slightly better, although not working can still spark community alarm bells if it seems that the father may have lost his job and was not in his caring situation due to a family choice. Theo, who left his job in the high-tech sector says, 'Everybody assumed I was laid off.' James, a gay and recently divorced father who took a four-month paternity leave says, 'I think there is still a stigma for men with staying at home particularly around other men. I can't tell you how many times people ask as a first liner, "So, what do you do for a living?" When I answered, "I stay at home," most wondered, "Well, what happened?"'

Henry, who is currently out of work, remarks that his lower social class combined with the fact that he is currently out of work may be the reason why his house is not seen as an acceptable option for his daughter's sleepovers: 'My daughter sleeps over at a friend's place right across the street, and her friend never comes back. I push it, in the sense that it isn't fair. I actually try to mention it to the parents and stuff, but it's no big deal. They live in a nice big detached house. The girl has two full sets of parents that both live in nice big detached houses with multiple cars, that kind of thing. And I live in this town house co-op place.'

Jacob, a physician in training (who used to be a carpenter) says that sleepovers have not been a problem at his house, either for his two sons or for his eleven-year-old daughter. He reflects that this and his acceptance as a frequent helper in his children's schools may be rendered unproblematic partly because his is a high-status occupation: 'I am involved in the school. I help out on field trips. I go in and help to read whatever I can. I am also the head-lice coordinator. Once or twice a month I go and look at heads! I know the teachers and the principal and a lot of the kids. I also know them from ringette and hockey. I feel very accepted. Being a doctor may be part of it. It might be different if I was a plumber.'

A key resource of hegemonic masculinity – that of social status acquired through being a family provider, especially in a high-income or high-status profession – helps to increase fathers' ability to cross into socially acceptable moral identities as caregivers, while also cushioning them from being viewed with suspicion. What is playing out here are the links between hegemonic masculinity and earning. In effect, the economically unsuccessful male caring for children represents a form of double jeopardy because he is judged as being a failed male (e.g., not a breadwinner) (Thorne, 1993, 161) and as a deviant man (e.g., a primary caregiver). On the other hand, a man who is visibly providing economically for his family, or has temporarily left a career that allows him to do this, often feels more comfortable in himself and more accepted in his community as a caregiver.

Resources of Masculinity: Heterosexuality

Issues of social acceptability are especially acute for gay fathers, many of whom can face extra scrutiny over their role with children. Most of the gay fathers in my study confront multiple jeopardy (King 1990; cited in Ward, 2004, 82) discrimination because both gender and sexuality work against them. Six out of the nine gay fathers in the study mention that their communities do not know they are gay, or where they have come out, the response has been largely cold and unaccepting. Several examples can be given here. Aidan is a fifty-one-year-old divorced and gay father of a twenty-year-old daughter who now lives with him as she attends college in Toronto. He reflects on how he came out when she was in high school, and he was living in a small 'redneck town' of about a thousand inhabitants: 'That was hard [laughs]. When Helena started primary school, I was president of the PTA. And vice president of the Royal Canadian Legion. When I came out, if you will, there were a lot of shocked faces. People essentially just got quiet. People clearly felt quite awkward.'

Issues of exclusion on the basis of gender and sexuality are well expressed by Jean Marc, a French-Canadian forty-three-year-old gay and divorced father of seven-year-old twin boys. He lives in a small town in Ontario, and his ex-wife has sole custody. He took a four-month parental leave when his twins were infants and is very involved in their lives. It has been a gradual process, however since, following his coming-out, he was shunned by his wife and her family:

> I thought that she would be accepting and that she would understand this. It was the opposite. The kids were removed from the house. I was told to get out. I cried for a week. I was clinically depressed for quite some time. What really helped me was Gay Fathers of Toronto. And I got some counselling. It really hurt me that Monique didn't want joint custody. That really cut me to the quick. I think she was absolutely terrified of me taking the kids to Toronto and maybe bringing them into some kind of immoral lifestyle.

Even though Jean Marc is now involved with the children again, he is nevertheless disinclined to come out to the school and the wider community because he fears that its members, particularly if teachers know he is gay, will think less of him: 'I think it's important that I go and meet their teachers. I have not met any of their teachers yet [long sigh]. I am perhaps somewhat timid. I don't know. I just didn't know what to expect. It's a situation where their teacher is married to a police officer in the town. Everybody knows me. I want them to know that, hey, I'm a good father. I'm involved. And you may have heard that I'm gay and that's absolutely correct. But I'm not some riffraff off the street.'

Three of the nine gay fathers have had more successful border crossings due to greater community acceptance of diversity in parenting, combined with organizations that have provided both support and information for gay fathers in their coming-out processes. Such resources are more available in larger urban settings where there is a rich heterogeneity of lifestyles and a positive acknowledgement of such choices. Bernard, for example, who lives in Toronto and has shared custody of a four-year-old son with two lesbian mothers, finds his situation is palatable since 'there are other children at the school who have two dads or two moms. So he is not alone there. We live in a progressive area.' Similar stories of acceptance are told by Ray and Carson, who have adopted an infant girl and are 'embraced by the community,' and for Harrison, who has organized meetings for Gay Fathers of Toronto and has built up a support network and an awareness around gay fathering in his community.

In attempting to 'successfully cross the gender divide' (Thorne, 1993, 61), gay fathers often have to demonstrate that they can blend into parenting settings so that gender and sexuality lose critical significance. The intersections of gender, class, and sexuality can act as powerful resources of masculinity to cushion, or exacerbate in a negative way, men's presence here. Men of low income or lower social status as well as gay men highlight the constantly shifting gender borders and that the everyday spaces that men and women inhabit represent power and processes of inclusion and exclusion (Buss, 2004; G. Rose, 1993). These gender borders, or boundaries, are thus both spatial and ideological (Buss, 2004; Thorne, 1993).

Fathers without Mothers: '... Like a Mother'

In writing about the moral transformations experienced by women in the process of becoming mothers, McMahon writes that 'becoming a mother can provide some women with symbolic and relational opportunities for human experiences, that, when experienced by men have been called heroic: that is, transformative of self and potentially redemptive of society' (265). In chapter 4, I referred to some of the emotional shifts that occur as a result of men on their own caring for children. In that chapter, I described Roy, a sole custodial father, who was forced to find the 'soft father' within himself because, when he was being harsh with his four-year-old son, he didn't 'have that mother side in the house, a mother to turn around to me and say, "would you just go away?" And for her to take care of things.' Golin, an African-Canadian sole-custody father of four school-age children has to 'remind' himself to 'set boundaries' because he can 'get lost in the nurturing.' The fluidity of motherly and fatherly nurturing becomes especially apparent when mothers are temporarily or permanently unavailable, thus providing spaces and moments for men to experience 'symbolic and relational opportunities for human experiences.'

Other examples can be given here of fathers developing unexpected feelings of responsibility that, in McMahon's terms, are 'transformative of self.' In the case of Manuel and Julie, her many years of shift work and her reduced time at home encouraged, or existed parallel to, Manuel's development of the kind of moral identity and responsibility that resembles mothering. Manuel begins to speak and Julie poignantly completes his sentence:

> MANUEL For me, it was like I had given birth to them. Since they were born, something was put on Lyse and Enrique. I am going to look after them. I am going to be here all the time. I think it was like an emotional and physical attachment to them. It wasn't just like a father but it was –
> JULIE – like a mother.

Ray, gay father of an adopted baby girl, initially thought that 'I wouldn't be able to give her that enchanted attention that I saw mothers have with children.' Yet he expresses his overwhelming surprise at the discovery of his profound connection with his daughter: 'I'm just overwhelmed by her. I'm just crazy about her. There's no precedent for my behaviour. I am completely surprised by it.'

For Ryan, a military general and a sole-custody father of two, his time on his own with his children 'has been an incredible growing experience for me because I have been very male orientated my whole life, and now I have had to broaden the way I approach life. Whereas if I had stayed married, I probably would have kept going on my own little track. *I've become much more in tune.*'

Although resources of masculinity (social class and heterosexuality) and having the opportunity to parent in spaces and times without the presence of the child's mother can increase the social acceptability and the moral verification of fathers as primary or shared caregivers, is it the case that these fathers also cross into new moral identities as fathers? That is, do such measures allow fathers to begin to chip away at binary conceptions of mothering and fathering so that the differences between mothering and fathering become less influential and the similarities between these as identities and practices are emphasized?

Moral Transformations in Fathers

McMahon asks, 'And what do moral implications for children hold for men's identities?' (McMahon, 1995, 264). From my work on fathering, I infer that when women move over, or are temporarily emotionally and practically unavailable, men can come to know the depths of what it means to be fully responsible for a child. It is this responsibility for others that profoundly changes them as men. That is, having the opportunity to care engenders changes in men that can be seen as moral transformations. Three such changes can be mentioned. First, fathers notice personal changes in themselves as men. Second, many come to recognize the value and the skill involved in caregiving work. Third, men begin to question what social commentators have referred to as 'male stream' concepts of work, and to adopt perspectives traditionally espoused by women on the need for work-family balance.

GENERATIVE CHANGES IN FATHERS:
'MY HARD EDGES HAVE SOFTENED'

A first change as a result of caregiving is that fathers note ensuing personal and generative (Hawkins, Christiansen, Sargent, & Hill, 1993; Hawkins & Dollahite, 1996) changes as they make the shift from worker to carer. Aaron, for example, who used to be lawyer in a 'cut-throat' environment 'where you have to be strong' says that 'my hard edges have softened' and he has had a steep learning curve 'about sharing, feelings, and spending time with them, sort of mellowing out a little.' In a similar way, many fathers also find that their time at home gives them the opportunity to reflect on what it is they actually want to do once they return to the workforce. Frank, who has been at home with two children for four years, considers that this time has been 'a real personal-growth experience for me' and would not have realized that his strengths and interests are in social work and not in accounting, his previous field. In his words, 'When you're wrapped up in everyday work, you don't reflect on where you are and where you're going.'

THE VALUE OF CAREGIVING WORK:
'IT'S THE HARDEST WORK I HAVE EVER DONE'

Second, many fathers mention that parenting is the most difficult job they have ever done. Archie, at home for seven years, says, 'It's the hardest work I have ever done in my whole life' and 'it's like I have a full-time job but I don't get paid.' Men also come to appreciate how vitally important, yet socially devalued, caregiving work is. They thus add their voices to the chorus of generations of women who have argued for the valuing of unpaid work (Crittenden, 2001; Luxton, 1997; Luxton & Vosko, 1998; Waring, 1998). Joe, an Aboriginal stay-at-home father of two says, 'This Mr. Mom business – here I am complaining about it, and women have been putting up with for hundreds of years.'

Rory, who was mentioned in the introduction to this book, sees caring for his son Tristan as a 'job,' and more specifically *his* job: 'I know what my job is here ... I will make sure that everything is going right in Tristan's life, because that is my job.'

WORK-FAMILY BALANCE ISSUES

For some fathers there is a change in their perceptions of an adequate home-work balance. This is particularly the case for stay-at-home fathers, many of whom are adamant that they can arrange their working hours to remain very involved with their children if and when they go back to full-time employment. While issues of home–work balance have been configured for decades as largely women's issues, with women being the ones who make adjustments in work schedules to accommodate children (Brannen & Moss, 1991; Hochschild, 1989), stay-at-home fathers come to join their female partners in recognizing the need for what researchers have recently termed greater 'work–life integration' (Johnson, Lero, & Rooney, 2001). In two-parent families, many men commented that their ideal home–work arrangement was that both parents worked part-time, or that one parent worked from home.

Craig, for example, notes that he has changed as a result of being at home with his twin sons: He says, 'Dads don't have that drive when they walk in the door from work to connect with their kids. Some dads do if they have a certain personality, but I would say a good majority of dads say, "I've got to decompress. I want to read my paper. Leave me alone – that kind of thing."' Nevertheless, Craig says that he anticipates that when he goes back to work, 'I think I'll miss them terribly through the day. I think I'm very bonded with them.'

As mentioned in the opening of this book, Sam, who has been at home for five years, thinks that his wife, a lawyer, should also have the opportunity to stay home for a while. He speaks from his recognition of the benefits of close and sustained connection with his children and the loss that occurs if parents do not take this 'chance in your life to do that': 'if we had another child, I would want to go back to work and have my wife stay at home. If you don't have a chance to raise them yourself, that is a great loss.'

Conclusions

This chapter has unpacked the question, 'Do men mother?' through the lens of moral responsibility and has demonstrated that the demand for mothers to meet a level of social acceptability, as identified by Sara Ruddick, is bound by many gendered structural and ideological constraints. Framing social acceptability as a set of moral responsibilities and the shoulds and oughts of parenting, women feel judged for not caring enough while fathers who are primary caregivers feel judged for not earning. The recurrent comments of feeling as if they have failed as a man or that they are not being a good man underpin many of the narratives of fathers who have given up earning or have pushed earning into a secondary place in their lives.

As I have argued throughout this chapter, caring for others is intricately connected to 'people's identities as moral beings,' which 'are being constructed, confirmed and reconstructed – identities as a reliable son, a generous mother, a caring sister or whatever it might be' (Finch & Mason, 1993, 170). Similarly, fathers work to find a sense of what it means to be a good father from within a social and cultural location and 'with reference to other people' (Finch & Mason, 1993, 61). While judged as earners, fathers are also differentially judged as caregivers when they can be viewed as incompetent or through a community lens that is marred with suspicion. In spite of enormous changes in the social conditions under which men parent, there are still residues of a social fear around close relations between men and children, particularly between men and the children of others. Such suspicions differ from rural to urban areas and are expressed in other ways for low-income fathers and gay fathers. Nevertheless, what is striking is how the gendered quality of such scrutiny cuts across class, ethnicity, and sexuality. Both women and men comment on this.

This chapter has put forward several ways of understanding how deeply gendered structures and expectations come to matter in the lives of women and men. These include men and women's social worlds, the gendered ideologies and psy complexes that transmit gendered ideas and ideals, and the weight of hegemonic masculinity in relation to earning and the devaluation of the traditionally feminine. Finally, embodied aspects of parenting matter greatly in how men and women feel about themselves as parents – and how they feel they are viewed by others. The sites where embodiment matters in the social acceptability and the practical and moral movements of fathers on the social landscapes of parenting include recent versions of the moms and tots groups (community playgroups), schoolyards, classrooms, female-dominated venues, as well as single fathers' hosting girls' sleepover parties.

Martha McMahon has argued that 'men and women tend to experience themselves and self-other relationships in gendered ways because social situations are deeply gendered, both in the structures that organize them and in the expectations we bring to them' (McMahon, 1995, 269). It may well be the case that parenting itself, in particular contexts and times, is the best example of borderwork. Set within 'deeply gendered' structures and expectations, the view that mothering and fathering are separate, but relational, identities pervades my interviews with fathers and mothers. This is found in mothers' and fathers' descriptions of a mother's extra-special bond (whether envisioned as symbolic or real), the tendency for mothers to invest greater worry about children, and their overwhelming propensity to take over the care of children at the end of their employment day.

If gender borders exist in parenting responsibilities, I would argue they are most firmly rooted with regard to moral responsibilities. Yet there is some variation in the firmness of the gender borders. In this vein, this chapter draws on Barrie Thorne's discussion of 'resources of masculinity' and how they can assist men to cross gender borders. Being economically successful and exhibiting definitive signs of heterosexuality can assist fathers with easier transitions whereby they feel capable as caregivers or, more important, feel that they are judged as capable by others. A low-income or unemployed father faces a form of double jeopardy, whereby he feels judged as a *failed* male for not being a primary or successful breadwinner and as a *deviant* man in his role as a primary caregiver. A gay father often faces what theorists have termed multiple jeopardy because gender, sexuality, and, in some cases, social class work against him.

While, as persuasively argued by McMahon, many women experience profound moral transformations when they become mothers, my study, as detailed in this chapter, indicates that such transformations can also occur for fathers. Fathers find that their 'hard edges have softened,' they recognize the value in caring work, and they articulate a commitment to taking on what has traditionally been a balancing act for women – that of combining family responsibilities with paid employment. Some authors have argued that such moves symbolize mothering practices and identities (see Risman, 1987, 2004; Coltrane, 1996), but my argument is that these fathers are not mothering and they are not mothers. Rather, a key insight that emerges from this study is that these *fathers are reconfiguring fathering and masculinities*.

This latter point will be further developed in the final chapter of this book, where I pull together the three responsibilities in order to reflect on the 'Do men mother?' question and to show how the question itself draws attention to what is revealed as well as obscured within it. I also draw together my study's key theoretical and empirical contributions and suggest areas for further investigation.

PART THREE

Conclusion and Postscript: Men and Fathering

7 Conclusion: Men Reconstructing Fathering

Introduction: Old Beginnings

I began this book describing unexpected feelings of vertigo as I listened to stay-at-home fathers speak about their relationships with the children. Approaching its end, I return to the initial stages of my project on fatherhood and to a particular incident with a small group of single fathers that took me by surprise. It occurred in the winter of 2000, when I had invited some fathers to Carleton University to participate in a series of focus groups. The first was with five sole-custody fathers. It was a bitterly cold Canadian night, and fathers shyly trooped in and sat at the long table we had set up in a classroom. After about two hours of speaking about their experiences as single fathers and some of the issues of importance to them, I asked them a final question that reached into the realm of possibilities: 'In an ideal world, what resources or supports would you like to see for single fathers?'

As I sat waiting for one of them to start the discussion, I expected to hear that they wanted greater social support and societal acceptance, more programs and policies directed at single fathers. What I heard instead was an awkward silence that filled the room. I waited. The silence continued. Feet shuffled under the table. 'Well?' I probed. 'Any volunteers?' Steve, a sole-custody father of four children living in a small town outside Ottawa, spoke first: 'An ideal world would be one with a father and a mother. We'd be lying if we pretended that wasn't true. How can there be an ideal world without a mother for the children?'[1] Nods of agreement followed, along with murmurs of approval for Steve's response. This had not occurred to me. The complete intertwining of mothering and fathering, especially for fathers, had simply not crossed my mind as a possible answer. Many fathers had such bitter experiences of separation and divorce, so I had expected them to make a special claim for fathers as primary caregivers.[2] Instead, what these fathers exhibited in their quiet statements and nods of agreement was a strong sense of the connectedness of mothering and fathering and the relational deficits felt by men in the absence or loss of a significant relationship in their lives.

These ideas were confirmed again and again in my individual interviews with single fathers. Indeed, as mentioned in chapter 2, the interviews were haunted by the unseen presence of the child's mother. Perhaps most notable is how the majority of fathers' interviews open with a remark about the children's mother. Each of my interviews with fathers began with the simple question, 'How did you come to be in this situation of primary caregiver of your children?' Separated and divorced fathers always begin their narratives by describing a stark moment of rupture, most notably when their wives leave. Dennis, an Aboriginal-Chinese father, begins his story this way: 'Her mom and I didn't get along.' Mick, a truck driver and sole-custody father, started with: 'Her mom, my ex-wife, was an alcoholic.' Morgan, a joint-custody father of two, commences his fathering story as follows: 'Not to sound bitter or anything, but she left me for another man.'

Many stay-at-home fathers provided similar openings to their narratives. Gary, a stay-at-home father of three began with 'How did I come to be a stay-at-home father? My wife owns her own business. She's a hairdresser, and because I'm a carpenter I'm also very flexible with the hours. So it worked out that we did this.'

Joe, an Aboriginal father at home with two preschool daughters, starts his interview by saying, 'I wasn't working. Well, *she* decided. She said "I'm pregnant, and one of us has to stay at home with the baby. I don't want daycare." I agreed. I said, "Okay, you make a lot more money than I can." So that's when it started.'

Throughout my four years of interviewing fathers and in the writing of this book, I have often returned to those unexpected beginnings to ponder what they mean as examples of mothering and fathering. There are several important revelations in these seemingly simple acts of beginning their fathering narratives *with mothers*. First, fathers rely profoundly on mothers to define their own fathering. As detailed in chapters 4, 5 and 6 of this book, the mother-led quality of fathering emerges as a key finding in this study (see also Backett, 1982; Cowan & Cowan, 2000; Daly, 2002; Deutsch, 1999; Gerson, 1993; Greif, 1985; Lewis, 1986;

McBride & Mills, 1993; Parke, 1996; Stueve & Pleck, 2003). A related point is that fathers do not identify themselves as mothers or refer to the work they do as mothering. Men view themselves as fathers, and their fathering practices and identities evolve in relation to those enacted by mothers. Thus, while it is not always clear what the essence of fathering *is*, what is certain for men is that it *is not* mothering.

Second, the relational losses felt by men when their marriage breaks down were stronger than I would have anticipated. It is as though hegemonic masculinity, with its emphasis on autonomy and self-reliance, collapses in those moments of crisis to reveal the hidden influences of more stereotypical feminine qualities of connection, relationships, and interdependence. Several fathers made it clear to me that they were looking for another women to replace the mother of their children. Even more memorable were the moments in a few interviews with divorced fathers when I was overwhelmed by the depth of emotion expressed by men about these losses. One father, Christian, who was seventy-one years old, looked back over thirty years to the time when his marriage was dissolving. He began to sob as he recalled how they broke the news to their young son: 'I remember it well. He was sitting on the couch in his pyjamas, and we asked him what he would think if we separated.' Later when he had regained his composure, Christian added, *'Where there are wounds, they do heal. But there are always scars.'*

In addition to these findings on the relational and distinctly felt qualities of mothering and fathering, the mother-led dance within parenting, and the unexpected relational losses and scars that underpinned many of the single-father narratives, there are several concluding points that I want to develop in this final chapter. First, I return to the 'Do men mother?' question and pull together the varied dimensions of my response. Ultimately I deconstruct the question. Second, I underline the key theoretical and empirical contributions that can be gleaned from this study and, where implicated, suggest areas for future study. Finally, the book ends with a few select reflections on changing mothering and fathering.

Do Men Mother?

Three Responsibilities: Emotional, Community, and Moral

This book has aimed to solve the puzzle of women and domestic responsibility by focusing on men's role. As indicated in my introduction, I have sought to describe, name, and understand the care that men provide, specifically in terms of the way this care is organized, experienced, and understood and with what repercussions for men, women, children, families, and society. In order to grapple with this question of men and care, this book has been positioned around a question that has often been asked, assumed, or argued in scholarship and popular thinking on men, women, and mothering. The idea that men can mother has, quite simply, been argued too many times to ignore. My response has been to chart a path between a positive and negative answer by drawing attention to both the similarities and differences between men's and women's ways of parenting.

In chapter 4 ('Emotional Responsibility'), I respond to the question Do men mother? by investigating the issue of emotional responsibility or, in Sara Ruddick's terms, the first demand on mothers for preservation or protective care. This study of men as primary caregivers provides a partially affirmative answer to the question of men and mothering by highlighting that men care and nurture in ways that very much resemble what are often considered maternal responses. The overwhelming picture painted by both mothers and fathers is that the practices of mothering and fathering have much in common. Nevertheless, at the edges of these sometimes symmetrical practices, gender differences play out in several ways. As described in chapter 4, there are differences between mothers and fathers in their overall style of nurturing, with fathers emphasizing fun, playfulness, physical activities, sports, the outdoors, practicality in emotional response, and the promotion of independence and risk taking with older children. The examples of men roughhousing with infants, getting the children outdoors, being physical and active, and the promotion of children's independence occurred too often in the narratives to ignore. While some fathers certainly do not fit this mould in all instances, the majority of fathers do.[3] An example of how fathers and mothers differ in approach to emotional responsibility is well summarized by Penny, who says in her couple interview with her husband, Carl, 'There *are* differences, such as nursing, which only I can do. And in the stereotype that has actually borne out in our situation of you being more rough and tumble and me being the more cuddly one.'

In chapter 5 ('Community Responsibility'), I build on Sara Ruddick's second demand on mothers, to facilitate children's social growth, as I explore a broadly held idea of community responsibility as an integral part of mothering. This robust conception of the domestic implies that caring for children occurs not only within households but also between households and between households and other social institutions (i.e., schools, doctors' and dentists' offices, workplaces, and community venues). The fathers in my study give varied names to community responsibility, including *the higher care, administration* (as opposed to *maintenance*) and *seeing the need* (as opposed to *'filling the need'*). While mothers, in both joint-custody and stay-at-home-father families, still take on most of the organization and networking related to children's lives, there have been tremendous changes in households and communities, with fathers taking a greater share of this work and responsibility. Most notably, some sole-custody and stay-at-home fathers take on most of this responsibility and devise their own strategies for accomplishing this part of parenting. Fathers also develop their own parenting networks, through their involvement in children's sports and in community activities and by connecting with other fathers who are taking advantage of increased fathering programs in community settings. In chapter 5, I describe four styles of paternal involvement in community responsibility; these include fathers being *assistants, partners,* or *managers.* Across all these approaches to parental responsibility, the majority of fathers are also *network builders,* as they construct their own distinct paternal networks that exit alongside female-dominated ones.

The third and final responsibility, that of moral responsibility for children, is very much tied up with the shoulds and oughts of what it currently means to be a good mother or a proper mother and a good father or a responsible father. Chapter 6 argues that in spite of dramatic changes in the past few decades in women's and men's lives as workers and as caregivers, the changes have not been fully felt at the level of ideology nor in gendered normative assumptions about what has been referred to as the balance between 'cash and care' (Hobson & Morgan, 2002, 2; see also Beaujot, 2000).

Across the three responsibilities, I have employed the concept of borderwork to capture the constant emphasis on gender differences in parenting. As drawn from the work of Barrie Thorne, borderwork illuminates how, in particular places and times (whether measured in years passing or by the stages of child rearing), gender boundaries or borders are sometimes erected. In chapter 4, I draw attention to two recurring instances of borderwork in fathers' and mothers' narratives of emotional responsibility: first, gendered responses to the child who is hurt or has fallen down, and second, deeply held beliefs in the intimate connection between mother and child. In chapter 5, instances of borderwork in community responsibility highlight the contexts where gender differences exist as fathers create and maintain community networks; included here are men in female-dominated playgroups, fathers and girls' sleepovers, and beliefs in gender-divergent friendship patterns, especially around children.

The five examples described in chapter 4 and chapter 5 can also be useful to show borderwork in relation to moral responsibility. Fathers' and mothers' practices and identities are, in Goffman's terms, both practical and moral; that is, mothers and fathers make decisions in practical and relational terms but also in terms of how they think they ought to act in gendered social worlds. In chapter 6, I elaborate on this point and argue that mothering and fathering as separate moral identities may constitute one of the best examples of borderwork in adult life. Much like memories of schoolyard contests where girls and boys are opposed, mothering and fathering, particularly in the early years, can also present a striking gender divide in adult life.

Mothering and fathering are also deemed borderwork because the processes by which men come to be primary caregivers start with the deeply marked gender division between moral expectations for mothers and fathers – when mothers take on a different moral identity to that which is socially, culturally, and ideologically prescribed. It is as though fathers look across this metaphorical gender divide to what women are doing and then co-construct their own actions in relation, sometimes in reaction, to those maternal decisions and movements. Many of the fathers made a point of saying that they did not grow up expecting to be primary caregivers. As described in chapter 4, most fathers interviewed for this study believe that fathers and mothers have a different connection to their children and that the one held by the mother is stronger, vaster, and more profound. Their words throughout this book represent only a fragment of the many pages of interview transcripts that record fathers' views on this. Tom says that his wife is 'more inclined to go the extra mile to be emotionally connected', while Alistair notes that 'women are more sensitive and more inclined to be emotionally involved.' Mitchell observes that the mother-child tie 'may be a spiritual connection,' Shahin comments in exasperation that 'the bond is vaster in women' and that 'I could never be a woman; I would die of exhaustion', while Sasha says, 'That is what men do not have – that extra, extra-special thing with the children.'

Yet in spite of such strong affirmations of gender differences in

parenting and distinct practices and identities of mothering and fathering, my interviews with fathers and mothers also reveal significant
movement and flow within households that disrupt the seemingly
binary picture. As shown in my discussion of border crossings, woven
through chapters 4, 5, and 6, women's mothering, space, time, and
embodiment can matter greatly in some contexts, while ethnicity, social
class, and sexuality matter in others. As demonstrated throughout this
book, intersectionality plays out in various ways, with gender often the
axis of differentiation in parenting but with diverse and unique intersections mapped out between gender, class, ethnicity, and sexuality in
relation to emotional, community, and moral responsibilities.

Movement and Flow between Responsibilities

We can also discern intimate linkages among emotional, community,
and moral responsibilities. The taking-on of emotional responsibility,
for example, has implications for the ways in which fathers' moral
responsibilities are framed and felt within society. As detailed in chapter 6, fathers who have the opportunity to be emotionally connected to
their children can experience generative changes that influence their
understanding of masculinities and what it means to be a man in contemporary society. Moreover, fathers taking on parts of the emotional
responsibility for children can help to alleviate mothers' worries and
guilt that they are not doing enough for their children. The moral
responsibility to care has been a source of women's strength and
power, but when it is a compulsion to care rather than a choice, moral
responsibility can also become a source of tremendous grief, depression, and sadness (see Mauthner, 2002).

There are also links between community responsibility and moral
responsibility. Fathers spending time in community spaces with young
children can help alleviate community suspicions of men and their relationships with children and challenge the expectations and assumptions that only women can care for children. Moreover, women being
freed from all or most of the community responsibility for children
opens up the opportunity to pursue their own interests – be they personal, political, economic, or social. Would Kate Reddy, the protagonist
in Alison Pearson's novel, have stood 'distressing' pies in the middle of
the night if she had a husband who could help with the baking for her
daughter's school social event? Many of the men in my study do indeed
take on baking and cooking in equal or greater measures than the

women in their lives. As Harry says, 'My wife would get upset. They'd phone from the church and ask her to make something. She'd say, "I don't do the cooking or baking in this house. You ask my husband!"'

While the moral responsibilities for caring and earning are deeply ingrained and certainly do not shift easily, men's greater involvement with children of all ages does, in the words of Thorne (1993, 133), begin to 'chip away at traditional ideologies and hold out new possibilities' of differently framed moral responsibilities that have an impact on men, women, and children. Alexander, a law professor who took two periods of parental leave to care for his daughters, reflects on what would happen if 'gender and childcare operate differently':

> There is a historical sexual ambiguity operating between men and girls. We know that history – sexual abuse. This could relate to the fact that men have not been so deeply engaged with childcare. But I wonder if, culturally, men were much much more engaged in childcare, more involved with their kids, would it feel entirely different? Maybe if gender and childcare operated differently, there wouldn't have been that stark break in terms of that physical and emotional connection between father and daughter. And I could still have that – a different kind of physical connection with [his oldest daughter] Katherine.

The Problem with the Question Itself

As detailed in chapter 1, the Do men mother? question can engender agreement or disagreement, approval or disapproval. Working with the matter of men and mothering over the past four years and speaking to over a hundred fathers and a small group of mothers, I have arrived at the view that studying fathers' caregiving through the lens of men and mothering limits our views of fathers' caring. Further, I believe that the question itself is flawed. Listening to, and theorizing from, men's narratives and practices with the question 'Do men mother?' or even 'Can they mother?' implies that we are looking at fathering and fathers' experiences of emotional, community and moral responsibilities through a maternal lens. Thus, other ways of nurturing are pushed into the shadows and obscured (see also Lupton & Barclay, 1997; Richards, 1982; Smith, 1998; Stueve & Pleck, 2003). As argued in chapter 1, studying men's practices through female-centred identities and practices is not dissimilar to the types of scholarship strongly criticized by feminists scholar – that of studying women's lives through male-centred lenses. Questioning equality in whose terms means recognizing that men's terms may be missed if we use dominant understandings gleaned from research on women and mothering.

With regard to the issue of emotional responsibility, a maternal lens misses the ways that fathers promote children's independence and risk taking, while their fun and playfulness, physicality and outdoors approach to caring for young children are viewed only as second best, or invisible, ways of caring. Similarly, in terms of growth or community responsibility, the use of a maternal lens means that we miss the creative ways that fathers are beginning to form parallel networks to those that have traditionally been developed by and existed for mothers.

In addition to the problems that arise from the use of a maternal lens to study fathering, the question Do men mother? is also problematic for three other reasons. First, it carries the subversive implication that there is an 'ideal' kind of mother and also holds women firmly to the moral responsibility that they will be primary caregivers of children. While Ruddick writes against this assumption in the second edition of *Maternal Thinking* – recognizing that 'there is nothing foreordained about maternal response' (1995, xi) – her decision to nevertheless call this work mothering and not caring or parenting does inadvertently fall into the trap of holding mothers to a particular mother-child model (see Dietz, 1985), to a 'motherhood mandate' (see Russo, 1976), and to an ideology of 'intensive mothering' (Hays, 1996) that belie the complexity and diversity of mothering in practice. We know from research on low-income and single mothers throughout the world that many women mother in ways that combine what would be considered maternal and parental skills (Clarke, 1957; Collins, 1994; Scheper-Hughes, 1992; Segura, 1994), and that 'motherhood is a culturally formed structure with various meanings and subtexts' (Segura, 1994, 226).

Second, to claim that men can mother on the grounds that mothering is 'construed as *work* rather than as an *identity*' (Ruddick, 1995, xi; emphasis added) is to hold a distinction between practice and identity. While theoretically and heuristically interesting, it remains an untenable distinction because, in everyday practices, there is often a blurred line between who people think they *are* and what they *do*. I would argue that differing contexts can produce varying sets of identities and attitudes (Connell, 1987; Griffin, 1989; Thorne, 1993), but identities are nevertheless produced *in* and *through* social situations and through people's relationships with others (Bhabha, 1994; Gilligan, Brown, &

Rogers, 1990; Ireland, 1994).[4] As detailed in this book, mothers not only care for their children as maternal practice but also feel strong moral assumptions weighing on them as caregivers, just as men feel the heavy burden of social expectations and moral assumptions that they be breadwinners.

Third, to call fathers' practices of caregiving 'mothering' may render invisible other mothers who are also in the picture. For all the primary-caregiving fathers, there is often a mother somewhere on the scene. As stated in chapter 2, mothers are very present in the fathers' narratives. Sole-custody fathers, in a situation in which the mother has left or plays a secondary role, often look for another mother to share the care of their children – their own mother, an aunt, a sister, a female neighbour or a caregiver. In the nine gay-father households, there is a mother or other mothers actively involved in the children's lives. For stay-at-home fathers, mothers do not give up their caring, and most of them comment on the conflicts embedded in their decision to be at work while their male partner stays at home. As described in chapter 4, Denise, for example, wrestles with the possibility that she might be replaced as primary caregiver but is reassured when her young son calls her name in the middle of the night. As Nina states so strongly at the beginning of chapter 6, 'I'm perfectly comfortable with saying he's their primary caregiver ... but don't say that he's their mother. *I'm their mother!*'

The question 'Do men mother?' cuts to the heart of issues of gender equality and gender differences in contemporary society. I'm in agreement with Ruddick, who says, 'I remain unconvinced by arguments that there not only are but should be distinct paternal and maternal "roles" and "tasks"' (Ruddick, 1997, 206). Similarly, like Risman I agree that 'men *can* mother' (Risman, 1998, 46) and like Coltrane and Ruddick, I accept that 'maternal thinking' is something that fathers can develop (Coltrane, 1989, 489; Ruddick, 1995). Nevertheless, while they *can* develop ways of being and thinking that emulate what we consider stereotypical mothering behaviour or what Marilyn Friedman has called the 'symbolically feminine' (Friedman, 1993, 2000), fathers *do not* mother in practice, partly because mothering itself is a richly varied experience and institution (Rich, 1986). They also do not mother because the everyday social worlds, the embodied experiences of women and men, and the larger 'gender regime' (Connell, 1995, 2000) do not permit eliding of the two institutions and distinct identities. Rather than comparing fathers to mothers, we require novel ways of listening to and theorizing about fathers' approaches to parenting.

More effective questions to be grappled with are ones that explore how fathers enact their parental responsibilities and ultimately how they reinvent fathering.

Theoretical, Empirical, and Methodological Contributions of the Study

In addition to these points on the 'Do men mother?' question, this study also provides for several theoretical, empirical, and methodological contributions to the study of domestic life and to our understandings of gender differences and gender equality.

Methodological Insights: Gaining Access to Relational and Interactional Labour

The methodological contributions of this research evolved gradually as I moved step by step through the intellectually rich experience of conducting and constructing knowledge with and from men. As a woman navigating my way into male territory, I felt like an anthropologist in a foreign land. In grappling with narratives that differed from my own life experience, I employed several methodological strategies. First, I made an epistemological shift from subjects to narratives; that is, I did not attempt to *know* fathers but, rather, I attempted to *know something about their narratives*. Indeed, I have come to the view that this may be, as it were, *as good as it gets* for a researcher who is striving to make bold knowledge claims about the messy, illusive, and complex stories that emerge from people's everyday lives. A second methodological strategy is that I created interpretive communities to help make sense of fathers' and mothers' stories (see also Fish, 1980; Siltanen, Willis, & Scobie, under review). A final strategy, one that underpinned all the research in this book, is that of my reflexive stance as a researcher. Taking a reflexive position engenders interesting questions about how we name the lenses we use to make sense of social science narratives and the fine lines between ethnography and auto-ethnography (see Ellis, 2004; Ellis & Bochner, 2001). One way of working with this issue is highlighted in chapter 2, where I draw on a compelling metaphor from a the novel *Fugitive Pieces* by Anne Michaels. When I first came across the metaphor of the gossamer wall as a way of describing the intimate line that both divides and unites two people, it took my breath away. This image came back to me when I was writing about the challenges of distinguishing the line where my own thoughts ended and those of my research respondents began. I thus reflect, in chapter 2, on three gossamer walls that exist for us as researchers: between ourselves and our shadow selves; between ourselves and our research respondents; and between researchers and readers.

Aside from these general reflections on qualitative research, the arguments developed throughout this book underline some of the methodological concerns inherent in conducting research on domestic life, and particularly on domestic responsibility (see Doucet, 2001b; Leslie, Anderson, & Branson, 1991). The topic of housework is, as discussed in chapter 3, laden with sensitivity and differences of opinion as to who does it and how much gets done. Ultimately, household work and childcare, and especially domestic responsibilities, are intrinsically relational activities and identities. As described in chapters 4, 5 and 6, emotional, community, and moral responsibilities for children of all ages encompass feelings and activities deeply rooted in social relationships of interdependence that change over time. Taking responsibility for children and for the domestic life of children is not simply about tasks and burdens. It requires both labour and love (Graham, 1983). It implies knowing what needs to be done based on identified needs and acting to fill, or find others to fill, the needs (Balbo, 1987; Tronto, 1989; Sevenhuijsen, 1998). It is eminently interactional and is located in the social world of relationships between parents and children, and between parents and other people who are involved in caring for and having some responsibility for children. Quite simply, the responsibility for children cannot be reduced to tasks or time allocations.

There are strong methodological implications that arise from these points. The importance of interviewing both women and men, ideally together as well as separately, cannot be overstated. Both mothers and fathers have distinct and complementary perspectives on what actually occurs in domestic and intimate spaces, and both have vantage points on how mothering and fathering, as practices and identities, intersect or run parallel to each other.

Finally, this study draws attention to the need for innovative and creative methods of data collection to encourage women and men to discuss and reflect on the quality and locations of domestic work and responsibilities as well as what might shift their persistently gendered characteristics. As noted in chapter 2, the Household Portrait technique for collecting data on the division of domestic labour used in my couple interviews is just one participatory and visual tool that encourages couples to discuss the matters with each other. Indeed, one of the reasons why domestic responsibility has been insufficiently and inadequately defined and theorized may be related in part to the methods used to collect data on task distribution from individuals rather than focusing on the relational, ambiguous, taken-for-granted, invisible, and negotiated quality of domestic responsibility (but see Carrington, 1999). This work, as discussed in chapter 3, also interrogates the central terminology used in this field of study: that of 'gender *divisions* of domestic labour.' While the work of domestic life can certainly be *divided* between family members, the fact that it has strong relational dimensions leads me to suggest that this should be termed gender *relations* and *divisions of labour*.

Widening Our Understanding of Domestic Work and Responsibility

A key contribution of this book is that of widening current understandings of domestic work and responsibility. I have argued for a conception of domestic labour that includes non-routine maintenance work (i.e., household repair, renovation, and construction), and community work. These are areas where stay-at-home fathers *do* make strong contributions both to domestic labour and to the domestic economy. This is not to underplay arguments for greater symmetry between women and men's divisions of domestic labour, which is still largely weighted on the side of women, but it allows for greater visibility and recognition of what men actually *do*. Community labour such as involvement in school, community councils, and children's sports are places where fathers may find a comfortable fit that accounts for their gendered upbringing, their sense of masculinity, and their fathering.

A second way that my work helps broaden our conception of the domestic is that it confirms observations made over fifteen years ago by the British sociologist Lydia Morris when she argued that greater research was needed on 'the question of the permeability of household boundaries.' She wrote, 'Extra-household linkages have, however, remained an unelaborated aspect of the household approach in UK research, although there is sufficient evidence to suggest that this may represent a worthwhile topic for investigation' (Morris, 1990, 3).

The findings in this book confirm her view (see also Bell & Ribbens, 1994; Hertz, 1997; Hertz & Ferguson, 1998; Hessing, 1993; Uttal, 1996). Although much research has focused on the connections between paid work/employment and households/families, less emphasis has been given to the links between the social institution of the family and the wider 'institutional arena' of the community (Doucet, 2000; Goetz, 1995,1997). In addition, much can be gleaned from research on black families in the United States and from research in developing countries where inter-household and inter-institutional relations are more solidly explored and addressed (e.g., Collins, 1994, Moser, 1993).

Above and beyond these points on the widening of domestic *work*, a valuable contribution of the research in this book is in its theoretical and empirical understandings of domestic *responsibility*, most notably the responsibility for children. This work also expands on recent in-depth theorizing about the responsibility for children. Building on the excellent insights of Lamb (1987), which draws on the distinction between engagement, accessibility, and responsibility, my work delves further into the quality, layers and location of this responsibility. Particular aspects of identity and emotional work are implicated in planning and organizing children's activities (see also Leslie et al., 1991; Pleck & Mascaidrelli, 2004; Pleck & Stueve, 2001; Stueve & Pleck, 2003). An original contribution is my argument for a wider spatial dimension to responsibility, one that incorporates the community so that responsibility resides not only in domestic spaces but also between households, and between households and other social institutions (schools, health institutions, community centres, and extracurricular activities) (see chapter 5) Furthermore, I have argued that the responsibility for children is simultaneously relational and interactional (chapter 4), both material and moral (see chapter 6), and that taking on responsibility is part of the processes of women and men 'doing gender' within households and communities.

Expanding Our Understanding of Parenting and Paid Work

The sixty-six stay-at-home fathers in this study on fathering call into question the continuing use of the terms *stay-at-home father* or indeed *stay-at-home parent*. As I discussed in chapter 3, these fathers represent three patterns of combining caring and employment that entail taking a break from employment, retraining, seeking to move into another kind of career, or more commonly combining part-time or flexible work hours with the changing caring needs and demands of young children. While the particularities of each situation are diverse, all these fathers had creatively carved out a unique relationship between their unpaid and paid work activities. Just as Anita Garey (1999) uses the metaphor of weaving to discuss the ways that mothers blend com-plex routines of employment, motherhood, and community work, stay-at-home fathers are building new models of employment and fatherhood, which represent not only changes in the institution of fatherhood but also potential shifts in relations between women and men in the social institutions of work, home, and community.

For *all* the stay-at-home fathers in my study, the decision to relin-quish full-time employment is the result of a mix of factors that include variations of the following: his wife/partner has the higher income with employment benefits and a stronger career interest (at this stage of their lives); the parents share strong views on the importance of home care; the fact that there is a paucity of good childcare facilities in Canada; the cost of childcare; and, in some cases, a child with particu-lar developmental, physical, or health needs. Although the decision is not an easy one for many of these fathers, the majority are in a position of taking on part-time employment or leaving the labour market for a short period to retrain or to begin retraining once their children reach a particular age. Like many Canadian mothers, these fathers are part of a growing trend to voluntary part-time employment in Canada (Marshall, 2000). While this 'choice' is driven by the development of a competitive service-based global economy, and while many workers are disadvantaged by the marginalized status of part-time work,[5] a man's decision to stay home can also be seen as part of workers' seek-ing greater flexibility and balance between their work and home lives.[6] Women are more likely to choose part-time work while they raise chil-dren, but this study demonstrates that fathers are also seeking creative alternatives to managing paid employment and caregiving.

Maternal Gatekeeping

In chapters 4 and 5, I discuss parenting as a mother-led dance, in that mothers in joint-custody and two-parent households play a key role in determining the ways that fathers take on the emotional and commu-nity responsibility for children. Such findings can be seen as confirma-tion of a growing body of literature on maternal gatekeeping; the scholarship explores and explains how some mothers, in and outside marriage, demonstrate ambivalence about highly involved fathering. They may thus act as gatekeepers in order to mediate and control paternal involvement (Allen & Hawkins, 1999; DeLuccie, 1995; Dien-hart & Daly, 1996; Seery & Crowley, 1999). Put succinctly, maternal gatekeeping is defined as 'a collection of beliefs and behaviors that ultimately inhibit a collaborative effort between men and women in family work by limiting men's opportunities for learning and growing through caring for home and children' (Allen & Hawkins, 1999, 200). This concept of maternal gatekeeping has at least three dimensions: mothers setting rigid standards; external validation of a distinct mothering identity; and gender-differentiated parenting. According to these three criteria, are the fourteen women in this study gatekeepers?

Setting of rigid standards for housework or childcare that fathers must meet is not the case for the mothers interviewed as part of my research project. Certainly, as described in chapter 3, some of the women start out with higher expectations for housework, but these become modified not only with the arrival of children but with their return to work while their male partner is the more home-based parent. In a few cases where income is available, housecleaning services are used to alleviate conflict over housework standards.[7] As also discussed in chapter 3, housework is a sensitive issue. In most households, men seem to be less focused on housekeeping and more on household maintenance and renovations. Moreover, they put playing with children and getting outdoors with the children ahead of household chores. As detailed in chapters 4, 5 and 6, such an approach is related to several issues: differing social expectations and moral identities about men, women, and domestic space; men's resolve to differentiate their parenting from that of women; their intent to instil an active and physical approach to caregiving; and their desire to enact their parenting in what feels like a more masculine style.

With regard to standards of child rearing, most women start out as the experts, largely due to pregnancy, breastfeeding, and maternity leave. In most two-parent households, fathers rely on women to set the style of parenting, and they build and adapt their own to complement their female partners'. As described in chapter 4, men are more likely to promote independence in their children, while women are more likely to be protective. Yet in cases where women are not available or not invested in a strong maternal identity, fathers do come to take on a more protective stance and struggle with what are often viewed as more maternal issues, such as letting go of their children. Setting standards for the way children should be cared for does not seem to occur in these two-parent households; while it may occur in joint-custody households (see Braver & Griffin, 2000; Fagan & Barnett, 2003), it was not discussed at any length by the fathers in this study.

How do my findings relate to the second dimension of maternal gatekeeping, that of gender differentiation in parenting? As depicted in chapters 4, 5 and 6, there are some gender differences in parenting but also a great deal of similarity. As I have argued throughout this book, space, time, and embodiment matter greatly in determining where and how parenting will be experienced, and observed, as gender-differentiated.

A final dimension of maternal gatekeeping is that of a distinct mothering approach and identity. Most of the women in this study do hold on to a special mothering identity, thus confirming the research of many other scholars on mothering. In chapter 6, I write that this is a moral identity, which encompasses how women and men feel they *should* act in society. It also relates to the symbolic power of mothering, which is something the majority of men and women refer to. Statements by men that 'she's the mother' or by women that 'I am still the mother' or 'Don't call him the mother' reverberate throughout the narratives of mothers and fathers. As pointed out by Sarah Allen and Alan Hawkins, 'doing family work is a way to validate a mothering identity externally as it is the primary source of self-esteem and satisfaction for many women'; it can also be the case that this primary source of identity 'does not automatically mean that they are inhibiting more collaborative arrangements of family work' (Allen & Hawkins, 1999, 204). It is important to point out that however strong the maternal identity is for the mothers in my study, it is just one of many identities. According to the work of British sociologists, the female partners of stay-at-home fathers exhibit a clear *mother/worker integral gendered morality* in that they value both paid employment and mothering and devote considerable time and identity resources in both of these (Duncan & Edwards, 1999; Edwards, Duncan, Reynolds, & Allred, 2002).

A further unique finding from this research is that maternal gatekeeping occurs in several sites and ways. The research conducted thus far on this concept has focused on its occurrence in households between a woman and a man. My work shows how it is enacted by couples in households, but it also occurs in *communities*, between mothers and *other* fathers. Perhaps the best illustrations of this are in chapter 5, when a woman came, in the words of Archie 'to check me out' because he was reading to the kids in the schoolyard or when Martin felt excluded in the mothers' group because a woman was uncomfortable breastfeeding in front of him. It could well be that the times and places where maternal gatekeeping occurs in communities

are those in which male embodiment is viewed as intrusive or threatening, either to women or to children.

Several interesting questions about gatekeeping emerge from this
study. The first is on the relationship between women who gatekeep
and the length and experience of maternity leave or parental leave taken
by women and/or men. For example, is maternal gatekeeping more
likely in households where women take long maternity leaves? Conversely, does it occur less in households where men take some parental
leave? Second, do men take on *paternal gatekeeping* in domestic and community life, and if so, where and when? Finally, is there any relation
between women's sense of responsibility as expressed by a need to
protect children and the extreme gender-differentiated experiences of
women and men regarding issues of violence and sexual abuse? Could
it be that there is a symbolic relationship between women's maternal
gatekeeping and a larger societal fear that hovers around the history of
male violence and sexual abuse? Such thoughts began to enter my analysis after I reflected on the words of one father, Alexander, speaking
about the loss of his close relationship with his stepdaughter: 'There is
a historical sexual ambiguity operating between men and girls. We
know that history – you know, sexual abuse.'

Finally, what emerges as particularly interesting in this study is the
idea of women moving over and creating space for men. Metaphorically, the image of borders (borderwork) and gates (gatekeeping) can
be joined here. It is women, however, who lead in taking down this
gender border, or opening the gate, so that men can also participate
fully in parenting. This idea of opening and closing borders or gates
provides for a more dynamic concept of maternal gatekeeping and the
recognition that while it may occur in particular spaces and times, it
does shift and change and even disappear.

Gender Equality and Gender Differences

As outlined in chapter 1, there are many ways for the theoretical concepts of gender equality and gender differences to intersect in social
life. Illuminated by this data on primary caregiving fathers, several key
insights gleaned from this study can feed back into the theoretical
debates.

NOT DIFFERENCES, BUT DISADVANTAGES
The approach taken in this book has been informed by the work of the

feminist legal scholar Deborah Rhode and particularly her point that the critical issue should not be difference 'but the difference difference makes' (Rhode, 1989, 13; added emphasis) or, put differently, where differences turn to disadvantages. Specifically, in chapter 3, I discuss the conceptual and empirical difficulties with attempting to delineate the contours and composition of an 'equal' division of labour, while in chapters 4, 5 and 6, I attend to the ebb and flow of differences over time in households and communities. There are, as mentioned above, variations in women's and men's parenting narratives. Yet sometimes these differences are not disadvantages or inequalities but simply differences per se, as rooted in the gendered upbringing of men and women (e.g., 'I grew up as a boy'), dominant gendered approaches to forming and maintaining friendships and networks (e.g., 'It's just not easy for a guy'), the gender-based composition of caring work, identities, and associated spatial contexts within which caring is done (e.g., 'estrogen-filled worlds') and the expectations that come to bear on what women and men do, or are seen to do (e.g., 'I felt like I wasn't being a good man').

Furthermore, it is important to be mindful that the question of the difference differences makes is exceedingly difficult to answer in all contexts since, as articulated in chapter 3, how differences come to matter can be subjectively imbued. What is certain is that differences do not always lead to disadvantages and difference does not always mean unequal. In this vein, my work veers away from some of the well-known studies on primary-caregiving fathers, where concepts of 'shared equally' 'equal parenting' or 'co-mothering' are employed to describe the work and identities of women and men in parenting (Deutsch, 1999; Ehrensaft, 1984, 1987; Kimball, 1988; Risman, 1987; Smith, 1998). My view remains that it is tremendously difficult to measure equality in household life, and it is perhaps best judged against how one's participation in domestic life allows for personal, social, economic, and political opportunities outside the home, all of which aid in the larger struggle for women's and men's social and economic equality (see also Doucet, 1995b). My belief is that gender difference, unlike dominant approaches in feminist sociology, can co-exist with equality and, indeed, what should be emphasized is gender symmetry rather than gender equality.

EQUALITY ON WHOSE TERMS?
In chapter 1, I pointed out that many feminist scholars over the past few decades have cautioned that different methodological, theoretical,

and political tools are required when we study diverse groups of persons. In the context of this work on fathering, I have argued that we must employ different lenses and hearing aids when we study men in female-dominated domains of social life. I thus turned the question 'Do men mother?' on its head and maintained that the question, while still asked and contended vigorously by social scientists, could well be replaced by questions and lines of inquiry that provide alternative ways to speak about men's experiences in caregiving. The related question of equality on whose terms reminds us of the need to provide ample space for men's narratives of care and to resist the impulse to investigate and theorize them against maternal standards. Adopting such a stance, with room for theoretical or empirical surprises, indeed offers innovative ways of describing and theorizing men's nurturing practices and ultimately provides novel ways to think about emotional responsibility and community responsibility (see chapters 4 and 5).

STRADDLING EQUALITY AND DIFFERENCE

My last point on equality and differences builds on the point above on questioning the terms under which equality is sought. Accommodating both gender equality and differences means striving for equality in social conditions set up around a male work norm while simultaneously questioning the terms under which that equality would be achieved, and thus altering those terms while still working towards them. In chapter 1, I lay out a theoretical position that combines both gender equality and gender differences. In relation to caregiving, taking such an approach has two large implications. First is the need to both value care work and critique the conditions within which it occurs. Men who are actively involved in caregiving readily articulate the value and extreme importance of this work. Indeed, as I described in the introduction to this book, fathers' voices engendered a form of vertigo in me when I first heard them narrating the joys and burdens of raising children.

Yet it is important to add that these voices represent partial representations of the larger issues of what it would mean to have a society truly committed to caregiving (Fisher & Tronto, 1990; Larrabee, 1993; Noddings, 2003; Sevenhuijsen, 1998, 2000; Tronto, 1993). In addition to valuing of care, we must also call for structural and ideological changes including viewing and counting housework and childcare as *work* in census data and in national GDP accounting (Crittenden 2001; Luxton and Vosko 1998; Waring 1998); the importance of universal high-quality childcare (Mahon & Michel, 2002; Jenson 2002); and flexible working options for both parents (Brandth & Kvande 2001; Moss & Petrie, 2002).

Intersectionality

This book has been based on the narratives of 118 fathers and fourteen heterosexual couples. The category of primary-caregiving father is further disaggregated into single fathers and stay-at-home fathers, along with a select few shared-caregiving fathers and fathers on parental leave. Diversity of experience is perhaps best reflected in the participation of nine gay fathers, four Aboriginal fathers, fifteen fathers from visible minorities, and a diverse representation across social class, as measured by income and education levels. What distinguishes this study from others on shared-caregiving couples is the high level of diversity achieved, particularly relating to ethnicity, sexuality, and social class.

I began the study with the clear intention of finding a diverse group of fathers. As detailed in chapter 2, the task was not an easy one, as it took more than three years and multiple strategies to gain a sample with a good level of diversity across social class, ethnicity, and sexuality. If gaining diversity in sampling was difficult, the task of analysing the processes and meanings of the interplay of differences between women and men posed even greater challenges. That is, the ways that multiple differences interact, and indeed *matter*, are hardly straightforward. In this vein, I draw on recent concerns in feminist literature that address the challenges of studying and analysing intersectionality (McCall, 2005) and recognizing that 'not all differences are created equally' and that at times 'counting and ranking' inequalities may be a sound political strategy' (Ward, 2004, 83). As demonstrated throughout this book, issues of intersectionality play out in varied ways, with *gender* often being the main axis of differentiation in parenting. There are, however, diverse and unique intersections being mapped out between gender, class, ethnicity, and sexuality in relation to emotional, community, and moral responsibilities (see chapters 4, 5 and 6).

We know that, structurally, fathers of ethnic minorities are disadvantaged, particularly recently arrived immigrants (see chapter 3). In this study, class, based on education levels and earnings, negatively marks the lives of the single Aboriginal fathers as well as the recently arrived immigrant fathers whose educational qualifications are not fully recognized in Canada. Where fathers of ethnic minorities have high educational qualifications achieved in Canada and/or are married to high-income women, the disadvantages they may face as ethnic minority fathers recede. They still face some cultural barriers, but these can be partly mediated by fluency of language and the advantages bought by living in middle-class neighbourhoods with good schooling and community resources. Moreover, while particular cultural ideas might promote a high degree of gender difference in parenting, these can be also be influenced by social networks, choice of marriage partner, or education. What is notable is that for immigrant fathers who remain embedded in their particular cultural community within the larger Canadian society, ideas are more likely to change slowly. This is the case for the Somali immigrant fathers in this study.

Perhaps the greatest difficulties in gaining social acceptance as caregivers are faced by gay fathers. Indeed, most of the gay fathers in my study confront 'multiple jeopardy' (King 1990; cited in Ward, 2004, 82) in discrimination because gender, sexuality and, in some cases, social class work against them. The intersections of gender, class, and sexuality can act as powerful resources for masculinity to cushion, or exacerbate in a negative way, men's active fathering roles, particularly in community settings. Throughout chapters 5 and 6, examples from my interviews with fathers illustrate the subtle fears that persist in community settings about close relations between men and children, particularly between men and the children of others. Such suspicions differ between rural and urban areas and seem to be more pervasive for low-income fathers and gay fathers. Nevertheless, in spite of differences between men, the gendered quality of such scrutiny cuts across class, ethnicity, and sexuality.

Masculinities

This book has also explored two key questions in relation to men and masculinities. I began my study on fathers as primary caregivers with the desire to engage with David Morgan's compelling claim that 'one strategy of studying men and masculinities would be to study those situations where masculinity is, as it were, *on the line*' (1992, 99; emphasis in original). Thus, *do* fathers who are primary caregivers put masculinity on the line, or do they reconfigure that same line according to what is defined as masculine or feminine? Second, I wanted to know whether engaged fathering confirms or challenges current theoretical understandings of masculinities. Since there is a strong connection between hegemonic masculinity and the devaluation of the feminine, what happens to dominant or hegemonic conceptions of masculinities when men are heavily invested in caring, one of the most female-dominated and feminine-defined areas of social life?

Fathers do not put their masculinity on the line but rather are actively reconstructing masculinities to include aspects of traditional feminine characteristics. Fathers' narratives, as detailed in chapters 4, 5 and 6, are filled with visible and inchoate contradictions, which tell how fathers are both determined to distance themselves from the feminine but are also, in practice, radically revisioning masculine care and ultimately our understandings of masculinities.

The effects of this revisioning of masculinity can be heard in these fathers' narratives because they speak partly from the borders of the most traditional arena of men's dominance within the 'gender order,' that of paid work. When men take on strong identities as caregivers and, in the case of stay-at-home fathers, partially or fully relinquish their identities as primary breadwinners, it is inevitable that processes of personal and social shuffling and readjustment will occur. Perhaps most notable is that fathers' relation to paid work begins to shift, their meanings of work are dramatically altered, and men begin to take on perspectives that are more aligned with women's social positioning (Gilligan, 1982, 1993) and ultimately 'feminine' (Noddings, 2003) or 'feminist' (Friedman, 1993, 2000; Stoljar, 2000; Tronto, 1989) vantage points. Fathers grappling with how to be 'a good man' (Marc) while also recognizing the 'softening' (Aaron) that occurs while intimately involved in caregiving suggests the need to move beyond current theorizations on masculinities to develop other theoretical tools and approaches. To cite again the work of Jeff Hearn and David Morgan, 'the experience of masculinity is far from uniform and that *new ways of theorizing these differences need to be developed*' (Hearn and Morgan, 1990, 11; emphasis added).

What do these men's lives mean for our understanding of changing masculinities? As discussed in chapter 1, Connell's work has been one of the most well cited in explicating various masculinities. His fourfold classification identifies these as the following: first, hegemonic masculinity is perhaps most strongly identified '*as the opposite of femininity*' (Connell, 2000, 31); *subordinated* (especially gay masculinities), *marginalized* (exploited or oppressed groups such as ethnic minorities), and *complicit* masculinities (those organized around the complicit acceptance of what has come to be termed the 'patriarchal dividend') (Connell, 1995, 2000; my emphasis).

I would maintain that these men's stories do not represent any one of the key masculinities (hegemonic, subordinate, marginalized or complicit) but rather that men move constantly between them. Drawing again on Connell's recent work, narratives of male care, represent processes 'of internal complexity and contradiction' as well as the 'dynamics' of changing and evolving masculinities (Connell, 2000, 13). He further writes that 'masculinities are not fixed' nor are they 'homogenous, simple states of being,' but instead are 'often in tension, within and without' and that 'such tensions are important sources of change' (Connell, 2000, 13). Living and working for sustained periods as primary caregivers, the fathers described throughout my book are in a unique position to create new forms of masculinity. They do so through delicate balancing acts of simultaneously embracing and rejecting both femininity and hegemonic masculinity. They provide 'abundant evidence that masculinities do change. Masculinities are created in specific historical circumstances, and as those circumstances change, the gender practices can be contested and reconstructed' (Connell, 2000, 13–14).

As men move between femininities and masculinities, between achieving some version of equality or symmetry with women while emphasizing masculine differences, I would argue that *men are, in fact, radically revisioning caring work, masculine conceptions of care, and ultimately our understandings of masculinities.* Indeed, fathers' narratives take us beyond a recent debate in the academic literature on masculinities (Brandth & Kvande, 1998; Dryden, 1999; but see Plantin, Sven-Axel, & Kearney, 2003). This is the issue of whether active fathering reproduces or challenges hegemonic masculinity. The fathers' narratives address the ways that men are creating *new kinds of masculinities* by bringing together varied configurations of masculinities and femininities. Indeed, our understandings of men's lives and their subjective conceptions of masculinities could, for example, benefit from long-standing feminist debates on the intricate links between theoretical and empirical concepts of justice and care, autonomy and connection, and individual rights and relational responsibilities (Benhabib, 1992; Doucet, 1995b; Gilligan, 1988; Kittay, 1999; Minow & Shanley, 1996; Sevenhuijsen, 1998, 2000; Tronto, 1993, 1995). That is, men's practices and identities of caregiving go beyond current conceptions of masculinities and femininities and may reflect philosophical and political concepts of self, identity, and subjectivity that embrace varied degrees of dependence, independence, and interdependence as well as varied versions of 'relational autonomy'(Friedman, 1993, 2000).

Embodiment

If, as laid out in chapter 1, it is the case that 'bodies do matter' (Messer-schmidt, 1999, 122), how *do* they matter in fathering and mothering narratives? Throughout this book, I have attempted to make concrete the embodied quality of mothers' and fathers' narratives and to bring such parental embodiment into sociological understandings of mothering and fathering. I have argued that there are contexts – times and spaces – when, indeed, embodiment does matter a great deal and there are other contexts where it is negligible or inconsequential. Yet what continually astounded me in this work was the *weight of embodiment* in fathers' narratives. While this impact of bodies waxes and wanes through the narratives and through the flow of parental time, it nevertheless emerges as one of the stronger themes in my work, even though I certainly did not ask anyone to speak about it directly, nor did I start out with embodiment as an area of inquiry. Whereas dominant approaches in this field of study assume that men and women are interchangeable disembodied subjects within and between households, my work emphasizes that fathers and mothers are embodied subjects who move through domestic and community spaces with inter-subjective, relational, moral, and normative dimensions framing these movements.

This *weight* of embodiment is very present in chapters 4, 5 and 6. In chapter 4 ('Emotional Responsibility'), it figures in the ways that fathers give greater symbolic and practical significance to the role that mothers play with children. Both fathers and mothers assert the influence of female embodiment – pregnancy, birth, breastfeeding, and post-birth recovery as well as the metaphoric example of a mother's hug ('longer,' 'tighter,' 'deeper') – as having greater weight in emotional responsibility. Fathers' embodiment also comes to figure in the ways that men focus on physical activities, being outdoors, playing, and doing sports with their children, all drawing on a notion of masculine embodiment as strong, physical, and muscular (Burstyn, 1999).

In chapter 5, fathers' narratives draw attention to the way they must move cautiously as embodied actors in female-dominated community playgroups and in settings where they are placed in close relation to preteen and teen girls. Drawing on Goffman as well as varied sociological work on how men and women 'do gender' (Thompson & Walker, 1989; West & Zimmerman, 1987), I note the perceptible presence of the 'social gaze' on men and that fathers, at varied moments and in particular sites, can feel both suspicion and surveillance as they enter community settings with children.

In chapters 5 and 6, I also detail how fathers cross the borders and boundaries of restrictive masculine definition around caregiving; they do so by negotiating their way into female-dominated venues, creating alternative spaces for men and ultimately revisioning the variable and negotiable meanings of male embodiment.

The care of others is, quite simply, deeply embodied. Caring is filled with interactive, relational, and moral dimensions. Moreover, caregivers are watched by others who also care. One father, Luke, offered a simple sentence on the blend of emotional and embodied qualities in care. He said, 'We all leave marks on those we care for.' Moreover, as mothers' and fathers' narratives stretched across time to their own fathers and mothers, to grandmothers and grandfathers, and to the inner reaches of childhood memories, a poignant point from Connell is relevant here: *'Bodily experience is often central in memories of our own lives, and thus in our understanding of who and what we are'* (Connell, 1995, 53; my emphasis).

In addition to the theoretical, empirical, and methodological insights that emerge from this research on primary-caregiving fathers, it also lends itself to reflections on the potential for positive social change. These new beginnings are discussed below in the final section of this concluding chapter.

New Beginnings

Moral Transformations in Men

Chapter 6 illustrates some of the moral transformations that occur in fathers who are actively involved in caring for their children. Specifically, three key ways in which this happens are personal generative changes in fathers; their recognition of the value and difficulty of caregiving work; and their commitment to join women in the sharing of work–family responsibilities. In addition to these changes, one of the most radical points emerging from this study relates to the work's political implications and to the potential role of men in the social recognition and valuing of unpaid work (Armstrong & Armstrong, 1993; Doucet, 2005a; Luxton, 1980, 1997; Luxton & Vosko, 1998).

Freed somewhat from the breadwinner imperative, the fathers in this study, particularly the stay-at-home fathers, can be viewed as representing some of what Karin Davies refers to in her Swedish study of women, work, and time (Davies, 1990, 1994). She argues that decisions to work part-time or to take time off from work constitute 'breaking the pattern' out of 'wage labour as the over-riding structure and an unconditional adherence to male time' (Davies, 1990, 217). She further maintains that 'by limiting the time spent in wage labour, a soil is provided whereby visions of what is important to fight and strive for can find space' (Davies, 1990, 208). Although she wrote about women more than two decades ago, the views of Davies as applied to men have a particularly powerful effect because the 'the over-riding structure' and 'male time' that she refers to have strong connections to masculinity, particularly hegemonic masculinity. It is men's overall privileged access to the rewards of paid employment and their concurrent lesser role in the care of dependent others, that partly account for the dominance and the associated 'patriarchal dividend' (Connell, 1995) from which men benefit. The slow process of critical resistance documented here by fathers as they comment on concepts of 'male time' constitutes some unravelling of their relation to the structural effects of hegemonic masculinity.

It is also important to mention that fathers' increasing share of caregiving work represents a reversal of a trend that many authors have repeatedly mentioned over the past two decades. This is an increasing pattern whereby middle class families with ample economic resources rely on other lesser-paid women (e.g., nannies and housekeepers) to take up domestic work and childcare (Bakan & Stasiulis, 1997; Coltrane, 2003). Paying others to perform domestic services such as childcare and housework is ultimately passing on women's traditional domain from one group of women to another, thus hardening the boundaries that exist around gender and caring. The end result is that childcare and domestic labour remain as devalued women's work wherein an ever-broadening lower tier of women are paid meagre wages to perform a 'modified housewife' role while other women do work considered more socially valuable. As phrased eloquently by one author, this model seems to trap us into 'endlessly remaking the world in the same image: some people in the public sphere, the world of power, of importance, and some people in the

private sphere, rocking the cradle but never really ruling the world'
(Rothman, 1989, 103).

The fathers described in this book seem to be assisting with breaking out of this cycle of gender imbalance between 'the private sphere'
and 'the world of power.' They do this in four ways. First, they partially redress the class and gender imbalances implicated in the way
that caregiving is currently organized in most societies. Second, the
personal transformations that men undergo as a result of being highly
involved in caregiving may also be the key to the way gender changes,
for this generation and the next (Coltrane, 1989, 1996; Deutsch, 1999;
Deutsch, Servis, & Payne, 2001; Gerson, 1993; Hochschild, 1989; Rissman, 1998). Third, fathers can be viewed as responding not only to
Rothman's ideas but even more profoundly to Dorothy Dinnerstein's
lament a quarter century ago in her classic book *The Mermaid and the
Minotaur* (1977) wherein she elaborated on the many societal and psychological imbalances that occur in a society when one gender does the
metaphoric 'rocking of the cradle' while the other 'rules the world.'
Finally, giving Davies's work credit, we see she acknowledges that 'it is
up to women to exert influence' since they are more likely to have
'experience of rejecting male time' and thus 'concrete knowledge and
understanding of how we can produce and reproduce new forms of
daily life ... which are not so oppressive' (1990, 247). My study suggests
that primary caregiving fathers are stuck in a distinctive position as
well. Indeed, adding fathers' voices to the issues can also 'exert influence' very loudly indeed, both theoretically and politically.

Moral Transformations in Women

When men and women both partake in the work and responsibility for
the care of children, tremendous generative changes occur not only for
men but also for women. As the women in my study went back to
work while their male partners stayed at home, they alternated
between relief and a sense of regret, loss, and guilt. Yet the latter feelings were short-lived, as all the women admitted that once they
grappled with initial feelings of doubt and regret, they went on to
experience the freedom to explore their own interests and to combine
parenting and other challenges in ways that are often reserved only for
men. As well expressed in Deutsch's study on parenting, 'Relinquish-
ing a traditional maternal identity wasn't always easy. But when others
saw that their own freedom to work and achieve meant that they actu-

ally felt happier with their children, it was easier to adopt a new standard of motherhood' (Deutsch, 1999, 212).

When men participate actively in fathering, the moral identity of mothers can begin to change so that the restrictive shoulds and oughts widen to include both relationality *and* autonomy, as well as interdependence, dependence, and independence. As discussed above, in my reflections on changing masculinities, femininities widen to embrace more masculine aspects and women, like men, thus move between masculinities and femininities. If, as McMahon (1995) has argued, motherhood entails a moral transformation of one's identity, it may be the case that being a mother with an actively involved co-parent means entirely different moral transformations. Such findings have also been hinted at in work on gay couples that has argued that they can more fully share domestic divisions of labour and the care of children without the gender constraints that frame who should be earning and who should be caring (see Carrington, 1999; Doucet & Dunne, 2000; Dunne, 1996).

As part of these changes, some women claim that they learn from the ways that their male partners parent and, specifically, from their more relaxed styles (see also Deutsch, 1999; Hays, 1996). Partly uninhibited by the constraints of the moral responsibility to care and the judgements brought to bear on what it means to be a good mother or a proper mother, fathers can bring a sense of ease to this role. Natasha, whose partner, Tom, has been home for seven years, finds this freedom surprisingly refreshing and goes as far as to say that such qualities can make men excellent caregivers:

> Any woman that hears about a man who says he'd love to stay home with his kids, she says, 'well, you have no idea how much work it is.' She just kind of rolls her eyes and says, 'He wouldn't last a week.' Not true. For a woman it's a lot of work to stay at home because she creates a lot of work. And men, when they stay at home, they don't create work. They create fun and play, and then when they have to work, they get down to it and they work. And they don't do the whole stress trip. And they don't do the anxiety trip and the guilt trip that women do. Maybe we're products of our society, but on the whole I think that men are great caregivers, actually.

Flow and Change in Mothering and Fathering: 'A Wonderful Flexibility'

A final point that emerges from this work is that change and evolution must be built into our understandings of parenting and domestic life. Methodologically, this underlines the importance of repeat interviewing rather than one-time visits to households and, where possible, longitudinal studies. Substantively, one intriguing question on long-term gender change that emerges from this study is hinted at in chapter 4: what will be the possible effects of active fathering on children, particularly daughters? That is, will dominant paternal patterns of emphasizing play, sports, risk taking, and independence come to matter if and when such daughters become parents?

The issue of flow and change is also important because there is a tendency for mothers and fathers, and for observers of domestic life, to overemphasize gender differences in parenting and to downplay gender similarities. As detailed in chapter 4, while most fathers point to deep-seated differences between mothers and fathers in relation to emotional responsibility, the daily practices of caregiving are much less gender bifurcated. Particularly within the stay-at-home-father households, at varied times and in diverse spaces, individuals and couples move back and forth between primary and secondary parenting. Such movements were reflected, indeed, almost as a mirror image, in the individual and couple interviews as men and women vascillated on who took on emotional and community responsibilities, in what contexts, and at which times.

Some of the explanation for the ways that beliefs about gender differences supersede actual practices can be found in the concept of ideology, as discussed in chapter 6. Ideologies about gender and parenting act in taken-for-granted ways, much like 'the "spontaneous" quality of common sense' with its transparency its 'naturalness,' its refusal to examine the premises on which it is grounded' (Purvis & Hunt, 1993, 479). In spite of the power of ideology, the stories told throughout this book reveal the potential elasticity of gendered agency in dominant social structures and the promise of greater opportunities for women and men to make choices based on inclinations, skills, interests, and lifestyle issues rather than on the dictates of gender.

Finally, flow and change imply an intricate relation between parents and not simply a *division* of labour. This book has argued for a multilayered relational approach to parenting as well as for a recognition of the way particular households live in relation to other social institutions (workplaces, schools, community organizations, other households, medical institutions, and government policy) and especially to the community in which these are embedded. Parenting is, in short, interactive and co-created between parents and others (see also Backett, 1982, 1987; Cowan & Cowan, 1992; Fox, 1998, 2001; LaRossa & Larossa, 1981). This view has also been taken in a recent article by a large group of international writers on themes of men and masculinities in ten European countries. The authors point out that '[r]elatively little work has been carried out on men as carers' and that '[f]urther exploration of the complex dynamics surrounding negotiations between women and men in relationships regarding housework, parenting and emotional work would be welcome' (Hearn et al., 2002, 399). This research underlines some of these complex dynamics between women and men.

The interactive and evolving quality of parenting is well etched in many of the couple interviews. Tom and Natasha, for example, reflect on the ebb and flow in their styles and commitments to emotional and community responsibility and the concurrent chipping-away at deeply felt ideological conceptions and moral responsibilities for them as parents. Tom summarizes this when he says, 'It's been a hard road, but the trick is to just say it's never ending. It's not static. When the kids are growing up, their needs are different, from one day to the next. They'll cling to each of us for different stuff. They crave different things from each of us.'

Claire says in her couple interview with her husband, Alistair, 'There is a movement, a flow, there is allowance in the way that we do things that accepts change.' Even more evocative is her metaphor of how she could replace Alistair and he could replace her, like a part of the body growing back to replace one that has been lost. I end the book with this poignant metaphor as a way of thinking about mothering and fathering as constantly evolving in relation to each other:

CLAIRE Alistair's mom lost part of a lung, half of a lung, a few years ago to cancer. And the lung has actually grown to fill that space. *I don't know if you can tell that the tissue is different now. But it has grown to take over that space.* And in terms of your study, I think it's hard to imagine bringing up the kids without Alistair. But if something happened to him, maybe I would in a sense grow to fill some of the father vacuum. Just as a single man would grow to fill some of the mother vacuum. Part of what is different from being a mother and a father is the expectations of those roles.

ALISTAIR And yet we are sharing a lot of things that in a previous generation, wouldn't have happened ... And there are key times when you have handled the economic responsibility in the family that normally would have been handled by the man. *And it gave us a wonderful flexibility to be able to do all that we have done.*

Postscript: Revisiting an Epistemology of Reception

A book that tells a story about active fathering is bound to be read and received in multiple ways. As I come to its end, I remain troubled by the way it may be read. The concept of 'the epistemology of reception,' which I introduced in chapter 1, reminds me to consider 'how and under what circumstances social scientific knowledge is received, evaluated, and acted upon and under what circumstances' (May, 1998, 173). Specifically, and briefly, there are three ways in which I hope this work will, and *will not*, be read and used.

GENDER DIFFERENCES OR GENDER EQUALITIES

In making the argument that men do not mother, is this book claiming that there are irreconcilable differences between women and men? Although I am quite certain that, against my strong hopes, this book may be used to make that claim simply on the basis of reductive thinking about that one point, my intention has been to provide a nuanced and non-binary response. If I was forced to reduce my argument to its essence, it would be to say that there are gender differences and similarities in parenting. Moreover, what matters most in framing differences between women and men are space, time, and embodiment, along with the social conditions within which women and men are raised and the ways that social institutions are structured by gendered practices and ideologies. While my argument remains, largely in response to those who argue the contrary within the terms of that debate, *men are not mothers* and *fathers do not mother*, there are times and places where men's caregiving is so impeccably close to what we consider mothering that gender seems to fall completely away, leaving only the image of a loving *parent* and child.

The problem that I am alluding to here is less the issue of my arguments and more the larger political backdrop against which these debates are waged. Specifically, my work may well be heard and picked up by those groups who argue from the political and religious right and who insist on innate differences between women and men, mothering and fathering. Such groups include international chapters of the Promise Keepers or the Fatherhood Responsibility Movement that emphasize and promote ideals of fathers as family breadwinners and heads of the household and mothers as natural primary caregivers and supplementary or non-earners (Coltrane, 1997, 2001; Gavanas, 2002; Messner, 1997). Support for men's involvement in the family can unwittingly turn into arguments about essential differences between women and men or about the moral superiority of particular family forms. This latter argument is dealt with in the next section.

WHAT KIND OF FAMILIES?
The work of the American sociologist Scott Coltrane illuminates well the unexpected link between promoting active fathering and the dangers of it being used to promote a particular narrow model of *the family*. He laments, 'As a researcher who studies how and why men get involved in raising children and maintaining households, I share the goal of making men more aware of the benefits of assuming domestic duties and getting involved in the details of raising children. What troubles me, however, is the narrow vision of family perpetrated by these moral entrepreneurs' (Coltrane, 2001, 390).

These 'moral entrepreneurs' include American associations such as the National Fatherhood Initiative, the Marriage Movement, and the Promise Keepers, all varied hybrids of political and religious organizations that have brother associations in many Western countries. According to Coltrane, the groups have many beliefs in common, including the need for legal marriage, divorce being unacceptable, and men as the natural heads of household. 'Promoting a cultural idea of fathers as family patriarchs, mothers as natural caregivers, and heterosexual married couples as the only legitimate households in which to raise children will only serve to marginalize and punish the increasing numbers of families who do not fit this idealized form' (Coltrane, 2001, 309–10).

There are certainly such 'moral entrepreneurs' in Canada, where there are chapters of groups such as the Promise Keepers as well as dozens of organizations that lobby for fathers' rights (e.g., Fathers for Justice and Fathers for Family Justice). Yet the political landscape is also notably different for this sparsely populated yet geographically larger country that lies north of the United States. Two aspects of the Canadian political terrain are worth drawing attention to in this regard. First, same-sex marriage was legalized across Canada by the *Civil Marriage Act* enacted on July 20, 2005.[1] While the action was denounced by the religious and political right, the Canadian government still saw fit to recognize varied forms of marriage and ultimately several models of family. Second, Canada now has one of the most generous parental leave policies in the world, which is available to either the father or the mother. In these two pieces of legislation, what has been particularly striking is the positioning of men within the family. In the first instance, Canada recognizes two men as constituting a family and entitled to legal benefits that were traditionally confined to heterosexual married couples. Second, employed Canadian men are eligible for parental leave; this means not just taking a day off for the birth of the child or a few days or weeks of vacation or sick leave but rather an entitlement to a full thirty-five weeks of paid leave.

A further point in this debate is one of historical and cultural sensitivity. While social commentators, both scholarly and popular, lament the decline of the traditional family, it is important to be cognizant of the fact that there has always been tremendous diversity in families and that the mythical nuclear family has never actually been the ideal form or the dominant form at any point in Western history (Coltrane, 1996, 2001; Coontz, 1992, 2005; Stacey, 1993). This is particularly the case when we examine the experiences of working-class, low-income, ethnic-minority, immigrant, and gay families. Moreover, families continue to change and evolve, and it could well be argued that the family form most idealized in popular culture and memory, that of the breadwinner father and child-rearing mother, has been replaced by multiple new family forms. These new forms, for which Judith Stacey has coined the umbrella term *postmodern family*, include some of the families that have populated this book; they include single parent families (both single-father and single-mother families), blended families, two-household families with joint custody of children, cohabiting couples, lesbian and gay families, stay-at-home-father families, and varied kinds of two-income families (see Cheal, 1991, 1999; J. Lewis, 2003; Stacey, 1990).

FATHERING AT WHATEVER COST?
The final troubling area of the epistemology of reception is that this book may be read as an argument that fathers should be involved with

their children, no matter what the cost. Do children need fathers? Are fathers necessary to children's lives? Constantly discussed in academic, media, and popular forums in many countries, the argument that children need their fathers is, however, made most vehemently by men's rights and fathers' rights advocates. While there have always been men who feel disadvantaged in society, the proliferation of such groups in most Western countries in the past twenty years has been nothing short of overwhelming.[2] Consisting of predominantly white, heterosexual, and middle-aged men, they are composed of fathers' rights advocates and non-custodial fathers' groups who accord much of the blame for their problems to women (for an overview, see Coltrane 1997; Messner 1997; Kimmel 1999; Coltrane 2001; Farrell 2001; Flood 2002; Coltrane 2004; Flood 2004). As well described by Michael Flood, an Australian pro-feminist writer,[3] such groups 'believe that men's right to a fair negotiation in child custody settlements, to a fair trial in domestic violence cases, and to fair treatment in the media have all been lost. Responsibility and blame for these problems is attributed to women, the women's movements and feminism' (Flood, 2004).

There are others who argue that active fathering is beneficial for men (Palkovitz, 2002; Snarey, 1993), for couples (Cowan & Cowan, 1992; Hyeyoung & Raley, 2005; Nomaguchi, 2003), and for children (Lamb, 2000; Pleck & Mascaidrelli, 2004). It is the latter scholarship, written in multi-disciplinary journals that espouse a variety of diverse, yet sound, academic arguments that fuels work such as mine. That is, their intention is to increase fathering involvement largely for the sake of children and healthy families and communities, but not as part of a larger political, ideological struggle between women and men. My view is that positive and nurturing parenting by mothers and/or fathers is the critical issue, rather than the necessary prescribed presence of any particular father per se.

At the end of this book, an additional cautionary note is necessary to add to the issue of men's equality with women in child rearing. Like many fathering researchers, I have made the plea that we need to understand men on their own terms and not through female-centred approaches (Doherty, Kouneski, & Erickson, 1998; Hawkins, Christiansen, Sargent, & Hill, 1993; Hawkins & Dollahite, 1996; LaRossa & Reitzes, 1995). Nevertheless, there is a difference between this call and the argument by feminist scholars that male lenses should not be used to study women. Quite simply, the structural backdrop that accompanies these questions is different, asymmetrical, and indeed unequal.

These stories of resistance and change, promise and potential on the part of men, as narrated throughout this book, must be framed against structural relations between women and men. Women's opportunities in paid work, in education, in politics have certainly widened and increased gradually throughout the past half century. Nevertheless, women continue to face disadvantages, particularly in the realms of paid work and politics, where their representation at the highest levels in both of these spheres has remained sparse in all countries.

It is thus important to recognize that arguing for men's greater involvement in childcare is to encourage men's entry into what is arguably the primary domain where women hold power and responsibility. Quite simply, there are differential costs to this call for greater participation of the other gender. Active fathers, as individuals, may lose some power and authority in the workplace when they trade 'cash for care' but men as a gender still benefit from the ever-present 'patriarchal dividend' (Connell, 1995) that accrues to males in society. The same is not true for women. While men may come to appreciate, as has been argued throughout this book, the joys and rewards of caregiving, it is still women who overwhelmingly pay the social and economic price for care in society. Ann Crittenden's words are a subtle reminder of how, in spite of the rhetoric of involved fathering, women still maintain the responsibility, with all its concomitant pleasures and burdens for children. She writes, 'For all the changes in the last decades, it is still women, not men who adjust their lives to accommodate the needs of children; women who do what is necessary to make a home; women who forgo status, income, advancement, and independence' (2001, 27).

The fathering stories recounted in this book are marginal ones; they sit quietly on the borders of most men's lives in most contemporary societies. R.W. Connell poignantly cautions that 'the gender order does not blow away at a breath' and notes that 'the historical process around masculinity is a process of struggle in which, ultimately, large resources are at stake' (2000, 14). We are reminded of the need to move beyond vignettes of everyday caring to focus on wider gendered relations and the need for greater structural changes and policy measures to assist both women and men to achieve work-life integration (Folbre, 1994, 2001; Fraser, 1997; Gerson, 1993; Hobson, 2002; Plantin et al., 2003). My modest hope is that this book will be read as a small step towards such social change.

APPENDICES

APPENDIX A: WHO ARE THE FATHERS?

Table A.1. Single Fathers

Name and City	Age	No. of children	Ages of children	Ethnicity	Relationship status	Years as primary caregiver	HH income	Occupation	Education
1. Al Small town, Ontario	38	1	7	White	Divorced; sole custody	1	50,000	Electrician/general contractor	Technical college
2. Bernard City in Ontario	42	1	4	White	Co-parenting (informal joint custody with two lesbian mothers	4	50,000	Payroll specialist	University
3. Christian Rural Ontario	71	1	29	White German Canadian	Divorced; joint custody	15	70,000	Retired, formerly engineer/business	Post-graduate
4. Dennis Ottawa	28	1	10	½ Aboriginal and ½ Chinese	Sole-custody father. Child's mother lives in another province		Under 20,000	Restaurant chef	Less than high school
5. Devon Ottawa	26	1	7	White	Divorced; sole custody	2.5 years	50,000	Electrical technician	Technical college
6. Dick Vancouver, British Columbia	46	2	3 3	White	Divorced; sole custody	2.5 years	N/A	Web consultant	Some college
7. Doug Ottawa	40	1	9	White	Divorced; joint custody. Also took 3 months parental leave	6	70,000	Audit manager	University
8. Earl Ottawa	55	3	31 24 21	White (Hebrew)	Divorced and sole custody for 5 years. Then remarried	5	80,000	Business	Post graduate
9. Edward Small city, Ontario	46	2	19 16	White	Divorced gay father. Has joint custody with his ex-wife	10	80,000	Business	University
10. Gilbert Rural Ontario	46	1	11	Aboriginal (grew up on a reserve)	Sole-custody father	5	30,000	Salesclerk	High school

Table A.1. (*Continued*)

Name and City	Age	No. of children	Ages of children	Ethnicity	Relationship status	Years as primary caregiver	HH income	Occupation	Education
11. Golin Ottawa	42	4	13 10 9 6	African Canadian (20 years in Canada)	Sole-custody father	5	50,000	Information technology in government	Post-graduate
12. Greg City in Quebec	31	1	5	Italian Canadian	Joint-custody father	5	50,000	Respiratory therapist	Community college
13. Harrison Toronto	54	1	22	White	Divorced gay father; sole custody	22	Over 100,000	Consultant	University
14. Henry Ottawa	48	2	12 8	British Canadian	Sole-custody father	5	80,000 (when working)	Looking for work (technology consultant)	University
15. Jack Fredericton, New Brunswick	45	3	17	White	Sole-custody father	4 years joint custody, 2 years sole custody	55,000	Government scientist	Post-graduate
16. Jacob Ottawa	35	3	12 9 7	White	Sole-custody father	2.5	70,0000	Previous: carpenter. Currently physician in training	Post-graduate
17. Jared Ottawa	49	1	14	White	Widowed	3	Under 20,000	Disability for 3 years	Less than high school
18. Kent Moncton, New Brunswick	44	3	11 9 7	White	Divorced; joint custody	5	50,000	Public servant	University
19. Kevin Small town Ontario	42	4	12 11 9 7	White	Divorced; sole custody	3.5	70,000	Car salesman	High school
20. Kofi Montreal	44	2	13 11	African Canadian (20 years in Canada)	Divorced; sole-custody father	9	70,000	University professor	Post-graduate

Table A.1. (*Continued*)

Name and City	Age	No. of children	Ages of children	Ethnicity	Relationship status	Years as primary caregiver	HH income	Occupation	Education
21. Len Small town, Quebec	45	1	17	French Canadian	Divorced; joint custody	6.5	50,000	Mailman (letter carrier)	High school
22. Lester Rural Ontario	50	1	11	White	Divorced; joint custody	10	70,000	Police officer	Community college
23. Logan Small town, Ontario	54	3	12 12 10	White	Divorced; joint custody	9	70,0000	College professor	Post-graduate
24. Lorne Small city, northern Ontario	45	3	20 18 14	White	Divorced; sole custody	4	85,000	Mill foreman	High school. Some college
25. Mick Ottawa	45	1	16	White	Divorced; sole-custody father	13	50,000	Transport truck driver	High school
26. Morgan Ottawa	45	2	13 10	White	Divorced; joint custody	7	45,000	Graphic artist and designer	Community college
27. Osie Ottawa	47	2	15 12	African Canadian (20 years in Canada)	Joint custody for 10 years. Sole custody for 3 years	13	50,000	Self-employed software training	University
28. Nestor Toronto	35	2 (twins)	12 12	White	Divorced; sole custody	2	60,000	Small business	High school
29. Nicholas Halifax, Nova Scotia	35	2	5 2	White	Separated	1	70,000	Self-employed and post-graduate student	University
30. Reid City in Ontario	39	4	17 15 11 10	White	Divorced; sole custody.	8	Varies. Between 25,000 and 100,000	Technology consultant	Technical college
31. Ron Victoria, British Columbia	53	2	10 7	White	Divorced; sole custody	6.5	25,000	Web designer	Community college
32. Roy Ottawa	31	1	3	White	Never married; sole custody since his son was 4 months old	2.5	50,000	Military	High school

Table A.1. (Concluded)

Name and City	Age	No. of children	Ages of children	Ethnicity	Relationship status	Years as primary caregiver	HH income	Occupation	Education
33. Ryan Ottawa	44	2	14 7	White	Divorced; sole custody (going back to court soon)	2.5	80,000	Military	University
34. Sasha Ottawa	33	3	14 12 10	African Canadian (20 years in Canada)	Divorced; joint-custody father	8	Under 20,000	Dancer and dance teacher	High school
35. Seamus Ottawa	55	4	All adults	White (Irish Canadian)	Widowed	15	70,000	Insurance representative	High school
36. Stephen Small town, Quebec	32	1	4	White	Never married; sole custody	2.5	N/A	Marketing consultant	High school
37. Stuart Ottawa	38	2	10 8	White (German Dutch)	Divorced; sole custody	8	75,000	Self-employed	University
38. Vincent Ottawa	50	1	5	White (Scottish German)	Divorced; joint custody (not legal)	5	Over 100,000	Speech writer	Post-graduate
39. Wally Small town, Ontario	42	1	10	White	Divorced (married three times); sole custody	5	20,000	Post office	High school
40. Wayne Ottawa	42	2	14 12	Polish Canadian (emigrated to Canada)	Widowed	8	80,000	Engineer	University

Table A.2. Stay-at-home Fathers

Name and City	Age	No. of children	Ages of children	Ethnicity	Relationship status	Years as primary caregiver	HH income	Occupation	Education
1. Aaron Ottawa	51	2	8 10	Jewish, wife is French Canadian	Married	9	100,000	Previously lawyer; now writer	Post-graduate.
2. Adam Ontario (rural)	42	3	17 15 11	White	Married	10	100,000 (now)	Previously stay-at-home dad, then part-time student Now; govt economist	University
3. Ahmed Ottawa	52	3	10 10 10 (triplets)	Iranian	Married	3	24,000	Free-lance journalist, part-time student	University
4. Alistair Ottawa	42	2	13 10	White	Married	1	60,000	Writer	University
5. Andre Ottawa	32	3	6 5 5	White	Married	2	Under 20,000	Not employed; on disability	High school
6. Andrew Ottawa	42	2	7 5	White	Married	2	100,000	Engineer, planning to retrain as teacher	Post-graduate
7. Andy Ottawa	30	1 (& 1 due)	3	Italian/Sicilian	Married	2½	60,000	Not employed	Post-graduate
8. Archie Ottawa	39	2	6 4	White	Married	5	Over 100,000	Previously gas service technician; now: Not employed	University
9. Austin Calgary	47	2	13 6	White	Married; wife has cancer	2	N/A	Internet consultant	University
10. Benoit Montreal	37	2	6 3	White, French Canadian	Married	2	75,000	Full-time dad	University
11. Blair Ottawa	43	4	21 14 12 8	White	Married	8	120,000	Film producer	University
12. Bruce Ottawa	35	2	6 4	White; wife is black	Married	5	80,000	Not employed	University

Table A.2. (Continued)

Name and City	Age	No. of children	Ages of children	Ethnicity	Relationship status	Years as primary caregiver	HH income	Occupation	Education
13. Cameron Ottawa	32	2 plus a foster child (19)	2 6 months	White	Married	2½	40,000	Not employed	University
14. Carl Ottawa	35	2 (& 1 due)	4 2½	White	Married	4	50,000	Previously book-store manager; not employed	University
15. Craig Ottawa	40	2 (twins)	4 4	White	Married	3½	40,000	Part-time in hard-ware store	High school
16. Eduardo Ottawa	37	1 (& 1 due)	3	Latino	Married	1	40,000	Previously interna-tional development; currently student	Post-graduate
17. Ed Rural Ontario	37	3	3.5 2	White	Married	3	N/A	Part-time student	Masters (post graduate)
18. Frank London Ontario	37	2	5 2	White	Married	4	60,000	Previously account executive; now studying part-time to be a social worker	University
19. Gary Ottawa	37	3	7 5 2 months	White	Married	7	60,000 (+ some property)	Carpenter/ landlord	University
20. Graeme Ottawa	44	2	3 3 months	White	Married	1	45,000 90,000 (when he is working)	N/A	High school. Some college
21. Harry Rural Ontario	46	2	9 6	White	Married	9	60,000	Rural farmer; jewellery maker	Technical College
22. Helmut Ottawa	41	2	8 6	White	Married	4	50,000	Education con-sultant	University
23. Howard Ottawa	44	2	9 7	White	Married	6	Over 100,000	Formerly software engineer; currently not employed	University

Table A.2. (Continued)

Name and City	Age	No. of children	Ages of children	Ethnicity	Relationship status	Years as primary caregiver	HH income	Occupation	Education
24. Hubert Ottawa	36	3	9 5 1½	Chinese	Married	1	30,000	Chef	High school
25. Jarabee Ottawa	35	2	3 1	Somali; wife from Ethiopia	Married	2	Under 20,000	Polling research (evenings and weekends); wife studying English	University
26. Jerome Fredericton, New Brunswick	44	2	11 6	White	Married	11	60–90,000	Works a few hours a week in wife's (pediatrician) office	University
27. Jesse Ottawa	37	1	3	White, partner is French Canadian	Married (common law)	2	60,000	Artist and media arts	University
28. Jimmy Rural Ontario	34	1*	4	White	Married (common law)	4	30,000	Auto mechanic	High school
29. Joe Ottawa	55	2	4 2	Aboriginal	Married	4	60,000	Not employed	Less than high school
30. Kyle Small town, Ontario	53	2	12 9	White; wife is German Canadian	Married	1 year at home, other years as shared	Under 20,000	Part-time town councillor; wife works part-time as librarian	University
31. Luke Ottawa	43	2	15 13	White	Married	14	100,000	Caregiver for mentally challenged (works shifts)	Technical college
32. Lewis Ottawa	38	2	4 1	White	Married	1	50–70,000 depending on who is working	Business	University
33. Manuel Ottawa	53	2	20 18	Latino	Married	7	80,000	Special education teacher	University
34. Marc Ottawa	53	2	18 15	White	Married	15	75,000	Freelance writer and martial arts instructor	University

*Jimmy also has one child from a former relationship who is living in another province.

Table A.2. (Continued)

Name and City	Age	No. of children	Ages of children	Ethnicity	Relationship status	Years as primary caregiver	HH income	Occupation	Education
35. Martin Ottawa	40	1	1½	White (Czech Canadian)	Married	1	While home, 50,000	Previously insurance, then guide-dog training	University
36. Maurice Ottawa	30	2	4 1	Black	Married	1	60,000	Previously military; now restaurant manager	Technical college
37. Mitchell Ottawa	38	3	7 3 3	White	Married	7	60,000	Retired naval officer	University
38. Norman Ottawa	39	1	5	White	Married	4	1000,000	Retired early	University
39. Owen Ottawa	41	2	11 8	White	Married	8	70–80,000	Actor, carpenter	Post graduate
40. Patrick Small town, Ontario	38	2	4 2	White	Married	1	70,000	Business	University
41. Peter Ottawa	38	2	6 4	White	Married	5	70–80,000	Desktop publishing	University
42. Richard Ottawa	38	3	7 2 1 month	White, French Canadian	Married	2	60,000	Formerly electronic technician	Technical college
43. Rick Ottawa	47	2	17 13	White	Married	10	80–100,000	Writer	University
44. Robert Rural Quebec	45	2	6 4	White French Canadian	Married	3	70,000	Previously owned business; currently not employed	High School
45. Robin Ottawa	36	2	3 1	White	Married	2	45,000	Part-time security guard	University
46. Rory Calgary, Alberta	53	1	4	White	Married	4	Over 100,000	Previously: oil and gas industry	University
47. Sam Ottawa	40	2	6 3	White	Married	5	100,000	Driving instructor	High school

Table A.2. (*Concluded*)

Name and City	Age	No. of children	Ages of children	Ethnicity	Relationship status	Years as primary caregiver	HH income	Occupation	Education
48. Samatar Ottawa	67	11	3–39	Somali (12 years in Canada)	Third wife. His wife is studying; he is home with their 3-year-old	1	N/A	Retired business man	High school
49. Shahin Ottawa	42	1	6	Iranian	Married	6	90,000	Cabinet maker and carpenter	University
50. Shane Ottawa	32	1	4	White	Married	4	100,000	Writer	High school
51. Theo Ottawa	34	4	4 3 2 1	White	Married	2	85,000	At home full time; previously computer engineer	Post-graduate
52. Tom Small town, Quebec	38	3	8 5 3	White	Married (common-law)	8	Over 100,000	Trained as a counsellor	University
53. William Ottawa	49	3	12 11 8	White, married to an Iraqi	Married	4	45,000	Book publisher (small press)	University
FATHERS ON PARENTAL LEAVE									
54. Ray Ottawa	36	1	5 months	White	Gay father living with partner; adopted a baby in an open adoption	5 months (unpaid parental leave)	50,000	Writer and co-owner of a small business	University
55. Matthew Ottawa	35	1	9 months	White	Married	3 months	100,000	Refrigerator repair	Technical college
56. Griffith Ontario	44	2	3 3 mos	White	Married	9 months (paid and unpaid parental leave)	90,000	Business	High school and some college
57. Walter Ottawa	38	1	9 mos	White	Married; parental leave (taking it for 1 year; some paid, some unpaid)	9 mos – taking one year	130,000 (when he is working)	Business	University

Table A.3. Both Stay-at-home and Single Fathers

Name and City	Age	No. of children	Ages of children	Ethnicity	Relationship status	Years as primary caregiver	HH income	Occupation	Education
1. Alexander Small town, Ontario	45	3	15 10 3	White	Married 12 years; in process of separating – will share custody	Shared and primary at different point; mainly primary over 10 years; took two parental leaves	90,000	Professor	Post-graduate
2. Brandon Rural Ontario	49	3	18 13 12	White	Divorced; sole custody; has worked from home	3 (works from home)	Under 20,000	Organic farmer	University
3. Burt Ottawa	41	1	11	White	Single	10 (working flexibly when child was young)	80,000	Computer consultant	Technical college
4. Bruno Ottawa	49	2	16 14	Italian Canadian (Brazilian mother)	Divorced Sole custody	14 Worked nights when children were young and cared for them during day (with help from his mother)	80,000	Advertising	High school
5. Dean Rural Quebec	50	3	16 14 10	White	Separated; shared custody	Was stay-at-home father for 3 years	80,000	Marketing Consultant	University
6. Emmett Small town, Ontario	34	1	9	White	Divorced; was stay-at-home father for 6 years; now fighting for shared custody	6 as stay-at-home father	Under 20,000	Community development leader	University
7. James Toronto	33	1	3.5	White	Separated gay father	1.5 years as stay-at-home father; now joint custody	50,000	Manager with a charity	High school; some university
8. Johnny Ottawa	36	1	12	White	Divorced, sole custody	6 as sole custody and periods of being at home as well	Under 20,000	Unemployed; previously radio broadcaster	Less than high school

Table A.3. (*Concluded*)

Name and City	Age	No. of children	Ages of children	Ethnicity	Relationship status	Years as primary caregiver	HH income	Occupation	Education
9. Jude Rural Saskatchewan	44	6	23 19 14 14 11 8	Aboriginal (lives on reserve)	Separated; joint custody	5 years at home; now joint custody father	Under 20,000	Teacher's aid	Less than high school
10. Leslie Small town, Alberta	33	3	9 7 5	White	Divorced gay father	3 years as stay-at-home father; now joint custody father (5 years)	20,000 (his gay partner makes 15,000)	Graphic designer	High school
11. Lucas Ottawa	59	2	27 23	White (Canadian Finnish)	Divorced; joint custody; was stay-at-home father for 3 years	3 at home + joint custody for 15	50,000	Consultant	Post-graduate
12. Paul Ottawa	26	1	6	White	Never married; sole custody (not legal) Also at home working as a visual artist	3	Under 20,000	Visual artist (self-employed)	University
13. Victor Ottawa	50	2	12 8	White (Italian)	Stay-at-home; now separated	Home for 12, separated for 3	Under 20,000	Musician	Less than high school

Table A.4. Shared care giving fathers

Name and City	Age	No. of children	Ages of children	Ethnicity	Relationship status	HH income	Occupation	Education
1. Ayan Ottawa	50	1	13	Somali (12 years in Canada)	Married; he is raising his cousin's son	N/A	Previously teacher, now student	University in Somalia
2. Aidan Toronto	51	1	20	White	Divorced gay father; daughter lives with him now that she is at university	Over 100,000	Computer manager	Post-graduate
3. Dalmar Ottawa	52	4	24 21 18 13	Somali (10 years in Canada)	Married; highly involved father	50,000	University lecturer	Post-graduate
4. Ghedi Ottawa	49	3	10 7 4	Somali (10 years in Canada)	Married; his wife (also Somali) is studying to be a nurse. He shares the care of the children	40,000	Previously doctor in Somalia; now as administrative assistant (government)	Post-graduate in Somalia
5. Pedro Ottawa	50	2	17 12	Latino (10 years in Canada)	Married; highly irvolved father	50,000	Social worker	University
6. Leandros Ottawa	45	1	10	Greek	Married	80,0000	Self-employed real estate	University
7. Jean-Marc Small town, Ontario	43	2 (twins)	7 7	French Canadian	Divorced gay father. His wife has sole custody, but he is highly involved. Took parental leave when twins were babies	50,000	Public sector employee	University
8. Morris Toronto	57	2	27 23	White	Married (heterosexual) gay father; openly gay within his heterosexual marriage. He stayed with his wife initially for the children's sake and now for companionship	Over 100,000	Self-employed consultant	High school

Table A.5. Couples Interviewed

Names	Stay-at-home father status (SAHD)	Ages*	No. of children	Ages of children	Ethnicity (self-defined)	Household Income (Canadian dollars)	Occupation
1. Peter & Linda	SAHD for 5½ years; home-based Web designer (6–12 hours per week)	38 36	2	6 4	White	80,000	Peter Web designer Linda high school teacher
2. Richard & Aileen	SAHD for 2 years	40 35	3	7 2 2- mos.	Aileen white Richard white, French Canadian	50,000	Richard previously electric technician Aileen federal government public servant
3. Manuel & Julia	SAHD for 7 years. She worked shift work for many years. He now works full time in special education	Early 50s	2	20 18	Manuel latino Julia white	83,000	Manuel latino Julia white
4. Shahin & Louise	SAHD 6 years Self-employed carpenter	Early 40s	1	3	Shahin Iranian Louise French Canadian	100,000	Shahin carpenter/renovator Louise laywer
5. Mitchell & Nina	SAHD for 7 years	Early 40s	3	6 4 year old twins	Mitchell white Nina German Canadian	60,000	Mitchell former naval officer Nina clinical psychiatrist
6. Joe & Monique	SAHD for 4 years	55 32	2	4 2	Joe Aboriginal Monique white	60,000	Joe mainly unskilled labour Monique laywer
7. Gary & Kathy	SAHD for 7 years. She is self-employed and does not get maternity leave; he has worked flexibly as a self-employed carpenter and landlord of one small building	Late 30s	3	7 5 2 months	White	60,000	Gary carpenter/landlord Kathy self-employed hair-dresser

Table A.5. (Concluded).

Names	Stay at home father status (SAHD)	Ages*	No. of children	Ages of children	Ethnicity (self-defined)	Household Income (Canadian dollars)	Occupation
8. Carl & Penny	SAHD for 4 years	Mid 30s	2 and she is pregnant with 3rd	4 2.5	White	50,000	Carl former bookstore manager Penny government civil servant
9. Tom & Natasha	SAHD for 7 years. Has done occasional contracts of part-time work, but mainly at home	Early 40s	3	7 6 4	White Natasha Dutch Canadian	Over 100,000	Tom counsellor Natasha family physician
10. Martin & Denise	SAHD for over 1 year; now works 3 days a week	42 36	1	4	White Martin Czech Canadian	80,000	Martin insurance industry, then trained guide dogs, now back to insurance Denise communications in government
11. Craig & Mary Claire	SAHD for 4 years. Works 2 nights a weeks at Home Hardware store	Early 40s	2	4-year-old twins (they were triplets but one died)	White	40,000	Craig previously worked in auto parts Mary Claire psychiatric nurse
12. Ghedi & Sara	Shared care giving	42 35	3	10 7 4	Somali (in Canada 10 years)	40,000	Ghedi was a doctor in Somalia; now works as a admin assistant in government Sara studying nursing
13. Alistair & Claire	SAHD for one year while his daughter was an infant	41 42	2	13 10	White	60,000	Alistair a novelist Claire completing her PhD studies
14. Theo and Lisa	SAHD for 3 years	35 35	4	5 4 3 2	White	85,0000	Theo formerly computer engineer Lisa computer engineer

* Ages are given in range in cases where consecutive interviews (individual father interview, focus group interview, and couple interview were held over a three to four year period).

APPENDIX B: 'COAXING' FATHERS' STORIES

B. 1: Focus Groups with Fathers*
Aide-Memoire

1. Introductions
   - Name
   - Number, ages, and gender of children
   - How and when did you become a primary caregiving father?
   - Previous or present employment?
   - Anything else you would like to share with the group?

2. Day-to-Day Life as a Father
   - (Points of entry and points of exclusion) (see diagram below)

3. Mothering and Fathering
   - When men are primary caregivers, are they mothering?
   - Do you think women and men care for children differently?
   - Is there a 'masculine' concept of care?

4. Proposals and Desired Changes
   - In your view, what are the three advantages/ best parts about being a stay-at-home dad (or a single dad)?
   - In your view, what are the three disadvantages/ worst parts about being a stay-at-home dad (or a single dad)?
   - If you could construct an ideal world for stay-at-home fathers (or single fathers), what would it look like and how would you get there?

5. Gains and Losses
   - What have you gained from being a stay-at-home father (or a single father)?
   - What have you lost?
   - Is there a gap between what you expected and what you have experienced?
   - What would you like people to know about stay-at-home fathers (or single fathers)?

---

* Used as a guide for single-father groups and stay-at-home-father groups.

Fathers' Focus Group

Day-to-Day Life as a Father

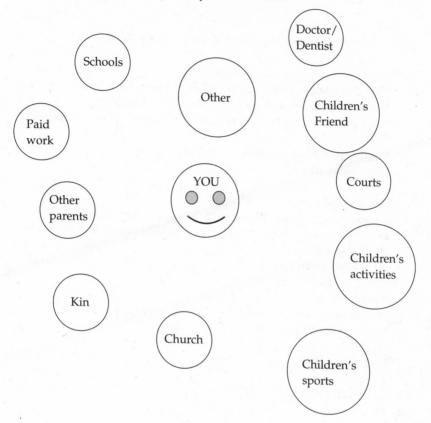

B.2: Focus Group with Somali Fathers

1. Introductions
   - Name:
   - Number, ages, and gender of children:
   - Previous or present employment:
   - When did you come to Canada:
   - Your situation as a father (Single? Shared? Primary?):

2. Background on Your Fathering in Canada
    - How has your fathering changed as a result of being in Canada?
    - Is this a positive or negative change in your view?

3. Daily Routine
    - Your main tasks and responsibilities in your household?

4. Wider Community and Social Support
    - If you need help with raising the children, whom do you turn to (friends, family, community organizations, community elders)?
    - What are some of the important issues that you turn to others for help with?
    - Which parent takes the children to the doctor or dentist?
    - Who deals with education issues?

5. Mothering and Fathering
    - Do you think these are different sets of practices and activities?
    - Do you think fathers care for children in a different way than the mother does? If so, how?
    - What is most important to you in your role as a father?

6. Parenting Role Models
    - Do you draw on your parents as role models for your parenting?
    - Your mother? Your father? Others?

7. Other Issues?

B.3: Individual Interviews with Fathers
Aide-Memoire

I. Background Information
    (i) *Demographics about You and Your Children*
        - Age:
        - Relationship Status:
        - Ethnic background:
        - Address:
        - (If applicable) E-mail address:
    (ii) *Children*:
        - Number:

- Ages:
- Names of children:
- How long have you been the primary caregiver of your child(ren)?

(iii) *Work Information*:
  - Are you currently employed?
  - (If applicable) Occupation (previous or present):
  - If employed, hours worked per week:
  - What is your spouse/partner's occupation?
  - Income? (or) income range for you and for your partner:
  - Under 20,000
  - 20,001–39,999
  - 40,000–59,999
  - 60,000–99,999
  - Over 100,000

Education:

II. Interview's Five Themes
  (i)   *Background on How You Came to Be Primary Caregiver*
    - How did you come to be here?

  (ii) *Typical Day and Week*
    - Tell me about a typical day.
    - A typical week?

  (iii) *Community Relationships*
    - I am interested in knowing about your life as a father in relationship to the community that you live in and the organizations and institutions that you are associated with.
    - How have you been treated as a primary caregiver: in the community? In the playground? In the school? In parenting groups?
    - Friendships: Do you have close friendships? Who?
    - Do you have a lot of friends who are fathers?
    - Anybody who helps you with the children? Provides support and guidance?
    - Do you connect with other parents?
    - Do you spend time with any other fathers?
    - Where, when?
    - Do you belong to any fathering organizations?

Figure B.1. Household Portrait: Richard and Aileen

Richard	Mainly Richard (with Aileen helping)	Shared Equally	Mainly Aileen (with Richard helping)	Aileen
Cooking evening meal (weekdays)	Taking out garbage	Buying of minor household (kitchen) items	Changing beds	Cleaning stove
Cooking evening meal (weekends)	Vacuuming	Buying furniture	Household cleaning – kitchen	Household cleaning – bathroom
Watering plants	Making breakfast	Repairing clothes	Reading childcare books/magazines for parenting ideas	Laundry – doing it
Shopping for groceries	Buying major household appliances	Setting disciple and following through	Son turns to … when upset	Tidying up and dusting
Washing floors	Garden – vegetable	Buying children's clothes	Family contacts (letters, phone calls)	Ironing
Making daily lunches for Elizabeth	Making beer, wine, or other	Promoting children's independence		Laundry – putting away
Garden – flowers	Bedtime routine	Buying Christmas presents		Household cleaning – bedrooms
Minor repairs – plumbing, electrical	Reading to the children	Making decisions about children's behaviour		Cleaning toilet
Indoor painting	Bath-time routine	Making children's doctor appointments		Washing up
Washing windows	Sports	Planning meals		Decorating house
Mowing lawn	Taking photos	Long-term planning of children's activities		Feeding cats
Car maintenance	Feels they have the overall responsibility for the children's lives			Weekend lunch
Outdoor painting	Organizing children's birthday parties			Making bed
Renovations				Worry
Snow blowing				Sending Christmas cards
Cleaning cat litter				Remembering birthdays and sending cards
Making jams/preserves				Making photo albums
Making baby food				Organizing social events with friends
Baking				Deciding what needs doing re housework
Physical play				

Figure B.1. (*Concluded*)

Richard	Mainly Richard (with Aileen helping)	Shared Equally	Mainly Aileen (with Richard helping)	Aileen
Creative play				
Homework				
Elizabeth turns mainly to … when upset				
Evening play				
Library				
Attending to children at night if they awaken				
Outdoor activities				
Cooking for guests				
Household bills				
Overall budgeting and financial management				
Overall planning and management of children's day-to-day activities				
Parent-teacher meetings				

(iv) *Ideas on Mothering and Fathering*
      (These questions were handed to fathers on a sheet in the face-to-face
      interviews).
      - Are men and women different?
      - Is *being* a mother different from *being* a father?
      - Are the practices/activities of mothering and fathering different?
      - Do you think fathers *care* for children in a different way than mothers
        do?
      - How would you describe yourself as a father (e.g., five adjectives)?

(v) *Your Own Family of Origin and Parenting Role Models*
      - Tell me about your own mother and father (or your caregivers as you
        were growing up).
      - Can you use five adjectives to describe each of your parents (or care-
        givers)?
      - Who are your role models in parenting?

(vi) *Conclusions*
      - Are there any issues that I haven't covered that you think are impor-
        tant?
      - What do you hope might come out of a project like this?
      - Do you know of any other fathers who might be willing to partici-
        pate in the project?
      - How did you find out about the project?

B.4: Internet Interview

*Are you (or have you been) a father who is the primary caregiver of your
children?*

If so, I would like to hear from you for the purposes of research. As part of an
ongoing research project funded by the Social Sciences and Humanities
Research Council of Canada, I want to build up a profile of fathers as primary
caregivers. To my knowledge this is the first attempt to investigate fathers as
primary caregivers via the Internet. Only your help will make it a success.
There are about fifty-five questions, and it should take about ten to fifteen minutes to complete.
   To respect your anonymity, the form you submit is sent to a cgi-bin. Your
name and email address are not attached unless you choose to provide them in

the spaces below. As a further precaution, you could use a public access terminal (e.g., a library, CyberCafe or Computer Lab). Or you can print off the questionnaire and send it directly to me:

Professor Andrea Doucet
Department of Sociology and Anthropology
Carleton University
1125 Colonel By Drive
Ottawa, Ontario
Canada K1S 5B6

CATEGORIES OF THE INTERVIEW:
- Background information: Characteristics of fathers who take this leave
- Issues of why you came to be a primary caregiver
- Experience: How fathers experienced the situation
- Mothering and fathering
- Social networks, friendships, and support
- Policy changes

I. BACKGROUND INFORMATION
1. Name (optional):
2. Are you interested in being contacted for any follow-up research?
   Yes ☐ No ☐
3. If yes, then please provide email address (optional):
4. Relationship: married (including common law) ☐ divorced ☐
   separated ☐ single widower ☐ cohabitation (opposite gender partner) ☐
   cohabitation (same gender partner) ☐ other ☐
5. Age:
6. City:
7. Province:
8. Rural ☐ urban ☐
9. Ethnicity:
10. How many children do you have?
    - How old is your first child?
    - How old is your second child?
    - How old is your third child?
    - How old is your fourth child?
    - How old is your fifth child?
    - How old is your sixth child?

11. More than six children? What are their ages and gender?
12. How long were you, or have you been, the primary caregiver of your children:
13. Income:
14. (If applicable) partner/ wife's income:
15. Combined family income:
16. Your education level:
17. Occupation:

II. WHY DID YOU CHOOSE TO BE PRIMARY CAREGIVER?

1. I chose to be the primary caregiver of my children because I was (we were) dissatisfied with other childcare options.
   - Strongly agree ☐ Agree ☐ Agree somewhat ☐ Disagree ☐ Strongly disagree ☐
2. I took leave of absence from work or quit work in order to stay home with children.
   - Strongly agree ☐ Agree ☐ Agree somewhat ☐ Disagree ☐ Strongly disagree ☐
3. I chose to be the primary caregiver of my children because we (I) wanted home care for children.
   - Strongly agree ☐ Agree ☐ Agree somewhat ☐ Disagree ☐ Strongly disagree ☐
4. I chose to be the primary caregiver of my children because I was already unemployed, so childcare was a convenient solution.
   - Strongly agree ☐ Agree ☐ Agree somewhat ☐ Disagree ☐ Strongly disagree ☐
5. I chose to be the primary caregiver of my children because I am (was) a student with a flexible schedule.
   - Strongly agree ☐ Agree ☐ Agree somewhat ☐ Disagree ☐ Strongly disagree ☐
6. I chose to be the primary caregiver of my children because one salary was sufficient to live on.
   - Strongly agree ☐ Agree ☐ Agree somewhat ☐ Disagree ☐ Strongly disagree ☐
7. I chose to be the primary caregiver of my children because my partner/ wife makes a very high salary.
   - Strongly agree ☐ Agree ☐ Agree somewhat ☐ Disagree ☐ Strongly disagree ☐
8. I chose to be the primary caregiver of my children because my partner/ wife is career oriented.

- Strongly agree ☐ Agree ☐ Agree somewhat ☐ Disagree ☐ Strongly disagree ☐

9. I chose to be the primary caregiver of my children because I am less career oriented than my partner.
   - Strongly agree ☐ Agree ☐ Agree somewhat ☐ Disagree ☐ Strongly disagree ☐

10. I chose to be the primary caregiver because I separated from my partner and was in a better position to take this on.
    - Strongly agree ☐ Agree ☐ Agree somewhat ☐ Disagree ☐ Strongly disagree ☐

11. I chose to be the primary caregiver because I took parental leave.
    - Strongly agree ☐ Agree ☐ Agree somewhat ☐ Disagree ☐ Strongly disagree ☐

12. I am primary caregiver and I share responsibilities with another.
    - Strongly agree ☐ Agree ☐ Agree somewhat ☐ Disagree ☐ Strongly disagree ☐

13. Other (specify):

III. HOW FATHERS EXPERIENCED THE SITUATION

1. In your view, what have you gained from this experience?
2. In your view, what have you lost as a result of this experience?
3. What advice would you like to offer to fathers who are approaching this same situation?
4. Overall, this experience has been: very positive, positive, not positive
5. Explain, including the best and worst aspects ...

IV. MOTHERING AND FATHERING

1. The job of mothering and fathering is the same job.
   - Strongly agree ☐ Agree ☐ Agree somewhat ☐ Disagree ☐ Strongly disagree ☐
2. Mothering and fathering are different sets of activities.
   - Strongly agree ☐ Agree ☐ Agree somewhat ☐ Disagree ☐ Strongly disagree ☐
3. Mothers do more creative activities with the children.
   - Strongly agree ☐ Agree ☐ Agree somewhat ☐ Disagree ☐ Strongly disagree ☐
4. Fathers do more physical play and sports with the children.
   - Strongly agree ☐ Agree ☐ Agree somewhat ☐ Disagree ☐ Strongly disagree ☐
5. Mothers are more nurturing than fathers.

- Strongly agree ☐ Agree ☐ Agree somewhat ☐ Disagree ☐ Strongly disagree ☐
6. Fathers are more disciplinarian than mothers.
   - Strongly agree ☐ Agree ☐ Agree somewhat ☐ Disagree ☐ Strongly disagree ☐
7. With the exception of birthing and breastfeeding, a father can do everything that a mother can do.
   - Strongly agree ☐ Agree ☐ Agree somewhat ☐ Disagree ☐ Strongly disagree ☐
8. Mothers do housework better than fathers.
   - Strongly agree ☐ Agree ☐ Agree somewhat ☐ Disagree ☐ Strongly disagree ☐
9. Fathers are different from mothers.
   - Strongly agree ☐ Agree ☐ Agree somewhat ☐ Disagree ☐ Strongly disagree ☐

Explain:

V. SOCIAL NETWORKS, FRIENDSHIPS, AND SUPPORT

1. I have ____ friend(s): one ☐ a few ☐ quite a few ☐ many ☐
2. In general I think that women make friends differently than men do.
   - Strongly agree ☐ Agree ☐ Agree somewhat ☐ Disagree ☐

Explain:

3. Women have more social networks than fathers do, and I think this makes a difference in the experience of parenting.
   - Strongly agree ☐ Agree ☐ Agree somewhat ☐ Disagree ☐

Explain:

4. It is important for me to have social networks and friends who can assist me as a parent.
   - Strongly agree ☐ Agree ☐ Agree somewhat ☐ Disagree ☐
5. Comments on your social networks and friends as a father:

VI. POLICY CHANGES

I would like to see the following changes that would help fathers and/or parents:

1. High-quality day care (in varied settings and with different choices available to parents)
   - Most important ☐ Very important ☐ Important ☐ Not a priority ☐ Not feasible ☐
2. Tax breaks for a stay-at-home parent

- Most important ☐ Very important ☐ Important ☐ Not a priority ☐ Not feasible ☐
3. More flexible working options so that parents could work and care for children.
   - Most important ☐ Very important ☐ Important ☐ Not a priority ☐ Not feasible ☐
4. Parenting courses for mothers and fathers.
   - Most important ☐ Very important ☐ Important ☐ Not a priority ☐ Not feasible ☐
5. Paid parental leave for one year available to either the mother or the father.
   - Most important ☐ Very important ☐ Important ☐ Not a priority ☐ Not feasible ☐
6. Other (explain):
7. Is there anything else you would like to add/recommend/suggest?

APPENDIX C

Data Analysis: The Listening Guide

At the core of the Listening Guide are the interchangeable words *listening* and *reading* so that one reads interview transcripts as though he or she was still listening to the person in the interview setting. Furthermore, it employs multiple and successive 'readings' of interview transcripts 'each time listening in a different way' (Brown 1998, 33). I used four readings in my work on fathers: the first was for the central storyline combined with a reader-response reflexive strategy; the second traced the 'I,' or central protagonist, in the narrative; the third and fourth drew the analysis out from the research subjects and their narratives to their nexus of social relationships and then even further into wider structural relations. These readings, as briefly described below, are not entirely representative of the way other researchers have used the Listening Guide but reflect the assumption that methods are not recipes that can be applied in uniform ways across projects (Mauthner & Doucet, 2003; see also Law, 2004, Charmaz, 2006). That is, while methods begin with particular ontological and epistemological conceptions, these can be transformed as they move through the hands and minds of varied researchers.

Reading 1: Reading the Story and Reading Myself in the Story

The Listening Guide begins with a reading for plot or narrative. Combining 'the basic grounded theory question' which is 'what is happening here?' (Charmaz, 2006, 168; see also Glaser and Strauss, 1967) with elements from narrative analysis, I read carefully through a selection of twenty-five interview transcripts using a coloured pencil to highlight recurring words, themes, events, protagonists, the central plot, subplots, and key characters. As a woman working with men's narratives, I was quite concerned to reflect on my responses to the narratives, and thus even more compelling than the reading for the storyline was the 'reader-response' element in that I read myself in the text, watching for how I was responding to being back in the research relationship and how this was occurring, initially at a biographical and emotional level, and then through the tracing of my theoretical responses.

More than just paying lip service to reflexivity, this first reading of interview transcripts offers a concrete way of putting oneself into continuing relationship with research subjects as well as offering a concrete way of 'doing reflexivity' (see Mauthner & Doucet, 2003). In practical terms, the Listening Guide suggests the use of a worksheet technique for this reading, whereby the respondent's words are laid out in one column and the researcher's reactions and interpretations are laid out in an adjacent column (Gilligan, Brown, et al., 1990; Brown & Gilligan, 1992). This allows the researcher to examine how and where some of her own assumptions and views – whether personal, political, or theoretical – might affect her interpretation of the respondent's words, or how she later writes about the person.

I conducted this and all of the readings of transcripts both alone and in small groups. Working with other colleagues highlighted the fact 'that people have more than one way to tell a story and see a situation through different lenses and in different lights' (Gilligan et al., 1990, 95). Through undertaking such in-depth analyses, I found that several biographical factors seemed to matter in the way I maintained relationships with the fathers who participated in my study. Specifically, I drew on my reflexive positioning as a white middle-class woman raised in a working-class family, my memories of growing up in a household with three brothers, and my more recent parenting knowledge. Moreover, I felt myself drawn into understanding and theorizing the narratives of fathers from difficult working-class backgrounds. My memories of our house on Main Street – on the working-class, Catholic side of town, near the paper mill and the 'low rental' houses – translated into my identification with narratives from low-income backgrounds or ones from small towns where tolerance for diversity was largely stifled. I read such narratives with a tacit understanding, as they brought me back to a place of familiar stories and rhythms.

In the case of less familiar stories, I widened my interpretive community and brought colleagues, research assistants, and friends with varied social locations who could help me to make sense of areas of experience that I was less familiar with. For example, throughout the process of group-based analysis, colleagues who had a familiarity with alcoholic family backgrounds helped me to interpret the narratives of fathers whose family patterns were rooted in alcoholism or substance abuse. To assist me with interpreting the narratives of gay fathers and fathers of ethnic minorities, I involved several research assistants and colleagues in analysis of transcripts, or in conversations, so as to gain understanding of areas of experience and social identities that I was less familiar with.

Reading 2: An 'I' Reading (Reading for Research Subjects)

One of the most powerful aspects of the Listening Guide is that it allows for a metaphorical space for the subject to 'speak' within the interpretation of his or her textual record, the transcript. This occurs through a second reading of an interview transcript, which attends to the particular *person* in the interview transcripts, and to the way this person speaks about her/himself and the parameters of her or his social world. Put differently, this reading involves 'directing my attention to the way the person speaks about herself is designed to highlight or amplify the terms in which she sees and presents herself ... I listen to her voice and attend to her vision and thus make some space between her way of speaking and seeing and my own' (Gilligan, Brown, et al., 1990, 103). It 'represents an attempt to stay, as far as it is possible, with the respondents' multi-layered voices, views and perspectives rather than simply and quickly slotting their words into either our own ways of understanding the world or into the categories of the literature in our area' (Mauthner & Doucet, 1998, 132). This process centres our attention on the active 'I' that is telling the story; amplifies the terms in which the respondent sees and presents herself; highlights where the respondent might be emotionally or intellectually struggling to say something; and identifies those places where the respondent shifts between 'I', 'we', 'you,' or 'it,' which can signal some change in the respondent's perceptions of self and their relationship to the events or phenomenon being discussed.

In concrete terms, I did this reading by using a coloured pencil to trace the 'I' in the interview transcripts, and I also worked with the interview transcripts on the computer screen, ultimately distilling them into 'I story' or an 'I poem' (Gilligan, 2002; Gilligan, et al., 2005) which is a streaming sequence of 'I' and 'we' statements. For example, in the case of Dennis, a half-Chinese and half-Aboriginal sole-custody father of an eight-year-old girl, the beginnings of his 'I poem' look something like the following:

I'm half Chinese, half Native
I grew up on a reserve
I had my hair permed ...
I was Hawaiian ... Somalian ...
I was passed for Greek, Italian ...

Yeah, it's gotten easier ...

Her Mother and I didn't get along ...
I found out that she was pregnant with her after we had broken up ...
I just told her that I'd be there for her as a father ...
I didn't want to separate the two kids ...
I tried to do that for awhile and then
I decided to come from Winnipeg to Toronto,
I figured there was nothing for me to do out there and
I had to do something good for myself...
I came to Toronto ...
I was going to school,
I had a job ...

I flew up there and picked her up, flew back, spent Christmas...
She was six ...
I spent most of the time bringing her up,
If I was working, I was working ...
I would be jumping back and forth from work and home
So, we bonded pretty quickly.
Her Mother wasn't ... a very nurturing person ...
I sent her back out there ...
I had called back a couple weeks later
She was at home by herself at about eight o'clock ... ten o'clock at night ...
I was trying to call my father and the police and so on to get them over to the house ...
I've heard rumors about it before ...

I got a private investigator ...
I called social services,
I called all her old neighbours and family that knows what she's like ...
I decided okay,
I'm going to fight for custody ...
I had decided that I wasn't telling her family ...
I figured they'd all just up and disappear,
That's the kind of people they are.
I was doing this...
I went through that this summer.
So, social services got on their butt really hard...
She jumped up screaming ... shouting ... swearing to give her to her father

Cause he wants her anyway, and walked out ...
All I had to do is get my lawyer to do up the papers,
I went out there,
She signed them
And that was that.

The 'I' reading, or the construction of an 'I' poem, puts the narrator in the transcript at the centre, at least for one heuristic moment. Its simple and yet powerful effect is in how it reminds us to listen to 'how she (he) speaks of herself (himself) before we speak of her (him)' (Brown & Gilligan, 1992, 27–8). In the case of Dennis above, following his 'I' revealed a man whose identity was often misinterpreted (*'I'm half Chinese, half Native, I was Hawaiian ... I was passed for Greek, Italian...'*), and who sets himself up as the heroic saviour of his child, who is morally distinct from his ex-girlfriend and her family (*'That's the kind of people they are'* while *'I just told her that I'd be there for her as a father'*). It also underlines how he went to great, indeed heroic, ends to wrest his daughter from that family into his own (*'I got a private investigator ... I called social services, I called all her old neighbours and family that knows what she's like'*).

This reading was also useful in illuminating how fathers spoke about themselves as men and as fathers and how they navigated through the 'shoulds' and 'oughts' of masculinities and parenting. That is, this reading revealed the gaps and contradictions in their stories, the dimensions of insecurities, personal tensions, feelings of inadequacy as they travelled through 'complex maternal worlds' (Bell & Ribbens, 1994), their feelings of being judged as a 'failed male' in terms of earning (Doucet, 2005) as well as feeling under sporadic surveillance as embodied actors moving on female-dominated terrain (Doucet, in press).

While providing brief streams of light into what could be metaphorically construed as the inner worlds of fathers, the 'I' reading also revealed the extent of contradiction in some of the fathers' narratives and further emphasized the limits of understanding experience and subjectivity. While fully aware of long-standing debates on the need to historicize and contextualize experience and subjectivities and the dangers of speaking about transparent subjects (e.g., de Laurentis, 1994; Scott, 1994; Weedon, 1987), I nevertheless clung to the view that there was some 'relationship between people's ambiguous representations and their experiences' (Hollway & Jefferson, 2000, 3) and that there was a 'knowing subject' (Code, 1995; Smith, 1996; Stanley, 1994) that I could, at the very least, even partially know within the account being given. Yet as I analysed my interviews with fathers and as I struggled to get at fathers as subjects, it gradually dawned on me that the subjects behind and within these stories were largely inaccessible. This was partly due to what researchers have identified as the difficulties for men with disclosing vulnerability (Daly, 1993) and partly because of the highly political context within which fathering, particularly single fathering, occurs (Mandell, 2002 Doucet, 2004). Noticing that some fathers, such as Dennis, constructed their stories as 'heroic narratives' (see also Presser, 2004), I began to pay less attention in my analysis to integrity or credibility of the 'I' in the story and focused on concerns that are more broadly taken up in ethnomethodological work (see ten Have, 2004), and which are also dealt with in Ian Plummer's 'sociology of stories,' including the critical questions of what 'brings people to the brink of telling' and 'how people come to construct their stories' (Plummer, 1995a, 1995b).

Aware that stay-at-home fathers worry about appearing masculine and single fathers face bitter custody battles, I abandoned any illusion of accessing subjectivities, even the possibility of attaining a 'reflexively constituted subject' (Mauthner & Doucet, 2003). As result of this epistemological shift, I gave greater emphasis to narratives and came to the view that rather than knowing subjectivities, all I could know was their narratives or *narrated subjectivies* (see also Benhabib, 1999, McNay, 2000, Somers, 1994). One consequence of this move was that in my writing on fathers I have been very deliberate to speak about *fathers' narratives* as one of my key sources of data and not fathers or *fathers' experiences*.

These first two readings, as described above, are the staples of the Listening Guide approach in that researchers using this method of data analysis would be encouraged to undertake it as a way of understanding the narratives being told, the place of the researcher in interpreting and retelling the narratives and giving initial primacy to understanding research subjects as the narrators of their stories. Generally speaking, researchers have conducted two or more further readings that can vary depending on their research topic. These latter readings move the analysis out from the relationship between researchers and research and bring theoretical lenses to interview data. Specifically, I have focused these latter readings on the location of subjects and their narratives, first, into local matrices of social networks and relationships and then, second, into wider patterns of social structure, ideologies, or discourses.

Readings 3 and 4: Theoretical Readings

In the third reading of interview transcripts, recognizing the eminently social and relational quality of parenting children, I traced for respondents' accounts of their intimate relational worlds by focusing on friendships, social networks, and social support. This third reading is further informed by feminist theoretical insights that have critiqued and replaced individualist and autonomous conceptions of agency with more relational concepts of subjects and selves (Benhabib, 1992, 1995; Friedman, 1993, 2000). In the case of Dennis, I read for his relationships with other parents, with the institutional actors who were central in his daughter's life (teachers, health care workers, caregivers), and with social networks created around his daughter through her friends and through the activities she took part in. This reading pulled out issues of emotional responsibility (see chapter 4) and community responsibility (see chapter 5).

Finally, in a fourth reading, I explored the intersections of class, ethnicity, sexuality, and gender in social institutions (community, schools, health institutions, work and family) while also focusing on structured power relations and dominant ideologies. Broadly speaking, the fourth reading is informed by fundamental principles gleaned from structuration theory (Bourdieu 1977, 1992; Giddens 1984) as well as concepts of the 'gender order' (Connell 1987, 1995) and 'relations of ruling' (Smith 1987, 1999). This latter reading moves the local, particular, micro-level, subject-centred emphasis out into more macro-level, structural, material, and ideological levels. Again in relation to Dennis, issues of gender, ethnicity and class mattered in his parenting, particularly in his access to minimal financial resources and social capital, his difficult background living between an Aboriginal reserve and then making the transition into low-income housing in the city. Ideological conceptions of fathers as breadwinners and mothers as primary carers also played a role in Dennis's constant search for a girlfriend to help him care for his daughter. I also read for theoretical issues of embodiment, masculinities, the relation between gender equality and gender differences, and intersections between race, class, sexuality, and gender. Some of these findings are covered under the themes of moral responsibility (chapter 6), intersectionality (woven throughout the book), and borderwork (chapters 4, 5, and 6).

Notes

Introduction: Do Men Mother?

1 All names used in this book are pseudonyms. Any identifying characteristics such as names of other persons in their narratives, the names of compa-
nies, schools, and organizations are also changed. Effectively, all proper
nouns have been changed. The names of cities, towns, and provinces have
remained unchanged except for those cases where I felt that a person might
be identified due to some particularities of his or her story.

2 Many of the longer excerpts from interviews have been edited for clarity. I
did this reluctantly, at the request of the editors at University of Toronto
Press, in order to balance readability with the many extensive quotations
taken from the interviews conducted with fathers and mothers. Through
this process, however, I paid particular attention that the meanings of the
interviews were not changed and where repetition was needed to enhance
a point, I left it in. Where repetition or rambling sentences detracted, rather
than enhanced, what I understood to be the central focus of the quote, I
removed these. Having done all but three interviews myself, I had a strong
sense of where the interview excerpts could be cut back and where they
should not be cut. This represents another one of the many decisions that a
researcher makes in relation to how much of respondents' voices to include
and how much to edit.

3 This statement that 'today's fathers are more involved in their children's
lives than fathers of previous generations' has to be tempered with the
observation that there have always been highly involved fathers. Ralph
LaRossa has, for example, pointed out that we need to 'acknowledge the
variety or fathering styles in the past' and that 'we would do well to
broaden our perspective to allow for the fact that there *were* men in the past

who cared for children – changing diapers and getting up in the middle of the night' (LaRossa, 1997, 195).

4 Sara Ruddick has argued that men's greater participation in the daily dramas of care would create revolutionary change in society as well as in social conscience: 'It is now argued that the most revolutionary change we can make in the institution of motherhood is to include men in every aspect of childcare ... Again and again, family power dramas are repeated in psychic, interpersonal, and professional dramas, while they are institutionalized in economic, political, and international life. Radically recasting the power-gender roles in these dramas might just revolutionize social conscience' (Ruddick, 1983, 89).

5 Much analysis of the ways in which national governments have dealt both with women's employment and the issue of the care of children has drawn on Esping-Andersen's or Walter Korpi's threefold understandings of welfare states. These three models, according to Esping-Andersen and Korpi, respectively, include 'social democratic' or 'dual earners' (i.e., Scandinavian countries); 'liberal regime' or 'market-oriented' (i.e., the United States, Canada, the United Kingdom, New Zealand, Australia); and 'general family support' or 'conservative' (i.e., Austria, Belgium, France, Germany, Italy). Clearly, as with all heuristic models, there are overlaps between the models as well as times where particular countries do not fit neatly into any of these models (Esping-Andersen, 1999; Korpi, 2000; Orloff, 2002, 2004). Indeed, even within Canada, there are variations as to how state policy and parenting intersect (Bernard & Saint-Arnaud, 2004; Jenson, 2002)

6 In spite of such enthusiasm over the radical potential of men's involvement in care work, more sobering analyses of this possibility gradually came to be articulated in the 1980s and 1990s. Many commentators began to point out that the greater participation of men across the varied versions of global kitchens, bathrooms, and children's rooms could only be regarded as one small step towards transformative social change. As Iris Marion Young astutely saw it, 'It has not taken feminists long, however, to see that the matter is not simple' since the '[g]ender division of parenting is only one of the many institutional structures that produce and maintain the oppression of women' (Young, 1984, 142–3). More recently, Jane Flax, in a revisiting of Dinnerstein's work, has also reconfirmed the point made by Young two decades earlier: 'From my view of gender, it follows that changing one feature of social organization will not transform the whole' (Flax, 2002).

7 In addition to calling for men's involvement in caregiving as a way of challenging a gendered stalemate in caregiving, feminist scholars and activists

have also noted the importance of other measures. In relation to the specific issue of housework and childcare, several lines of argument have been put forth and include, for example, the valuing of unpaid work (Fraser, 1997; Folbre, 1994); its inclusion in census data as well as in national GDP accounting (Crittenden, 2001; Luxton & Vosko, 1998; Waring, 1988); universal high-quality childcare (Mahon, 2002; Jenson, 2002); and flexible working options for both parents (Brandth Kvande, 2001; Moss, 1996).

8 The fathering literature has drawn attention to key obstacles to greater fatherhood involvement including, for example, the role of work in fathers' lives (Deutsch, 1999; Dowd, 2000; Pleck, 1985); parental modelling after one's own father (Coltrane, 1996; Cowan & Cowan, 1987; Daly, 1993; Pleck, 1985; Snarey, 1993a); maternal gatekeeping from wives or female partners (Allen & Hawkins, 1999a; Parke, 1996; Pleck, 1985); co-constructed processes of 'doing gender' by both mothers and fathers (Berk, 1985; Coltrane, 1989, 1996; Risman, 1998; West & Zimmerman, 1987); gender ideologies (Deutsch, 1999; Hochschild, 1989), discourses of fatherhood (Dienhart, 1998; Lupton & Barclay, 1997; Mandell, 2002), and gender differences in the creation and maintaining of community parenting networks (Doucet, 2000, 2001b).

9 In her book *Mother Nature: A History of Mothers, Infants and Natural Selection*, Sarah Blaffer Hrdy does not argue that men can mother, but she does frame the issue of men and caregiving in terms of mothering when she explores the question of 'why males don't mother more' (1999, 209).

10 It is important to acknowledge that Ruddick's eloquent and provocative work on mothering and maternal thinking is framed by large moral, epistemological, philosophical, and political aims that link 'maternal thinking and a global peace politics though 'envision[ing] a world organised by the values of caring labour' (1995, 135).

11 The past several decades have witnessed dramatic international growth in the share of women who are part of the paid work force. In 2003, 57 per cent of all Canadian women aged fifteen and over had jobs, up from 42 per cent in 1976. There have been particularly sharp increases in the employment rate of women with children. In 2003, 72 per cent of all women with children under age sixteen living at home were part of the employed workforce, up from 39 per cent in 1976. In Canada, women with children, though, are still less likely to be employed than women without children; in 2003, 79 per cent of women under age fifty-five without children had jobs while 63 per cent of women with children under age three were employed and 69 per cent of women whose youngest child was age three to five was employed. Women with pre-school-age children are still less likely than

those with school-age children to be employed; in 2003, 66 per cent of women with children under age six were employed, compared with 77 per cent of those whose youngest child was age six to fifteen (Statistics Canada, 2003).

12 The number of families with stay-at-home mothers has declined over recent decades, as single-earner families have become less common. Yet between 1976 and 1997, the proportion of families with stay-at-home fathers increased from 1 per cent of all families to 6 per cent. In 2002, there were 985,300 stay-at-home mothers compared with 110,700 stay-at-home fathers; put differently, about one out of every ten stay-at-home parents is male. The father who stays at home to look after the children is, on average, forty-three years old, less likely to have a post-secondary education than a father who is earning outside the home (51.3 per cent compared with 64 per cent), and less likely to have been in a managerial or professional position. The length of time out of the workforce varies by gender, but this has been increasing gradually for men and decreasing for women. In 2002, 35 per cent of stay-at-home mothers and 26 per cent of stay-at-home fathers had been out of work for five years or more. Those mothers and fathers who had left the workforce in the previous twelve months cited very different reasons for leaving: loss of a job (57 per cent of men, 33 per cent of women); personal or family responsibilities (44 per cent of women and only 5 per cent of men) and other reasons, such as returning to school or a disability (24 per cent or women and 39 per cent of women) (Marshall, 1998; Statistics Canada, 2002b).

13 This category of stay-at-home father has consistently increased with slight fluctuations up and down over the past ten years, owing to the increasing number of dads at home as well as more dads willing to use this label. There was a low of 80,300 in 1997 and a high of 110,700 in 2002. Ontario has, by far, the highest number of stay-at-home fathers (42 per cent) with 46,100, followed by Quebec with 22,600 (20 per cent). In 2002, the highest numbers of stay-at-home dads per major city are the following: Toronto (20,800), Vancouver (9,300), Montreal (8,500) Ottawa (4,200), Calgary (2,700) and Edmonton (2,300) (Statistics Canada, 2000b).

14 The public saliency of this issue is well revealed in the fact that in the winter of 2005, the United States held its tenth convention for stay-at-home-dads. The convention included multiple workshops on varied themes related to fathering, keynote speakers, personal networking, and book signings.

15 According to Statistics Canada, in 1986, the year following major amendments to the Divorce Act, mothers won custody more than three-quarters

of the time and fathers 15 per cent of the time, with joint custody and other arrangements making up the remaining 10 per cent. In 2000, custody of 37.2 per cent of dependents was awarded to the husband and wife jointly, thus continuing a fourteen-year trend of steady increases in joint-custody arrangements. In 2002, for the first time, fewer than half of children whose parents sought court-ordered custody were placed in the care of their mother. For the 35,000 dependent children for whom custody was determined though divorce proceedings, sole custody of 49.5 per cent of the children was awarded to the mother, 8.5 per cent to the father, and 42 per cent to joint custody. Under a joint-custody arrangement, dependents do not necessarily spend equal amounts of their time with each parent (Statistics Canada, 2003). It is important to point out, however, that these figures give us only a partial picture of custody awards in Canada since they include only cases decided formally by courts. According to Boyd (2002), the numbers of mothers with custody are much higher when non-divorce-court awards and those for separated common-law relationships are included.

16 Also according to the OECD, one of Canada's strengths is its Employment Insurance Act of 2001, providing paid parental leave for almost a year as a 'very important contribution to both equal opportunity for women and infant well-being and development' (OECD, 2004, 5).

17 In Quebec, the provincial government introduced a public childcare system, based on day-care centres and private homes. In 1997, the initial cost to parents was $5 a day, although in 2003, this increased to $7 a day. Quebec currently accounts for about 40 per cent of regulated childcare centres in Canada. There have been some criticisms of Quebec's system and gradual changes made to increase quality, nutrition, and worker-child ratios (CBC, 2004; Jenson, 2002).

1. Studying Men, Mothering, and Fathering

1 Issues of gender equality and difference have, in fact, run through feminist theory for centuries, perhaps most notably back to one of the first full-length books advocating women's equality with men, that of Mary Wollstonecraft's *Vindication of the Rights of Women* (Wollstonecraft, 1992 [1792]). In the past few decades equality and difference have been constantly intertwined, both politically and theoretically. They recurred, for example, throughout the 1970s, with debates in the United States over the proposed Equal Rights Amendment and in the 1980s with the publication of Carol Gilligan's book *In a Different Voice* (1982), and then through the late 1980s and the 1990s with Italian, Dutch, and French feminists pulling out com-

plex strands of variations in the thinking about equality and differences (Bock and James, 1992; Bono and Kemp, 1991; Kemp and Bono, 1993, Cavarero, 1993) (Gisela Bock & James, 1992; Bono & Kemp, 1991; Cavarero, 1993; Nancy Fraser & Bartky, 1992; Grosz, 1989). There are no simple or neat answers to this theoretical debate and to the issues raised. This theoretical and political conversation has, nevertheless, persisted because it builds on well-worn disputes over whether and how women and men are different or the same, the interplay between the social and the embodied, and how equality might be achieved in spite of, or through the incorporation of, differences.

2 Popular television programs that highlight gender differences in parenting include Tim Allen's *Tool Time* (which produced new shows from 1991 to 1999), *According to Jim* (with Jim Belushi) and *Everybody Loves Raymond*.

3 It is important to point out that neither Nancy Fraser nor Nancy Folbre fit squarely into the gender differences strand; however, like that of many feminists, their work at times draws on these debates in order to make strategic arguments. Both authors actually work *between* issues of gender equality and gender differences.

4 There have been internal tussles between women writing on caregiving and whether or not feminists value caregiving enough while they work to transform the unequal, taken-for-granted, or oppressive conditions under which it is performed (see, for example, the debate between Ahlander & Bahr, 1995; Riley & Kiger, 1999).

5 In a similar vein, Jane Flax maintains that what feminists should seek to end is 'not gender, not differences, and certainly not the feminine, but rather domination' (Flax, 1992, 194).

6 By *power relations* Connell is referring, for example, to how the 'main axis of power in the contemporary European/US gender order is the overall subordination of women and the dominance of men' (Connell, 2002, 24).

7 By *production relations*, Connell refers to the deeply rooted gender divisions of paid and unpaid work, where women do most of the caring work, consistently earn lower wages than those of men, and participate in gender-stratified labour markets. Connell also notes that 'equal attention should be paid to the economic consequences of gender division of labor, specifically the benefits accruing to men from unequal shares of the products of social labor (i.e. *'the patriarchal dividend'*)'(Connell, 2000, 25).

8 The third aspect of gender relations, according to Connell, is *emotional relations* or *cathexis*. While Connell's work (1987, 1995, 2000) configures emotional relations mainly in terms of sexual desire, my book also considers emotional relations as issues of emotional connection and normative

expectations around gendered propensities and responsibilities for caring and 'emotional labor' (Hochschild, 1983).

9 Fourth and finally, Connell writes about *symbolism*: 'we often understand gender differences through symbolic oppositions rather than through images of gradation, and this reinforces belief in gender dichotomy' (Connell, 2000, 26). Symbolism exists in images of masculinity and femininity, of men and women in popular culture, in language and in normative understandings. Certain areas of social life are frequently defined as masculine and others as feminine with, for example, sports often associated with the masculine and caring with the feminine (Connell, 2000, 154). As explored in this book, gender differences as 'symbolic oppositions' come into play in understandings of mothering and fathering as identities, practices, and as institutions.

10 See also Melody Hessing's (1993) Canadian study of female clerical workers,' which details strategies for managing employment and domestic life and the significance of household networks in sustaining gender divisions of labour.

11 While there has been much debate on the usefulness of the concept 'masculinities' (Clatterbaugh, 1998; Hearn, 1996), I hold with Connell that 'we need some way of talking about men and women's involvement in the domain of gender' and that masculinities and femininities remain theoretically useful concepts to assist us with making sense of understanding gender relations as well as 'gender ambiguity' (Connell, 2000, 16–17).

12 Many social scientists who study bodies and embodiment also draw on Michel Foucault (1973, 1977, 1979), Pierre Bourdieu (1984, 1992) or Emile Durkheim (1895 [1982], 1912 [1995]).

13 In a similar manner, Linda Nicholson, in an article devoted to 'interpreting gender,' eloquently argues for a view whereby 'the body does not disappear from feminist theory' but rather 'it becomes a variable rather than a constant,' as well as a *map* that varies depending on where it is placed: 'Thus I am advocating that we think about the meaning of *woman* as illustrating a map of intersecting similarities and differences. Within such a map the body does not disappear but rather becomes an historically specific variable whose meaning and import are recognized as potentially different in different historical contexts' (Nicholson, 1994, 83).

14 Elsewhere, I draw on two other points from Goffman (Doucet, in press). The first is 'body techniques,' a concept that Goffman borrows from M. Mauss (1979); the second is inter-subjectivity, or *inter-corporeality*, which builds on the work of Merleau-Ponty (1964, 1968).

15 By noting the moral quality of Goffman's analysis of body techniques,

Crossley is highlighting Goffman's symbolic interactionist roots (see also Denzin, 1970) and the way people are judged on their 'bodily norms.'

16 Thorne is drawing on the work of Fredrik Barth and his introduction to *Ethnic Groups and Boundaries* (1969). She writes, 'This notion comes from Fredrik Barth's analysis of social relations that are maintained across ethnic boundaries without diminishing the participants' sense of cultural difference and dichotomized ethnic status' (Thorne, 1993, 64).

2. Knowing Fathers' Stories through Gossamer Walls

1 All names used for characters from the researcher's past are pseudonyms.

2 According to Normin Denzin, 'Symbolic interactionism takes as a fundamental concern the relationship between individual conduct and forms of social organization, most centrally social groups. This perspective grants the human the ability to carry on conversations with himself and asks how selves emerge out of the social structure and social situations' (Denzin, 1970, 260). As for the Aubie boys, it is important to acknowledge that they did indeed 'turn out very well without a mother to raise them.'

3 There are, or course, many different ways to 'do' ethnography, and the term itself and the accomplishment of ethnographies are determined by the epistemologies and ontologies underpinning the conducting of the ethnography (Denzin, 1994; Guba & Lincoln, 1998; Hammersley, 1998; Hammersley & Atkinson, 1983).

4 To recruit respondents, I was fortunate to have the assistance of one particularly extroverted research assistant who was very good at approaching men walking with infants and young children in parks, in shopping malls, and in bookstores.

5 Like the well-known British fatherhood researcher Charlie Lewis, I had in mind a sample of 'one hundred fathers' (Lewis, 1986). I thus interviewed 101 fathers, and a further 17 fathers participated through an Internet interview.

6 Education levels, for example, were as follows: 28 per cent of the fathers had a high school education (or less than high school); 13 per cent had attended technical or community college; 44 per cent had attended university, and 15 per cent had post-graduate university degrees (i.e., business, law, engineering, teachers' college, social work degree, a master's degree or a Ph.D.).

7 Of the eighty-nine in-depth interviews, sixty were transcribed verbatim, whereas the final twenty-nine were transcribed selectively. Transcription costs are considerable since it takes six to eight hours to transcribe one hour of tape. Focus groups were recorded and partially transcribed, and notes

were taken at the group and afterwards. All the couple interviews were transcribed verbatim.

8 The process of developing the Household Portrait technique was informed by principles from non-formal participatory education and my experience as a participatory research trainer and facilitator (1986–89) with UNICEF and the United Nations Development Programme in Central and South America (see Doucet, 1996, 2001; Srinivasan, 1977, 1990).

9 The Household Portrait technique examined domestic tasks as well as responsibility for them and for children, for financial management, and for household maintenance and repair. A standard list of household tasks was drawn up, with unique variations for some households. The list was based on information gleaned from a short background questionnaire sent to all couples as well as from the literature on gender divisions of labour (e.g., Berk, 1985; Brannen & Moss, 1991; Pahl, 1984). Variations between households in task definition were found depending on the number and ages of children; household type and amount of household repair and maintenance undertaken; household income and the ability to buy in services; the contribution of older children to household work; and some households' own particular additions to the list of household work tasks (i.e., walking the dog; getting firewood; bedtime talks; confidences; and responding to children's emotional needs in a practical way. One example of the latter is that of helping a child to find a stolen bike (see Doucet, 1996, 2001).

10 With the Household Portrait, a sixth, though less frequently used, point on the scale allowed couples to indicate where hired help or older siblings assisted in housework and childcare tasks.

11 The Web surveys were analysed at the end only to further support findings from the interviews and were viewed as supplementary data in relation to the more in-depth interviews.

12 Lois McNay, in her theoretical work on subjectivity and agency, has also called for an analytic move from subjects to narratives and an appreciation of Paul Ricoeur's work on narrative (Ricoeur, 1985) and the ways that it shows a sense of temporal fluctuation in narratives (McNay, 2000).

13 While approximately one-quarter of the accounts were retrospective, my analysis of the accounts was that they were not treated differently from the more current accounts, except to place them in differing social contexts from which these stories are produced. What was notable was that the details of fathers' daily and weekly routines were largely lost over time when fathers looked back to their years at home. In responding to my question asking them to 'describe a typical day and a typical week,' fathers looking back spoke in large sweeps as they cobbled together varied memo-

ries, whereas current stay-at-home fathers provided rich contextual details about the routines and activities of caregiving.

14 Those who joined my interpretive community included a gay man, two transgendered persons, a black woman, as well as several colleagues and research assistants of varied educational and social backgrounds. In addition, having lived in South America for six years, I could appreciate the pressures of machismo for Latino fathers and for fathers of Italian heritage.

3. Understanding Fathers as Primary Caregivers

1 Some recent films with well-known actors portraying primary-caregiving fathers are, for example, *I am Sam* (Sean Penn), *The Shipping News* (Kevin Spacey), *Jersey Girl* (Ben Affleck) and, more comically, three men coming to grips with caring for an infant in the 1987 hit film *Three Men and a Baby* (Tom Selleck, Ted Danson, and Steve Guttenberg).

2 Recent novels with primary-caregiving fathers include *Man and Boy* (Parsons, 1999) and *Househusband* (Hudler, 2002) and *Housebroken: Confession of a Stay-at-Home Dad* (Eddie, 1999).

3 I made exceptions to the rule of fathers being a primary caregiver for at least one year only if there were other features of the father's experience that were interesting. In the case of Ray, a gay father of an adopted baby girl, he had been home on a self-financed parental leave when I interviewed him; Matthew was the first person in his male-dominated profession of mechanical repair to take a parental leave; and Hubert, a Chinese-Canadian father, was at home for only six months.

4 Besides Manuel and Julie, there were only four couples out of the fourteen interviewed (thus approximately one-third) who could be viewed as being in a situation with the father as primary caregiver during his time at home. These couples had the following in common: the man clearly identified first with the children and not with paid work; he did not talk about his paid work (past or present) very much in our interview; he set the domestic routine, and his female partner fitted into it; his wife or female partner did not heavily identify with the mothering persona and/or were willing to let go of being the primary caregiver so that the father could take it on; and the mother had a very demanding career. In addition to Manuel and Julie, the other couples of the fourteen interviewed that fitted into this pattern were Tom (trained as a counsellor) and Natasha (a physician); Richard (formerly an electronics technician) and Aileen (a federal public servant); Shahin (a

cabinetmaker/carpenter) and Louise (a lawyer), and Theo (formerly an engineer in a high-tech company) and Lisa (an engineer in a high-tech company).

5 The one gay father married to a woman is Morris, who has two grown children; like the majority of gay married fathers described by Dunne, this man was open about his sexuality to his wife, and she was reportedly supportive about her husband's gay lifestyle (see Dunne, 1999, 4).

6 The majority of stay-at-home fathers had partners living with them while they were at home (64/66). For the six fathers who were both single and at home, only one father was raising his child without any participation of the child's mother.

7 Craig was in fact initially a father of triplets, but one infant died.

8 The number of hours worked varied with fathers working few hours when their children were preschool or in half-day kindergarten and increasing their working hours when children were in school full time.

9 Women still tend to do more unpaid domestic work than men (Bianchi, Milkie, Sayer, & Robinson, 2000; Coltrane & Adams, 2001; O'Brien, 2005). According to Statistics Canada, in 2001, about 21 per cent of women aged fifteen and over devoted thirty hours or more to unpaid household work a week, compared with 8 per cent for men (Statistics Canada, 2003a).

10 One example of difficulties with measuring household labour emerges through recent commentary on how Arlie Hochschild's (1989) highly cited statistics on fathers' low contributions of time to domestic labour excluded what fathers did on weekends as well as tasks such as 'shopping, administrative services, repairs, and waiting in line (Levine & Pittinsky, 1998, 24–5). Scott Coltrane, to his credit, includes non-routine work such as household repairs, car repairs, exterior painting, and other tasks more traditionally considered male tasks (Coltane, 1996, 65–6) as well as 'driving and play routines with the children' (Coltrane, 1996, 66).

4. Fathers and Emotional Responsibility

1 Perhaps the most well known instigator of this debate is Carol Gilligan (1982) and her book *In a Different Voice*. It is astounding that nearly a quarter century after its first printing, it is still amply cited in scholarship on care or other aspects of female-dominated practice. Two decades of scrutiny, critique, and appreciation of this work is rooted in Gilligan's claim that there is a moral orientation, 'a different voice,' which is often associated

with women. This 'care voice' or 'the ethic of care' is characterized by a commitment to maintaining and fostering the relationships in which one is woven (Gilligan, 1982, 19) and an ethic that emphasizes 'attachment, particularity, emotion and intersubjectivity' (Cole & Coultrap-McGuin, 1992, 4–5). In contrast, the 'justice voice' or the 'ethic of justice' – associated mainly with the work on moral development by Gilligan's colleague and mentor, Lawrence Kohlberg, as well as with the work of the liberal political theorist John Rawls – emphasizes individual rights, equality, autonomy, fairness, rationality, a highly individuated conception of persons, and a concept of duty that is limited to reciprocal non-interference (Gilligan, 1982). In responding to the perception that *different* implied *women*, Gilligan's work initially caused a 'storm of controversy' (Jaggar, 1990, 249) around the problematic equation of women with care and the associated dangers of essentializing women's caregiving. Gilligan, in response, consistently maintained that though the care voice is heard most often in women, it can also be heard in men (Gilligan, 1986).

2 I am grateful to Carol Gilligan for pointing this out to me.

3 All but one of the gay fathers felt that they parented in a mainly masculine way, drawing on similar patterns of behaviour to heterosexual fathers – emphasizing sports and play, outdoor activity, risk taking, and the promotion of independence.

4 The pattern is also in evidence for the nine gay fathers in the study. Three fathers indicate that they are not really sports oriented, whereas the other six are. Of the three who claim not to be interested in sports, the one with an infant says that he nevertheless plays with children at playgroup more than the mothers do.

5 Sport itself also needs to be socially and historically located (Burstyn, 1999). According to Michael Messner, '[M]odern sport is a "gendered institution" in that it is a social institution constructed by men, largely as a response to a crisis of gender relations in the late nineteenth and early twentieth centuries. The dominant structures and values of sport came to reflect the fears and needs of a threatened masculinity. Sport was constructed as a homosocial world, with a male-dominant division of labour that excluded women. Indeed, sport came to symbolize the masculine structure of power over women' (Messner, 1992, 16).

6 Recent literature on boys in school highlights how these processes begin in boyhood, when exhibiting signs of emotion marks boys as wimps (Pollock, 1987) and as 'polluting the male ideal' by 'conveying qualities of softness, emotion and embodiment that are dangerously feminine' (Prendergast & Forrest, 1998, 167).

5. Fathers and Community Responsibility

1 There are several dimensions of community responsibility and the social growth of children, including the work of creating and maintaining community networks around children; kin work; planning birthday parties and special occasions; organizing and keeping track of children's activities; and long-term planning of children's social development. In this study, issues of community responsibility are directly explored through joint couple interviews as well as in the interviews conducted with individual fathers.

2 These numbers are gleaned from the narratives of fourteen fathers in the fourteen couple interviews and in the seventy-nine individual interviews (sixty-two in person and twenty-seven by telephone).

3 Gordon Campbell is the premier of the province of British Columbia. A great deal of publicity surrounded his arrest for drunk driving when he was on holiday in Hawaii in January 2003.

4 For gay fathers, the issue of networking for their children was complicated by the ways that their coming out was responded to by their community. For the two fathers in this study who are parenting in a non-heterosexual context (Ray and his partner as well as Bernard and two lesbian mothers), their long-standing identities as gay men living in communities open to diverse family models meant that they were faced with issues similar to heterosexual fathers, such as navigating complex maternal worlds. As fathers coming out from heterosexual marriages, they confronted different community reactions to, first, the dissolution of their marriages, and second, combining their newly revealed gay identity and practices with fathering.

5 In the U.K., there has been an enormous proliferation of fathering organizations and community organizations focused on fathers. Similarly, there are now several well-developed organizations that attend to the needs and interests of stay-at-home fathers (see www.homedad.org.uk).

6 In the United Kingdon, for example, fathers are currently eligible for two weeks' paid paternity leave, but a three-month paid paternity leave is currently being debated by the ruling Labour party (www.homedad.org.uk). Moreover, the government has set a goal of extending paid maternity leave to one year (by the end of its next Parliament, 2009–2010, which includes the right for a mother to transfer a portion of her maternity pay and leave to the father (Moss & O'Brien, 2005). In the Scandinavian countries of Denmark, Norway, and Sweden, fathers have had access to parental leave for some time now, and there is a tradition of strong fathering involvement with children. In Denmark, fathers may take thirty-two weeks of paid

parental leave (Rostgaard, 2005); in Norway, fathers are eligible to share part of the forty-three weeks of paid parental leave extended to each family, while four weeks are set aside for the father only (as a father's quota) (Brandth & Kvande, 2005). In Sweden, parents have access to 480 days of paid leave with 60 days for the mother, 6 days for the father and the remaining 360 days as a family entitlement that either parent can use (Chronholm & Haas, 2005).

6. Fathering, Mothering, and 'Moral' Responsibility

1 This particular line of thinking is also very much in line with interactionist perspectives on 'doing gender,' where women and men are viewed as participating in the construction and maintenance of asymmetrical gender relations (West & Zimmerman, 1987). There are thus expectations of what women and men should do and these expectations are disrupted, such as in the example of men as primary caregivers and women as primary breadwinners, and women and men can feel a sense of breaking away from the dominant norm.

2 I am using the concept of household strategies in the way that Claire Wallace does, considering 'the agency of the social actors and the ways in which they may use all forms of work in organizing their lives' while also recognizing 'the various structural and cultural circumstances in which they operate and how household members perceive that environment' (Wallace, 2002, 288).

3 My concept of social institution is similar to that developed in the work of Anne Marie Goetz, who writes extensively on gender and development and who draws, in turn, on both R.W. Connell (Connell, 1995) and Anthony Giddens (Giddens, 1984). Goetz makes three critical arguments about social institutions (Goetz, 1995, 1997). First, she argues that they are 'best understood as frameworks for socially constructed norms which function to limit choice' (Goetz, 1997, 6). Second, 'they provide structure to everyday life, making certain forms of behavior predictable and routine, *institutionalizing* them' (Goetz, 1997, 6). Third, she draws attention to both structure and agency involved in social institutions, noting that there is a 'human dimension in the construction of institutions' that 'alerts us to the fact that they are not immutable or "natural" approaches to organizing human relationships' (Goetz, 1997, 7). In arguing for social institutions as 'historically constructed frameworks for behavioral rules and generators of experience,' she posits that it is not difficult to understand the obstacles to changing institutional patterns.

4 The definition of ideology that I am drawing on is akin to that described by Trevor Purvis and Alan Hunt in their well-known piece on ideology and discourse in which they argue that ideology works in a taken-for-granted way, much like common sense or tacit knowledge. They write, 'It is precisely the "spontaneous" quality of common sense, its transparency, its "naturalness," its refusal to examine the premises on which it is grounded, its resistance to correction, its quality of being recognizable which makes common sense, at one and the same time, "lived," "spontaneous" and unconscious' (Purvis & Hunt, 1993, 479).

5 As I discussed at length in chapter 2, my emphasis throughout this book is on narratives rather than on conceptions of self. Thus, I focus on how people talk about themselves as mothers and fathers, and as women and men. Specifically, I examine how women and men take on different moral preconceptions about their roles and identities as parents.

6 Three pieces of evidence provided me with access to women's and men's views on mothering and fathering. First were there Household Portraits, which were constructed by thirteen of fourteen couples in their couple interviews. Second were the detailed descriptions of daily routines and practices described by fathers in their individual interviews when they were asked to 'tell me about a typical day' as well as a typical week. Third were answers by women and men to the direct questions about mothering and fathering (see appendix B.3).

7. Conclusion: Men Reconstructing Fathering

1 It is important to point out that there were no gay fathers in this focus group and that there would likely have been different responses in a group with gay fathers.

2 Indeed, many fathers' rights groups do make such special claims for fathering rights and can at times be highly critical of women, mothers, and feminists (see Boyd, 2002).

3 This coheres with recent American research on fathering. According to Coltrane and Adams, for example, fathers spend about four times as much time doing sports with children as mothers and spend more time in play or leisure with children than doing housework with them (Coltrane & Adams, 2001)

4 I am especially grateful to Jane Ireland for assisting me with these points.

5 Such employment has been variably termed as non-standard employment (Krahn, 1991, 1995), contingent employment (Polivka & Nardone, 1989), precarious employment (Vosko, 2000; Vosko, Zukewich, & Cranford, 2003),

or temporary employment (Galarneau, 2005). Whatever its name, this is employment heavily characterized as part-time, temporary (e.g., short contracts, casual or seasonal work), or self-employment. Such jobs increased almost twice as rapidly as permanent employment in recent years and accounted for almost one-fifth of overall growth in paid employment between 1997 and 2003. These jobs share low wages, insecure working conditions, limited access to social benefits and statutory entitlements (i.e., employment insurance, maternity leave and parental leave).

6 Between 1997 and 1999, voluntary part-time employment rose from 69 per cent of all part-time workers to 73 per cent. This further represented 14 per cent of all employment in Canada.

7 It is the case that Canadian households are increasingly buying household cleaning services (one-tenth of husband-wife households in 2000); a key factor that determines the decision to buy domestic help is not only the household income but even more important is the wife's share of the household income. According to a report from Statistics Canada: 'Buying domestic help is not just a matter of having sufficient household income. It is also matters whose income it is. Consider two husband-wife households, identical in every respect except that the husband makes 75 percent of the income in one household while the wife makes 75 percent in the other … [T]he second household will be roughly twice as likely to pay for home services' (Palameta, 2003, 15).

Postscript: Revisiting an Epistemology of Reception

1 The Civil Marriage Act was introduced by Prime Minister Paul Martin's Liberal government in the Canadian House of Commons on February 1, 2005, as Bill C-38. Prior to its passage, court decisions in eight of ten provinces (including the three most populous) and one of three territories had already legalized the issue of marriage licences to same-sex couples; this had applied to about 29.2 million Canadians (89.7 per cent of the population) living in provinces and territories where same-sex marriages are legal. Most legal benefits commonly associated with marriage had been extended to cohabiting same-sex couples since 1999.

2 Some of these groups include the Lone Fathers Association, the Men's Rights Agency, the Men's Confraternity, Fathers Without Rights, the Shared Parenting Council, Dads Against Discrimination, and many others.

3 According to Flood, pro-feminist men, while diverse in their specific beliefs and political commitments, nevertheless share many key feminist understandings of society. He writes, 'We believe that women as a group suffer

inequalities and injustices in society, while men as a group receive various forms of power and institutional privilege. The current, dominant model of manhood or masculinity is oppressive to women, as well as limiting for men themselves. We also recognise the costs of masculinity: conformity to narrow definitions of manhood comes with the price tag of poor health, early death, overwork and emotionally shallow relationships. We believe that men must take responsibility for our own sexist behaviours and attitudes and work to change those of men in general. Both personal and social change are vital. Just as there is substantial diversity and disagreement within feminism, there is diversity among pro-feminist men. One area of disagreement for example is over the extent to which men are also limited or harmed by the gender relations of society. Some men emphasise the privilege that men receive by virtue of being men in a patriarchal or male-dominated society, while others emphasise the ways in which both men and women are constricted by gender roles' (Flood, 2002).

References

Adams, M., & Coltrane, S. (2004). Boys and Men in Families: The Domestic Production of Gender, Power and Privilege. In R.W. Connell (Ed.), *The Handbook
of Studies on Men and Masculinities* (pp. 230–48). Thousand Oaks, CA: Sage.

Ahlander, N.R., & Bahr, K.S. (1995). Beyond Drudgery, Power, Equity: Toward
an Expanded Discourse on the Moral Dimensions of Housework in Families.
Journal of Marriage and the Family, 57, 54–68.

Allen, S.M., & Daly, K. (2002). *The Effects of Father Involvement: A Summary of the
Research Evidence.* Carleton Place, ON: Father Involvement Initiative –
Ontario Network.

Allen, S.M., & Hawkins, A.J. (1999). Maternal Gatekeeping: Mothers' Beliefs
and Behaviors That Inhibit Greater Father Involvement in Family Work.
Journal of Marriage and the Family, 61, 199–221.

Andrews, M. (1991). *Lifetimes of Commitment: Aging, Politics, Psychology.* Cambridge: Cambridge University Press.

Arber, S., & Ginn, J. (2004). Aging and Gender: Diversity and Change. In P.
Babb (Ed.), *Social Trends, No. 34.* London: TSO.

Armstrong, P., & Armstrong, H. (1993). *The Double Ghetto* (3rd ed.). Toronto:
McClelland and Stewart.

Bader, E. & Doucet, A. (2005). *Canadian Community Organizations and New
Fathers: A Report of the New Fathers' Cluster of the Father Involvement Research
Alliance.* Policy Report. Guelph: University of Guelph.

Bacchi, C.L. (1990). *Same Difference: Feminism and Sexual Difference.* London:
Allen and Unwin.

Backett, K. (1982). *Mothers and Fathers: A Study of the Development and Negotiation of Parental Behaviour.* London and Basingstoke: Macmillan.

Backett, K. (1987). The Negotiation of Fatherhood. In M. O'Brien (Ed.), *Reassessing Fatherhood* (pp. 74–90). London: Sage.

Bakan, A.B., & Stasiulis, D. (Eds.). (1997). *Not One of the Family: Foreign Domestic Workers in Canada*. Toronto: University of Toronto Press.

Balbo, L. (1987). Crazy Quilts: Rethinking the Welfare State Debate from a Woman's Point of View. In A.S. Sassoon (Ed.), *Women and the State* (pp. 45–71). London: Unwin Hyman.

Barker, R.W. (1994). *Lone Fathers and Masculinities*. Avebury, U.K.: Aldershot.

Barnett, R.C., & Baruch, G.K. (1987). Determinants of Fathers' Participation in Family Work. *Journal of Marriage and the Family, 49*, 29–40.

Barnett, R.C., Marshall, N.L., & Pleck, J.H. (1992). Men's Multiple Roles and their Relationship to Men's Psychological Distress. *Journal of Marriage and the Family, 54*(3), 358–67.

Barth, F. (1969). Introduction. In F. Barth (Ed.), *Ethnic Groups and Boundaries* (pp. 9–38). Boston: Little, Brown.

Barthes, R. (1977). The Death of the Author (S. Hearth, Trans.). In R. Barthes (Ed.), *Image-Music-Text* (pp. 142–8). London: Fontana Paperbacks.

Beaujot, R. (2000). *Earning and Caring in Canadian Families*. Peterborough, Ont: Broadview Press.

Beauvais, C. (2001). *Literature Review on Learning Through Recreation (Discussion Paper No. F-15)*. Ottawa: Canadian Policy Research Network.

Bell, L., & Ribbens, J. (1994). Isolated Housewives and Complex Maternal Worlds: The Significance of Social Contacts between Women with Young Children in Industrial Societies. *The Sociological Review, 42*(2), 227–62.

Beneson, J.F. (1990). Gender Differences in Social Networks. *Journal of Early Adolescence, 10*, 472–95.

Benhabib, S. (1992). *Situating the Self*. Cambridge: Polity Press, 1992.

Benhabib, S. (1995). Feminism and Postmodernism. In S. Benhabib, J. Butler, D. Cornell & N. Fraser (Eds.), *Feminist Contentions: A Philosophical Exchange* (pp. 17–34). New York and London: Routledge.

Benhabib, S. (1999). Sexual Difference and Collective Identities: The Global Constellation. *Signs: Journal of Women in Culture and Society, 24*(2), 335–62.

Berk, S.F. (1985). *The Gender Factory: The Apportionment of Work in American Households*. New York: Plenum.

Bernard, P., & Saint-Arnaud, S. (2004). *More of the Same: The Position of the Four Largest Canadian Provinces in the World of Welfare Regimes*. Ottawa: Canadian Policy Research Networks.

Bhabha, H.K. (1994). *The Location of Culture*. London and New York: Routledge.

Bianchi, S.M., Milkie, M., A., Sayer, L.C., & Robinson, J.P. (2000). Is Anyone Doing the Housework? Trends in the Gender Division of Household Labor. *Social Forces, 79*(1), 191–228.

Bird, S.R. (1996). Welcome to the Men's Club: Homosociality and the Maintenance of Hegemonic masculinity. *Gender & Society, 19*(2), 120–32.

Blankenhorn, D. (1995). *Fatherless America*. New York: Basic Books.

Bock, G. (1992). Equality and Difference in Nationalist Socialist Racism. In S.
James (Ed.), *Beyond Equality and Difference: Citizenship, Feminist Politics and
Female Subjectivity* (pp. 89–109). London and New York: Routledge.

Bock, G., & James, S. (Eds.). (1992). *Beyond Equality and Difference: Citizenship, Feminist Politics and Female Subjectivity*. London and New York:
Routledge.

Bolak, H.C. (1997). When Wives Are Major Providers: Culture, Gender, and
Family Work. *Gender & Society, 11*(4), 409–33.

Bono, P., & Kemp, S. (Eds.). (1991). *Italian Feminist Thought: A Reader*. Oxford:
Blackwell.

Bordo, S. (1997). *Twilight Zones: The Hidden Life of Cultural Images from Plato to
O.J.* Berkeley: University of California Press.

Bott, E. (1957). *Family and Social Networks*. London: Tavistock.

Bourdieu, P. (1977). *Outline of a Theory of Practice*. Cambridge: Cambridge University Press.

Bourdieu, P. (1984). *Distinction: A Social Critique of the Judgment of Taste*. London: Routledge.

Bourdieu, P. (1992). *The Logic of Practice*. Cambridge: Polity Press.

Boyd, S.B. (2003). *Child Custody, Law and Women's Work*. Don Mills, ON: Oxford
University Press.

Bozett, F.W. (1988). Gay Fatherhood. In C.P. Cowan (Ed.), *Fatherhood Today:
Men's Changing Role in the Family*. New York: Wiley.

Bradbury, B. (1984). Pigs, Cows and Boarders. Non-wage Forms of Survival
among Montreal Families, 1861–1881. *Labour/Le Travail, 14*(Autumn 1984),
9–46.

Bradbury, B. (1993). *Working Families: Age, Gender and Daily Survival in Industri-
alizing Montreal*. Toronto: McClelland and Stewart.

Braidotti, R. (1991). Introduction: Dutch Treats and Other Strangers: Reading
Dutch Feminism. In J.J. Hermsen and A. van Lenning (Eds.) (A. Lavelle,
Trans), *Sharing the Difference: Feminist Debates in Holland* (pp. 1–16). London
and New York: Routledge.

Brandth, B., & Kvande, E. (1998). Masculinity and Child Care: The Reconstruction of Fathering. *The Sociological Review, 46*(2), 293–313.

Brandth, B., & Kvande, E. (2001). Flexible Work and Flexible Fathers. *Work,
Employment and Society, 15*(2), 251–67.

Brandth, B., & Kvande, E. (2002). Reflexive Fathers: Negotiating Parental Leave
and Working Life Gender. *Work and Organization, 9*(2), 186–203.

Brandth, B., & Kvande, E. (2005). Leave Policies and Research: Norway. In P. Moss (Ed.), *Leave Polices and Research: Overviews and Country Notes*. Brussels: Centre for Population and Family Studies (CBGS).

Brannen, J., & Moss, P. (1991). *Managing Mothers: Dual Earner Households After Maternity Leave*. London: Unwin Hyman.

Braver, S.L., & Griffin, W.A. (2000). Engaging Fathers in the Post Divorce Family. *Marriage and Family Review, 29*, 247–67.

Brittan, A. (1989). *Masculinity and Power*. Oxford: Basil Blackwell.

Brown, L.M. (1998). *Raising Their Voices: The Politics of Girls' Anger*. Cambridge, MA: Harvard University Press.

Brown, L.M., & Gilligan, C. (1992). *Meeting at the Crossroads: Women's Psychology and Girls' Development*. Cambridge, MA: Harvard University Press.

Bumpus, M.F., Crouter, A.C., & McHale, S.M. (1999). Work Demands of Dual-Earner Couples: Implications for Parents' Knowledge About Children's Daily Lives in Middle Childhood. *Journal of Marriage and Family, 61*(4), 465–76.

Burawoy, M. (2000). Introduction: Reaching for the Global. In M. Thayer (Ed.), *Global Ethnography: Forces, Connections, and Imaginations in a Postmodern World* (pp. 1–40). Berkeley: University of California Press.

Burawoy, M., Burton, A., Ferguson, A.A., Fox, K., Gamson, J., Gartrell, N., et al. (Eds.). (1991). *Ethnography Unbound: Power and Resistance in the Modern Metropolis*. Berkeley: University of California Press.

Burkitt, I. (1999). *Bodies of Thought*. London: Sage.

Burstyn, V. (1999). *The Rites of Men: Manhood, Politics, and the Culture of Sport*. Toronto: University of Toronto Press.

Buss, D.E. (2004). The Spaces of International Law and the Places of Feminist Theory. In D. Buss and M. Ambreena (Eds.), *International Law: Modern Feminist Approaches*. Oxford: Hart Publishing.

Cairns, R.B., Perrin, J.E., & Cairns, B.D. (1985). Social Structure and Cognition in Early Adolescence: Affiliative Patterns. *Journal of Early Adolescence, 5*, 339–55.

Campbell, M.L., & Gregor, F. (2002). *Mapping Social Relations: A Primer in Doing Institutional Ethnography*. Aurora, ON: Garamond Press.

Carrigan, T., Connell, R. W., & Lee, J. (1985). Toward a New Sociology of Masculinity. *Theory and Society, 14*, 551–604.

Carrington, C. (1999). *No Place like Home: Relationships and Family Life among Lesbians and Gay Men*. Chicago: University of Chicago Press.

Cavarero, A. (1993). Towards a Theory of Sexual Differences. In P. Bono (Ed.), *The Lonely Mirror: Italian Perspectives in Feminist Theory* (pp. 189–221). London and New York: Routledge.

CBC (2004). *In Depth: Day Care in Canada*, October 25, 2004.

Chafetz, J.S. (1991). The Gender Division of Labor and the Reproduction of Female Disadvantage: Toward an Integrated Theory. In R.L. Blumberg (Ed.), *The Triple Overlap* (pp. 74–96). Newbury Park, CA: Sage.

Charmaz, K.C. (2006). *Constructing Grounded Theory: A Practical Guide through Qualitative Analysis.* London: Sage.

Cheal, D. (1991). *Family and the State of Theory.* Toronto: University of Toronto Press.

Cheal, D. (1999). *New Poverty: Families in Postmodern Society.* Westport, CT: Greenwood Publishing.

Chodorow, N. (1978). *The Reproduction of Mothering: Psychoanalysis and the Sociology of Gender.* Berkeley and Los Angeles: University of California Press,.

Chronholm, A., & Haas, L. (2005). Leave Policies and Research: Sweden. In P. Moss (Ed.), *Leave Polices and Research: Overviews and Country Notes.* Brussels: Centre for Population and Family Studies (CBGS).

Clarke, E. (1957). *My Mother Who Fathered Me: A Study of the Family in Three Selected Communities in Jamaica.* London: G. Allen & Unwin.

Clatterbaugh, K. (1998). What Is Problematic about Masculinities? *Men and Masculinities, 1*(1), 24–45.

Code, L. (1988). Experience, Knowledge and Responsibility. In M. Griffiths & M. Whitford (Eds.), *Feminist Perspectives in Philosophy* (pp. 187–204). Bloomington: Indiana University Press.

Code, L. (1995). How Do We Know? Questions of Method in Feminist Practice. In S.D. Burt & L. Code (Eds.), *Changing Methods: Feminists Transforming Practice.* Peterborough, ON: Broadview.

Cohen, P.N. (2004). The Gender Division of Labor: 'Keeping House' and Occupational Segregation in the United States. *Gender & Society, 18*(2), 239–52.

Collins, P.H. (1994). Shifting the Center: Race, Class and Feminist Theorizing about Motherhood. In E.N. Glenn, G. Chang & L.R. Forcey (Eds.), *Mothering: Ideology, Experience and Agency* (pp. 45–65). London and New York: Routledge.

Collins, P.H. (2000). *Black Feminist Thought: Knowledge, Consciousness, and the Politics of Empowerment* (2nd ed.). London and New York: Routledge.

Coltrane, S. (1989). Household Labor and the Routine Production of Gender. *Social Problems, 36*(5), 473–90.

Coltrane, S. (1994). Theorizing Masculinities in Contemporary Social Science. In M. Kaufman (Ed.), *Theorizing Masculinities* (pp. 39–60). Thousand Oaks: Sage.

Coltrane, S. (1996). *Family Man: Fatherhood, Housework, and Gender Equity.* New York and Oxford: Oxford University Press.

Coltrane, S. (1997). Scientific Half-Truths and Postmodern Parody in the Family Values Debate. *Contemporary Sociology, 28*(1), 7–10.

Coltrane, S. (2000). Research on Household Labor: Modeling and Measuring the Social Embeddedness of Routine Family Work. *Journal of Marriage and the Family, 62* (November 2000), 1208–1233.

Coltrane, S. (2001). Marketing the Marriage 'Solution': Misplaced Simplicity in the Politics of Fatherhood: 2001 Presidential Address to the Pacific Sociological Association. *Sociological Perspectives, 44*(4), 387–418.

Coltrane, S. (2004). Fathering: Paradoxes, Contradictions, and Dilemmas. In L. Ganong (Ed.), *Handbook of Contemporary Families: Considering the Past, Contemplating the Future* (pp. 224–43). Thousand Oaks, CA: Sage.

Coltrane, S., & Adams, M. (2001). Men's Family Work: Child-Centered Fathering and the Sharing of Domestic Labor. In N.L. Marshall (Ed.), *Working Families: The Transformation of the American Home* (pp. 72–102). Berkeley: University of California Press.

Combahee River Collective. (1983). The Combahee River Collective Statement. In B. Smith (Ed.), *Home girls: A Black Feminist Anthology* (pp. 264–74). New York: Kitchen Table Women of Color Press.

Connell, R.W. (1987). *Gender and Power.* Cambridge: Polity Press.

Connell, R.W. (1995). *Masculinities.* London: Polity Press.

Connell, R.W. (2000). *The Men and the Boys.* Berkeley: University of California Press.

Coontz, S. (1992). *The Way We Never Were: American Families and the Nostalgia Trap.* New York: Basic Books.

Coontz, S. (2005). *Marriage: A History.* New York: Viking.

Cowan, C.P., & Cowan, P.A. (2000). *When Partners Become Parents* (2nd ed.). Mahwah, NJ: Erlbaum.

Cowan, C.P., & Cowan, P.A. (Eds.). (1987). *Men's Involvement in Parenthood: Identifying the Antecedents and Understanding the Barriers.* Hillsdale, NJ: Erlbaum.

Crittenden, A. (2001). *The Price of Motherhood: Why the Most Important Job in the World Is Still the Least Valued.* New York: Henry Holt.

Crossley, N. (1995a). Merleau-Ponty, the Illusive Body and Carnal Sociology. *Body & Society, 1*(1), 43–63.

Crossley, N. (1995b). Body Techniques, Agency and Intercorporeality: On Goffman's Relations in Public. *Sociology, 29*(1), 133–49.

Crossley, N. (2001). Embodiment and Social Structure: A Response to Howson and Inglis. *The Sociological Review, 49*(3), 318–26.

Csordas, T.J. (1990). *Embodiment and Experience: the Existential Ground of Culture and Self.* Cambridge: Cambridge University Press.

Daly, K. (1993). Reshaping Fatherhood: Finding the Models. *Journal of Family Issues, 14*, 510–30.

Daly, K. (1996). *Families and Time: Keeping Pace in a Hurried Culture.* Thousand Oaks, CA: Sage.

Daly, K. (2002). Time, Gender, and the Negotiation of Family Schedules. *Symbolic Interaction, 25*(3), 323–42.

Davies, C.A. (1999). *Reflexive Ethnography: A Guide to Researching Selves and Others.* London and New York: Routledge.

Davies, K. (1990). *Women, Time and Weaving the Strands of Everday Life.* Avebury, U.K.: Gower Publishing Company.

Davies, K. (1994). The Tension between Process Time and Clock Time in Care Work: The Example of Day Nurseries. *Time and Society, 3*, 276–303.

De Lauretis, T. (1994). The Essence of the Triangle, or Taking the Risk of Essentialism Seriously: Feminist Theory in Italy, the U.S. and Britain. In N. Schor & E. Weed (Eds.), *The Essential Difference* (pp. 1–39). Bloomington and Indianapolis: Indiana University Press.

DeLuccie, M.F. (1995). Mothers as Gatekeepers: A model of Maternal Mediators of Father Involvement. *The Journal of Genetic Psychology, 156*(1), 115–27.

Denzin, N.K. (1970). Symbolic Interactionism and Ethnomethodology. In J.D. Douglas (Ed.), *Understanding Everyday Life: Toward the Reconstruction of Sociological Knowledge* (pp. 259–84). Chicago: Aldine Publishing Company.

Denzin, N.K. (1994). The Art and Politics of Interpretation. In Y. S. Lincoln (Ed.), *Handbook of Qualitative Research.* London: Sage.

Deutsch, F.M. (1999). *Halving it All: How Equally Shared Parenting works.* Cambridge, Massachusetts: Harvard University Press.

Deutsch, F.M., Servis, L.J., & Payne, J.D. (2001). Paternal Participation in Child Care and Its Effects on Children's Self-Esteem and Attitudes Towards Gender Roles. *Journal of Family Issues, 22*(8), 1000–24.

DeVault, M. (1991). *Feeding the Family: The Social Organization of Caring as Gendered Work* Chicago: University of Chicago Press.

DeVault, M., & McCoy, L. (2003). Institutional Ethnography: Using Interviews to Investigate Ruling Relations. In J.F. Gubrium (Ed.), *Inside interviewing: New Lenses, New Concerns* (pp. 369–94). London: Sage.

Di Leonardo, M. (1987). The Female World of Cards and Holidays: Women, Families and the World of Kinship. *Signs, 12*(3), 440–53.

Dienhart, A. (1998). *Reshaping Fatherhood: The Social Construction of Shared Parenting.* London: Sage.

Dienhart, A., & Daly, K. (1996). Men and Women Co-creating Father Involvement in a Nongenerative Culture. In D.C. Dollahite (Ed.), *Generative Fathering: Beyond Deficit Perspectives* (pp. 147–66). Thousand Oaks: Sage.

Dietz, M.G. (1985). 'Citizenship with a Feminist Face': The Problem with Maternal Thinking. *Political Theory, 13*(1), 19–37.

Dinnerstein, D. (1977). *The Mermaid and the Minotaur: Sexual Arrangements and Human Malaise.* New York: Harper Colophon Books.

Doherty, G., Friendly, M., & Beach , J. (2003). *OECD Thematic Review of Early Childhood Education and Care: Canadian Background Report.* Paris: OECD.

Doherty, W.J., Kouneski, E.F., & Erickson, M.F. (1998). Responsible Fathering: An Overview and Conceptual Framework. *Journal of Marriage and the Family, 60,* 277–92.

Dollahite, D.C., Hawkins, A.J., & Brotherson, S.E. (1997). Fatherwork: A Conceptual Ethic of Fathering as Generative Work. In D.C. Dollahite (Ed.), *Generative Fathering: Beyond Deficit Perspectives* (pp. 17–35). Thousand Oaks, CA: Sage.

Doucet, A. (1995a). *Gender Equality, Gender Differences and Care: Toward Understanding Gendered Labor in British Dual Earner Households.* Unpublished doctoral dissertation, University of Cambridge, Cambridge, UK.

Doucet, A. (1995b). Gender Equality and Gender Differences in Household Work and Parenting. *Women's Studies International Forum, 18*(3), 271–84.

Doucet, A. (1996). Encouraging Voices: Towards More Creative Methods for Collecting Data on Gender and Household Labor. In S. Lyon (Ed.), *Gender Relations in the Public and the Private.* London: Macmillan.

Doucet, A. (1998). Interpreting Mother-Work: Linking Methodology, Ontology, Theory and Personal Biography. *Canadian Woman Studies, 18*(2 & 3), 52–8.

Doucet, A. (2000). 'There's a Huge Difference Between Me as a Male Carer and Women': Gender, Domestic Responsibility, and the Community as an Institutional Arena. *Community Work and Family, 3*(2), 163–84.

Doucet, A. (2001a). Can Boys Grow into Mothers? Maternal Thinking and Fathers' Reflections. In A. O'Reilly (Ed.), *Mothers and Sons: Feminism, Masculinity and the Struggle to Raise Our Sons* (pp. 163–82). New York and London: Routledge.

Doucet, A. (2001b). You See the Need Perhaps More Clearly than I Have: Exploring Gendered Processes of Domestic Responsibility. *Journal of Family Issues, 22*(3), 328–57.

Doucet, A. (2004). Fathers and the Responsibility for Children: A Puzzle and a Tension. *Atlantis: A Women's Studies Journal, 28*(2), 103–14.

Doucet, A. (2005). 'It's Almost like I Have a Job but I Don't Get Paid': Fathers at Home Reconfiguring Work, Care and Masculinity. *Fathering: A Journal of Theory, Research, and Practice about Men as Fathers, 2*(3), 277–304.

Doucet, A. (2006). "Estrogen-Filled Words": Fathers as Primary Caregivers and Embodiment. *The Sociological Review, 23* (4), 695–715.

Doucet, A., & Dunne, G.A. (2000). Heterosexual and Lesbian Mothers Challenging 'Feminine' and 'Male' Conceptions of Mothering. In S. Abbey (Ed.), *Mothers and Daughters: Connection, Empowerment and Transformation* (pp. 103–120). Savage, Maryland: Rowman and Littlefield.

Doucet, A., & Mauthner, N.S. (2002). Knowing Responsibly: Ethics, Feminist Epistemologies and Methodologies. In T. Miller (Ed.), *Ethics in Qualitative Research* (pp. 123–45). London: Sage.

Dowd, N.E. (2000). *Redefining Fatherhood*. New York: New York University Press.

Dryden, C. (Ed.). (1999). *Being Married, Doing Gender: A Clinical Analysis of Gender Relationships in Marriage*. London: Routledge.

Duncan, S. (2003). *Mothers, Care and Employment: Values & Theories* (Working Paper No.1). Bradford, UK: ESRC Research Group for the Study of Care, Values and the Future of Welfare.

Duncan, S., & Edwards, R. (1999). *Lone Mothers, Paid Work and Gendered Moral Rationalities*. London: Macmillan.

Dunne, G.A. (1996). *Lesbian Lifestyles: Women's Work and the Politics of Sexuality*. London: Palgrave Macmillan.

Dunne, G.A. (1999). *The Different Dimensions of Gay Fatherhood*. London: Report to the Economic and Social Research Council.

Durkheim, E. (1895 [1982]). *The Rules of Sociological Method*. London: MacMillan.

Durkheim, E. (1912 [1995]). *The Elementary Forms of Religious Life* (K.E. Fields, Trans.). New York: Free Press.

Economic and Social Research Council. (2004). *Welfare and Single Parenthood in the UK, 2005*

Eddie, D. (1999). *Housebroken: Confessions of a Stay at Home Dad*. Toronto: Random House.

Edwards, R., Duncan, S., Reynolds, T., & Allred, P. (2002). *A Mother's Instinct? Paid Work, Partnering and Childcare, Working Paper 26*. Bradford: University of Bradford.

Edwards, R. (1990). Connecting Method and Epistemology: A White Woman Interviewing Black Women. *Women's Studies International Forum, 13*(5), 477–90.

Ehrensaft, D. (1984). When Women and Men Mother. In J. Trebilcot (Ed.), *Mothering: Essays in Feminist Theory* (pp. 41–61). Totowa, NJ: Rowman and Allanheld.

Ehrensaft, D. (1987). *Parenting Together: Men and Women Sharing the Care of their Children*. London: Collier Macmillan Publishers.

Ellis, C. (2004). *The Ethnographic I: A Methodological Novel about Autoethnography.* Berkeley, CA: AltaMira Press.

Ellis, C., & Bochner, A.P. (2001). *Ethnographically Speaking: Autoethnography, Literature, and Aesthetics.* Berkeley, CA: AltaMira Press.

England, K. (1994). Getting Personal: Reflexivity, Positionality and Feminist Research. *Professional Geographer, 46*(1), 80–9.

Epsing-Andersen, G. (1999). *Social Foundations of Postindustrial Economies.* New York: Oxford University Press.

Esping-Andersen, G. (1999). *Social Foundations of Postindustrial Economies.* New York: Oxford University Press.

Fagan, J., & Barnett, M. (2003). The Relationship between Maternal Gatekeeping, Paternal Competence, Mothers' Attitudes about the Father Role, and Father Involvement. *Journal of Family Issues, 24*(8), 1020–43.

Farrell, W. (2001). *Father and Child Reunion: How to Bring the Dads We Need to the Children We Love.* New York: Jeremy P. Tarcher/Putnam Publishers.

Fathers Direct. (2004). *U.S. Statistics on Step parents/Children.* Retrieved January 15, 2005.

Ferree, M.M., Lorber, J., & Hess, B. (1999). *Revisioning Gender.* Thousand Oaks, CA: Sage.

Finch, J. (1989). *Family Obligations and Social Change.* London: Polity.

Finch, J., & Mason, J. (1993). *Negotiating Family Responsibilities.* London: Routledge.

Fineman, M. (1992). The Neutered Mother. *University of Miami Law Review, 45,* 653–69.

Fineman, M. (1995). *The Neutered Mother: The Sexual Family and Other Twentieth Century Tragedies.* New York: Routledge.

Fish, S. (1980). *Is There a Text in This Class? The Authority of Interpretive Communities.* Cambridge, MA: Harvard University Press.

Fisher, B., & Tronto, J. (1990). Towards a Feminist Theory of Caring. In M.K. Nelson (Ed.), *Circles of Care: Work and Identity in Women's Lives* (pp. 35–62). New York: State University of New York Press.

Fisher, M., & Connell, R.W.M. (2002). *Masculinities and Men in Nursing.* Paper presented at the 3rd College of Health Sciences Research Conference 'From Cell to Society,' Leura, Australia.

Flax, J. (2002). Reentering the Labyrinth: Revisiting Dorothy Dinnerstein's *The Mermaid and the Minotaur. Signs: Journal of Women in Culture and Society, 27*(4).

Flood, M. (2002). *Frequently Asked Questions about Pro-Feminist Men and Pro-Feminist Men's Politics.* www.xyonline.net (3rd edition).

Flood, M. (2004). Backlash: Angry Men's Movements. In S.E. Rossi (Ed.), *The*

Battle and the Backlash Rage On: Why Feminism Cannot Be Obsolete (pp. 261–78). Philadelphia: Xlibris Press.

Folbre, N. (1994). *Who Pays for the Kids? Gender and the Structures of Constraint.* London: Routledge, Chapman and Hall.

Folbre, N. (2001). *The Invisible Heart: Economics and Family Values.* New York: The New Press.

Foucault, M. (1973). *The Birth of the Clinic: An Archaeology of Medical Perception.* London: Tavistock.

Foucault, M. (1977a). *Discipline and Punish: the Birth of the Prison.* London: Tavistock.

Foucault, M. (1977b). What is an Author? In M. Foucault (Ed.), *Language, Counter-memory, Practice: Related Essays and interviews* (pp. 113–38). Ithaca, NY: Cornell University Press.

Foucault, M. (1979). *The History of Sexuality, vol.1: An Introduction.* London: Allen Lane/Penguin.

Fox, B. (1998). Motherhood, Changing Relationships and the Reproduction of Gender Inequality. In A. O'Reilly (Ed.), *Redefining Motherhood* (pp. 159–174). Toronto: Second Story Press.

Fox, B. (2001). The Formative Years: How Parenthood Creates Gender. *Canadian Review of Sociology and Anthropology, 38*(4), 373–90.

Fox, B. (Ed.). (1980). *Hidden in the Household: Women's Domestic Labour Under Capitalism* Toronto: The Women's Press.

Frank, R. (1999). Research on At-Home Dads. In C. Cooper (Ed.), *At-Home Dad Handbook.* St. Paul, Minnesota: Curtis Cooper.

Fraser, N. (1997). After the Family Wage: A Postindustrialist Thought Experiment. In N. Fraser (Ed.), *Justice Interruptus: Critical Reflections of the 'Postsocialist' Condition* (pp. 41–66). New York: Routledge.

Fraser, N., & Bartky, S.L. (Eds.). (1992). *Revaluing French Feminism: Critical Essays on Difference, Agency, and Culture.* Bloomington: Indiana University Press.

Fraser, N., & Gordon, L. (1997). A Geneaology of 'Dependency': Tracing a Keyword of the U.S. Welfare State. In N. Fraser (Ed.), *Justice Interruptus: Critical Reflections on the 'Postsocialist' Condition* (pp. 121–50). London: Routledge.

French, S. (1993). *Fatherhood: Men Write about Fathering.* London: Trafalgar.

Friedman, M. (1993). Beyond Caring: The Demoralization of Gender. In M.J. Larrabee (Ed.), *An Ethic of Care: Feminist and Interdisciplinary Perspectives* (pp. 258–74). London: Routledge.

Friedman, M. (2000). Autonomy, Social Disruption and Women. In N. Stoljar (Ed.), *Relational Autonomy: Feminist Perspectives on Autonomy, Agency, and the Social Self* (pp. 35–51). New York and Oxford: Oxford University Press.

Fuss, D. (1989). *Essentially Speaking: Feminsim, Nature and Difference*. London: Routledge.

Galarneau, D. (2005). Earnings of Temporary Versus Permanent Employees. *Perspectives on Labour and Income, Statistics Canada, 6*(1).

Garey, A.I. (1999). *Weaving Work and Motherhood*. Philadelphia: Temple University Press.

Gatens, M. (1996). *Imaginary Bodies: Ethics, Power and Corporeality*. London: Routledge.

Gavanas, A. (2002). The Fatherhood Responsibility Movement: The Centrality of Marriage, Work and Male Sexuality in Reconstructions of Masculinity and Fatherhood. In B. Hobson (Ed.), *Making Men into Fathers: Men, Masculinities and the Social Politics of Fatherhood* (pp. 213–44). Cambridge: Cambridge University Press.

Geiger, B. (1996). *Fathers as Primary Caregivers*. Westport, CT: Greenwood Press.

Gershuny, J.I. (2001). *Changing Times*. New York: Oxford University Press.

Gershuny, J.I., & Pahl, R E. (1979). Work Outside Employment: Some Preliminary Speculations. *New Universities Quarterly, 34*, 120–35.

Gerson, K. (1993). *No Man's Land: Men's Changing Commitments to Family and Work*. New York: Basic Books.

Giddens, A. (1984). *The Constitution of Society: Outline of the Theory of Structuration*. Cambridge: Polity Press.

Gilligan, C. (1982). *In a Different Voice: Psychological Theory and Women's Development*. Cambridge, MA: Harvard University Press.

Gilligan, C. (1988). Remapping the Moral Domain: New Images of the Self in Relationship. In B. Bardige (Ed.), *Mapping the Moral Domain: A Contribution of Women's Thinking to Psychological Theory and Education* (pp. 3–19). Cambridge, Mass.: Harvard University Press.

Gilligan, C. (1993). Reply to Critics. In M.J. Larrabee (Ed.), *An Ethic of Care: Feminist and Interdisciplinary Perspectives* (pp. 207–14). New York and London: Routledge.

Gilligan, C. (2002). *The Birth of Pleasure*. New York: Alfred A. Knopf.

Gilligan, C., Brown, L.M., & Rogers, A. (1990). Psyche Embedded: A Place for Body, Relationships and Culture in Personality Theory. In S. Frank (Ed.), *Studying Persons and Lives*. New York: Springer.

Gilligan, C., Spencer, R., Weinberg, K.M., & Bertsch, T. (2005). On the Listening Guide: A Voice-Centered Relational Method. In S.N. Hesse-Biber & P. Leavy (Eds.), *Emergent Methods in Social Research* (pp. 253–72). Thousand Oaks, CA: Sage.

Ginn, J., & Arber, S. (2002). Degrees of Freedom: Do Graduate Women Escape the Motherhood Gap in Pensions? *Sociological Research Online, 7*(2).

Glaser, B.G., & Strauss, A. L. (1967). *The Discovery of Grounded Theory: Strategies for Qualitative Research*. Chicago: Aldine Publishing Company.

Goetz, A.M. (1995). Institutionalizing Women's Interests and Accountability to Women in Development. *IDS Bulletin, 26*(3), 1–10.

Goetz, A.M. (1997). Introduction: Getting Institutions Right for Women in Development. In A. M. Goetz (Ed.), *Getting Institutions Right for Women in Development*. London: Zed Books.

Goffman, I. (1963). *Behaviour in Public Spaces*. Glencoe: Free Press.

Goffman, I. (1969). *The Presentation of Self in Everyday Life*. Garden City, NY: Doubleday.

Goffman, E. (1972). *Relations in Public*. Harmondsworth: Penguin.

Goffman, E. (1987). The Arrangement between the Sexes. In M. Hill (Ed.), *Women and Symbolic Interaction* (pp. 51–78). Winchester, MA: Allen and Unwin.

Graham, H. (1983). Caring: A Labor of Love. In D.A. Groves (Ed.), *A Labor of Love: Women, Work and Caring* (pp. 13–30). London: Routledge and Kegan Paul.

Graham, H. (1983b). Do Her Answers Fit His Questions? Women and the Survey Method. In E. Gamarnikow (Ed.), *The Public and the Private* (pp. 132–47). London: Tavistock.

Gray, J. (1992). *Men Are from Mars Women Are from Venus: The Classic Guide to Understanding the Opposite Sex*. New York: HarperCollins Publishers.

Greenstein, T.N. (1996). Gender Ideology and Perceptions of the Fairness of the Division of Labor: Effects on Marital Quality. *Social Forces, 74*(3), 1029–42.

Gregson, N., & Lowe, M. (1993). Renegotiating the Domestic Division of Labour: A Study of Dual Career Households in Northeast and Southeast England. *The Sociological Review, 41*(3), 475–505.

Gregson, N., & Lowe, M. (1994). *Servicing the Middle Classes: Class, Gender and Wages and Domestic Labour in Contemporary Britain*. London and New York: Routledge.

Greif, G.L. (1985). *Single Fathers*. Lexington, MA: Lexington Books.

Griffin, C. (1989). 'I'm Not a Women's Libber, but ...': Feminism, Consciousness and Identity. In D. Baker (Ed.), *The Social Identity of Women* (173–93). London: Sage.

Grosz, E. (1989). *Sexual Subversions: Three French Feminists*. Boston: Allen and Unwin.

Grosz, E. (1995). *Space, Time and Perversion*. London: Routledge and Kegan Paul.

Guba, E.G., & Lincoln, Y.S. (1998). Competing Paradigms in Qualitative Research. In Y.S. Lincoln (Ed.), *The Landscape of Qualitative Research* (pp. 195–220). Thousand Oaks, Calif.: Sage.

Hamilton, R. (2005). *Gendering the Vertical Mosaic: Feminist Perspectives on Canadian Society* (Second Edition ed.). Toronto: Pearson.

Hammersley, M. (1998). *Reading Ethnographic Research* (Second Edition ed.). Essex, UK: Addison Wesley Longman.

Hammersley, M., & Atkinson, P. (1983). *Ethnography: Principles in Practice*. London: Tavistock.

Hansen, K.V. (1992). Our Eyes Behold Each Other: Masculinity and Intimate Friendships in Antebellum New England. In P.M. Nardi (Ed.), *Men's Friendships* (pp. 35–58). Newbury Park, CA: Sage.

Hawkins, A.J., Christiansen, S.L., Sargent, K.P., & Hill, E.J. (1993). Rethinking Fathers' Involvement in Child Care: A Developmental Perspective. *Journal of Family Issues, 14*(4), 531–49.

Hawkins, A.J., & Dollahite, D.C. (1996). *Generative Fathering: Beyond Deficit Perspectives*. Thousand Oaks, CA: Sage.

Hays, S. (1996). *The Cultural Contradictions of Motherhood*. New Haven: Yale University Press.

Haraway, D. (1991). *Simians, Cyborgs and Women: The Reinvention of Nature*. New York: Routledge.

Harding, S. (1993a). Rethinking Standpoint Epistemologies: What Is Strong Objectivity? In L. Alcoff & E. Potter (Eds.), *Feminist Epistemologies* (pp. 49–82). London: Routledge.

Hearn, J. (1996). Is Masculinity Dead? A Critique of the Concept of Masculinity/Masculinities. In M. Mac an Ghaill (Ed.), *Understanding Masculinities* (pp. 202–27). Buckingham, UK: Open University Press.

Hearn, J., & Morgan, D.H.J. (1990). Men, Masculinities and Social Theory. In D.H.J. Morgan (Ed.), *Men, Masculinities and Social Theory*. London: Unwin Hyman.

Hearn, J., Pringle, K., Muller, U., Oleksy, E., Latti, E., Chernova, J., et al. (2002). Critical Studies on Men in Ten European Countries: (1) The State of Research. *Men and Masculinities, 4*(4), 380–408.

Hekman, S. (1999). Backgrounds and Riverbeds: Feminist Reflections. *Feminist Studies, 25*(2), 31–42.

Hertz, R. (1997). A Typology of Approaches to Child Care: The Centerpiece of Organizing Family Life for Dual-Earner Couples. *Journal of Family Issues, 18*, 355–85.

Hertz, R., & Ferguson, F. I. (1998). Only One Pair of Hands: Ways that Single Mothers Stretch Work and Family Resources. *Community, Work and Family, 1*(1), 13–37.

Hessing, M. (1993). Mothers' Management of their Combined Workloads: Clerical Work and Household Needs. *Canadian Review of Sociology and Anthropology, 30*(1), 37–63.

Hobson, B. (2002). *Making Men into Fathers: Men, Masculinities and the Social Politics of Fatherhood*. Cambridge: Cambridge University Press.

Hobson, B., & Morgan, D.H.J. (2002). Introduction: Making Men into Fathers. In B. Hobson (Ed.), *Men, Masculinities and the Social Politics of Fatherhood* (pp. 1–21). Cambridge: Cambridge University Press.

Hochschild, A.R. (1983). *The Managed Heart: Commercialization of Human Feeling*. Berkeley: University of California Press.

Hochschild, A.R. (1989). *The Second Shift*. New York: Avon Books.

Hochschild, A.R. (1997). *The Time Bind: When Work Becomes Home and Home Becomes Work*. New York: Henry Holt.

Hofferth, S.L. (2003). Race/Ethnic Differences in Father Involvement in Two-Parent Families: Culture, Context, or Economy. *Journal of Family Issues, 24*(2), 185–216.

Hollway, W., & Jefferson, T. (2000). *Doing Qualitative Research Differently: Free Association, Narrative and the Interview Method*. London: Sage.

HomeDad.org.UK. (2005). *Welcome to HomeDad UK*. Retrieved 15 January 2005.

hooks, b. (1981). *Ain't I a Woman? Black Women and Feminism*. Boston: South End Press.

Howson, A., & Inglis, D. (2001a). The Body in Sociology: Tensions Inside and Outside Sociological Thought. *The Sociological Review, 49*(3), 297–317.

Hrdy, S.B. (1999). *Mother Nature: A History of Mothers, Infants, and Natural Selection*. New York: Pantheon Books.

Hudler, A. (2002). *Househusband*. New York: Ballantine Books.

Hughes, K.D. (2000). Restructuring Work, Restructuring Gender: Women's Movement into Non-Traditional Occupations in Canada. In A. Verma (Ed.), *Restructuring Work and the Life Course*. Toronto: University of Toronto Press.

Hughes, K.D. (2005). *Female Enterprise in the New Economy*. Toronto: University of Toronto Press.

Hyeyoung, W., & Raley, R.K. (2005). A Small Extension to 'Costs and Rewards of Children: The Effects of Becoming a Parent on Adults' Lives.' *Journal of Marriage and Family, 67*, 216–21.

Ireland, J. (1994). *Gender, Work and Identity in the Lives of Women and Men in Nursing and the Engineering Trades in the South of England*. Unpublished doctoral dissertation, University of Cambridge, Cambridge.

Irigaray, L. (1993). *An Ethics of Sexual Difference* (G.C. Gill, Trans.). Ithaca, NY: Cornell University Press.

Irigaray, L. (1994). *Thinking the Difference: For a Peaceful Revolution* (K. Montin, Trans.). New York: Routledge.

Jackson, M. (1995). *The Mother Zone: Love, Sex, & Laundry in the Modern Family.* New York: Henry Holt.

Jaggar, A.M. (1990). Sexual Difference and Sexual Equality. In D.L. Rhode (Ed.), *Theoretical Perspectives on Sexual Differences* (pp. 239–54). New Haven and London: Yale University Press.

Jain, A., & Belsky, J. (1997). Fathering and Acculturation: Immigrant Indian Families with Young Children. *Journal of Marriage and the Family, 59*, 873–83.

James, E., Edwards, A., & Wong, R. (2003). *The Gender Impact of Pension Reform: A Cross Country Analysis.* Washington, DC: World Bank.

Jenson, J. (2002). Against the Current: Child Care and Family Policy in Quebec. In S. Michel (Ed.), *Child Care Policy at the Crossroads* (pp. 309–32). New York: Routledge.

Johnson, K.L., Lero, D.S., & Rooney, J.A. (2001). *Work-Life Compendium 2001: 150 Canadian Statistics on Work, Family and Well-Being.* Guelph, Ontario: Centre for Families, Work and Well-Being, University of Guelph.

Johnson, M.M. (1988). *Strong Mothers, Weak Wives: The Search for Gender Equality.* Berkeley: University of California Press.

Kane, M.J., & Disch,L. (1993). Sexual Violence and the Reproduction of Male Power in the Locker Room: A Critical Analysis of the Lisa Olson 'Incident.' *Sociology of Sport Journal, 10* (4), 331–52.

Kaufman, M. (1999). Men, Feminism, and Men's Contradictory Experiences of Power. In J.A. Kuypers (Ed.), *Men and Power* (pp. 59–83). Halifax: Fernwood Books.

Kimball, G. (1988). *50–50 Parenting: Sharing Family Rewards and Responsibilities.* Lexington, MA: Lexington Books.

Kimmel, M.S. (1994). Masculinity as Homophobia: Fear, Shame and Silence in the Construction of Gender Identity. In M. Kaufman (Ed.), *Theorizing Masculinities* (pp. 119–41). Thousand Oaks, CA: Sage.

Kimmel, M.S. (1999). Clarence, William, Iron Mile, Tailhook, Senator Packwood, Spur Posse, Magic ... And Us. In M. Messner (Ed.), *Men's Lives* (Fifth ed., pp. 540–51). Boston: Allyn and Bacon.

Kittay, E.F. (1999). *Love's Labor: Essays on Women, Equality and Dependency.* New York and Oxford: Oxford University Press.

Klein, R.D. (1983). How We Do What We Want to Do: Thoughts about Feminist Methodology. In G. Bowles & R.D. Klein (Eds.), *Theories of Women's Studies* (pp. 88–104). London: Routledge.

Korpi, W. (2000). Faces of Inequality: Gender, Class and Patterns of Inequalities in Different Types of Welfare States. *Social Politics, 7*, 127–91.

Krahn, H. (1991). Non-Standard Work Arrangements. *Perspectives on Labour and Income, Statistics Canada, 4*(4), 35–45.

Krahn, H. (1995). Non-Standard Work on the Rise. *Perspectives on Labour and Income, Statistics Canada, 7*(4), 35–42.

Kremarik, F. (2000). Family Affair: Children's Participation in Sports. *Canadian Social Trends (Statistics Canada), Autumn 2000*, 20–4.

Kristeva, J. (1987). *Tales of Love* (L. Roudiez, Trans.). New York: Columbia University Press.

LaBier, D. (1986). *Modern Madness: The Hidden Link Between Work and Emotional Conflict*. New York: Simon and Schuster.

Lamb, M.E. (2000). The History of Research on Father Involvement: An Overview. *Marriage and Family Review, 29*(2/3), 23–42.

Lamb, M.E. (Ed.). (1981). *The Role of the Father in Child Development*. New York: John Riley.

Lamb, M.E. (Ed.). (1987). *The Father's Role: Cross-Cultural Perspectives*. Hillsdale, NJ: Erlbaum.

Lamb, M.E., Charnov, E., & Levine, J.A. (1987). A Biosocial Perspective on Parental Behavior and Involvement. In A. Rossi (Ed.), *Parenting Across the Life Span* (pp. 11–42). New York: Academic Press.

Lamb, M.E., & Day, R.D. (Eds.). (2004). *Reconceptualising and Measuring Father Involvement*. New Jersey: Lawrence Erlbaum Associates.

Landes, J. (1980). Wages for Housework- Political and Theoretical Considerations. In E. Malos (Ed.), *The Politics of Housework* (pp. 195–205). London and New York: Allison and Busby.

LaRossa, R. (1997). *The Modernization of Fatherhood*. Chicago and London: University of Chicago Press.

LaRossa, R., & Larossa, M.M. (1981). *Transition to Parenthood: How Infants Change Families*. London: Sage.

LaRossa, R., & Reitzes, D.C. (1995). Gendered Perceptions of Father Involvement in Early 20th Century America. *Journal of Marriage and the Family, 57*, 223–229.

Larrabee, M.J. (Ed.). (1993). *An Ethic of Care: Feminist and Interdisciplinary Perspectives*. New York and London: Routledge.

Law, J. (2004). *After Method: Mess in Social Research*. London and New York: Routledge.

Lesko, N. (Ed.). (2000). *Masculinities at School*. London: Sage.

Leslie, L.A., Anderson, E.A., & Branson, M.P. (1991). Responsibility for Children: The Role of Gender and Employment. *Journal of Family Issues, 12*(2), 197–210.

Levine, J.A., & Pittinsky, T.L. (1998). *Working Fathers: New Strategies for Balancing Work and Family.* San Diego: Harcourt Brace Longmans.

Lewis, C. (1986). *Becoming a Father.* Milton Keynes, UK: Open University Press.

Lewis, J. (2003). *Should We Worry about Family Change?* Toronto: University of Toronto Press.

Lieblich, A., Tuval-Mashiach, R., & Zilber, T. (1998). *Narrative Research: Reading, Analysis, and Interpretation.* Thousand Oaks, CA: Sage.

Longino, H.E. (1993). Subjects, Power and Knowledge: Description and Prescription in Feminist Philosophies of Science. In L. Alcoff & E. Potter (Eds.), *Feminist Epistemologies* (pp. 101–20). London: Routledge.

Longino, H.E. (2002). *The Fate of Knowledge.* Princeton and Oxford: Princeton University Press.

Lorber, J. (1994). *Paradoxes of Gender.* New Haven: Yale University Press.

Lupton, D., & Barclay, L. (1997). *Constructing Fatherhood: Discourses and Experiences.* London: Sage.

Luxton, M. (1980). *More than a Labor of Love: Three Generations of Women's Work in the Home.* Toronto: Women's Press.

Luxton, M. (Ed.). (1997). *Feminism and Families: Critical Policies and Changing Practices.* Halifax: Fernwood Publishing.

Luxton, M., & Corman, J. (2001). *Getting By in Hard Times: Gendered Labour at Home and on the Job.* Toronto: University of Toronto Press.

Luxton, M., & Vosko, L.F. (1998). Where Women's Efforts Count: The 1996 Census Campaign and Family Politics in Canada. *Studies in Political Economy, 56* (Summer 1998), 49–82.

Mac an Ghaill, M. (1994). *The Making of Men: Masculinities, Sexualities, and Schooling.* Buckingham: Open University.

Maccoby, E.E. (1990). Gender and Relationships: A Developmental Account. *American Psychologist, 45,* 513–20.

Mahon, R., & Michel, S. (2002). *Child Care Policy at the Crossroads: Gender and Welfare State Restructuring.* London: Routledge.

Malos, E. (1980). *The Politics of Housework.* London and New York: Allison and Busby.

Mandell, D. (2002). *Deadbeat Dads: Subjectivity and Social Construction.* Toronto: University of Toronto Press.

Mandell, N., & Sweet, R. (2004). Homework as Home Work: Mothers' Unpaid Educational Labour. *Atlantis: A Women's Studies Journal, 28*(2), 7–18.

Mann, C., & Stewart, F. (2000). *Internet Communication and Qualitative Research: A Handbook for Researching Online.* London: Sage.

Marks, L. (2004). Feminism and Stay at Home Motherhood: Some Critical

Reflections and Implications for Mothers on Social Assistance. *Atlantis: A Women's Studies Journal, 28*(2), 73–84.

Marshall, K. (1998). Stay-at-Home Dads. *Perspectives on Labour and Income, Statistics Canada, Spring 1998,* 9–15.

Marshall, K. (2000). Part-time by Choice. *Perspectives on Labour and Income, 1*(2), 5–12.

Marshall, K. (2003). Benefiting from Extended Parental Leave. *Perspectives on Labour and Income, Statistics Canada, 4*(3), 5–11.

Marsiglio, W. (1993). Contemporary Scholarship on Fatherhood: Culture, Identity and Conflict. *Journal of Family Issues, 14*(4), 484–509.

Marsiglio, W., Amato, P., Day, R.D., & Lamb, M.E. (2000). Scholarship on Fatherhood in the 1990s and Beyond. *Journal of Marriage and Family, 62,* 1173–191.

Martin, P.Y. (2003). 'Said and Done' Versus 'Saying and Doing': Gendering Practices, Practicing Gender at Work. *Gender and Society, 17*(3), 342–66.

Maushart, S. (1999). *The Mask of Motherhood: How Becoming a Mother Changes Everything and Why We Pretend It Doesn't.* New York: New York Press.

Mauss, M. (1979). *'Body Techniques' in Sociology and Psychology.* London: Routledge and Kegan Paul.

Mauthner, N.S. (2002). *The Darkest Days of My Life: Stories of Postpartum Depression.* Cambridge, MA: Harvard University Press.

Mauthner, N.S., & Doucet, A. (1998). Reflections on a Voice Centred Relational Method of Data Analysis: Analysing Maternal and Domestic Voices. In R. Edwards (Ed.), *Feminist Dilemmas in Qualitative Research: Private Lives and Public Texts* (pp. 119–44). London: Sage.

Mauthner, N.S., & Doucet, A. (2003). Reflexive Accounts and Accounts of Reflexivity in Qualitative Data Analysis. *Sociology, 37*(3), 413–31.

May, T. (1998). Reflexivity in the Age of Reconstructive Social Science. *International Journal of Social Research Methodology, 1*(1), 7–24.

McBride, B.A., & Mills, G. (1993). A Comparison of Mother and Father Involvement with their Preschool Age Children. *Early Childhood Research Quarterly, 8,* 457–77.

McCall, L. (2005). The Complexity of Intersectionality. *Signs: Journal of Women in Culture and Society, 30*(3), 1771–800.

McMahon, M. (1995). *Engendering Motherhood: Identity and Self-Transformation in Women's Lives.* New York: The Guilford Press.

McMahon, M. (1996). Significant Absences. *Qualitative Inquiry, 2*(3), 320–36.

McNay, L. (2000). *Gender and Agency: Reconfiguring the Subject in Feminist and Social Theory.* Cambridge: Polity Press.

Mead, G.H. (1962). *Mind, Self, and Society* (2nd ed.). Chicago: University of Chicago Press.

Mederer, H.J. (1993). Division of Labor in Two-Earner Homes: Task Accomplishment versus Household Management as Critical Variables in Perceptions about Family Work. *Journal of Marriage and the Family, 55*, 133–45.

Meehan, E., & Sevenhuijsen, S. (Eds.). (1991). *Equality, Politics and Gender*. London: Sage.

Mellor, P., & Shilling, C. (1997). *Re-Forming the Body: Religion, Community and Modernity*. London: Sage.

Merleau-Ponty, M. (1962). *The Phenomology of Perception* (C. Smith, Trans.). London: Routledge and Kegan Paul.

Merleau-Ponty, M. (1964). *Signs*. Evanston: Northwestern Press.

Merleau-Ponty, M. (1965). *The Structure of Behaviour*. London: Methuen.

Merleau-Ponty, M. (1968). *The Visible and the Invisible*. Evanston, IL: Northwestern University Press.

Messerschmidt, J. (1999). Making Bodies Matter: Adolescent Masculinities, the Body, and Varieties of Violence. *Theoretical Criminology, 3*(2), 197–220.

Messner, M.A. (1987). The Meaning of Success: The Athletic Experience and the Development of Male Identity. In H. Brod (Ed.), *The Making of Masculinities: The New Men's Studies* (pp. 193–209). Boston: Allen and Unwin.

Messner, M.A. (1990). Boyhood, Organized Sports, and the Construction of Masculinities. *Journal of Contemporary Ethnography, 18*(4), 416–44.

Messner, M.A. (1992). *Power at Play: Sports and the Problem of Masculinity*. Boston: Beacon Press.

Messner, M.A. (1997). *Politics of Masculinities: Men in Movements*. Thousand Oaks, CA: Sage.

Messner, M.A. (2000). Barbie Girls versus Sea Monsters: Children Constructing Gender. *Gender & Society, 14*(6), 765–84.

Michaels, A. (1996). *Fugitive Pieces*. Toronto: McClelland and Stewart.

Miles, M.B., & Huberman, M.A. (1994). *Qualitative Data Analysis: An Expanded Sourcebook*. London: Sage.

Milkie, M.A., & Peltola, P. (1999). Playing All the Roles: Gender and the Work Balancing Act. *Journal of Marriage and the Family, 61*(4), 476–90.

Miller, M. (1983). *Men and Friendships*. Boston: Houghton Mifflin.

Mingione, E. (1988). Work and Informal Activities in Urban Southern Italy. In R. E. Pahl (Ed.), *On Work: Historical, Comparative and Theoretical Approaches* (pp. 548–78). Oxford: Basil Blackwell.

Mink, G. (1995). *The Wages of Motherhood: Inequality in the Welfare State 1917–1942*. Ithaca, NY: Cornell University Press.

Minow, M., & Shanley, M.L. (1996). Relational Rights and Responsibilities: Revisioning the Family in Liberal Political Theory and Law. *Hypatia, 11*(1), 4–29.

Mirande, A. (1988). Chicano fathers: Traditional Perceptions and Current Realities. In C. P. Cowan (Ed.), *Fatherhood Today: Men's Changing Role in the Family.*
New York: Wiley.

Mishler, E.G. (1986). *Research Interviewing: Context and Narrative.* Cambridge,
MA: Harvard University Press.

Monaghan, L.F. (2002). Hard Men, Shop Boys and Others: Embodying Competence in a Masculinist Occupation. *The Sociological Review, 50*(3), 334–55.

Morgan, D.H.J. (1992). *Discovering Men.* London: Routledge.

Morgan, D.H.J. (1996). *Family Connections: An Introduction to Family Studies.*
Cambridge: Polity Press.

Morris, L. (1985). Local Social Networks and Domestic Organisations: A Study
of Redundant Steelworkers and Their Wives. *The Sociological Review, 33*(2),
327–42.

Morris, L. (1990). *The Workings of the Household: A US-UK Comparison.* Cambridge: Polity Press.

Moser, C. (1993). *Gender Planning and Development:* Theory, *Practice and Training.* London: Routledge.

Moss, P., & Petrie, P. (2002). *From Children's Services to Children's Spaces: Public
Policy, Children and Childhood.* London: Routledge.

Moss, P., & O'Brien, M. (2005). Leave Policies and Research: United Kingdom.
In P. Moss (Ed.), *Leave Polices and Research: Overviews and Country Notes.* Brussels: Centre for Population and Family Studies (CBGS).

Naples, N.A. (2003). *Feminism and Method: Ethnography, Discourse Analysis, and
Activist Research.* New York and London: Routledge.

Nardi, P.M. (1992). 'Seamless Souls': An Introduction to Men's Friendships. In
P.M. Nardi (Ed.), *Men's Friendships* (pp. 1–14). Newbury Park, CA: Sage.

Nelson, L.H. (1993). Epistemological Communities. In L. Alcoff & E. Potter
(Eds.), *Feminist Epistemologies* (pp. 121–60). New York and London: Routledge.

Nettleton, S., & Watson, J. (Eds.). (1998). *The Body in Everyday Life.* London and
New York: Routledge.

News, U.S.C.B. (Writer) (2004). 'Stay-at-Home' Parents Tops 5 Million, Census
Bureau Reports. Washington, DC: U.S. Department of Commerce.

Nicholson, L. (1994). Interpreting Gender. *Signs: Journal of Women in Culture and
Society, 20*(11), 79–105.

Noddings, N. (2003). *Caring: A Feminine Approach to Ethics and Moral Education*
(2nd ed.). Berkeley: University of California Press.

Nomaguchi, K.M., & Milkie, M.A. (2003). Costs and Rewards of Children: The
Effects of Becoming a Parent on Adults' Lives. *Journal of Marriage and Family,
65,* 356–74.

O'Brien, M. (1987). Patterns of Kinship and Friendship among Lone Fathers. In M. O'Brien (Ed.), *Reassessing Fatherhood: New Observations on Fathers and the Modern Family* (pp. 225–45). London: Sage.

O'Brien, M. (2005). *Shared Caring: Bringing Fathers in the Frame* (EOC Working paper Series No. 18). Manchester: Equal Opportunities Commission.

O'Brien, M., & Shemilt, I. (2003). *Working Fathers: Earning and Caring*. Manchester, UK: Equal Opportunities Commission.

O'Connor, J.S., Orloff, A.S., & Shaver, S. (1999). *States, Markets, Families, Gender, Liberalism, and Social Policy in Australia, Canada, Great Britain and the United States*. Cambridge: Cambridge University Press.

O'Donnell, M., & Sharpe, S. (2000). *Uncertain Masculinities: Youth, Ethnicity and Class in Contemporary Britain*. London: Routledge.

OECD (2004). *Early Childhood Education and Care Policy: Canada Country Note*. Paris: Organisation for Economic Co-operation and Development: Directorate for Education.

Offen, K. (1992). Defining Feminism: A Comparative Historical Approach. In S. James (Ed.), *Beyond Equality and Difference: Citizenship, Feminist Politics and Female Subjectivity* (pp. 69–88). London and New York: Routledge.

Oliker, S.J. (1989). *Best Friends and Marriage: Exchange among Women*. Berkeley: University of California Press.

Oliver, K. (Ed.). (1993). *Ethics, Politics, and Difference in Julia Kristeva's Writings*. New York: Routledge.

Orloff, A.S. (2002). *Women's Employment and Welfare Regimes: Globalization, Export Orientation and Social Policy in Europe and North America* (No. Social Policy and Development Programme paper Number 12). Geneva: United Nations Research Institute for Social Development.

Orloff, A.S. (2004). *Farewell to Maternalism: State Policies and Mothers' Employment*. Paris, France: Paper prepared for the Annual Conference of RC 19, September 2–4.

Pahl, R. (2000). *On Friendship*. Cambridge, UK: Polity.

Pahl, R.E. (1984). *Divisions of Labour*. Oxford: Basil Blackwell.

Pahl, R.E. (1995). *After Success: Fin-de-Siècle Anxiety and Identity*. Cambridge: Polity Press.

Palamet, B. (2004). Low Income among Immigrants and Visible Minorities. *Perspectives on Labour and Income, Statistics Canada, 5*(4).

Palkovitz, R. (2002). *Involved Fathering and Men's Adult Development: Provisional Balances*. Mahwah, NJ: Lawrence Erlbaum Associates.

Parke, R.D. (1996). *Fatherhood*. Cambridge, MA: Harvard University Press.

Parr, J. (2001). Notes for a More Sensuous History of Twentieth Century Canada: The Timely, the Tacit and the Material Body. *Canadian Historical Review,* *82*(4), 720–45.

Parsons, T. (1999). *Man and Boy.* New York: Simon and Schuster.

Pearson, A. (2002). *I Don't Know How She Does It: The Life of Kate Reddy, Working Mother.* New York: Knopf.

Pease, B. (2000). *Recreating Men: Postmodern Masculinity Politics.* London: Sage.

Pérusse, D. (2003). New Maternity and Parental Benefits. *Perspectives on Labour and Income, Statistics Canada, 4*(3), 12–15.

Phillips, A. (1991). *Engendering Democracy.* Cambridge: Polity Press.

Plantin, L., Sven-Axel, M., & Kearney, J. (2003). Talking and Doing Fatherhood: On Fatherhood and Masculinity in Sweden and England. *Fathering, 1*(1), 3–26.

Pleck, E.H., & Pleck, J.H. (1997). Fatherhood Ideals in the United States: Historical Dimensions. In M.E. Lamb (Ed.), *The Role of the Father in Child Development.* New York: Wiley.

Pleck, J.H. (1985). *Working Wives, Working Husbands.* London: Sage.

Pleck, J.H., & Mascaidrelli, B.P. (2004). Parental Involvement: Levels, Sources and Consequences. In M.E. Lamb (Ed.), *The Role of the Father in Child Development* (4th ed.; pp. 222–71). New York: Wiley.

Pleck, J.H., & Stueve, J.L. (2001). Time and Parental Involvement. In K. Daly (Ed.), *Minding the Time in Family Experience: Emerging Perspectives and Issues* (pp. 205–26). London: JAI Press.

Plummer, K. (1983). *Documents of Life.* London: George Allen and Unwin.

Plummer, K. (1995a). An Invitation to a Sociology of Stories. In J. McGuigan (Ed.), *Studies in Culture: An Introductory Reader* (pp. 333–45). London: Arnold.

Plummer, K. (1995b). *Telling Sexual Stories: Power, Change, and Social Worlds.* London: Routledge.

Polivka, A.E., & Nardone, T. (1989). On the Definition of 'Contingent Work.' *Monthly Labor Review, 112*(12), 9–16.

Pollack, W. (1998). *Real Boys: Rescuing Our Sons from the Myths of Boyhood.* New York: Owl Books.

Popenoe, D. (1993). American Family Decline, 1960–1999: A Review and Appraisal. *Journal of Marriage and the Family, 55,* 527–42.

Popenoe, D. (1996). *Life without Fathers: Compelling New Evidence That Fatherhood and Marriage are Indispensable for the Good of Children and Society.* New York: The Free Press.

Potuchek, J.L. (1997). *Who Supports the Family: Gender and Breadwinning in Dual Earner Marriages.* Stanford, CA: Stanford University Press.

Prendergast, S., & Forrest, S. (1998). 'Shorties, Low-Lifers, Hardnuts and Kings': Boys, Emotions and Embodiment in Schools. In S.J. Williams (Ed.), *Emotions in Social Life: Critical Themes and Contemporary Issues* (pp. 155–72). London and New York: Routledge.

Presser, L. (2004). Violent Offenders, Moral Selves: Constructing Identities and Accounts in the Research Interview. *Social Problems, 51*(1), 82–101.

Pruett, K. (2000). *Fatherneed: Why Father Care Is As Essential As Mother Care for Your Child*. New York: Broadview Press.

Pulkingham, J. (1994). Private Troubles, Private Solutions: Poverty among Divorced Women and the Politics of Support Enforcement and Child Custody Determination. *Canadian Journal of Law and Society, 2*, 351–64.

Purvis, T., & Hunt, A. (1993). Discourse, Ideology, Discourse, Ideology, Discourse, Ideology ... *British Journal of Sociology, 44*(3), 473–99.

Radin, N. (1982). Primary Care-Giving and Role Sharing Fathers. In M.E. Lamb (Ed.), *Non-Traditional Families: Parenting and Child Development* (pp. 173–204). Hillsdale, NJ: Erlbaum.

Reid, H.M., & Fine, G.A. (1992). Self-Disclosure in Men's Friendship: Variations Associated with Intimate Relations. In P.M. Nardi (Ed.), *Men's Friendships* (pp. 132–52). Newbury Park, CA: Sage.

Reissman, C.K. (1993). *Narrative Analysis*. Newbury Park, CA: Sage.

Reissman, C.K. (2003). Analysis of Personal Narratives. In J.F. Gubrium (Ed.), *Inside Interviewing: New Lenses, New Concerns* (pp. 331–46). London: Sage.

Rhode, D.L. (1989). *Justice and Gender: Sex Discrimination and the Law*. Cambridge, MA: Harvard University Press.

Rhode, D.L. (Ed.). (1990). *Theoretical Perspectives on Sexual Difference*. New Haven, CT: Yale University Press.

Ribbens-McCarthy, J., Edwards, R., & Gillies, V. (2000). Moral Tales of the Child and the Adult: Narratives of Contemporary Family Lives under Changing Circumstances. *Sociology, 34*(4), 785–803.

Rich, A. (1986). *Of Woman Born: Motherhood as Experience and Institution* (Second ed.). New York: Norton.

Richards, M.P.M. (1982). How Should We Approach the Study of Fathers? In M. O'Brien (Ed.), *The Father Figure*. London: Tavistock.

Ricoeur, P. (1985). *Time and Narrative*. Chicago: University of Chicago Press.

Riley, P.J., & Kiger, G. (1999). Moral Discourse on Domestic Labor: Gender, Power, and Identity in Families. *The Social Science Journal, 36*(3), 541–548.

Risman, B.J. (1987). Can Men Mother? Life as a Single Father. *Family Relations, 35*, 95–102.

Risman, B.J. (1998). *Gender Vertigo: American Families in Transition*. New Haven and London: Yale University Press.

Risman, B.J. (2004). Gender as a Social Structure: Theory Wrestling with Activism. *Gender & Society, 18*(4), 429–50.

Risman, B.J., & Johnson-Sumerford, D. (1997). Doing It Fairly: A Study of Feminist Marriages. *Journal of Marriage and the Family, 60*(1), 23–40.

Robinson, B.E., & Barret, R.L. (1986). *The Developing Father: Emerging Roles in Contemporary Society*. New York: Guilford.

Rose, G. (1993). *Feminism and Geography: The Limits of Geographical Knowledge*. Minneapolis: University of Minnesota Press.

Rose, N. (1991). *Governing the Soul: The Shaping of the Private Self*. London: Routledge.

Rose, N. (1996). Identity, Genealogy, History. In P. du Gay (Ed.), *Questions of Cultural Identity* (pp. 128–51). London: Sage.

Rostgaard, T. (2005). Leave Policies and Research: Denmark. In P. Moss (Ed.), *Leave Polices and Research: Overviews and Country Notes*. Brussels: Centre for Population and Family Studies (CBGS).

Rothman, B.K. (1989). Women as Fathers: Motherhood and Childcare under a Modified Patriarchy. *Gender & Society, 3*(1), 89–104.

Rubin, L. B. (1985). *Just Friends: The Role of Friendship in Our Lives*. New York: Harper and Row.

Ruddick, S. (1983). Maternal Thinking. In J. Treblicot (Ed.), *Mothering: Essays in Feminist Theory* (pp. 213–30). Totowa, New Jersey: Rowman and Littlefield.

Ruddick, S. (1995). *Maternal Thinking: Towards a Politics of Peace* (Second ed.). Boston: Beacon.

Ruddick, S. (1997). The Idea of Fatherhood. In H.L. Nelson (Ed.), *Feminism and Families* (pp. 205–20). New York and London: Routledge.

Russell, G. (1983). *The Changing Role of Fathers*. St. Lucia, Australia: University of Queensland Press.

Russell, G. (1987). Problems in Role-Reversed Families. In M. O'Brien (Ed.), *Reassessing Fatherhood: New Observations on Fathers and the Modern Family* (pp. 161–82). London: Sage.

Russo, N.F. (1976). The Motherhood Mandate. *Journal of Social Issues, 32*, 143–53.

Sanchez, L., & Kane, E.W. (1996). Women's and Men's Constructions of Perceptions of Housework Fairness. *Journal of Family Issues, 17*(3), 358–87.

Sargent, P. (2000). Real Men or Real Teachers? Contradictions in the Lives of Men Elementary Teachers. *Men and Masculinities, 2*(4), 410–33.

Sassoon, A.S. (1987). Introduction: The Personal and the Intellectual, Fragments and Order, International Trends and National Specificities. In A.S.
Sassoon (Ed.), *Women and the State: The Shifting Boundaries of Public and Private* (pp. 13–42). London: Unwin Hyman.

Scheper-Hughes, N. (1992). *Death without Weeping: The Violence of Everyday Life
in Brazil.* Berkeley: University of California Press.

Scott, A., & Morgan, D.H.J. (Eds.). (1993). *Body Matters.* London: Taylor and
Francis.

Scott, J.W. (1988). *Gender and the Politics of History.* New York: Colombia University Press.

Scott, J.W. (1992). Experience. In J. Butler & J.W. Scott (Eds.), *Feminists Theorize
the Political* (pp. 22–40). London: Routledge.

Scott, J.W. (1994). A Rejoinder to Thomas C. Holt. In J. Chandler, A.I. Davidson
& H. Harootunian (Eds.), *Questions of Evidence: Proof, Practice and Persuasion
across the Disciplines* (pp. 397–400). Chicago: University of Chicago Press.

Seale, C. (1999). *The Quality of Qualitative Research.* London: Sage.

Seale, C. (2002). Qualitative Issues in Qualitative Inquiry. *Qualitative Social
Work, 1*(1), 97–110.

Seery, B.L., & Crowley, M.S. (1999). Women's Emotion Work in the Family:
Relationship Management and the Process of Building Father-Child Relationships. *Journal of Family Issues, 21*(1), 100–27.

Segura, D.A. (1994). Working at Motherhood: Chicana and Mexican Immigrant
Mothers and Employment. In L.R. Forcey (Ed.), *Mothering: Ideology, Experience and Agency* (pp. 211–33). London and New York: Routledge.

Seidler, V. (1992). Rejection, Vulnerability and Friendships. In P.M. Nardi (Ed.),
Men's Friendships (pp. 15–34). London: Sage.

Seidler, V. (1997). *Man Enough: Embodying Masculinities.* London: Sage.

Sevenhuijsen, S. (1998). *Citizenship and the Ethics of Care: Feminist Considerations
on Justice, Morality and Politics.* London: Routledge.

Sevenhuijsen, S. (2000). Caring in the Third Way: The Relation between Obliga-
tion, Responsibility and Care in Third Way Discourse. *Critical Social Policy: A
Journal of Theory and Practice in Social Welfare, 25*(1), 5–38.

Sharma, U. (1986). *Women's Work, Class and the Urban Household: A Study of
Shimla, North India.* London: Tavistock.

Shields, J. (2003). *No Safe Haven: Markets, Welfare, and Migrants* (No. 22).
Toronto: Joint Centre of Excellence for Research on Immigration and
Settlement (CERIS).

Shilling, C. (1993). *The Body and Social Theory.* London: Sage.

Siltanen, J., Willis, A., & Scobie, W. (under review). Separately Together:

Working Reflexively as a Team. *International Journal of Social Research Methodology*.

Silver, C. (2000). *Being There: The Time Dual-Earner Couples Spend with their Children*. Ottawa: Statistics Canada.

Simmons, R. (2002). *Odd Girl Out: The Hidden Culture of Aggression in Girls*. Orlando, FL: Harcourt Books.

Smart, C. (1991). The Legal and Moral Ordering of Child Custody. *Journal of Law and Society, 18*(4), 485–500.

Smith, C.D. (1998). 'Men Don't Do this Sort of Thing' A Case Study of the Social Isolation of Househusbands. *Men and Masculinities, 1*(2), 138–72.

Smith, D. (1987). *The Everyday World as Problematic: A Feminist Sociology*. Milton Keynes, UK: Open University Press.

Smith, D. (1996). Telling the Truth after Postmodernism. *Studies in Symbolic Interaction, 19*(3), 171–202.

Smith, D. (1999). *Writing the Social: Critique, Theory and Investigations*. Toronto: University of Toronto Press.

Snarey, J. (1993). *How Fathers Care for the Next Generation: A Four-Decade Study*. Cambridge, MA: Harvard University Press.

Somers, M.R. (1994). The Narrative Constitution of Identity: A Relational and Network Approach. *Theory and Society, 23*(5), 605–50.

Spelman, E. (1988). *The Inessential woman*. Boston: Beacon Press.

Spence, L. (2002). *Girls' Friendships and Social Networks*. Unpublished doctoral thesis, Carleton University, Ottawa.

Srinivasan, L. (1977). *Perspectives on Non-Formal Adult Learning*. Boston: World Education.

Srinivasan, L. (1990). *Tools for Community Participation: A Manual for Training Trainers in Participatory Techniques*. New York: PROWWESS/United Nations Development Program.

Stacey, J. (1990). *Brave New Families: Stories of Domestic Upheaval in Late Twentieth-Century America*. Boston: Basic Books.

Stacey, J. (1993). Good Riddance to the Family: A Response to David Popenoe. *Journal of Marriage and the Family, 55*, 545–47.

Stack, C. (1974). *All Our Kin: Strategies for Survival in a Black Community*. New York: Harper and Row.

Stanley, L. (1994). The Knowing Because Experiencing Subject: Narratives, Lives, and Autobiography. In K. Lennon & M. Whitford (Eds.), *Knowing the Difference: Feminist Perspectives in Epistemology* (pp. 132–148). London: Routledge.

Statistics Canada. (2002b). *Labour Force Survey, Annual Average 2002 / Family*

Characteristics of Single Husband–Wife Families (Table 2). Ottawa: Statistics Canada.

Statistics Canada. (2003). *Women in Canada: Work Chapter Updates* (Catalogue No. 89F0133XIE). Ottawa: Statistics Canada.

Statistics Canada. (2003a). *Canada E-Book.* Ottawa: Statistics Canada.

Stoljar, N. (2000). Autonomy and Feminist Intuition. In N. Stoljar (Ed.), *Relational Autonomy: Feminist Perspectives on Autonomy, Agency, and the Social Self* (pp. 94–111). New York and Oxford: Oxford University Press.

Stueve, J.L., & Pleck, J.H. (2003). Fathers' Narratives of Arranging and Planning: Implications for Understanding Parental Responsibility. *Fathering, 1*(1), 51–70.

Sullivan, O. (1996). Time Co-ordination, the Domestic Division of Labour and Affective Relations: Time Use and the Enjoyment of Activities within Couples. *Sociology, 30*(1), 79–100.

Tam, P. (2003). Fathers Can Mother Children Too. *The Ottawa Citizen,* 8 April.

Taylor, C. (1990). Embodied Agency. In H. Pietersma (Ed.), *Merleau-Ponty: Critical Essays.* Washington, DC: University Press of America.

Taylor, J.M., Gilligan, C., & Sullivan, A. (1997). *Between Voice and Silence: Women and Girls, Race and Relationships.* Cambridge, MA: Harvard University Press.

Thompson, L., & Walker, A. (1989). Gender in Families: Women and Men in Marriage, Work and Parenthood. *Journal of Marriage and the Family, 51*(4), 845–71.

Thorne, B. (1993). *Gender Play: Girls and Boys in School.* Buckingham, UK: Open University Press.

Tolman, D.L. (2002). *Dilemmas of Desire: Teenage Girls Talk about Sexuality.* Cambridge, MA: Harvard University Press.

Townsend, N.W. (2002). *The Package Deal: Marriage, Work, and Fatherhood in Men's Lives.* Philadelphia: Temple University Press.

Tronto, J. (1989). Women and Caring: What Can Feminists Learn about Morality from Caring? In S. Bordo (Ed.), *Gender/Body/Knowledge: Feminist Reconstructions of Being and Knowing* (pp. 172–87). New Brunswick and London: Rutgers University Press.

Tronto, J. (1993). *Moral Boundaries: A Political Argument for an Ethic of Care.* New York and London: Routledge.

Tronto, J. (1995). Care as a Basis for Radical Political Judgements (Symposium on Care and Justice). *Hypatia, 10*(2), 141–49.

Ungerson, C. (1990). The Language of Care: Crossing the Boundaries. In C. Ungerson (Ed.), *Gender and Caring: Work and Welfare in Britain and Scandinavia* (pp. 8–33). New York: Harvester Wheatsheaf.

Uttal, L. (1996). Custodial Care, Surrogate Care, and Coordinated Care: Employed Mothers and the Meaning of Child Care. *Gender & Society, 10*(3), 291–311.

Vosko, L.F. (2000). *Temporary Work: The Gendered Rise of a Precarious Employment Relationship.* Toronto: University of Toronto Press.

Vosko, L.F., Zukewich, N., & Cranford, C. (2003). Precarious Jobs: A New Typology of Employment. *Perspectives on Labour and Income, Statistics Canada, 4*(10), 16–26.

Wacquant, L.J.D. (1995). Pugs at Work: Bodily Capital and Bodily Labour among Professional Boxers. *Body & Society, 1*(1), 65–93.

Waddington, D., Chritcher, C., & Dicks, B. (1998). 'All Jumbled Up': Employed Women with Unemployed Husbands. In J. Edwards (Ed.), *Men, Gender Divisions and Welfare* (pp. 231–58). London and New York: Routledge.

Walker, K. (1994). 'I'm Not Friends the Way She's Friends': Ideological and Behavioral Constructions of Masculinity in Men's Friendships. *Masculinities, 2*(2), 38–55.

Walker, L. (2002). Home Making: An Architectural Perspective. *Signs: Journal of Women in Culture and Society, 27*(3), 823–36.

Wallace, C.D. (2002). Household Strategies: Their Conceptual Relevance and Analytical Scope in Social Research. *Sociology, 36*(2), 275–92.

Wallace, C.D., & Pahl, R.E. (1985). Household Work Strategies in an Economic Recession. In E. Mingione (Ed.), *Beyond Employment* (pp. 189–227). Oxford: Basil Blackwell.

Waller, M.M. (2002). *My Baby's Father: Unmarried Parents and Paternal Responsibility.* Ithaca, NY, and London: Cornell University Press.

Walzer, S. (1998). *Thinking about the Baby: Gender and Transitions into Parenthood.* Philadelphia: Temple University Press.

Ward, J. (2004). 'Not all Differences are Created Equal': Multiple Jeopardy in a Gendered Organization. *Gender & Society, 18*(1), 82–102.

Waring, M. (1998). *Counting for Nothing: What Men Value and What Women Are Worth.* San Francisco: Harper and Row.

Watson, J. (1998). Running Around like a Lunatic: Colin's Body and the Case of Male Embodiment. In J. Watson (Ed.), *The Body in Everyday Life* (pp. 163–79). London and New York: Routledge.

Way, N. (1998a). *Everyday Courage: The Lives and Stories of Urban Teenagers.* New York: New York University Press.

Way, N. (1998b). Using Feminist Methods to Understand the Friendships of Adolescent Boys. *Journal of Social Issues, 53*(4), 703–25.

Weedon, C. (1987). *Feminist Practice and Poststructuralist Theory.* Oxford: Blackwell.

West, C., & Zimmerman, R. (1987). Doing Gender. *Gender & Society, 1,* 30–7.

Wheelock, J. (1990). *Husbands at Home: The Domestic Economy in a Post Industrial Society.* London: Routledge.

Whitford, M. (1991). *Luce Irigaray: Philosophy in the Feminine.* London and New York: Routledge.

Williams, C.L. (1989). *Gender Differences at Work: Women and Men in Nontraditional Occupations.* Berkeley, California: University of California Press.

Williams, C.L. (1992). The Glass Escalator: Hidden Advantage for Men in the 'Female' Professions. *Social Problems, 39*(3), 253–67.

Williams, J. (2000). *Unbending Gender: Why Family and Work Conflict and What to Do about It.* Oxford and New York: Oxford University Press.

Williams, R. (1983). *Keywords: A Vocabulary of Culture and Society (revised edition).* New York: Oxford University Press.

Williams, S.J., & Bendelow, G. (1998). *The Lived Body: Sociological Themes, Emboides Issues.* London: Routledge.

Wollstonecraft, M. (1992 [1792]). *A Vindication of the Rights of Women.* London: Penguin.

Wright, P. (1982). Men's Friendships Women's Friendships and the Alleged Inferiority of the Latter. *Sex Roles, 8,* 1–20.

Yeung, W.J., Sandberg, J.F., Davis-Kean, P.E., & Hofferth, S.L. (2001). Children's Time with Fathers in Intact Families. *Journal of Marriage and the Family, 63*(1), 136–54.

Yogman, M.W., Cooley, J., & Kindlon, D. (1988). Fathers, Infants and Toddlers: A Developing Relationship. In C.P. Cowan (Ed.), *Fatherhood Today: Men's Changing Role in the Family* (pp. 53–65). New York: Wiley.

Young, I. M. (1984). Is Male Gender Identity the Cause of Male Domination? In J. Trebilcot (Ed.), *Mothering: Essays in Feminist Theory* (pp. 129–46). Totowa, NJ: Rowman and Allanheld.

Young, I.M. (1990a). *Justice and the Politics of Difference.* Princeton, NJ: Princeton University Press.

Young, I.M. (1990b). *Throwing Like a Girl and Other Essays in Feminist Philosophy and Social Theory.* Bloomington: Indiana University Press.

Index

Kofi, 83; Kyle, 102, 113, 116, 131, 182, 183, 195; Lester, 149–50; Logan, 81; Lorne, 120; Luke, 121–2, 131–2, 143–4, 156, 161, 167–8, 171, 187, 240; Marc, 185–6, 237; Martin, 90, 137, 140, 151–2, 153, 156, 231; Matthew, 125, 294n3; Maurice, 83, 122, 162; Mick, 62–3; Mohammed, 130; Morris, 295n5; Osie, 148; Owen, 155, 196; Paul, 147–8, 175, 185; Ray, 169, 205, 206, 294n3, 297n4; Robert, 103, 114, 188; Ron, 132; Rory, 4, 89, 149, 180, 208; Roy, 122, 129–30, 135, 205; Ryan, 83, 147, 148, 161, 191, 206; Sam, 3, 81, 92, 104, 183, 196, 208; Sasha, 121, 220; Steve, 215; Victor, 103; Vincent, 152, 155, 165, 170; William, 113, 129, 145. *See also* couples: individual

femininity: devaluation of, 122, 195–6, 237; distancing of fathering from, 122; hegemonic masculinity and, 37, 122; widening of, 243
feminism: difference, 21; equality, 23; fathers' rights groups and, 19–20; intersectional theory, 31; and men's involvement in caregiving, 7; and valuing of caregiving, 290n4
field trips, 190–1
50-50 Parenting (Kimball), 9
Finch, Janet, 176
Flax, Jane, 286n6, 290n5
Flood, Michael, 249, 300–1n3
focus groups, 55–6, 266–8
Folbre, Nancy, 22, 290n3
Fraser, Nancy, 22, 290n3
French, Sean, *Fatherhood,* 69
Friedman, Marilyn, 224

friendships: and avoidance of intimacy, 153, 154; border crossings in, 164; borderwork and, 44; of children, 155–6; cross-gender, 154–6, 168; gender differences in, 151–3, 152, 153, 161–3, 164; generalizations regarding, 162; hegemonic masculinity and, 153–4; men's, 152–3, 163, 165; related to children, 165; same-sex, 155–6; self-reliance and, 152–3, 154; spatial contexts of, 168; of women, 36
Fugitive Pieces (Michaels), 16, 46, 48, 65, 71, 225
Fuss, Diana, 29

Garey, Anita, 172, 228–9; *Weaving Work and Motherhood,* 92
Gatens, Moria, 40
gay fathers, 13, 54, 86–8; analysis of narratives, 67; border crossings by, 204–5; coming out by, 203–4, 297n4; discrimination against, 203; diversity among, 77; divorced, 86–8; and feminine qualities in fathering, 123; in heterosexual marriages, 86–8; Internet survey and, 61; joint custody and, 86–8, 204; masculine style of parenting by, 296n3; and mothering-fathering differences, 126; multiple jeopardy of, 203, 210, 236; in non-heterosexual partnerships, 86–8; organizations for, 204; and other mothers for children, 224; as primary caregivers, 86–8; recruitment of, 53; scrutiny of, 203, 236; social acceptability of, 203–5, 236; as sports oriented, 296n4; stay-at-home, 86–8

primary-caregiving fathers, 74–5, 76, 77–83; defined, 75; gay, 86–8; masculinity of, 38; in media, 294n1; mothers' responsibilities and, 75; research on, 9; role reversal and, 77–81; self-defined, 54, 75; self-identification as, 13, 76; studies on, 24

production relations, 33, 290n7

Promise Keepers, 22, 247

protective care, 111, 116, 117

psy complexes, 192, 193, 194

puberty, 121

Purvis, Trevor, 299n4

Radin, Norma, 75

Rawls, John, 296n1

recruitment: of diverse group of fathers, 235; of ethnic-minority fathers, 53; of fathers, 52–4, 63–4, 235; of gay fathers, 53; of low-income fathers, 53; strategy, 75–6; volunteering vs, 75–6

reflexivity, 47–8, 51–2, 71–2, 225

The Reproduction of Mothering (Chodorow), 7

research: Atlas.ti in, 65, 67, 68; background forms, 53; data analysis, 48, 278–84; data collection, 47–8, 226–7; data sources, 12–13; extension of theory in, 72; focus groups, 55–6; Household Portrait technique, 56–61, 78–80, 97–100, 101, 113, 166, 183, 226–7, 270–1, 293n9–10; Internet surveys, 55, 61, 272–7; interviews, 55–61, 65–8 (*see also* interviews); Listening Guide, 65–6; methodological limitations, 68–71; qualitative methods in, 52, 67; recruitment of fathers, 52–4 (*see also* recruitment); reflexivity in, 47–9, 51–2; sample fathers, 54; shadow others in, 49–52; snowball sampling, 53–4; subjectivity in, 47. *See also* gossamer walls

responsibility/ies, 10, 15–16; in caregiving, 34–6; gender and, 6; of mothers, 6; movement and flow between, 221–2; as relationships between people, 35; responses to, 34; shared, 141; spatial dimension of, 228; of women, 250. *See also* community responsibility; emotional responsibility; moral responsibility;

Rhode, Deborah, 26, 29, 233

Ribbens, Jane, 36

Rich, Adrienne, 66

Ricoeur, Paul, 293n12

risk taking, 196, 244

Risman, Barbara, 9, 32, 193, 224

Robinson, Bryan, 9

role reversals: primary-caregiving fathers and, 77–81; in sociability, 164

Rose, Nikolas, 192, 193

Rothman, B.K., 242

Ruddick, Sara, 16, 107, 133, 136, 140–1, 175, 209, 218, 224, 286n4; *Maternal Thinking*, 9–10, 111, 223

same-sex partnerships, 13, 54, 248

schools: classrooms (*see* classrooms); fathers in, 11, 148, 149–50, 157–8, 190–1; volunteers in, 78

schoolyards: borderwork and, 44; embodiment and, 41; father-daughter relationship and, 157–8; fathers in, 12, 138, 157–8

Seale, Clive, 48

DATE DUE

NOV 1 6 2007			
MAR 0 5 2009			

#47-0108 Peel Off Pressure Sensitive